Political Ideologies

Their Origins and Impact

Eleventh Edition

LEON P. BARADAT

MiraCosta College

Longman
Boston   Columbus   Indianapolis   New York   San Francisco   Upper Saddle River
Amsterdam   Cape Town   Dubai   London   Madrid   Milan   Munich   Paris   Montreal   Toronto
Delhi   Mexico City   São Paulo   Sydney   Hong Kong   Seoul   Singapore   Taipei   Tokyo

Senior Acquisitions Editor: Vikram Mukhija
Senior Marketing Manager: Lindsey Prudhomme
Editorial Assistant: Beverly Fong
Associate Production Manager: Scarlett Lindsay
Project Coordination, Text Design, and Electronic
  Page Makeup: S4Carlisle Publishing Services
Cover Design Manager: Wendy Ann Fredericks
Cover Photo: © Exactostock/SuperStock
Photo Researcher: Poyee Oster
Senior Manufacturing Buyer: Roy L. Pickering, Jr.
Printer and Binder: RR Donnelley – Crawfordsville
Cover Printer: RR Donnelley – Crawfordsville

Credits and acknowledgments borrowed from other sources and reproduced, with permission, in this textbook appear on the appropriate page within the text. Unless otherwise stated, all artwork has been provided by the authors.

Library of Congress Cataloging-in-Publication Data
Baradat, Leon P., 1940-
  Political ideologies : their origins and impact / Leon P. Baradat.—11th ed.
   p. cm.
  ISBN-13: 978-0-205-08238-4
  ISBN-10: 0-205-08238-6
  1. Political science—History—Textbooks. 2. Ideology—History—Textbooks. I. Title.
  JA83.B248 2011
  320.509—dc22

                                                          2010044244

Longman
is an imprint of

1 2 3 4 5 6 7 8 9 10 — DOC — 14 13 12 11

www.pearsonhighered.com

ISBN-13: 978-0-205-08238-4
ISBN-10:   0-205-08238-6

To Elaine,
wife, partner, and friend.

And in memory of
Gail Prentiss and Cruz Venegas,
two of our best friends.

BRIEF CONTENTS

DETAILED CONTENTS

CHAPTER 10
Fascism and National Socialism   237

CHAPTER 11
Ideologies in the Developing World   275

CHAPTER 12
Feminism and Environmentalism   304

PREFACE

Since the first edition of this book, we have witnessed many changes in the currents and undertows of world politics. The Cold War ended, and people became hopeful momentarily that the political waters would calm. However, although the frightening possibility of a nuclear confrontation between the superpowers has diminished, we still find ourselves confronted with a threatening environment. The Middle East festers, even more than before; religious fundamentalism engenders violence; political terrorism has become commonplace; racism divides peoples; nationalism and neo-fascism emerge again; hate groups are resuscitating; famine emaciates millions in the Developing World while the insatiable developed economies squander resources; at home a corporate state emerges as the middle class disappears and vast wealth siphons into the hands of the very few; meanwhile, the Earth is warming in response to overcharged industrialized economies, threatening unprecedented disaster; and the press of the world's exploding population on finite potable water, food supplies, breathable air, and other resources has become so acute as to cause serious people to wonder whether the Earth remains capable of sustaining us.

These problems, and many others demand solutions. To resolve our difficulties, we must have a firm understanding of our own values and political system so that our efforts can enhance what we cherish rather than sacrifice it. We must also realize that we have to work together with other people in the world, since, driven by a global economy, many of our problems span national boundaries, exceeding the capacity of single states to solve them. We must learn to deal with people who have values, views, and ideas different from our own.

This book is a good place to begin such a critical endeavor because a clear understanding of current world ideologies is essential if one is to grasp the political realities of our time.

NEW TO THIS EDITION

Besides a thorough updating of examples, detail, and data, the following items are either wholly new or considerably expanded in this edition.

- The mixed messages of the Obama administration's first year in the civil liberties, foreign policy, health care, immigration, and the environment.
- The recently developed variegations in conservatism: The Tea Party movement, the expanding political importance of religious extremists, and the growing incivility of its extremists.
- The Great Recession, its causes and its political fallout.
- The reemergence of authoritarianism in the Developing World and Russia.
- China's continuing economic miracle while maintaining a firm grip on the political system, but also suffering serious social, environmental, and health problems.

■ The transfer of power from Fidel to Raoul Castro.
■ Right-wing extremism mounting in Europe, Asia, and the United States.
■ The growing salience of Islamism.
■ Terrorism's increasing acceptance in certain quarters.
■ The West's declining interest in feminism, but its spreading strength in the Developing World.
■ The mounting jeopardy to the global environment, with global warming coming more clearly into focus as the culprit.

FEATURES

Pedagogy

I think of myself as a teacher, not an author. This book, therefore, is written as a vehicle for teaching some of the world's great political ideas. Several features have been incorporated into this book that will help the reader learn its contents more easily.

Each chapter begins with a preview of the material to be covered in the chapter. It is designed to alert students to the principal ideas developed in the text that follows. Equipped with this overview, the details in the chapter become more meaningful. At the end of each chapter, questions are provided that are designed to stimulate thought and discussion about the major themes in the chapter.

I have also included at the end of each chapter a bibliography that can be used in further pursuit of the subject. These lists are certainly not exhaustive, but they can be used as jumping-off places for more detailed inquiry into the subject.

The text also includes *italicized* words and phrases. When you encounter them, take special note of them: it is my way of saying this material is particularly important. The glossary and the index at the end of the book should also be especially useful. The names and concepts appearing in **boldface** in the text can be found in the glossary, and you should pay close attention to them as well.

Approach, Organization, and Coverage

Fundamentally this book arrays the important ideologies chronologically so students not only learn the discrete ideas but also witness modern political thinking evolve. It is critical that students recognize the relevance to their lives of these ideas, thus care is taken to offer apt examples and to demonstrate the interrelationship of theoretical concepts, and practical politics. To this end, great effort is made to display the social, intellectual, and political consequences of the transformational economic progression from handcrafted goods, through mechanization, to cybernetics. Finally, it is essential that students receive a balanced presentation of this controversial subject. Accordingly, an effort is made to discuss a broad range of points of view on each topic.

Chapter Content

Chapter 1 examines the origins and implications of ideologies. Special consideration is given to the Industrial Revolution's responsibility for generating the social and political issues leading to appearance of the ideologies, a theme continued throughout the book. Additionally, the differences between political philosophy and ideologies are explored.

In Chapter 2 students are introduced to the spectrum of political attitudes and it distinguishes between attitudes about change and values as motivations for policy choices.

Nationalism, the most powerful political idea of the past three centuries, is studied in Chapter 3 from the perspectives of its origins, its utility, and its prospects for continued efficacy in a world confronted with exploding populations and inadequate resources.

The next three chapters focus on the theory and practice of democracy. Chapter 4 surveys the theories of seventeenth-century philosophers whose ideas become the foundation for contemporary democratic practice.

Chapter 5 analyzes the adjustments to the democratic theory made necessary by its application to practical political situations. It takes particular note of the adjustments to theory made by leaders on the left and the right.

In Chapter 6 the practice of contemporary liberal democracy and the institutions used in its application are explored. In this and the preceding chapter, students are encouraged to think about the relationship of theory and actual political, economic, and social realities.

Chapter 7 introduces anarchism as a rejection of depersonalization in modern societies and it is considered from historical and contemporary perspectives.

Socialism is the subject of inquiry in the next two chapters. Chapter 8 studies the two fundamental approaches to socialism: humanistic and "scientific." It investigates the components of socialism and the ideas of socialist thinkers from Babeuf, through the Utopians, to Marx.

Consistent with the text's approach throughout, Chapter 9 examines socialism as it is applied to extant social and political circumstance.

A comparative analysis of fascism and National Socialism opens Chapter 10. It then goes on to discuss contemporary right-wing extremist movements abroad and in the United States.

The cultural diversity, economic strife, social complexity, and political turmoil in the Developing World, which give rise to its spectrum-spanning ideologies, are the focus of Chapter 11.

Finally, Chapter 12 explores the ideological aspects of feminism and the strengthening and weakening interests in them. It then concludes with a study of environmentalism as an ideology, including an exposition of deep and humanist ecologists.

ACKNOWLEDGMENTS

Whereas any inaccuracies in this book are completely my own responsibility, several people have made such substantial contributions to it that I take pleasure in mentioning them here. My deepest gratitude belongs to my wife, Elaine. Her unselfish help and her unfailing support over the years have been instrumental to the book's success. I am also indebted to our sons, Leon and René, who, in the early editions of the book, sacrificed time we might have spent together so that the book could be written.

For the lucidity the first edition enjoyed, all credit and many thanks go to Professor Julie Hatoff. Spending untold hours reviewing the manuscript, suggesting improvements, and correcting errors, Professor Hatoff was of invaluable assistance. Her conscientious attention to my misplaced modifiers, arbitrary punctuation, and eccentric spelling was very helpful, and I am most grateful to her. Additionally, I am indebted to Professor John Phillips of MiraCosta College for his many suggestions for improvement, and to the following reviewers for their corrections and suggestions: Shaheen Ayubi, Rutgers University–Camden; Lynda Barrow, Coe College; and JoAnne Myers, Marist College. I would also like to thank my editor Vikram Mukhija, editorial assistant Beverly Fong, production manager Scarlett Lindsay, compositon production editor Roxanne Klaas, and copyeditor Sue Grutz for their guidance and help throughout this process.

Besides those who did so much to make this book a reality, I would like to take this opportunity to express my gratitude to the people of California for providing an excellent and free public education system to its youth. Were it not for the opportunity to attend state-supported schools and colleges, I would almost surely not have received an education. In addition, I would like to single out three teachers who have had particular influence on my professional life and whose pedagogical and scholarly examples have been important inspirations. To N. B. (Tad) Martin, formerly professor of history at the College of the Sequoias, who has a grasp of history and a teaching ability worthy of emulation, my sincere appreciation. To Karl A. Svenson, former professor of political science at Fresno State University, whose lectures were memorable and whose advice was timely and sound, my heartfelt thanks. Finally, and most important, to David H. Provost, formerly professor of political science at Fresno State University, my lasting gratitude for the help, encouragement, scholastic training, and friendship he so abundantly extended. His example has been particularly meaningful to me.

A NOTE TO THE STUDENT

I would like to share with you a few thoughts about general education requirements. Responding to economic and social pressures, students understandably want to complete their studies so that they can begin to make a living. Courses that do not immediately translate into dollars are often viewed by students as superfluous impositions on their time. The course for which you are reading this book may be one of those offerings. Yet there is more to life than materialism, and we must learn to appreciate and enjoy what we are and who we are while we make a living. In fact, it is likely that we will make a better living, and probably live better, if we appreciate and understand the world in which we live.

Education is the major custodian of civilization. Its function is to transmit the knowledge and values of our civilization to each succeeding generation. General education courses are the principal vehicle by which this function is executed at the college level. They offer you the world's wisdom, a priceless treasure. Immerse yourself in them, savor them, absorb them, enjoy them. Let general education courses expose you to the intellectual wonders of our world, expanding your vision and deepening your appreciation of life so that, as educator Stephen Bailey wrote, "Later in life when you knock on yourself, someone answers."

LEON P. BARADAT

SUPPLEMENTS

Longman is pleased to offer several resources to qualified adopters of *Political Ideologies* and their students that will make teaching and learning from this book even more effective and enjoyable.

PASSPORT FOR INTRODUCTION TO POLITICAL SCIENCE   With Passport, choose the resources you want from MyPoliSciKit and put links to them into your course management system. If there is assessment associated with those resources, it also can be uploaded, allowing the results to feed directly into your course management system's gradebook. With over 150 MyPoliSciKit assets like video case studies, mapping exercises, comparative exercises, simulations, podcasts, *Financial Times* newsfeeds, current events quizzes, politics blog, and much more, Passport is available for any Pearson introductory or upper-level political science book.

MYSEARCHLAB   Need help with a paper? MySearchLab saves time and improves results by offering start-to-finish guidance on the research/writing process and full-text access to academic journals and periodicals.

THE ECONOMIST   Every week, *The Economist* analyzes the important happenings around the globe. From business to politics, to the arts and science, its coverage connects seemingly unrelated events in unexpected ways.

THE FINANCIAL TIMES   Featuring international news and analysis from journalists in more than 50 countries, *The Financial Times* provides insights and perspectives on political and economic developments around the world.

LONGMAN ATLAS OF WORLD ISSUES (0-205-78020-2)   From population and political systems to energy use and women's rights, the *Longman Atlas of World Issues* features full-color thematic maps that examine the forces shaping the world. Featuring maps from the latest edition of *The Penguin State of the World Atlas*, this excerpt includes critical thinking exercises to promote a deeper understanding of how geography affects many global issues. Available at no additional charge when packaged with this book.

GOODE'S WORLD ATLAS (0-321-65200-2)   First published by Rand McNally in 1923, *Goode's World Atlas* has set the standard for college reference atlases. It features hundreds of physical, political, and thematic maps as well as graphs, tables, and a pronouncing index. Available at a discount when packaged with this book.

Ideology

PREVIEW

Ideologies are predicated on the Age of Enlightenment belief that people could improve their conditions by taking positive action instead of passively accepting life as it came. This new belief was accompanied by the great economic and social upheaval caused by the mechanization of production (the earliest stage of the Industrial Revolution). Indeed, one of the major themes of this book is that ideologies are the result of attempts to develop political accommodations to the economic and social conditions created by the Industrial Revolution.

Political scientists do not agree on the exact definition of the term *ideology,* but their opinions have enough in common to allow us to support the following definition: *Political ideologies are usually simply stated and oriented toward masses of people. They are materialistic, activist, and often impatient with delay.*

Ideology and political philosophy are each theoretical conceptualizations of politics, but political philosophy is addressed to the individual and is more intellectually profound and introspective.

THE DEVELOPMENT OF IDEOLOGY

Prior to the modern era, with but a few brief exceptions, people were discouraged from seeking solutions to their problems. They were expected to do what they were told by their spiritual and temporal superiors. Politics had not yet become democratized. Ordinary people were not allowed to participate in the political system. Politics was reserved for monarchs heading a small ruling class. Indeed, the Prussian king and military genius Frederick the Great (1712–1786) once said, "A war is something which should not concern my people." In other words, politics was not the business of ordinary people. Rather than enjoy a voice in government, the masses were expected to work, producing material goods to sustain the state; they were not mobilized for political activity. In exchange for their obedience and productivity, the ruling class provided order and stability. Such was the social contract.

This attitude would be viewed as arrogant by contemporary observers, but only because every modern society is democratic in at least one sense of the word. *Every modern political system is motivational;* that is, leaders attempt to mobilize citizens to accomplish the political, economic, and social goals of the society. They are all intensely interested in involving their citizens in efforts to accomplish the objectives of the state, and ideologies are among the major tools used by modern governments to mobilize people. Consequently, modern ideologies call upon people to join in collective efforts. The goals of each ideology and the precise methods used to reach these goals are different, but they each call for mass mobilization and collective efforts to accomplish desired ends. In this sense, if in no other, ideologies are indispensable tools of the people who govern and of the people who are governed. As a consequence, familiarity with the most important ideologies is critical to one's understanding the world in which one lives.

The Source of Ideology

Knowledge, as it was commonly understood before the Enlightenment, was to be revealed by a superior wisdom; ordinary people were to understand and conform to such knowledge as best they could. Consequently, little questioning or challenging was encouraged among ordinary people, and naturally, change came very slowly as a consequence.

Gradually, however, people began to challenge this intellectual straitjacket. Some, such as Galileo Galilei, were punished for doing so. Galileo proved the Copernican theory that the Earth and other planets revolve around the sun, making it, and not the Earth, the center of the universe. Fearing that this assertion threatened the Catholic Church's primacy over truth, the pope had Galileo tried before the Inquisition and forced to recant. Of course, as Galileo must have known, the truth of the matter could not be suppressed forever.

Despite extreme efforts of the spiritual and temporal leaders to suppress "inconvenient truths," scholars and philosophers continued to probe and question, and in time, their efforts led to discoveries that revolutionized human existence. The net result of these accomplishments was the development of science and its practical application, technology. Success in early attempts to solve problems through the application of science, such as curing a disease or developing an important labor-saving device, gave people a new sense of empowerment. Liberation from the fetters of ignorance filled some with exhilaration, inquisitiveness, and inventiveness. Suddenly, after centuries of slavish obedience to tradition and conventional wisdom, the world became more rational and could be approached systematically. Invigorated by this secular epiphany, people were encouraged to apply human reason to an ever-widening range of problems.

In time, innovators developed machines that greatly increased productivity and drastically changed people's relationship to the things produced. Whereas production and consumption were once limited to the tiny quantities that could be fashioned by hand, the new technology permitted a previously unimagined abundance, thus introducing important economic, social—and eventually—political transformations. For example, the average worker was no longer actually making goods. Instead, workers found themselves simply the custodians of machines that wove fabric, forged steel, or carved wood.

Rather than building a whole carriage, for example, workers now found themselves on an assembly monotonously performing one tiny aspect of automobile production and then passing it on to the next person to contribute the next minute task. Eventually the vehicle is produced, but no one can claim credit for actually building it. Thus, industrialization brings abundance, but it also shrouds production with anonymity and something of the joy of accomplishment becomes lost.

These changes in productivity had enormous social effects. People who once led relatively healthy, albeit poor, lives in rural settings were brought together to live in cities. The workers' neighborhoods were crowded and unsanitary. Ironically, life became less social as people found themselves psychologically estranged from their neighbors at the very time when they were forced to share the same city block. For millennia, people had depended on a close relationship with the soil for the necessities of life. Now, suddenly, they found themselves divorced from the land. Urbanization and industrialization, accomplished by brutal methods during the eighteenth and nineteenth centuries, caused massive confusion and insecurity among most people. Ordinary people became disoriented and frightened. No longer could they produce most of the things they needed themselves. They were transformed into anonymous cogs of giant economic systems and, as such, were dependent

© Bettmann/Corbis

This scene of an eighteenth century cotton mill illustrates how dangerous the jobs assigned to children could be in the early Industrial Revolution. That the mill depicted was located in the state of Georgia reminds us that child labor exploitation existed no less in the United States than in any other industrializing society of the era.

for their well-being on people they did not know, in places they had never seen. Scholars, philosophers, and politicians made efforts to comprehend these events, to explain and rationalize them, and to accommodate the social and political changes they evoked in this "brave new world." Some of these rationalizations became political ideologies.

If the mechanization of production, the urbanization of society, and the separation of people from an intimate relationship with the land had been all that people had to face, the impact on human life would have been great indeed. However, even more turmoil lay ahead. Economic dislocation became a severe problem. Unemployment, depression, and inflation began to plague society and to disrupt the order of things to a degree previously not experienced. Workers became disoriented as the skills that had once been a major source of self-identification and pride were made unnecessary by automation. It became necessary to learn new skills to accommodate the new technology. At the same time, workers became dissociated from owners. Capital investment necessary to buy machines, factories, and resources became so great that owners had to spend their time managing their money (becoming capitalists); they were no longer able to work alongside their employees as they once had in their **cottage-industry** shops. Lulled by the monotony of the assembly line, workers became separated from their employers, estranged from impersonal managers, and ultimately alienated from their work.

Meanwhile, as family farms and businesses have disappeared, society has become increasingly mobile. Roots have disintegrated. Families, the most basic of all social units, have become dislocated from ancestral foundations, and the institution of the family itself seems to be dissolving, in the west at least, before our eyes. While we are being crowded closer together, we seem to be losing concern for one another. We are becoming increasingly isolated in a world filled with people. Ironically, we are developing a self-oriented world at the very time that we are becoming more and more dependent on others for our most basic needs. As the pace of change quickens and the basic institutions of society are weakened, change becomes virtually inevitable in societies ill-equipped to cope with it.

Although our economic success has presented us with new opportunities, it has also tended to exacerbate our social problems. Industrialization has produced great wealth for those who are fortunate enough to profit from it. For others, however, it has produced a new kind of slavery. The new slaves, be they neocolonial suppliers of cheap raw materials, industrial toilers, office workers, or even business executives and professionals, are exploited more fully than those of previous eras because of the efficiency of the modern system. For example, computers, BlackBerries, iPods, droids, and cell phones are usually presented to us by their vendors and enthusiasts as technologies that liberate people, and often they do. They are credited with increasing productivity, as indeed they have. But they also tether us to the workplace long after traditional business hours, extending the length of time we spend on the job. Employees who initially exalted at being allowed to telecommunicate, thus working from home, often find themselves compulsively checking their e-mail, cell phones, and BlackBerries for information, a process that quickly develops into ten-, or even twelve-hour days, rather than the standard eight hours. They become ensnared in an electronic bondage before they realize what is happening.

The gap between the user and the used, between the haves and the have-nots, is also increasing, threatening frightful results for a world that remains insensitive to it. In addition, industrialized economies have become voracious consumers of natural resources. Some of these vital commodities are, in fact, reduced to a very short supply. Competition for the remaining fuel and mineral resources increases the tension between industrialized and developing nations as well as among the industrialized nations themselves. As we come hard upon the earth's limits of some resources, certain foods, living space, water supplies, we witness the beginnings of what could become a devastating contest for survival the likes of which humankind has never yet experienced.

Many technical advances not only increase the demand for resources but also tend to increase the population and thus further escalate the demand for resources. Medical and nutritional discoveries have lengthened life expectancies and eradicated certain diseases so that today the world's population stands at almost 7 billion, a figure that will certainly increase by half again within the next half-century. Housing, clothing, and feeding these multitudes increases the drain on resources, causing scarcity and anxiety as competition for the remaining resources intensifies.

Prior to the present era, people relied on religion for answers to adversity, putting their faith unquestioningly in their God and in their priests. However, as **rationalism** developed and science seemed to contradict certain basic tenets of the church, people began to rely on science for solutions to their difficulties. The world became increasingly materialistic, decreasingly spiritualistic. Unfortunately, science brought humanity mixed blessings. For each problem it solved, it created new difficulties. Automobiles give us mobility, yet they also visit air pollution on their owners; birth control pills prevent unwanted children, but now ancient moral scruples are rejected and society faces venereal disease and AIDS in epidemic proportions; the computer has opened to us vast new opportunities, creating the Information Age, but it has also brought us eye strain, carpal tunnel obstructions, a dangerous loss of privacy, and it has expanded the workday enormously for many. Texting and other forms of electronic communications have increased our connections with others while, at the same time, impoverished personal relationships as face-to-face encounters are sacrificed by the substitution of cyberspaced ones and zeros. Nuclear energy offers cheap and virtually inexhaustible energy, yet as the accidents at Three Mile Island and Chernobyl attest, a mishap at a power plant can be disastrous; furthermore, although nuclear deterrence kept an uneasy peace until the Soviet Union collapsed, and although the United States

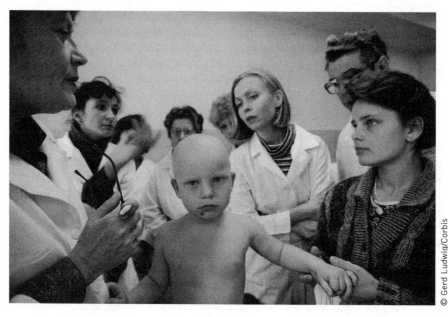

© Gerd Ludwig/Corbis

An anxious Soviet mother awaits the examination results of her child who suffered from the after-effects of the 1986 Chernobyl nuclear power plant accident.

and Russia are each now reducing the number of their aging nuclear warheads, their disarmament is far from total, and nuclear proliferation, witness current development in Pakistan, North Korea, and Iran—together with the new weapons the United States and Russia are producing—constitute a dire threat, one perhaps even more dangerous than that posed during the bipolar confrontation of the Cold War.

As if these problems were not enough, their impact has been magnified because they have been forced on us over an extremely brief period. Most of the developments just mentioned have occurred during the span of a few generations. People have never before experienced the rate of change they face today. We find ourselves catapulted into the future before we can fully understand the present or the recent past, and the more distant past—history—the indispensable text for progressive human social development, is being ignored so as to make room in the curricula for avalanches of new technical information. Such fundamental change, to say nothing of the rate at which it is occurring, has tended to disorient and confuse people. Values and institutions have become temporary. The industrialization of our economy has ignited social change, thus foisting upon us political transformation. It is, of course, political change with which we are concerned in this study. However, the political developments of the past several centuries have been fostered by economic and social conditions. The political ideologies described in later chapters may be viewed as *attempts to find a political accommodation to the social and economic conditions created by the* **Industrial Revolution.**[1] Madison, Marx, Mussolini, the Mullahs, and others developed their ideas in response to the conditions confronting them. If those conditions had been different, political thought would have been different. The two factors most responsible for the political world in which we now live are (1) *the belief that people can themselves take active steps that will improve their lives* and (2) *the Industrial Revolution.* Almost every modern social condition and political idea is supported by these two factors. The phenomenon of political ideologies is unique to our era because it is a response to a unique set of economic, social, and political circumstances.

IDEOLOGY DEFINED

The meaning of the word **ideology** is frequently debated. Dozens of different definitions have been suggested, and each has been challenged and contradicted. Indeed, political scientists cannot agree on whether ideology is a positive, negative, or neutral feature of modern society. While I have no hope of settling this controversy here, I do wish to discuss the origins of the term, explain its varying definitions, and arrive at a definition that will be useful to us during the rest of this study.

The Origin of the Term

It is generally agreed that the term *ideology* was first used by the French in the early nineteenth century, but we do not know for sure who coined it. Most of the evidence, however, indicates that the French noble and scholar **Antoine Louis Claude Destutt de Tracy** (1754–1836) probably originated the word. Writing at the turn of the nineteenth century,[2] he used the word *ideology* in

---

[1] I mean *industrialization* and *the Industrial Revolution* in the broadest sense. I am not using these terms to refer only to factory manufacture. The Industrial Revolution, as I view it, is still in progress. In the broader sense, the Industrial Revolution began when machinery was developed and set to the task of producing goods. Some people suggest that the transition from handmade to machine-made goods is all that the Industrial Revolution is about. But a broader view sees it continuing today. Having gone through stages of mechanization and automation, the Industrial Revolution continues to evolve and refine. Its most current phase, although probably not its last, is **cybernetics.**

Cybernetics in general has to do with the generation and exchange of information. As such, it has had a large impact on economics and production. The facet of cybernetics that is most at issue in this study is the aspect of production that finds machines (computers, for example) running other machines (robotic welders, for instance). This development not only has significant economic impact but also has important social and political implications for us and is evidence that the Industrial Revolution is still in progress. Indeed, the cybernetic transition may, in the long run, visit as much social and political turmoil upon society as did the original transition from handmade to machine-made goods.

[2] Interestingly, the first English version of De Tracy's most influential work, *Elements of Ideology,* was translated by Thomas Jefferson. It was published in English in 1817.

his systematic study of the Enlightenment. Like other thinkers of his time, De Tracy believed that people could use science to improve social and political conditions. To him, ideology was a study of the process of forming ideas, a "science of ideas," if you will. Ideas, De Tracy believed, are stimulated by the physical environment. Hence, *empirical learning* (the kind that is gained through experience) is the only source of knowledge. Supernatural or spiritual phenomena play no part in the formation of ideas.

Although the thrust of De Tracy's thought is psychological, thus not of immediate concern to us, two aspects of his theories should be noted. The first is *materialism*. Thought, according to De Tracy, is generated by material stimuli only, and the formation of an idea is a physical rather than a spiritual or mystical process. The scientific and materialistic basis of ideology will be pointed out later. For now, it is sufficient to note that materialism is a dominant theme in the concept of ideology.

The second important aspect of De Tracy's thought is that *social and political improvement* was its main goal. De Tracy wanted to apply the knowledge developed from his "science of ideas" to the whole society and thereby attempt to improve human life. Thus, ideology has been closely associated with politics from the beginning. It is therefore appropriate to give the word a political connotation unless a different context is indicated.

Karl Marx (1818–1883) and **Friedrich Engels** (1820–1895) developed a second theory about what ideology is. In *The German Ideology,* they contradict De Tracy on the subject. They argue that rather than a "science of ideas," ideology is nothing more than a fabrication used by a particular group of people to justify themselves. The concepts in an ideology were completely subjective, and they were used to justify the ruling class of society. Thus, the dominant political ideas, or ideology, of any society would always reflect the interests of the ruling class and, according to Marx and Engels, were based on incorrect interpretations of the nature of politics.

The distinguished German scholar Karl Mannheim (1893–1947) also studied ideology. While he basically agreed with Marx's conclusions, Mannheim contributed an analysis of ideology from a historical perspective. He compared the ideology of one historical era to that of another, arguing that no ideology could be fully understood unless this historical relationship was clear. No ideology, in other words, can be understood unless we grasp the ideas of the previous era and investigate the impact of the previous ideology on the current one.

Contemporary Definitions

Americans tend not to view political issues ideologically. Impatient with theoretical arguments, they consider ideologies idealistic and impractical concepts. Yet, political theory gives us statements of objectives by which to guide our actions and by which to assess our accomplishments. Without theory, political policy can be shortsighted and inconsistent. Further, ideologies are often used to persuade people to accomplish the goals of the state. Most political scientists readily agree that ideology is an important factor in our lives. Alas, they are no closer than earlier authorities to an agreement on exactly what the term means.

Frederick Watkins, in his insightful book *The Age of Ideology*, suggests that ideology comes almost entirely from the political extremes. Ideologies, he argues, are always opposed to the status quo. They propose an abrupt change in the existing order; therefore, they are usually militant, revolutionary, and violent. Watkins goes on to point out that most ideologies are stated in simplistic terms, utopian in their objectives, and usually display great faith in humankind's potential for finding success and happiness. Conservatism, lacking such optimism in human faculties, he writes, defends the status quo, resisting change, and thus is an *anti-ideology*, according to Watkins. Ideology emerged from the rationalist tradition, in which it was assumed that most problems could be solved if people applied reason rightly. As will be seen in Chapter 2, however, the conservative rejects this optimistic assumption about the capacity of human reason. Watkins, therefore, argues the conservative is opposed to the basic assumption of any ideology.

This particular point occasions some difficulty. It is true that conservatives are quick to argue that reason has its limits. Yet, they do not completely reject reason as a means by which political problems can be solved. To argue, therefore, that conservatism is not an ideology may be to misinterpret. Another modern commentator, David Ingersoll, suggests that each ideology includes an assessment of the status quo and a view of the future. The future is always represented as something better than the present or the past. Exactly what is better for the society is usually expressed in materialistic terms; for example, both Marx and Hitler envisioned a society of great bounty. In addition, Ingersoll asserts that each ideology contains a definite *plan of action* by which this better future can be attained. Indeed, the plan of action is central to any ideology, according to Ingersoll. Ideologies tend to convey a sense of urgency. Moreover, they are intended to stimulate people to achieve utopian objectives.

L. T. Sargent approaches the definition of ideology differently. He sees ideologies as based on the value systems of various societies. Yet, modern societies are complex and often contradictory. Thus, individuals within a society may not accept a single-ideology; they may appropriate parts of several ideologies, or they may become completely attached to a single idea system. In any event, Sargent makes the point that ideologies are simplistic in their approach to problem solving. Ideology, he writes, "provides the believer with a picture of the world both as it is and as it should be, and, in so doing . . . organizes the tremendous complexity of the world into something fairly simple and understandable."[3]

Finally, Terrence Ball cautions that developing too rigid a definition of ideology would be to miss the point. Rather than a phenomenon composed

---

[3]L. T. Sargent, *Contemporary Political Ideologies*, rev. ed. (Homewood, IL: Dorsey Press, 1972), p. 1.

of precise ingredients, Ball views ideology in more flexible and more academic terms. It is, he suggests, "an agenda of things to discuss, questions to ask, hypotheses to make. We should be able to use it when considering the interaction between ideas and politics. . . ."[4] For Ball, ideology exists whenever politics is motivated by intellectual rather than random impulses. Hence, the definition of ideology should not be construed narrowly or be understood to be dependent on any but the loosest criteria.

Clearly, the authorities do not agree on the definition of ideology. Opinions range widely, from the exclusive views of Watkins to the expansive perspective of Ball. In any case, it is clear that, at least for our purposes, five properties can be identified that are significant to the definition of ideology. It may be true, as Ball implies, that not all of these factors are essential for ideology, but, at the same time, these factors are both common and important in the ideologies we will study.

Ideology is first and foremost a *political term,* though it is often applied to other contexts. Second, ideology consists of a view of the present and a vision of the future. The preferred future is presented as a *materialistic* improvement over the present. This desirable future condition is often attainable, according to the ideology, within a single lifetime. As a result, one of the outstanding features of an ideology is its offer of hope. Third, ideology is *action-oriented.* It not only describes reality and offers a better future, but most important, it gives specific directions about the steps that must be taken to attain this goal. Fourth, ideology is *directed toward the masses.* If nothing else, Karl Marx, Benito Mussolini, Vladimir Lenin, Mao Zedong, and Adolf Hitler had one thing in common: They directed their appeal to the masses. They were interested in mobilizing huge numbers of people. Finally, because ideologies are directed at the masses, they are usually couched in fairly *simple* terms that can be understood by ordinary people. For the same reason, ideologies are usually *motivational* in tone, tending to call on people to make a great effort to attain the ideological goals. This mass appeal in itself implies confidence in people's ability to improve their lives through positive action. Remember, *all modern societies are democratic in this sense of the word.*

Applying these criteria to documents seemingly as different from one another as the *Declaration of Independence* and the *Communist Manifesto,* we can see that the two tracts are not only ideological statements, but are also very similar in important ways. Each of them is assuredly political. They each made statements about the world as seen by their authors and, implicitly at least, conjured how the world could be better. These observations were set out in common, assertive language appropriate for the times in which they were written, and they were each addressed to a wide readership. **Thomas Jefferson** wrote of the existence of certain inalienable rights and contended that governments were created to further these rights. He then went on to

---

[4]Terrence Ball and Richard Dagger, eds, *Ideals and Ideologies,* 2nd ed. (New York: Harper-Collins, 1995).

allege a large number of British violations of American rights. Similarly, Karl Marx focused on the essential equality of people and lamented that society had been divided into exploiting and exploited social classes. Finally, each document calls for action—the same action, interestingly enough—*revolution.* Each author claimed that the downtrodden have an inherent right to rise up and cast off their oppressors or exploiters.

In these terms, the two essays are virtually identical. They differ, of course. Jefferson focused on political factors and asserted the authority of natural law, but he confined his statement to explaining why the Anglo-American colonies were in rebellion against the British government. Any invitation for others to engage in rebellion could only be inferred. Marx, on the other hand, invoked what he understood to be economic laws governing people, and he called on workers *everywhere* to unite and to make themselves free. The theoretical differences and the intended focus of each essay aside, however, the two documents are remarkably similar as ideological statements.

Ideology and Philosophy

Finally, it may be useful to distinguish between philosophy and ideology. Previous eras enjoyed much more stable conditions than we now do. Although much was not known, almost everything was explained by spiritual or metaphysical propositions. Things were as they were because God intended them so, and, consequently, to question the basic order of life was certainly inappropriate and perhaps even heretical.

Government was the province of an elite. If actions were guided by theory at all, the theoretical base was normative and lodged in relatively complex tracts that only the best educated were likely to understand. Ordinary people were not involved in politics, nor were they expected to be acquainted with the goals or justifications for government beyond the most rudimentary principles. Accordingly, the *philosophy* that served as the theoretical base for the society was available to only a tiny percentage of the population.

Although each ideology is founded on a set of philosophical beliefs, philosophy is composed of three basic characteristics that distinguish it from ideology. First, philosophy tends to be *profound.* It attempts to penetrate the veneer of human existence and to address the actual meaning of life itself. To do so, it must deal with the subject in a very complex and holistic manner. It tries to analyze the totality of human experience to find the meaning contained therein and, by so doing, to produce generalizations by which future conduct can profitably be pursued and by which actions can be assessed. By contrast, ideology is uncomplicated and shallow. The world is usually explained in very simple terms, and little attempt is made to deal with the multitudinous variables we confront. Usually, "right" and "wrong" are made very clear, and people are simply asked to believe in them and to act accordingly.

Second, although philosophy can be the set of principles upon which an entire society bases its actions, it can also be taken up by a single *individual.*

Indeed, when reading philosophy, one is often struck by the feeling that the author is communicating directly with the reader and is not necessarily trying to reach a larger audience. Ideology, on the other hand, is addressed to huge numbers of people rather than to the individual. Ideology, as previously indicated, is the theoretical base for the mass mobilization upon which each modern nation is founded.

Third, philosophy tends to encourage *introspection*. The objective of philosophy is to explain the universe and help the reader find a place in it. Philosophy requires sustained contemplation and examines profound questions about the human condition. While philosophy may advise measures to improve society, *action is not its central focus—understanding is:* It is through greater understanding that human happiness is presumably achieved. Ideologies, instead, explain the world (albeit simply) and ask for people to take definite steps to improve their lives. Unlike philosophy, ideology invariably demands that people change the world to suit themselves. People are not asked to investigate the complex and underlying variables of human existence. Instead, they are called on to act, and this emphasis on action often demands suspension of contemplation. Indicative of the action orientation, Marx, himself holding a Ph.D. in philosophy, focused on this difference, saying, "The philosophers have only *interpreted* the world, the point is to *change it*" (emphases added).

While ideologies may ask people to transform themselves, the objective of such personal change is not limited to creating a better person. Instead, most ideologies are outwardly directed. People are to change themselves in order to be better able to modify the environment around them. Happiness of people in society is often juxtaposed to the condition of the world in which they find themselves, so that the world must be made to conform to the needs and conditions of the people who subscribe to a given ideology.

QUESTIONS FOR DISCUSSION

1. What important economic and social factors of the past two centuries contributed to the development of ideologies?
2. How does ideology relate to government and to politics?
3. In what ways have scholars viewed the nature and utility of ideologies?
4. What are the five traits common to most ideologies?
5. Differentiate between ideology and philosophy.

SUGGESTIONS FOR FURTHER READING

Arendt, Hannah, *On Revolution*. New York: Penguin Books, 1990.
Bell, Daniel, *The End of Ideology*. New York: Free Press, 1960.
Eagleton, Terry, *Ideology*. White Plains, NY: Longman, 1994.
Freeden, Michael, *Ideologies and Political Theory*. New York: Oxford University Press, 1998.

————, *Ideology: A Very Short Introduction.* Oxford: Oxford University Press, 2003.

Ingersoll, David E., and Richard K. Matthews, *The Philosophic Roots of Modern Ideology*, 2nd ed. Upper Saddle River, NJ: Prentice Hall, 1991.

Love, Nancy S., *Dogma and Dreams: A Reader in Modern Political Ideologies*, 3rd ed. Washington, DC: CQ Press, 2006.

Mannheim, Karl, *Ideology and Utopia*. London: Routledge and Kegan Paul, 1936.

Marx, Karl, and Friedrich Engels, *The German Ideology* (1846). London: Lawrence & Wishart, 1967.

Mudde, Cas, *The Ideology of the Extreme Right*. New York: Manchester University Press, 2000.

Tinder, Glenn, *Political Thinking*, 6th ed. New York: HarperCollins, 1995.

Torrance, John, *Karl Marx's Theory of Ideas*. New York: Cambridge University Press, 1995.

Watkins, Frederick M., *The Age of Ideology: Political Thought, 1950 to the Present*, 2nd ed. Upper Saddle River, NJ: Prentice Hall, 1969.

The Spectrum of Political Attitudes

PREVIEW

The terms *radical, liberal, moderate, conservative,* and *reactionary* are among the words most often used in political discourse. The concepts of political change and political values must be discussed in relation to these five terms in order to gain a clear understanding of what they represent. Radicals are people who find themselves extremely discontented with the status quo. Consequently, they wish an immediate and profound change in the existing order, advocating something new and different for society.

Considerably less dissatisfied, but still wishing to change the system significantly, are the liberals. All liberals share a belief in the equality, intelligence, and competence of people. Moderates find little wrong with the existing society, and their reluctance to change it is exceeded only by the conservatives. Differing from liberals in most respects, conservatives are dubious about bold efforts to improve the world for fear that incompetent meddling might, indeed, make things worse. Only the reactionaries reject current institutions and modern values. They would see society retrace its steps and adopt former political norms and policies.

Being clear about the values people hold is usually more revealing about the place they occupy on the spectrum than simply knowing what policy changes they advocate. Basically, people on the right of the political spectrum revere authority, tradition, elitism, and property rights, whereas those on the left emphasize political liberty, social change, human equality, and human rights.

Beyond these philosophical convictions, there are several other motivations that cause people to lean to the left or right. Psychological factors about the need for change are important. Economic circumstances also play a part. Age is another factor. Finally, one's view about the condition of human nature is probably the most important consideration in determining with which side of the spectrum one will identify. Each of these factors predisposes people's political attitudes about certain policy alternatives.

UNDERSTANDING THE SPECTRUM

Before studying specific ideologies, we should develop an understanding of certain basic political concepts. The terms *radical, liberal, moderate, conservative*, and *reactionary* are among the most commonly heard words in political discussion. Any coherent explanation of these political terms must be couched in terms discrete to a particular society because liberal or conservative positions on issues can differ from society to society. In this chapter we shall study the spectrum of political attitudes as it relates in the United States because that is the dominant audience for this book. Also, in order to study the subject, we must include consideration of two basic concepts: *change* and *values*. We will begin with an analysis of the concept of political change, and then turn to an investigation of the meanings of these terms as they relate to intent, or political values. Before proceeding, however, we should arrange the terms radical, liberal, moderate, conservative, and reactionary along a continuum in order to gain a graphic perspective on them. (See Figure 2.1.)

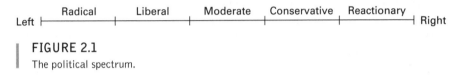

FIGURE 2.1
The political spectrum.

When they are arrayed from left to right in this fashion, we can see certain relationships among the terms with which we are concerned. For instance, the radical is at the far left of the spectrum, and the reactionary is at the opposite extreme. This alignment tells us something important. In politics, the term *radical* means an extremist of the left but not of the right.[1] In everyday conversation, on the other hand, the term radical is usually used simply to refer to something extreme, with no reference to either side of the spectrum or any particular philosophical conviction.

CHANGE, OR POLICY OPTIONS

People at each point on the political spectrum have an attitude about changing the existing political system (the **status quo**) by adopting certain policies or by pursuing certain courses of action.[2] Political change is endemic to any society.

---

[1]The terms *left* and *right* come to us from the French political experience. Those who generally supported the policies of the monarch were seated to his right, and those who proposed changes in the system were arranged to his left.

[2]While *status quo* means the extant conditions, one should take care not to be too literal about it when applied to positions on the spectrum. In this case, it should be understood to obtain only to fundamental things, like deep-rooted beliefs or foundational institutions. If a conservative, for example, wants to change a system in order to make it more conservative, or to make it conservative again, the wish for change is certainly conservative and not liberal or reactionary. Put differently, the mere fact that a conservative wishes a superficial change to an institution does not mean he or she is no longer conservative. Such an approach would make the terms we are studying meaningless. The deciding question is, is a particular policy intended to change society or keep it fundamentally the same?

By learning each group's attitude about fundamental changes, we will be taking a large step toward understanding what the terms radical, liberal, moderate, conservative, and reactionary mean.

Political change can be a very complex subject. With reference to the spectrum of political attitudes, we must actually learn four things about the change or policy option desired. First, we must determine the *direction*, forward or back, in which a proposed change would carry society. In other words, is the change progressive or retrogressive?

At this point, the reader should be on guard. Our society generally has a favorable bias toward progress. This is so because our ideological origins are rooted in eighteenth-century British liberalism, *classical liberalism*, which advocated progressive change. But, in fact, progress is not necessarily good or bad. It has no intrinsic value at all. *Progressive change* simply means a change from the status quo to something new and different in that society. Conversely, *retrogressive change* refers to a return to a policy or institution that has been used by that society in the past. For instance, the adoption of a universal compulsory government medical insurance program in the United States is a progressive policy because most people until 2018 are required to go to the marketplace to buy insurance. On the other hand, one might agree with the majority of the current U.S. Supreme Court that the states of the union are in some ways "sovereign." Such a stance has been rejected since the Civil War, so reasserting it at this point is quite retrogressive, or reactionary.

The watershed between progressive and retrogressive change lies between the conservative and reactionary sectors on the spectrum, and the line between these two sectors can be taken to represent no important change at all, or continuation of the status quo. (See Figure 2.2.) In other words, everyone to the left of the reactionary is progressive. Even conservatives are progressives in that, although they do not want a great deal of change to the status quo, the change they will allow is a transformation from what currently exists to that which the society has yet to experience. Only the reactionary wants a change from the status quo to something that existed previously.

Some people might protest that they consider themselves conservative or liberal, but that on a given issue they prefer a previous institution to the

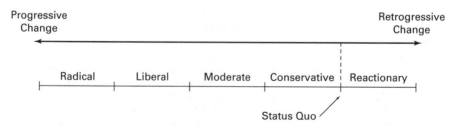

FIGURE 2.2
The position of status quo on the political spectrum.

present one. Does this make them reactionaries? Yes, it does—in relation to that particular issue. Although they might correctly consider themselves to be elsewhere on the spectrum as a general rule, they—like most of us—will find themselves at several different places on the spectrum in relation to a variety of specific issues. Few of us are absolutely consistent in our views, nor is there any particular reason to be so. Indeed, upon careful scrutiny, most people will find it difficult to place themselves in any single category because their attitudes on various issues will range over two or even more sectors on the spectrum. Typically, however, we can identify a general pattern; that is, we might find ourselves supporting liberal policies more frequently than any other position on the spectrum, and consequently, we might correctly characterize ourselves as liberals, even though our views on a few ideas might not be liberal.

The second thing one must determine when trying to locate desired policy options on the spectrum is the *depth* of a proposed change. Would the desired change amount to a major or a minor adjustment in the society? Would it modify or replace an institution that is fundamental to the society as it now exists? If so, what is the likelihood that the proposed change will cause unforeseeable and uncontrollable effects once it is implemented? For example, a proposal at the state level to require a course in introductory political science for graduation from college would undoubtedly inconvenience and annoy some students. However, such a policy change would probably have almost no disruptive effect on the society as a whole. On the other hand, if a state were to greatly reduce funding for its college system, the long-term impact is potentially enormous, changing thousands of lives and perhaps eventually affecting the society as a whole.

Once again, as with the direction of change, the watershed for the depth of change is at the line between conservative and reactionary, or at the status quo point on the spectrum. The farther people find themselves from the status quo, the more dissatisfied they are with the existing order and the more intense their desire for change. (See Figure 2.3.)

With the questions of the direction and the depth of change settled, the third aspect we must consider is the *speed* at which people want change to occur. Obviously, the more upset people are with the status quo, the more impatient they are likely to be, and, therefore, as a general rule, the more rapidly they would like to see the existing order transformed.

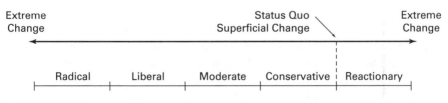

FIGURE 2.3
The desire for change as shown on the political spectrum.

The last factor we must consider regarding the concept of change is the *method* used to accomplish it. Political change can take place in a multitude of ways: officially or unofficially; legally, illegally, or extralegally; smoothly or abruptly; peacefully or violently. It is tempting for some people to conclude that those who would use violence to gain their political objectives are extremists. This, however, is not necessarily the case. True, violence is a major tool of certain extremist political groups. However, *violence is used by people at practically every point on the political spectrum.* The death penalty, property expropriation, chokeholds and certain other police techniques, and warfare itself are examples of forms of violence supported by people distributed all along the political continuum. Thus, it is unwise to jump to conclusions about the methods others use to accomplish their political goals.

It is possible, however, to make some generalizations about the methods employed for political change. For example, the farther we are from the status quo on the political spectrum, the more likely we are to find ourselves in opposition to the laws of the society. This is so because the law is a form of communication that sets forth the purposes, goals, and structures of the society. People who are opposed to those purposes, goals, or structures will necessarily be at odds with the law. Consequently, it is usually easier for conservatives to be law-abiding and patriotic, since they are satisfied with the system. Radicals, liberals, or reactionaries, by contrast, find it much more difficult to abide willingly by all the laws or to wave the flag as enthusiastically as their conservative counterparts.

Nevertheless, one should not assume from this discussion that conservatives would never violate the law to gain their political objectives. It sometimes happens that even those who control the laws of a society may not benefit from them at a given time. In such circumstances, it is not unlikely that an otherwise upstanding "pillar of society" would ignore or even violate the law. Examples include the refusal of corporations to comply with legally mandated health and safety requirements, stock market wizards and energy magnates defrauding ordinary people of billions, and ordinary people cheating on their taxes. It should be clear that the methods people use to achieve political change are complex. It is inaccurate to conclude that certain methods are the monopoly of a single sector of the political spectrum.

With the preceding general guide in mind, let us now turn to a consideration of each term on the political spectrum to determine the specific attitude of each group toward the concept of political change.

Radical

In general terms, a **radical** may be defined as a person who is extremely dissatisfied with the society as it is and therefore is impatient with less than extreme proposals for changing it. Hence, all radicals favor an immediate and fundamental change in the society. In other words, *all radicals favor revolutionary change.* The criterion that distinguishes one radical from another most clearly is the methods they would use to bring about a particular change.

All radicals want *immediate* change at society's *foundation*, but the less extreme among them do not insist on violence as the necessary vehicle by which to bring about social transformation. Indeed, one group of radicals, the *pacifists*, completely reject violence as a means to achieve justice. These people hold human rights to be of such great importance that no one, they believe, has the right to injure or kill another in pursuit of their political goals. Excellent examples of this attitude can be found in the careers of Mohandas Gandhi, Dr. Martin Luther King Jr., and labor leader Cesar Chavez. Each leader organized great movements demanding immediate and profound change, yet each refused to use violence to reach his goals, even after he had suffered violence at the hands of supporters of the status quo.

Even though not all radicals are violent and not all revolutions provoke conflict, radicals tend to be received by their adversaries with inordinately severe reactions. Owing a great debt to the philosophy of Jean Jacques Rousseau (1712–1778), contemporary radicals make the establishment terribly uncomfortable. Extreme leftists challenge the most cherished values and assumptions of society. They reject the institutions of the establishment, calling for a more humane, egalitarian, and idealistic social and political system. In fact, they demand a society which many of us desire in the ideal but which, for practical reasons or for reasons of expedience or lack of commitment, we have been unable or perhaps unwilling to create. Put differently, the radical causes us to wonder if indeed we did not fail—if we settled for a less than perfect world because it was more convenient. Thus, the idealism of radicals tends to place the rest of us on the defensive.

The radicals' contempt for society's values is so complete, their remedies so unorthodox, and, perhaps, the establishment's feelings of guilt at the thought that it may have failed so threatening that radicals are often feared with an intensity far beyond what is necessary to deal adequately with the challenge they pose. Accordingly, even though their numbers and influence do not demand such severe action, radical movements are often abjectly crushed. Examples of overreactions would be the official surveillance and harassment of leaders of the civil rights movement during the 1950s and 1960s, the same for leftists calling for peaceful relations between the United States and the Soviet Union and the People's Republic of China during the Cold War, and the same again for protesters of the Vietnam War (1960s and 1970s) and Afghanistan war. In some cases violence was used, like the 1968 brutalization by government officials of demonstrators at the Democratic National Nominating Convention in Chicago, who, while loud and vulgar, hardly constituted a clear and present danger to the republic. Even more egregious was the 1970 National Guard shooting at Kent State University of students protesting the war in Southeast Asia.

It must be quickly pointed out that extremists on the right have also suffered egregiously at the hands of the authorities. The FBI shootouts with the Weaver family on Ruby Ridge, Idaho (1992) and with the Branch Davidian sect in Waco, Texas (1993) are examples. But they were apparently the product of boorish and arrogant government officials, rather than frightened ones.

Kent State University News Service

In 1970, protesting students were fired upon by National Guard troops at Kent State University in Ohio. A 2010 analysis of an audiotape of the shooting revealed that someone may have given the order to fire on the students.

Liberal

Liberals are placed closer than radicals to the status quo point on the continuum because they are less dissatisfied with the fundamentals of society. Indeed, the liberal supports the basic features of that society. However, liberals are quick to recognize deficiencies in society and therefore are anxious to reform the system, favoring rapid and relatively far-reaching, progressive changes.

Today the term *progressive* is often used by liberals when describing themselves, because the term *liberal* has been effectively vilified in the United States by the right. However, there was a time when progressive had a discrete meaning. At the turn of the twentieth century the progressives, while remaining basically isolationists in foreign affairs, demanded leftists reforms in domestic policy. When President Woodrow Wilson led progressives to an internationalist foreign policy, liberal became the word of common currency for the mild left in American politics.

One of the most fundamental differences between the radical and the liberal is the attitude of each toward the law. Radicals are basically opposed to the political system that governs them, so they are apt to oppose the law because they see it as an instrument with which those who dominate the society maintain their control. Liberals, on the other hand, generally appreciate the concept of the law, and although they may want to change certain specifics of it, they will usually not violate it to accomplish their political objectives. Instead, they try to change the law through legal procedures. Liberals seek change in the system by several important means, but they reject attempts to revolutionize the system because they support its essentials.

Liberalism is one of the intellectual by-products of the Enlightenment, of the scientific method, and ultimately of the **Industrial Revolution**. During the medieval era, people looked heavenward for Divine relief from their wretched earthly existence. Faith in human potential, as well as esteem for humankind in general, was very low. However, the discoveries of inquisitive people such as Copernicus, Galileo, and Newton revolutionized people's attitudes toward themselves and their function in life. Through use of the scientific method, people began to make improvements in their material existence, and in so doing, they began to develop confidence in their ability to solve many problems that they had previously borne with little complaint. It was not long before people began to conclude that if physical difficulties could be solved through the use of human reason, perhaps the same could be done with social and political problems.

This speculation led to the keystone of liberalism: *Optimism about people's ability to solve their problems through the use of reason.* Accordingly, liberals are apt to apply reason to problems and to be confident that, if a solution can be found, it will be discovered by rational exercise, rather than by means less responsive to human will. Liberals, therefore, tend to address social difficulties with a vigor that conservatives see as meddlesome and dangerously overconfident. The liberals' willingness to "trifle" with "tried and true" social institutions in efforts to improve them causes conservatives—those who do not share such confidence in human reason—anxiety and disquiet.

Classical and Contemporary Liberalism Change has remained the major tool of liberalism throughout its long history. Consequently, its specific objectives have been revised from time to time. What was once desirable to liberals may be passé and unacceptable to them today, so that the exact meaning of liberalism has evolved over the years. For example, the original, or **classical liberals**, whose principal spokesman was **John Locke** (1632–1704), believed that all human beings were capable of being moral, competent, and intelligent. Further, Locke asserted that **natural law** (that is, certain rules of nature governing human conduct that could be discovered through the use of human reason) applied to all people in equal measure, thus assuring their fundamental moral equality.[3] Revering the individual above all things in society, classical liberals believed that government oppressed people when it had too much power—therefore, the less government the better, thus Thomas Jefferson's famous admonition, "That government governs best which governs least." In addition, private property

---

[3]Please note that "moral equality," as Locke understood it, meant only that all people were subject to the same moral prescriptions and limitations. No one had a greater right to kill or steal. The democratic implications of this belief are obvious. It should not be understood that Locke believed all people were equally moral.

was held in high esteem. Indeed, classical liberals believed that property was a **natural right** and that an individual's possessions were to be protected from government confiscation. But, liberals have since moved beyond Locke's views.

Contemporary liberalism, as will be seen in Chapter 5, was fathered by Jeremy Bentham (1748–1832), and its followers continue to uphold several of the notions developed by their classical predecessors. Still viewing people as intelligent creatures, contemporary liberals remain optimistic about our ability to improve life through reason. Change, therefore, is still a major tool of the liberal. Human equality is another concept that the liberal continues to support, but the basis for the assumption of equality has changed. Few liberals still believe in the concept of natural law. Instead, the contemporary liberal is more likely to argue that although there is a wide variety of differences among individuals, all people are equally human, and their equality with one another is a matter of great importance. Therefore, since no person is more or less human than any other, and since equals have no moral right to treat one another unequally, all people have the right to expect certain treatment and consideration from other people. These are called the **human rights** and are fundamentally the same as the natural rights.

In addition, contemporary liberals disagree with their classical counterparts about the nature of government. Modern liberals note that the concentration of wealth has deposited vast power in the hands of those who control the means of production, distribution, and exchange, and they posit that people with economic power will use it, in part, to sustain and increase power in their own hands, thus placing at a disadvantage those without economic power. Thus, it is logical to assume that, through time, the rules and power structure of society become increasingly unequal, with the well-to-do enjoying privilege and advantage over others. Thus, contemporary liberals are concerned that economic power can be as oppressive as political power.

In response to this bias, contemporary liberals believe government can be used by the economically weak to protect themselves against the oppression of the powerful. Discovering that some people have used their control of property to unfair advantage over less fortunate individuals, contemporary liberals temper their belief in the individual's right to accumulate property with their concern for the happiness of the society as a whole. Thus they tend to be more *egalitarian* (those who wish power and wealth to be more equally shared by all people) than the classical liberal. Moreover, rather than believing that government tends to deny human liberty, contemporary liberals believe they can use government to expand liberty by limiting oppression the wealthy would ordinarily impose on the poor.

Moderate

It is somewhat awkward to write about moderates because, unlike the other positions on the political spectrum, there is no philosophical foundation for this category. One could cite Aristotle's advice about seeking the Golden Mean, of course, but even this goal is more one of temperament than philosophy. One must be moderately something, either moderately liberal or moderately conservative. I introduce the moderate category only because it is so often used in political discussion to describe those who find themselves liberal or conservative about some things but not really committed with any degree of intensity to either side of the spectrum.

Moderates are fundamentally satisfied with the society, although they agree that there is room for improvement and recognize several specific areas in need of modification. However, they insist that changes in the system should be made gradually and that no change should be so extreme as to disrupt the society.

To say that being a moderate is only to take a mild stand on the issues is not to suggest that being moderate is always easy. Being moderate on an issue that engenders in most other people a highly emotional response can be very difficult indeed. For example, holding a moderate position on whether abortion should be legal could be problematic. Affirmative action, the death penalty, feminism, and the war in Afghanistan are other examples of issues on which the pro and con sides have so hardened that a less-than-absolutist stance can be unfairly seen as faint-hearted, ambivalent, and uncommitted.

Interestingly, like beauty, ideology often depends on the eye of the beholder. This phenomenon can currently be seen in relation to President Barack Obama. Petulant conservatives view his foreign policy in the Middle East; his pledge to vacate the alleged terrorist prisoners from the American naval base at Guantanamo, Cuba; his effort to reform the health care delivery system; and his policies to rejuvenate the economy as irresponsibly liberal and unconscionably disruptive. Meanwhile, bitterly disappointed, liberals regard his decision to send more troops to Afghanistan; his delay at closing down the prisons in Guantanamo; his refusal to completely end the "extraordinary renditions" (kidnapping suspected terrorists and sending them for "aggressive interrogations" to Syria, Egypt, and other places known for using torture); and his willingness to make huge compromises on public health reform as betrayals of liberalism. Disgruntled, they remind the president of the title of Jim Hightower's book, *There's Nothing in the Middle of the Road But Yellow Stripes and Dead Armadillos.*

Of course, either of these observations about Obama's policies may be true. In fact, both may be true. But it is also possible that, rather than being a stubborn ideologue, insisting his way is the only right way, he may simply be swallowing hard and behaving like a pragmatic, practical politician who wants to get something done. Politics, as the perceptive French politician Georges Clemenceau observed, is "the art of the possible": In politics, the ideal is often not possible.

Conservative

Conservatives are the most supportive of the status quo and therefore are reluctant to see it changed. Being content with things as they are does not suggest that conservatives are necessarily happy with the existing system, however.

Conservatives are often accused of lacking vision, but this charge is unfair. The difference between conservatives and liberals is not founded on the fact that the latter dream of achieving a better world, whereas the former think the status quo is the best conceivable existence. In fact, conservatives may desire a future no less pleasant than that of the liberals—a future free of human conflict and suffering. The essential difference between the two viewpoints rests on their respective confidence in when (or, indeed, whether) the ideal can be accomplished. Conservatives support the status quo not so much because they like it but because they believe that it is the best that can be achieved at the moment. Put differently, conservatives oppose change because they doubt that it will result in something better, not because they do not desire improvement.

Lacking confidence in society's ability to achieve improvements through bold policy initiatives, most conservatives support only very slow, incremental, and superficial alteration of the system. The most cautious of them often resist even seemingly minor change. They tend to see an intrinsic value in existing institutions and are unwilling to tamper with them, claiming that to do so might seriously damage that which tradition has perfected.

Of course, not all conservatives are equally resistant to change. Obviously, those closest to the status quo point on the spectrum are the least inclined to desire change. And, although it seems unlikely that many people are absolutely content with the system and are opposed to any change whatsoever, some people do take this position, and each of us could probably find some issues in which we would prefer no change at all. Still, most conservatives will accept some deviation from the status quo, be it ever so slight, and *the change they will accept is progressive.*

The primary reason conservatives are suspicious about the prospects of improving society through deliberate political policy is that *they do not believe human reason is powerful enough* to even completely understand, let alone solve, society's problems. Although they do not deny the existence of reason, they are wary of relying too heavily on it for solutions to human problems. Liberals and conservatives agree that people have complex natures composed of moral and immoral, rational and irrational impulses. They differ, however, on which attributes dominate. Liberals believe that human reason is powerful, that it can be successfully used to solve society's problems, and that it can also be employed by people to overcome impulses to do harm. Thus, liberals see human beings as trustworthy creatures who will normally behave themselves when left alone. Conservatives have less faith than liberals that people can use reason to restrain their animalistic impulses and their emotions; they mistrust human nature. Conservatives see people as relatively base and even somewhat sinister. They suspect the motives of others and tend to believe that, unless somehow deterred, people will take advantage of their unsuspecting or weaker fellows. Consequently, whereas liberals believe that little government control is normally necessary to ensure human compatibility, conservatives tend to favor authoritarian controls over the individuals in society. This explains why conservatives are the "law and order" advocates in society. They believe that unless police forces are large, laws harsh, and prisoners uncomfortable, people will not be deterred from crime.

Because they mistrust reason, conservatives often rely on **irrationalist**[4] rather than rationalist solutions to problems. To conservatives, reason is of limited use in making life better. They believe that human reason is severely limited. Although it can be used to deal with minor difficulties—technological improvements, for example—it cannot be counted on to successfully solve difficult problems such as eliminating poverty or ending war. Therefore, conservatives tend to place great reliance for dealing with society's problems on the passage of time, authority, institutions, religions, and traditions. For example, whereas liberals might try to solve a social problem such as poverty by creating a government program to eliminate it, the War on Poverty for example, conservatives are apt to eschew this rationalist approach and counsel that the matter be left to the "market" to decide. The market is beyond anyone's direct control. It operates in response to the demand and supply of hundreds of millions of individuals with no overriding scheme or management. Yet, conservatives often talk about the market as though it is guided by some sort of superhuman wisdom. Whether the approach works or not—strong arguments can be made on either side of this case—the point here is that conservatives prefer to leave the solution to major social problems to phenomena uncontrolled by deliberate rational acts.

Moreover, conservatives value longevity for its own sake and believe that one of the justifications for preserving a practice or an institution is the fact that it was worthwhile in the past. Obviously, this attitude encourages very little change in society.

Liberals and conservatives differ also with respect to the concept of human equality. Here again, we find a difference in emphasis dominating the debate between the two. Liberals recognize that people differ from one another: Some are stronger, more intelligent, better looking than others, and so on. But, the leftist argues, these are only superficial differences. The most important and determining feature of people is that they are all human, and they are each equally human; no one is more human than the other. Thus, if humanity is the most important of our features, and we are each equally human, equality must be the condition that predisposes our conduct toward one another. "When a black man bleeds, he bleeds red," they argue, emphasizing that beneath the surface all people are alike. Conservatives take the opposite view. They are quick to recognize the biological similarity among people but argue that this fact is relatively unimportant given the enormous variation in qualities among people. To the liberal protestation about everyone having red blood, conservatives respond by asking, "So what?" Emphasizing that crucial inequalities have always existed among people, conservatives insist that to attempt to construct a society on any other assumption is folly.

---

[4]The term *irrationalist* is not intended to imply that conservatives lack the rational or intellectual prowess of their opponents. In this book, the term *irrationalist* applies only to persons who see severe limitations in people's ability to solve problems through the use of reason.

Far from a simple academic debate, questioning the importance of human equality is fundamental to politics. Politics is largely caught up in the problem of how to distribute wealth and power justly in society. If one believes that human equality is fundamental, then there can be few moral arguments for distributing societies' benefits unequally. If, however, human equality is inconsequential—or does not exist at all—it would hardly be just to insist on an equal distribution of wealth and power.

Because liberals believe all people are equal, and further that human equality is the most compelling fact about people, they are *egalitarians*, believing a just society will take steps to distribute wealth and power equally. Just how equally wealth and power should be distributed depends upon one's view about how important human equality is. While all leftists believe it is the most compelling feature, only the most extreme leftists, certain radicals, demand that equality virtually eclipse all other qualities in determining the distribution of society's benefits. Whereas most other conservatives agree with reactionaries that human equality is a myth, because of the heavy influence of classical liberalism in the United States, American conservatives accept the principle of human equality. However, they oppose society's doing much to reward human equality because, although they agree that people are equal, they do not agree that human equality is important. Life, they aver, is like a race or contest. Equality is only the beginning point and therefore should not be rewarded. Instead, people's accomplishments throughout life should be rewarded. Although people are equally human, the rightists say, they did nothing to become human or equal and therefore deserve no particular political or social benefits because of it. Both of these are powerful arguments, and indeed, the way you come down on this issue will go a long way toward determining where you might find yourself on the spectrum.

Conservatism has, of course, long been a prominent political position, but it was not until Edmund Burke (1729–1797) put pen to paper that it was given a formal philosophical base. The well-governed society, Burke argued, is one in which people know their place. "The rich, the able, and the well-born" govern, whereas the people of lower social rank recognize their betters and willingly submit to their rule. Should they refuse—should the ordinary people try to govern themselves, as in France during Burke's time—the ultimate result can only be disaster, for nothing noble can come from the mediocre.

Burke was not content, however, to see the elite rule with no admonition for temperance, for although they were the best in society, they too were human and were afflicted with the same frailties as the commoners, albeit to a lesser degree. The elite, according to Burke, are responsible for ruling benevolently and effectively. Power is not to be used by the rulers to suppress the masses. Still, nothing good will result if either group pretends that inferior people share equal political rights with the ruling group. Decrying the "false" values of liberalism, Burke put his case bluntly when he wrote:

> The occupation of a hair-dresser, or of a working tallow-chandler, cannot be
> a matter of honor to any person—to say nothing of a number of other more

servile employments. Such description of men ought not to suffer oppression from the state; but the state suffers oppression, if such as they, either individually or collectively, are permitted to rule.

Interestingly, the present conservative position on private property is, to some extent, quite close to the classical liberal attitude, in that both regard private property as an inalienable right of the individual. The similarity ends there, however, since the conservative goes on to suggest that wealth is one of the important factors that distinguish one person's value to society from another's. Conservatives believe that the property right dominates virtually every other right. Consequently, government has no legitimate power to interfere with the individual's accumulation or use of private property unless this activity causes injury, death, or the destruction of another's property, and even those conditions are allowable under certain circumstances. For example, the American Chamber of Commerce and the National Association of Manufacturers are among the most vociferous opponents of the government mandating dramatic action to reduce emissions of greenhouse gases, which heavily contributes to global warming, even though the deleterious effect of climate change on human health, while debatable as to its exact extent, is indisputable as to its existence.

On the other hand, persuaded that people with great wealth often use their influence to stack the deck against the less fortunate, liberals tend to favor using government as an equalizer. Accordingly, they usually favor government regulation of business, arguing that likely irresponsible corporate behavior encouraged by the profit motive should be tempered by the law. In the case of pollution, liberals might assert that most people when shopping focus on the finished product, and its price, rather than the conditions under which it was produced. This lapse, however, should not be used as an excuse to allow manufacturers to knowingly endanger consumers.

Just as there are two distinctly different kinds of liberals, classical and contemporary, conservatism can also be divided. Whereas liberals tend to be egalitarians, conservatives tend toward *elitism*, favoring a stratified society based on one or another perception of merit. Those who are referred to as *Tories* closely follow the prescriptions of Burke. They make no bones about the fact that the excellent of society should rule, but at the same time, they should govern with dignity and benevolence. Tories look for leadership in a ruling class, one that has a civic duty to govern the less able. They call upon the rulers to ignore selfish impulse and govern in the interests of society as a whole. As Burke's statement above directs, the mediocre should certainly not rule, but neither should they be oppressed. Although it is a paternalistic approach, Toryism at least demands that the elite rulers govern with a social conscience and strive to do what is "best" for all people in society.

A second group, who are called the *entrepreneurs*, are much more individualistic and sometimes almost populist in their approach. Whereas the Tories look to an elite class to rule, the entrepreneurs might be seen as "democratic elitists," believing that the nation's leaders can come from any stratum of society. "The cream rises to the top," they believe, and the government and other social institutions should allow the greatest latitude possible for individual accomplishment. Otherwise, they might impede the excellent from excelling. In contrast to the Tories, the entrepreneurs demand less self-restraint and see government not as an obligation of one's station, but as an instrument by which superior individuals can better express their own authority. Instead of viewing government as a tool to shepherd society to noble goals, entrepreneurs want to limit government restraint on individual economic behavior so as to facilitate the elevation of the excellent and the devolution of the uncompetitive. Hence private enterprise, unregulated by the government, is the principal objective of the entrepreneurs. Columnist George Will and, to a much lesser extent, former president George H. W. Bush are American examples of Toryism. But the number of American Tories is very small today. Much more numerous are the entrepreneurs, who are led, at least symbolically, by former president Ronald Reagan, former Speaker of the House Newt Gingrich, and talk-show host Rush Limbaugh. Curiously, former president George W. Bush was also an entrepreneur. His policies were much closer to Ronald Reagan's than to his father's in that he had a simple "good" versus "evil" approach in foreign policy, and on the domestic side he pursued a classic supply-side economic policy (explained later in this chapter) and each sacrificed the environment at the altar of economic development. (See Chapter 12.)

Complicating the mix further is the recent emergence of two other strains of American conservatism: the *social conservatives* (sometimes called "theocons") and the *neoconservatives* (*neocons*). Focusing largely, although not entirely, on domestic policy, the social conservatives are closely associated with fundamentalist religious groups (Pentecostals, Evangelicals, Southern Baptists, Jehovah's Witnesses), who comprise about 25 percent of the U.S. population, Mormons, and Roman Catholics. Brushing aside the constitutional requirement of separation of church and state, these "true believers" insist that public policy unerringly reflect their Christian beliefs and insist that financial support of the U.S. government be given to their social organizations. (These efforts were remarkably successful under President George W. Bush, and, perhaps surprisingly to the theocons, many of their values and objectives are also endorsed by President Obama; witness Obama's support of Bush's faith-based initiatives, regardless of the entanglement of government funds and religious organizations.) Thus, the social conservatives are less interested than economic conservatives in tax cuts, low government spending, and balanced budgets. Instead, they focus on government support of Christian social issues (faith-based institutions), outlawing teaching Charles Darwin's theory of natural selection, securing government supported school vouchers and tax write-offs for students attending parochial schools, prohibiting abortion, banning same-sex marriages, and so forth.

While certainly mobilized before 2000 through Jerry Falwell's Moral Majority and the Christian Coalition led by Pat Robertson and Ralph Reed, the election of George W. Bush to the presidency galvanized this movement.

Bush's election and his fundamentalist rhetoric energized this element in the American body politic, and it became a powerful force in his support and a critical factor in his 2004 reelection. Since then, these religious extremists have become very aggressive in advancing their agenda.

It is important, however, to quickly note that while social conservatives agree on many things, they do not march in lockstep on all issues. For instance, Catholics oppose the death penalty, while fundamentalists strongly favor it. Fundamentalists are sure "the end time" (Armageddon) is near and that government policy—including the Iraq and Afghanistan wars, which are seen as "crusades against radical Islam"—should reflect that the end of the world is near.

Of course, not all Christians are extremists, but, a growing number of social conservatives, energized by the belief that their views are a manifestation of God's will, have led to two other interesting results. First, their emotional commitment to these issues have caused these activists to pursue them even to the extent of leading them to support pandering politicians who mouth desired platitudes about abortion, same-sex marriage, prayer in schools, and so forth, but then cast votes against the economic interests of these supporters.[5] Second, pursuing God's will, as they believe they do, they have grown dangerously impatient with other points of view. Dangerous because democracy is based on tolerance of ideas with which one might disagree. Some of these extremists, feeling themselves divinely deputized to defend the "truth" and that it is therefore not debatable, have increasingly resorted to obstructing meetings, shouting down opponents, and even doing violence (murdering doctors who perform abortions, for instance). This growing incivility and righteous extremism has also infected other elements of the right wing such as the Tea Party movement, thus causing more temperate people to turn away from the public discourse on some of our most important contemporary issues.

The Tea Party movement was a spontaneously formed group that in 2010 managed to dominate the Republican Party nominations in some states. A Libertarian-like group opposed to taxes and big government managed to get people with unorthodox views nominated—some elected—to office. Some of their candidates advocated seceding from the union, urging states not to enforce national law unless it is ratified by the state, the First Amendment does not apply to Muslims, Muslim children born in the United States are moles who will someday engage in terrorism, the national government's growing power may need a "Second Amendment solution," and ending popular election of United States senators. The list, by the way, goes on and on.

The second group of recently emerged conservatives is the neoconservatives who focus on foreign policy and were the most influential advisors to President George W. Bush in that field. Although a tiny group of people, the

---

[5]See Frank, Thomas, *What's the Matter With Kansas; How Conservatives Won the Heart of America*, (New York: Henry Holt and Co., 2004).

neocons are well financed and creative intellectually. These intellectuals posit that American values and institutions are superior to all others throughout the world, and with the demise of the Soviet Union, the United States is the victor of the Cold War and the world's sole superpower. It therefore has a responsibility to use its might to bring American virtues to the rest of the world. The 2001 American invasion and occupation of Iraq is a manifestation of this imperialist policy. Vice President Dick Cheney, Paul Wolfowitz, Douglas Feith, I. Lewis (Scooter) Libby, Richard Pearl, Robert James Woolsey Jr. (CIA director under President Clinton), John Podhoretz, and William Kristol are leading neocons and all held high government posts and/or exercised substantial influence during the Bush administration.

Their differences aside, all conservatives share similar goals. They revere tradition, history, and established institutions. Most important, because they are suspicious that human beings cannot make great improvements in society through rational and deliberate efforts, conservatives of every stripe are very reluctant to foster substantial change. ·

The foregoing positions among conservative camps have appeal, of course, but the conservative resistance to change is in itself very appealing to many people. In fact, it is not an exaggeration to suggest that of all the arguments made by conservatives to justify their ideology, the most attractive is the promise of political order. Radicals and liberals offer change, new ideas, and different institutions, but even if these were to succeed, the process of change itself would disrupt the society for a time. As it happens, large numbers of people have very low thresholds for political and social disorder. Thus, change—even though it might be for the better in the long run—disturbs them and they resist it. They are even willing to suffer a system that is somewhat harmful to their interests rather than go through any kind of abrupt dislocation in the pattern of their everyday lives. Order, then, is a powerful selling point for conservatism.

Reactionary

Of all the political actors discussed here, only the **reactionary** proposes retrogressive change; that is, reactionaries favor a policy that would return society to a previous condition or even a former value system. For example, we witnessed a reactionary revolution with the overthrow of the Shah of Iran in 1979. Without going into detail about the nature of the movement formerly headed by the Ayatollah Khomeini, we can see that his advocacy of a return to a literal application of the ancient laws in the Koran was clearly a reactionary legal posture. The policies of Iranian President Mahmoud Ahmadinejad and the Taliban's emergence in Afghanistan in the 1990s are also quite reactionary, as is the extreme Islamism movement. (See Chapter 11.)

In the United States, three movements with reactionary beliefs have recently become popular. The *Libertarian Party* lionizes the rights of the individual and thus calls for the reversal of the New Deal reforms of the 1930s and a return to the _laissez-faire_ policies that preceded them. Laissez-faire and the New Deal will be explained in detail later; for now, it is enough to point out that Libertarian ideology advocates a kind of rugged individualism and the abolition of government policies that try to mitigate the ill effects imposed on the less well-off when the well-heeled use their economic and political power. Although the Libertarian Party itself has not succeeded in winning many elections, the extreme right in the Republican Party espouses the Libertarian ideology, and that faction has, since 1994, been very powerful in both the Republican Party and its efforts in Congress. Another movement at the far right of American conservatism is the Tea Party movement.

Before we go further with the definition of reactionary, however, we should return to Figure 2.1 through 2.3 and note that they are distorted in one important respect. In these diagrams, the reactionary sector is no longer than any other sector, leading one to believe that a person at the extreme right of the reactionary sector is not more dissatisfied with the system than a person at the leftmost point of the conservative sector. In fact, the person farthest to the right among reactionaries is just as frustrated as the person at the leftmost point of the radical sector. To be accurate in this respect, the reactionary sector should actually be extended so that it is as long as all the progressive sectors combined. (See Figure 2.4.)

The closer reactionaries are to the status quo, the less impatient and frustrated they are and the more socially acceptable are their methods. However, just as the Marxist at the far left insists that no change without violence can be valid, the fascist at the extreme right argues that war is good in and of itself. All reactionaries reject claims to human equality and favor distributing wealth and power unequally on the basis of race, social class, intelligence, or some other criterion. By definition, reactionaries reject notions of social progress as defined by people to their left and look backward to other, previously held norms or values. Examples of reactionary movements beyond those just mentioned are various right-wing survivalist groups, neo-Nazis, the Ku Klux Klan, and extreme Christian fundamentalist sects like the Christian Identity Movement.

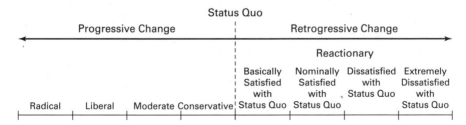

FIGURE 2.4
Reactionary sector detailed on the political spectrum.

VALUES, OR PERSONAL PHILOSOPHY

Having dealt with the concept of change, the reader is now prepared to distinguish among radicals, liberals, conservatives, and reactionaries. But the perceptive reader has probably begun to wonder whether one must know more about people than their attitudes toward change in order to completely understand their political orientation. For example, is it possible for a liberal and a reactionary to support exactly the same policy even when it proposes a basic change in the society? Yes, of course it is, thus the source of the old saw "politics can make strange bedfellows." The change itself is important, but not critical; much more significant is the anticipated result. Intent or expectation strikes at something much more fundamental in politics than simply the concept of change. It leads us to an investigation of basic political values and motivations.

For purposes of illustration, let us consider the volatile issue of abortion. On what grounds might abortion be supported or opposed? Although a pro-choice stance is usually seen as a liberal position, some conservatives have supported abortion, arguing that such a policy would reduce the number of unwanted children among the poor, thus indirectly reducing welfare costs. Liberals supporting a woman's right to choose an abortion do so for an entirely different reason, claiming that deciding whether to have an abortion is a totally private matter, one in which the government has no business interfering. Some people's notion of morality, it is argued, should not be allowed so much authority that it denies the individual's right to privacy.

Yet, are there not opponents of abortion? Of course, there are many; they also come from both sides of the continuum. Taking a traditionalist stance, conservative opponents assert that pregnant women are morally obliged to bear their children to term and that, except in extreme circumstances, they do not have the right to abort. On the other hand, liberals who oppose the death penalty because they reject society's right to take human life could oppose abortion for the same reason. Related issues, such as legalizing euthanasia, prostitution, narcotics use, and same-sex marriage, can be argued on similar grounds by the various antagonists. Clearly, then, intent, or the question of political values, is important to our study and bears further inquiry. Most people in our society have a fairly good understanding of human rights, since such rights appear in general terms in the Declaration of Independence and in specific terms in the Constitution of the United States, especially the Bill of Rights. Human rights include life; liberty; the pursuit of happiness; freedom of expression and religion, freedom from torture, *habeas corpus;* and so forth. These rights and liberties were incorporated into our political tradition by our country's founders, who were classical liberals.

The private property[6] right was originally thought to be an inalienable right proceeding to each individual from the natural law. Thus, it was referred

---

[6]Please note that in this book the term *property* is used in the broadest context. Hence, property refers not only to real estate but to all material items including money, clothing, furniture, and so forth.

to as a *natural right*. Classical economists such as John Locke, Adam Smith, and David Ricardo were convinced that people could not be truly free unless they were allowed to accumulate private property. It was not long, however, before liberals observed that the control of property by some people could be used to deny liberty to others. Accordingly, the property right was quickly relegated to a secondary position in the priority of rights. Today's liberals consider it a *social right*—one that can be granted, regulated, and denied by society based on its needs. Thus, the property right can be alienated from the individual if the group deems it appropriate. ⌊*Eminent domain*⌋ is a long-standing principal at law. It allows government to force an individual to sell private property if society has a pressing need for it—to build a freeway, for example.[7]

Indeed, leftists as close to Locke's time as Thomas Jefferson and Jean Jacques Rousseau refused to recognize property as an inalienable right. One of the most hotly debated phrases in the proposed Declaration of Independence of 1776 was "life, liberty, and the *pursuit of happiness*" (emphasis added). People more conservative than Jefferson, its author, argued that the phrase should be changed to read "life, liberty, and *property*" (emphasis added), just as John Locke had originally written.[8] Jefferson prevailed in that debate, of course.

Liberals challenge private property as a human right on the basis that no necessary logical link exists between ⌊human well-being⌋ and ⌊*private* property.⌋ Human rights are those things that are necessary to the species in order to lead a decent human life, and therefore cannot be justly denied by one human to another, since the two are equal. Close examination of the constituents of the phrase "life, liberty, and property" reveals that life is obviously an essential factor. Liberty is also fundamental if one accepts human equality as a reality. If people are equal, then no person has the moral right to subjugate another without consent. People, therefore, have the right to be free. Private property, however, does not enjoy similar status since it is not essential for people to lead a decent human life. Food, clothing, and housing are, of course, necessary for people to enjoy life, but these things need not be privately owned. Yielding to this logic, and impressed by the fact that some people use their control of property to the disadvantage of others, Jefferson penned the more general phrase "pursuit of happiness," and he successfully defended it against those who wished to substitute for it the term "property." Eleven years later, in 1787, while Jefferson was serving as U.S. ambassador to France, a much less liberal group of men gathered in Philadelphia to write a new constitution. Only scant mention was made of the rights of the people. Indeed, it was not

---

[7]Indeed, in a very controversial case, the Supreme Court of the United States ruled that local governments had the right to force the sale of private residential property so it could be developed for commercial use, thus increasing the city's tax base. (*Kelo* vs. *City of New London,* 2004.)

[8]Locke actually used the word *estate*, but *property* is commonly substituted for the term.

until the Fifth Amendment was adopted in 1791 that any general statement of inalienable rights appeared in the Constitution; that reference would read "life, liberty, and *property*"(emphasis added). Clearly, conservatives were in control of the country at the time.

As a general rule, we can conclude that those toward the left on the political spectrum tend to give the greatest emphasis to *human rights*, whereas those on the right tend to emphasize *property rights*. For example, if one were to ask a liberal whether a person has the right to refuse to sell a piece of property to an African American, he or she would certainly say, "No! As long as the African American has the money to buy the property, the seller has no right to refuse to sell." Notice that liberals are not unappreciative of the property right. Clearly, they insist that the prospective buyer have the amount of money asked by the seller. With that condition satisfied, however, the liberal would require that the sale be completed. In this case, the liberal's position is predicated on the assumption that an African American is morally equal to any other person and, therefore, should not be discriminated against because of race. The emphasis here is definitely on human rights.

On the other hand, if the same question were put to conservatives, their response would be different. They would probably say that although racial prejudice is unfortunate, if property owners insist on refusing to sell their property to a particular person on the basis of racial prejudice, they have every right to do so. Why? Because it is *their property*. Here the conservative recognizes the conflict between human rights and property rights, but the property right obviously supersedes the human right; property ownership prevails over equality. The conservative, unlike the contemporary liberal, might even argue that the property right is one of the human rights. Even if that were the case, close scrutiny of the conservatives' attitude toward various human rights would show them insisting that the property right dominates all other human rights.

The balance between human and property rights becomes increasingly one-sided as one moves toward the ends of the political spectrum. On the far left, **Karl Marx** predicted that communism would be democratic, allowing absolutely no private property or inequality. **Benito Mussolini** (1883–1945), at the opposite extreme, denied human rights entirely, insisting that people had no justification, no rights, no reason for being that was not bound up with the nation-state. Indeed, the individual's only function was to produce for the good of the state, and anyone who failed to do so could be liquidated.

To further dramatize the philosophical differences between left and right, let us consider the various goals that arise from their respective values. As mentioned earlier, the left is inclined toward egalitarianism. Socialism, generally thought to be a leftist economic theory, tends to level the society and produce material equality because one of its main goals is to reduce the gap between the haves and the have-nots in the society.

Politically, leftists advocate an egalitarian society as well. Radicals tend to propose pure democracy. Both Rousseau, the founder of modern radicalism, and Marx demanded that political power be shared equally by all people.[9] Liberals, on the other hand, accept representative government but insist that ultimate political power remain in the hands of the people.

By contrast, the right is unabashedly elitist. Capitalism is today a conservative economic system. This was not always so. **Adam Smith** (1723–1799), who fathered capitalism, was a classical liberal of the eighteenth century. Capitalism represented a liberal challenge to the mercantilist status quo of that time. (More will be explained about the conflict between capitalism and mercantilism in Chapter 5.) Today, however, capitalism *is* the status quo; consequently, support of this system in a capitalist country is necessarily a conservative position.

Capitalism tends to stratify society. Those who are successful are respected and rewarded. Those who are not are abandoned as failures. The net result is that society becomes hierarchical, an elitist circumstance thought desirable by people on the right.

Politically, rightists advocate an elitist structure as well. Believing that people are somewhat unequal and in need of guidance, conservatives and reactionaries favor a society in which superiors command and subordinates obey. The farther to the right we look, the more structured and *authoritarian* is the desired society, until at the extreme right we come to Mussolini's fascism. Mussolini saw his society as a sort of social pyramid. At the base were the masses, whose duty was to perform their functions as well as possible. At the top of the pyramid were the party members and, ultimately, the leader. The leader's function was to perceive good, justice, and right and to rule the society accordingly. The masses were expected to obey without question.

Leftists, by contrast, want to maximize *personal liberties*. Believing that people will generally be well behaved when left alone, liberals tend to want government to use a light touch in regulating individual activity. Another reason liberals tend to want the police power restrained is that they usually define acceptable human behavior more broadly: They tend to view fewer things as being wrong than do conservatives. Many liberals, for example, believe that "victimless crimes" should not be crimes at all. Prostitution, an act between consenting adults, is no one else's business, some leftists argue. On the other hand, most conservatives insist that prostitution is morally repugnant and must therefore remain illegal. Similarly, most conservatives believe that unprescribed use of narcotics should remain illegal and that the "drug

---

[9]Here each was referring to "relative equality," not "absolute equality." That is, ordinary people should enjoy the same political authority, possessing only one vote, for example, but obviously leaders need more power than do private individuals.

war" should continue. By contrast, most liberals contend that education and treatment are more effective than is police intervention in fighting drug abuse. A growing number of leftists argue that the drug war—this nation's longest war, having been declared by President Richard Nixon in 1972—clearly is not working and that it is actually counterproductive, because in their zeal to discourage drug abuse, the authorities are trampling on the civil liberties of innocent people. Some of them go on to suggest that the problem might be best solved by legalizing drug use. This, they aver, would take the profit away, thus removing drug pushers from the streets.

To suggest that liberals tend to be *libertarians* (people who wish to enhance individual liberties, but not to be confused with the Libertarian Party) and that conservatives tend to be authoritarian, using the police power more is true, so far as criminal law and civil liberties are concerned. However, the two switch sides when economic matters come to the fore. As a general rule, conservatives tend to fear people who do not have wealth, whereas liberals tend to be suspicious of people who do have it. Conservatives believe that people with wealth have it because they deserve it and that government power should protect them from attempts by the underclasses to take it from them. By the same token, they believe that government power should not impede people from using their property as they wish. Liberals, on the other hand, believe that people with economic power tend to use it unfairly to the disadvantage of the less fortunate. Accordingly, liberals are quick to use government power to regulate individual or corporate economic behavior. Here we see the right being the more permissive of the two.

Uncharacteristically, the left has recently demonstrated that it can be less tolerant than the right even about the exercise of civil liberties. Normally, the left accords people the greatest latitude in free expression, for example. Yet, over recent past years, in an attempt to discourage expressions of racism, sexism, and homophobia, the left has demanded that universities adopt language codes for students and that the media and public figures avoid the use of words that certain people may find offensive. These efforts to enforce a certain **political correctness** (PC) on society have been stoutly resisted by the right, and the controversy has treated observers to a curious reversal of roles: the left trying to *muzzle* free speech and the right defending it.

Finally, today's left tends toward *internationalism* and the right toward *nationalism*. Leftists speak of all people being sisters and brothers, arguing that national boundaries are artificial and unnecessary divisions setting people against one another. Marx, for instance, asserted that national boundaries were only artificial separations designed by capitalists to divide ordinary people and to distract them from their commonalities. Under socialism these frontiers would disappear because, he said, "working men have no country." Eventually the world would become a single socialist brotherhood. In an earlier generation, French revolutionaries borrowed from Rousseau, demanding a system dedicated to "Liberty, Equality, [and] *Fraternity*" (emphasis added).[10] Conversely, fascists exalt differences between individuals within a state and dissimilarities among states. As people are ranked according to their value within a society, fascists argue, so too will state dominate state until one state rises above all others. Less extreme rightists do not necessarily demand imperialistic dominance, but they are clearly nationalists, believing that their nation is better than others and that their national interest can be placed above others. (You will recall the neocon proposition about American superiority.) These ideas will be discussed more fully in the next chapter.

MOTIVATION

Many people suspect that economic pressures are the primary motivation for choosing a particular political position, and, indeed, this does appear to be an important factor. People who are doing well in society usually do not want it to change. By contrast, the poor have little to lose materially and much to gain from progressive change. Or so it can be supposed. Economics is not the only factor in the choice of political beliefs, however. There are plenty of poor conservatives, and one can easily find rich liberals. In fact, there is no single motivation for people's political attitudes. In the following paragraphs, we will discuss the most important factors besides economics that influence people's political choices.

Age is often a significant factor. Although we may have just emerged from an era (1980s–2007) in which young people tended to be among the most conservative people in society, this is rare historically. Usually, the young are more likely to be liberal than the elderly. This is probably because the older generations have a vested interest in the status quo that the younger generations have not yet acquired. Young people lack not only wealth, but also a sense of commitment and belonging. Fifty-year-olds are likely to feel that they have a stake in society, not only because they have helped create it, but also

---

[10]It is worth noting here that the fraternal, or social, aspects so prominent in the French Revolution were almost completely absent in the American Revolution. Because America enjoyed an abundance of land and natural resources, opportunity was not as severely restricted as in the more stratified European societies. Hence, the American Revolution was almost completely political in nature. No serious attempt was made to realign the social structure or to redistribute the wealth in America. Because our revolution simply constituted a transfer of power from the English to the American elite, it has not been a model for European revolutions. It is true that the success of the American Revolution encouraged Europeans to seek change in their own lives, but the changes needed in Europe were far more sweeping than those desired on the American side of the Atlantic. European revolutions became vehicles for economic and social change as well as for political transformation. Hence, the French Revolution is second only to the Industrial Revolution as the modern world's most influential upheaval, and it became the model for all subsequent European convulsions. Indeed, due largely to our unique social and economic environment, American politics has never been very similar to public affairs in Europe, a fact that sometimes causes serious misunderstanding on both sides.

because they have become used to it. The young have neither of these reasons to be committed to the system.

Some people are also more *psychologically suited* for liberalism or conservatism than others. To be a liberal, one must have a relatively high tolerance for disorder. Many people do not, so that even though they may not benefit materially from the system, they resist change because they fear disorder, and because they cannot be sure that the prospective change will actually leave them better off than before. Yet, some people seem to need almost constant change; the status quo never satisfies them.

Perhaps the greatest single determining factor in whether one will tend to the left or right is what one feels the *nature of people* to be. If one believes that people are essentially bad, selfish, and aggressive, then one is likely to lean to the right of the spectrum. Anyone who thinks that people are inherently evil will tend to rely on strict laws and firm punishment for violators in the belief that such measures are necessary to control errant behavior. On the other hand, people who believe their fellows to be essentially well meaning and rational will lean toward the left. They will try to avoid impeding human liberty by "unnecessarily" severe laws, and they will try to reason with offenders. People on the right tend to believe that prisons should be institutions for punishment, forcefully teaching transgressors to behave, whereas leftists see prisons as institutions for rehabilitation. Believing that denial of liberty is punishment enough, leftists hope to use penal institutions to school criminals in socially acceptable behavior and to give them skills that they can use to make a living honestly, thus avoiding a life of crime. The crux of the matter rests in assumptions about human nature: Are people impelled by greed and selfishness or are they motivated by more innocent aspirations? How one comes down on these questions will have a great deal to do with one's political views.

A practical example might help. Illegal immigrants are a growing problem, with an estimated 12 million undocumented people living in the United States today. What should be done to deal with this problem Mr. Conservative? "Get tough: Stop coddling these people. Make life here hard on them. Deny the interlopers health care, welfare, education, and other amenities. If need be, seal off the border and even use the military to intercept illegal crossings." Further, maybe we should reduce welfare payments to Americans, forcing them to go to work rather than leaving all those jobs to be done by foreigners.

Your solution Mr. Liberal? "Look, the illegals don't leave loved ones and familiar surroundings because they like to live in the bushes outside of our towns. They are attracted here by the money they can earn from people who illegally hire them. To keep them home, we should do what we can to help their native countries develop economies that are able to employ them, and we should adjust the wage scale here sufficiently so that American workers willingly take the jobs they now forfeit to foreign workers. If one can make more money from welfare than from taking menial jobs, is that the fault of welfare, or the wage scale in this country?"

THE CHANGING SPECTRUM

Just as people's views can modify over time, thus changing their location on the continuum, the spectrum can shift to the left or right while a person remains stationary. Ronald Reagan was a liberal New Deal Democrat in the 1930s. By the 1960s, he had become a reactionary Republican, and as such, he served two terms as governor of California (1967–1975) before becoming president of the United States (1981–1989). During Reagan's first term as governor, a reporter asked him why he had left the liberals. His answer was, "I didn't; they left me." Reagan was arguing that the things he wanted in the 1930s had been enacted and that he was satisfied with the achievement and did not want further change. Whether Reagan's assessment of himself was accurate is not important here; the critical thing is that if we were to remain unchanged in our political attitudes for thirty or forty years while the world changed around us, we might very well become reactionary after having been liberal because the status quo would have shifted so much in the meantime.

It is also appropriate to point out that the political spectrum of one society bears no particular similarity to that of any other society unless the status quo is the same in each. A given policy could be conservative in one society, liberal in another, and radical in a third. (See Figure 2.5.)

Let us assume that the issue we are dealing with is whether a pregnant woman has the right to have an abortion if she chooses not to carry the fetus to term. In the Netherlands, the right to an abortion is commonly accepted and quite legal. Some people in the society certainly oppose allowing abortions on demand, but there is a strong national consensus on the issue. Thus, a person in Holland supporting legal abortion on demand would be quite conservative on the issue, since this is supportive of a long established status quo.

In the United States, on the other hand, while the right to abortion is legal, the public is far from a consensus on the issue. And, unlike the Netherlands, it is usually illegal for federal funds to pay for abortions. Therefore, assuming

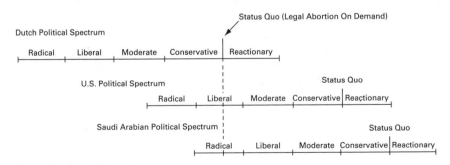

FIGURE 2.5
A comparison of political spectrums.

one in the United States supports abortion on demand is normally thought to be liberal on the issue, because it has not become a settled matter.

In Saudi Arabia, however, all induced abortions are illegal. Therefore, to support legalizing abortion on demand would be so far removed from the status quo as to be a radical position. Put differently, as far as induced abortions on demand are concerned, the political spectrum of the Netherlands is to the left of the United States' spectrum, while the Saudi spectrum is far to its right.

SPECIFIC POLICIES

At this point, it might be helpful to translate some of the previously discussed general ideological points into practical policy as related to U.S. politics. Basically, the politics of any country can be divided into two main arenas: foreign and domestic. Let us assume that the goals of our society can be generalized in the form of two major objectives: peace and prosperity. What specific policies might one expect from the establishment right and left in the United States in pursuit of the goals described above?

Foreign Policy

Believing that people are self-oriented and competitive, conservatives are likely to assume a relatively suspicious posture in dealing with foreign governments. Resorting to cliché, we can readily identify the slogan "The way to preserve the peace is to be prepared for war" as a distinctly conservative approach to foreign policy. Given this view, the hallmark of their relations with other states will be a strong military posture buttressed by mutual defense alliances with their friends against those whom they perceive as adversaries. Their foreign aid programs will tend to emphasize military assistance, thus strengthening their allies. The thrust of their policies will be directed at guarding against the incursions of their foes. Essentially, the world is viewed in adversarial terms, with the opponent seen as the aggressor. Because conflict is considered inevitable, little hope is held out for sustained amicable relations until the adversary conforms to the conservatives' views.

The liberal approach to foreign affairs is considerably different. Liberals do not believe that people are aggressive by nature. Further, they hold that people are capable of resolving their differences rationally. Warfare is regarded as abnormal, whereas peace and cooperation are considered natural to human beings.

Although liberals certainly do not ignore the martial aspect of foreign policy, they place much less emphasis on it than do their conservative counterparts. Their confidence in human reason is clearly apparent when they counter conservative militarism with the attitude that "the way to preserve the peace is to discover and eradicate the causes of war."

A Peace Corps worker helps Nepal peasants build terracing for their fields.

Courtesy Peace Corps

Libe

Deemphasizing military solutions, liberals tend to rely heavily on economic and technical aid to strike at what they conclude are the causes of war: poverty, disease, ignorance, intolerance, and so on. Further, liberals look to exchange programs among intellectuals, artists, and ordinary people as a means by which tensions can be reduced. This approach is based on the assumption that people will generally get along better if they understand one another; ignorance breeds fear, mistrust, anxiety, and conflict. Accordingly, liberals are likely to place great store on institutions such as the Peace Corps and the United Nations, institutions that conservatives view with suspicion. Liberals support these organizations because they believe that they give the greatest promise of letting rational beings solve their problems peacefully.

Obviously, neither of these positions is without contradiction. The right's suggestion that armed nations won't go to war is easily disproved, and one could argue with the left by asserting, "I know many people well whom I don't like. In fact, the better I get to know and understand them, the less I like them." Still, the generalizations introduced above are at the base of conservative and liberal foreign policy. The operative question is, are people rational and well intentioned, or are they incapable of controlling sinister impulses in their own nature?

Domestic Policy

As a general rule, it can be assumed that, all other things being equal, liberals will spend more on domestic programs than will conservatives. This principle also pertains to foreign policy, but to a lesser extent. Liberals not only spend more money but they also release it on a broader base in the society, among people who are apt to spend it again quickly. For their part, conservatives usually spend much less on domestic policy, and they release money among far fewer people—people who are also least likely to spend it again quickly. Consequently, liberal policies tend to place inflationary pressures on the economy by increasing the volume of money (the number of dollars in circulation) and the velocity of money (the frequency with which dollars are spent). Conservative policy reverses the liberal emphasis, thus exerting deflationary pressures on the economy.

Specifically, conservatives argue that ours is an advanced economy, one that needs a high degree of capital investment. The health of our economy is therefore dependent on a sound capital base. Although government involvement in the economy should be kept to a minimum, government should act to protect capital, the life's blood of the economy.

This view, referred to as **supply-side economics,** calls for money to be funneled from the government directly to big business by various means. (See Figure 2.6.) The theory suggests that the captains of industry will use the added revenue to increase productivity through capital investment (the purchase of factories and machinery, research and development, and so on) and will also improve the

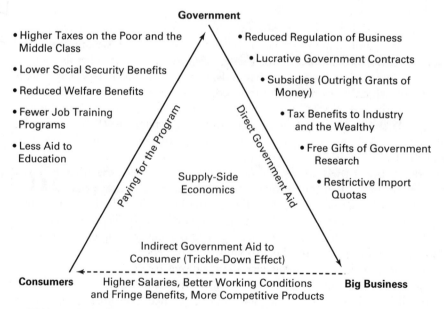

FIGURE 2.6
Supply-side economics.

condition of the workers by increasing wages, improving working conditions, and augmenting fringe benefits. Opponents call this largess "corporate welfare" and derisively refer to its purported benefits to the poor as the "trickle-down effect." These policies must be paid for by someone. Thus, conservative economic policies usually increase taxes on the poor and the middle class while reducing government services to them through cuts in social programs such as government aid to education, job training programs, Social Security, and so on. A classic recent example of policies like these can be seen in President George W. Bush's tax relief policies. In three separate tax reform laws, President Bush and the Republican Congress cut taxes by more than $2 trillion over a ten-year period. Meanwhile, critics argue that over 60 percent of the tax cuts have gone to the richest 20 percent of the public, with about 40 percent of the "recaptured" dollars going to the richest 1 percent of the public, who in fact assume only about 20 percent of the total income tax burden.

For their part, liberals argue that people, not big business, are the nation's principal resource. The benefits of direct government support should go to the people as a whole rather than to the wealthy. Having their spending power increased by government programs, people will purchase the goods produced by industry, thus affording it revenue to increase wages and capital investment.

However, these policies must also be paid for. So, liberals would reverse the policies of the supply-side approach, substituting what might be described as the *demand-side*, which increases government regulation and taxation of big business. (See Figure 2.7.) But since liberal policies are so much more

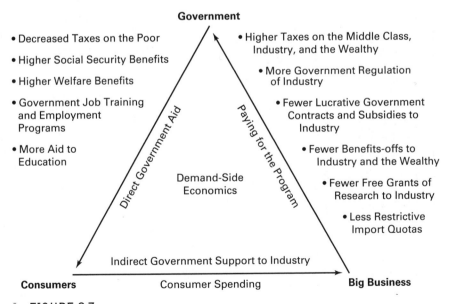

FIGURE 2.7

Demand-side economics.

Progressive Change   Status Quo   Retrogressive Change

Radical
Desires immediate, fundamental change. Is frustrated, impatient, and revolutionary. Some insist on violence, whereas others only tolerate it or reject it altogether.

Liberal
Desires rapid, far-reaching change. Believes people can improve their lives through the use of reason.

Classical Liberal
Believed in natural law. Believed private property was inalienable. Believed government oppressed people.

Contemporary Liberal
Believes private property is a social right. Believes government should be used to improve life through social engineering.

Moderate
Fairly contented with the society. Supports gradual change.

Conservative
Is active defending the status quo against change. Is pessimistic about human capacity to improve life through the use of reason. Depends on "tried and true" institutions. Believes private property is an inalienable right. Desires order.

Reactionary
Wishes things to be as they were. The frustration level of the extreme reactionary is equal to that of the extreme radical.

Left   Middle of the Road   Right

Supports: Support human rights
           Are rationalists
           Support egalitarianism
           Are suspicious that police power is used to oppress common people
           Will use government to protect people against the economic elite
           Are internationalists

Supports: Exalt property rights above all else
           Are irrationalists
           Are elitists
           Rely on police power to control threats to the status quo
           Oppose government involvement in the economy
           Are nationalists

FIGURE 2.8
Spectrum of political attitudes.

expensive than conservative programs, reversing the flow of money alone is not enough to cover the costs. Accordingly, besides increasing taxes on the wealthy, liberals would require the middle class to pay more taxes as well. Comprising the bulk of the taxpayers, and being less protected than the very wealthy or the very poor, the middle class is asked to carry the bulk of the tax burden under either plan.

The arguments by each side against the other's programs are familiar. Conservatives assert that liberal programs put everyone on the government dole, destroying individual initiative and making the recipients wards of the state. Liberals respond by contending that if individual initiative is destroyed by the grant of government aid, what happens to initiative in business under the supply-side approach? Quoting George Bernard Shaw, who said, "American capitalism is really socialism for the rich," liberals ask whether business is not made dependent upon government protection against competition by the supply-side model.

Liberals go on to argue that the trickle-down approach will not necessarily work. The government may release money to business in order to increase employment, for example, but business is likely to spend that money for its own purposes. Thus, the industrial owners may take greater profits from money the government meant for increasing jobs. After all, was it not just such a malfunction of the supply-side approach that caused the Great Depression and now the Great Recession?

"Ah," the conservatives respond, "if the supply-side is an inefficient method of releasing money into the economy, what of the demand-side? The government may give the poor money with which to buy milk for the children, but, all too often, it is spent on beer and cigarettes!" Round and round go the arguments. Each of us must decide to what extent either side is right.

Finally, the chart in Figure 2.8 is offered in the hope that it will give you a more complete picture of the spectrum and thus help you understand the material in this chapter.

QUESTIONS FOR DISCUSSION

1. What are the fundamental factors that precondition a person's attitude about the need for political change?
2. How can reactionaries, conservatives, liberals, and radicals be defined relative to their respective attitudes regarding change?
3. What fundamental values are common on the right and the left of the political spectrum, and how do these beliefs translate into public policy?
4. How do economics, belief about human nature, age, and psychology influence people's association with the political spectrum?
5. How can liberal and conservative approaches to foreign and domestic policy be compared and contrasted?

SUGGESTIONS FOR FURTHER READING

Buckley, William F., Jr., *Up From Liberalism*. New York: Hillman Books, 1961.

Burke, Edmund, *Reflections on the Revolution in France*. Chicago: Henry Regnery, 1955.

Crowder, George, *Liberalism and Value Pluralism*. New York: Continuum, 2002.

Dean, John W., *Conservatives Without Conscience*. New York: Viking, 2006.

Dewey, John, *Liberalism and Social Action*. Columbus, OH: Prometheus Publishing, 1999.

Friedman, Milton, and Rose Friedman, *Freedom to Choose*. New York: Harcourt Brace Jovanovich, 1980.

Kirk, Russell, *The Conservative Mind: From Burke to Eliot*. Washington, DC: Regnery, 2001.

Krugman, Paul, *The Conscience of a Liberal*. New York: W. W. Norton, 2009.

Ortega y Gasset, José, *The Revolt of the Masses*. New York: W. W. Norton, 1960.

Phillips, Kevin, *American Theocracy*. New York: Viking, 2006.

Pope, Daniel, *American Radicalism*. Malden, MA: Blackwell, 2001.

Raskin, Marcus, G., *Liberalism: The Genius of American Ideals*. Lanham, MD: Rowman and Littlefield, 2004.

Rawls, John, *Political Liberalism*. New York: Columbia University Press, 1993.

Sider, Ronald J., *The Scandal of the Evangelical Conscience*. Grand Rapids, MI: Baker Books, 2005.

Smith, Christian, *Christian America? What Evangelicals Really Want*. Berkeley: University of California Press, 2000.

Nationalism

PREVIEW

Nationalism, the theoretical expression of the nation-state, is the most powerful political idea of the past two centuries. As such, it has had an enormous impact on the modern world. The terms nation and state are often confused. *Nation* is a sociological term referring to a group of people who have a sense of union with one another. *State* is a political term that includes four elements: people, territory, government, and sovereignty.

The reason for the state's birth is probably quite practical, yet several theories of the origin of the state contradicting this likely fact have been historically important. The natural theory actually bases its definition of humanity on the existence of the state. The force theory suggests that the state emerged as the strong imposed their power on the weak. The divine theory contends that a particular people was chosen by God, whereas the divine right of kings theory regards the monarch as the personification of the state. The social contract theory suggests that people consciously create legitimate political power.

With the emergence of the nation-state, nationalism was developed as its ideological justification. Nationalism is used as a frame of reference as well as a yardstick by which to measure and assess people and policy. As a principal form of self-identification it can both unite and divide people.

Nationalism calls on people to identify with the interests of their national group and to support the creation of a state—a nation-state—to support those interests. Nationalism has become increasingly popular since the French Revolution. Leftists have supported it as a vehicle to improve the well-being of citizens, whereas rightists use it to encourage unity and stability. The end of the Cold War has seen many people who were formerly controlled by the Soviet Union assert their right to national self-determination. At the same time, however, Western European countries and North American states have taken steps toward international unions, and the Muslim world has toyed with the idea of a huge reactionary Pan-Islamic state. Although nationalism can be a positive influence, its limited vision can threaten conflict over scarce resources.

THE IMPORTANCE OF NATIONALISM

Nationalism is among the oldest, and unquestionably the most virulent, of all ideologies. It would be difficult to exaggerate the importance of this concept in contemporary politics. *Nationalism is the most powerful political idea of the past 200 years.* It has had a great impact on every person in every modern society. People have applauded policies pursued in the name of country they would have condemned for virtually any other reason. Millions of people have been sacrificed and died, property destroyed, and resources plundered, all in the name of the state. Yet, individuals have also risen to noble heights and made great contributions to humanity for the sake of the nation-state. As we will see in later chapters, nationalism is so powerful that it has dominated almost every other idea system. Indeed, only anarchism rejects the state, although certainly feminism, environmentalism, and socialism are uncomfortable with the state because these ideologies tend to appeal to humankind in general, rather than to the Danes, the Brazilians, the Indonesians, or the Gambians in particular. In all other ideologies, the state is given a role, and in some cases, it is given the dominant place. Moreover, the appeal of nationalism has recently reasserted itself in some former colonies which countries now find themselves split asunder by the conflicting and competing demands of different, once united, peoples. Therefore, it is essential that we take up the study of nationalism early in this book. Before we consider nationalism itself, however, let us examine two terms that are essential to understanding nationalism: *nation* and *state*.

Nation and State

The term **nation** is often used as a synonym for *state* or *country*. This is not technically correct, but the mistake is commonly made by political leaders as well as by ordinary people. To be precise, the term *nation* has no necessary political implication. Indeed, the concept of a nation is not political but social. A nation can exist even though it is not contained within a particular state or served by a given government. A nation exists when there is a union of people based on similarities in linguistic pattern, ethnic relationship, cultural heritage, or even simple geographic proximity.

Probably the most common feature around which a nation is united is ethnic background. One's *nationality* is often expressed in terms of ethnicity rather than citizenship. Thus, although some people will respond "American" when asked their nationality, it is not uncommon for loyal U.S. citizens to answer "Greek" or "Chinese" or "Colombian." These individuals are thinking of nationality as a cultural or ethnic term, not making a political comment. The fact that ethnic background can be the basis of a nation does not, however, mean that people must be related by blood to be members of the same nation. Switzerland, the United States, and Russia each include several ethnic groups, most of which have clear cultural differences. In fact, Russia contains almost 100 separate and distinct ethnic groups, and many of them have lived in what are parts of today's Russia for as long as, or longer than, the Russians themselves. Indeed, many republics in the Russian Federation are the ancient homelands of its disparate ethnic groups and are named after them: Buryatia, Chuvashia, Tuva, Udmurtia, for example.

Even when a nation is clearly identified by its ethnic makeup, the people of that nation can be divided into any number of different states. The German people are a good example. Basically, German people make up the bulk of the populations of Germany, however the Austrian and Dutch people are also Germanic, to say nothing of the inhabitants of several Swiss cantons (provinces). On the other hand, the Jews are a good example of a nation of people who, for a long time, had no country to call home. For thousands of years, Jews maintained their national identity, linked by strong cultural patterns as well as by ethnic relationships, but they had no state of their own, thus they lived in countries dominated by other national groups. Although their folklore promised a return to their homeland at some future time, the movement to set up a Jewish state in Palestine (known as *Zionism*) did not develop until the nineteenth century. Finally, in 1948, the state of Israel was created, and many Jews left their former homes for the new country. Today, there are 7.3 million people in the *state* of Israel, yet many members of the Jewish *nation* are still living in other lands. Both Russia and the United States, for example, have large Jewish populations.

By contrast with the Jews, the Polish nation has a long history of being encompassed by a state. Yet, from 1797 to 1919, Poland ceased to exist as a political entity, having been partitioned among its neighbors—Russia, Prussia, and Austria. The elimination of the Polish *state* did not spell the doom of the Polish *nation*, however. Bound together by a common language, intellectual tradition, history, geography, and religion, the Polish people continued to identify themselves as distinct from others, and following World War I, the Polish state was re-created. After a brief period of independence, Poland was conquered by the Nazis and then by the Soviet Union, and from World War II until 1989, Poland was governed by a Soviet-dominated communist government. If anything, the political ambiguity and foreign domination endured by Poland served to strengthen the people's feeling that they belonged to the Polish nation.

On the other hand, although a nation need not be organized into any particular state, it is indeed possible that a nation can evolve almost solely because its people identify with one another on the basis of residing in the same country. Switzerland is a good example of this phenomenon. Switzerland is composed of German, French, and Italian ethnic groups, but the experience of hundreds of years of isolation in the Alps has done much to forge a very strong Swiss national identity, even though the cultural diversity among its people remains clear and is celebrated and protected.

Geographical proximity alone, however, is seldom sufficiently cohesive to forge a nation from a diverse population. Iraq, created by the British in the early twentieth century with little thought to the ethnic complexity of its people, is composed of three main groups. Most of the Iraqis are Arabic, but they are divided against themselves into Shiite Muslims, comprising about 60 percent of the total population, and Sunni Muslims accounting for about 20 percent. The remaining 20 percent are mostly Kurds, a quite different ethnic group from the Arabs. Complicating matters more, these people find themselves further divided among often competing tribes, clans, classes, and political parties.

Although some people in Iraq feel loyal to Iraq itself, many more relate most closely to one of these other groups. Despite their minority status, the Sunni have dominated the country politically, and they now resist losing their privileged status. The Kurds want at least autonomy and probably independence. Predictably, the Shiites demand power commensurate with their share of the population. The 2003 American invasion proved ill-advised and very poorly planned, leading to a bloody insurrection. President George W. Bush would have been wise to heed the example of his father, President George H. W. Bush, who refused to end the 1991 Gulf War by occupying Iraq and unseating Saddam Hussein. As his son's less cautious policies later proved, the senior Bush concluded such a venture would dangerously destabilize Iraq, and the entire Middle East along with it. And, incredibly, our focus on Iraq led to our partial loss of control in Afghanistan to the once vanquished Taliban, causing another setback in the Middle East.

Only the addition of a large number of troops in 2007 led to the stabilization of the Iraqi situation. But the current removal of American troops from Iraq is only feeding our increased emphasis on the war in Afghanistan. Meanwhile, a growing number of people in the United States have concluded that we are out of our element being so deeply involved in the Middle East.

Politics can also be a source of national identity, although such affinity born of political factors alone is not common. Some people, usually in relatively new societies, have welded together in nationhood with politics as the main adhesive. The United States is a good example. We are a people who enjoy a very strong national identity. But what factors draw us together? Ethnicity is certainly not the focus of our nationhood. Though we speak a common language, English plays only a marginal role in making us one people; we never even made English the official national language. It is impossible to identify any cultural feature that is sufficiently cohesive to be the basis of American nationhood. Yet a nation we most assuredly are. The American nation is founded on a shared belief in certain political factors. It is forged by popular support of concepts that can best be assimilated in the notion of the state: flag, country, democracy, liberty, equality, tolerance. In fact, the American *nation* rests upon a bedrock of the *state* itself. Although most Americans do not consider themselves political beings, the fact that we find unity with one another primarily through the context of the state makes us among the world's most political people.

In contrast to the United States, the Soviet Union is an example of a failed attempt to create, out of a very diverse people, a single nation by political means. From 1917 to 1991, the Soviet Union was a single state composed of about 120 distinct national groups. Using Marxism-Leninism as the adhesive, Soviet leaders tried to create from their cosmopolitan society a single nation of people: *the new Soviet man* it was called. However, the various national groups within the country stubbornly resisted assimilation, preferring to maintain their traditional unique identities instead. Finally, in the late 1980s, when the communist system began to disintegrate, Soviet leader Mikhail S. Gorbachev loosened the Communist Party's totalitarian grip on the society. Responding to the new freedom, dozens of the national groups within the state loudly asserted their separate identities and many even demanded the right to political independence. Opposition to continued Russian control was a much more virulent motivation for dissolving the Soviet Union among the minority populations than was anti-communism.

Many people in the United States still believe that the American economic and military challenges brought the Soviet Union down. While competition with the United States certainly did not help Soviet stability, the greatest cause for its demise was the collapse of its attempted national union. Its diverse peoples insisted upon holding on to their traditional national identities, refusing to morph into the new Soviet man. For evidence of this, one need look no further than the last few weeks of the Soviet Union's existence. Mikhail Gorbachev was arrested by the hard-line party leaders on the eve before he was to sign a new treaty with the constituent parts of the Soviet state—the Union Republics (Russia, Ukraine, Estonia, Uzbekistan, etc.)—granting them more autonomy. When his arrest prevented this new arrangement, the ethnic components of the Union Republics refused to allow the continued predominance of the Communist Party and, led by Russia, the Union Republics, one by one, seceded from the Soviet Union in 1991. Suddenly, the Soviet Union was no more. It was replaced by fifteen independent countries, the former Union Republics. Subsequently, several minority national groups within most of these new countries have demanded independence, or at least autonomy, from the new states in which they now find themselves. The people of Chechnya have attempted to become independent from Russia through a long and bloody rebellion, the Gagauz Turks want freedom from Moldova, and Georgia has struggled against separatist movements among its Abkhazi and South Ossetia minorities. Although the bloodletting in most of these areas has ended, at least for the moment, it will take decades for these controversies to be sorted out. What is important for us at this point, however, is to note that, unlike in the United States, politics alone was not sufficiently strong in the Soviet Union to overcome the identities of the various national groups, and it therefore failed to coalesce them into a single nation.

One of the important reasons for the successful emergence of the American nation and the failure of the Soviet nation is that, unlike the people of the Soviet Union, the people of the United States (other than the Native Americans, who were simply overwhelmed and brushed aside) had to leave the old countries and immigrate to new ones. By contrast, the nations comprising the Soviet Union had been there for hundreds of years before the Bolshevik Revolution.

They did not go to a new politics, the new politics was imposed on them in their own land, and they ultimately rejected it.

Clearly, therefore, the term *nation* has no necessary political implications, but this is not at all true of the term *state*. Although we in the United States use the term *state* as a synonym for *province* (e.g., the state of Louisiana), the traditional usage of the word is as a synonym for *country*. Accordingly, a description of the state normally includes four elements: people, territory (a defined geographical space solely associated with a particular state), **sovereignty** (ultimate legal authority within a given territory), and government. A nation of people can find itself spread across the globe, and its existence is not necessarily determined by its association with any specific location. (The Kurdish people, for example, numbering about 20 million, finding themselves as minority groups within Turkey, Iran, Iraq, and Syria, form the largest national group that has no state of its own.) All states, however, have clear territorial boundaries. Moreover, these lands are served by governments that technically have final legal authority over all the people within their boundaries. The only characteristic necessarily shared by state and nation is people. When a nation of people manage to create a state of their own, however, the resulting political entity, the **nation-state,** is very important.

The Nation-State   The nation-state has become the principal form of political organization among modern people. Indeed, in political terms, part of the definition of a modern society is that it is organized into a nation-state. The term *nation* symbolizes the unity of a people; the term *state* formalizes the organization and structure of that union. One of the preeminent principals of the nation-state system is *national self-determination* (the right of national groups to organize themselves politically, forming nation-states). This idea developed wide currency during the twelfth century, and so it remains today, although it is far from perfectly adhered to, witness the Kurdish dilemma. Thus, since the turn of the twentieth century, the number of states has more than tripled and today is about 200. The nation-state has become a focal point around which people unify and through which they identify themselves and assess political events. So strong is the people's identification with the nation-state that political leaders often need only claim that a particular policy is in the *national self-interest* to satisfy many of their compatriots that the policy is justified.

This simplistic morality is striking for its power and authority, but it is also very troubling. Consider for a moment: If nation-state policy is primarily established and justified by narrow national self-interest, especially in a world confronted with dwindling resources, conflict among nation-states becomes almost inevitable. National self-interest raises selfishness among societies in the world to a level of acceptability that it would never achieve among individuals within a society. No modern state would legislate that any individual can do as he or she pleases solely on the basis that it is thought to be justified by personal self-interest. But that is the logic pervading the nation-state system, and it threatens chaos. If each nation-state's policy is determined primarily by what is best for that nation-state, then surely many such policies will be opposed by other nation-states on the grounds of their own national self-interest. In such an environment, the interests of the world as a whole are not considered, and given the extreme press of growing populations on vanishing resources, viscous international conflict over parochial policy becomes unavoidable.

The inherent shortsightedness of the nation-state system notwithstanding, it should be noted that although it is dominant today, the nation-state is only history's most recent authoritative form of political organization. Human beings rallied to several other political organizations before adopting the nation-state. Among these earlier forms are tribes, city-states, empires, and feudal baronies. Because the nation-state is only the latest in a long series of systems used as principal organs of political association, it is logical to expect that the usefulness of the nation-state will eventually become marginal, thus encouraging the evolution of yet another institution to someday replace it. At present, however, the nation-state remains dominant.

Before we move on to the next section, a word of clarification is appropriate. In the United States, the terms *nation* and *state* have specific meanings other than those just explained. In this country, as well as in several Latin American countries following our example, the term *state* has two meanings. It can mean *country*, as it traditionally has, or it can be used as a synonym for *province*. To complicate matters further, we used the word *nation* to refer to the central government. Thus, we pledge allegiance to the *Nation*, Congress is our *national* legislature, and a *national* law takes precedence over the laws of the *states*.

Theories of the Origin of the State

Although no definitive evidence exists, we are now fairly certain that the state evolved because society had a practical need for it. As people ceased their nomadic wanderings, private property became important. The state probably evolved as a way of organizing society to maximize the exploitation and distribution of resources, which had become limited when people stopped moving. Further, the instruments of the state (the law and government) were used to define, protect, and transfer property. Practical as is the probable reason for the origin of the state, it is mundane and unexciting, thus difficult to use in motivating people. In previous eras, politicians, theologians, and philosophers came up with several other more politically compelling ways to maximize the loyalty of citizens. There are probably elements of truth in some of these myths; most of them, however, are demonstrably inaccurate, and some are even fanciful. True or not, however, these theories have been believed by people and have motivated their political behavior. Thus, we consider the most important theories of the origin of the state.

The Natural Theory   Aristotle, the father of political science, is an early proponent of the **natural theory** of the origin of the state. He believed that people should constantly seek moral perfection, which they will probably never reach.

Still, the quest for moral perfection is the noblest of human pursuits. Humans, according to Aristotle, are social beings by nature; that is, they naturally gather together and interact with one another, thus forming a community. This congregation, Aristotle posited, takes place for reasons that go far beyond simple biological necessity. Indeed, a community is a necessary condition for human fulfillment. The formal organization of the community is the state. The formation of the state is a result of people's natural inclination to interact. Aristotle believed so firmly that the state was a society's natural environment that he claimed that people were human only within the state. An individual outside the state was either "a beast or a god," the state being the only environment in which one could be truly human. The state was the central institution in Aristotle's philosophy; it was not only the manifestation of our natural inclination to interact but also the vehicle through which the individual could achieve moral perfection. Expressing the same idea differently, Pericles (c. 495–429 B.C.E.), Athens's most esteemed statesman, said, "We alone regard a man who takes no interest in public affairs, not as a harmless but as a useless character."

To the ancient Greeks the state was not merely a natural phenomenon, it took on a much more important characteristic. Although it was made up of interacting individuals, it was actually greater than any single person or any group. It became an entity with a life, rights, and obligations apart from those of the people it served. This **organic theory** of the state was later supported by diverse people such as Thomas Aquinas, Rousseau, and Mussolini. Today's leftists also often refer to the organic society.

The Force Theory   The **force theory** actually embraces two schools of thought: one negative and the other positive. The original school, the negative one, goes back to ancient times. In this theory, the state was created by conquest; it grew out of the forceful domination of the strong over the weak. Therefore, the state was an evil thing that could be resisted in a righteous cause. As one might imagine, this negative application of the force theory has been dogma to revolutionary groups throughout the ages: to the early Christians resisting the Roman Empire, to medieval theologians trying to make the temporal authority subject to the spiritual, and to democratic insurrectionists leading the struggle against monarchical tyranny.

The positive expression of the force theory developed in Germany during the nineteenth century. Internal political divisions and external pressures had prevented the consolidation of Italy and Germany into modern political units until the late nineteenth century. A nationalistic spirit had been growing in Germany, however, since the Napoleonic Wars. It became exaggerated as a result of the frustration encountered by its proponents.

A positive theory of the forceful origin of the state was maintained principally by **Georg Hegel** (1770–1831) and **Friedrich Nietzsche** (1844–1900). Their theories form the basis of what is now called **statism**. They argued that the state was indeed created by force, but that rather than being evil, this feature dignified the state. Force was *not* something to be avoided. On the contrary, it was the primary value in society. It was its own justification: "Might makes right," as Nietzsche put it. The state, institutionalizing the power of the strong over the weak, simply arranged affairs as they should be. According to force theorists, the weak *should* be ruled by the strong; all of nature underscores this priority.

Some students of Hegel and Nietzsche have argued that the state is the most powerful form of human organization. As such, it is above any ordinary moral or ethical restraint and it is greater than any individual. It is not limited by something as insignificant as individual rights. (In Chapter 5, you will learn that in the eighteenth century, Edmund Burke held a similar view of the state's superiority over the individual.) Although certainly neither Hegel nor Nietzsche would have been sympathetic to fascism or Nazism, their theory that force justified action was used by Mussolini and Hitler for their own purposes; we shall return to a discussion of the ideas of these nineteenth-century philosophers in Chapter 10. For now, it is enough to remark that this version of the force theory is probably the clearest example of extreme nationalism: chauvinism. It puts the state above the people, giving government a status that cannot be equaled or surpassed. Thus, the institution itself has power separate from that of the people under it. The state is a self-contained being, an organic personality in and of itself, all-powerful and total.

The Divine Theory The **divine theory** is probably the oldest theory of the origin of the state. It is based on a fairly common assumption: Some people are God's chosen ones.

Saul, for example, was anointed by Samuel, the prophet of God, and Saul led the "chosen people" in the conquest of the Philistines. The Arabs conquered a vast empire and the Crusaders invaded the Middle East, both in the name of the "true religion," and Islamic fundamentalists, like the Jews, still claim that they are the chosen ones. Similarly, the Japanese during World War II, believing that they were favored by the sun goddess (Amaterasu) and convinced that their emperor was her direct descendant, willingly died in the emperor's cause, thinking salvation awaited them for such martyrdom. This belief still resonates politically in Japan. In 2000, Japanese Prime Minister Yoshiro Mori ignited loud protests both inside Japan and abroad by claiming that Japan was a "divine nation" with the emperor at its center.

Early Christian theologians used the concept of the divine origin of the state to their own advantage. The early fathers of the Church, Saint Ambrose (340–397), Saint Augustine (354–430), and Pope Gregory the Great (540–604), argued that spiritual and temporal powers were separate but that both came from God. Each of these thinkers was ambivalent about the relationship between the state and the Church. Augustine and Ambrose implied that the state was subject to the spiritual leadership of the Church, but neither pressed the point too far. Gregory, on the other hand, believed that the Church should bow to the state in all secular affairs. Gelasius I, who was pope from 492 to 496, first suggested the **two swords theory** as it was to be applied during the Middle Ages. The spiritual and secular powers were both essential to human life, but they could not be joined under a single person. The primary function of each was to contribute to the salvation of people. The state helped pave the way to paradise, providing peace and order and creating the atmosphere in which people could best serve God. The Church was responsible for developing the true spiritual doctrine and giving people guidance toward their heavenly goal.

None of the early Christian fathers would have disagreed with any of these positions. Gelasius I, however, went on to claim that the pope should take precedence over the state. He was the first to argue that the pope should be uncontradictable on questions of dogma. Further, he insisted that since the primary duty of both Church and state was to help people reach their eternal reward, the Church, being the *spiritual sword*, should prevail in disputes between these two basic institutions. John of Salisbury (1120–1180), a noted scholar, went even further than Gelasius I, stating that all temporal power actually came from the Church. Anyone who supported this theory would not question the superiority of the Church over the state.

The Roman Catholic Church was generally regarded as the greater of the "two swords" throughout the medieval period, and princes normally accepted this notion, often reluctantly. Gradually, however, the intellectual advances of the Renaissance led to religious and political changes. National monarchs began to claim authority over secular affairs. At the same time, the Reformation challenged the pope's spiritual absolutism.

Closer to home, the notion of *manifest destiny* was used to imply God's sanction for the United States conquering the North American continent and portions of the Pacific Ocean. Mormon doctrine teaches that the U.S. Constitution was divinely inspired, and a popular patriotic song suggests that "God shed his grace on thee." Even President Reagan's calling the Soviet Union the "evil empire" in 1983, President George W. Bush's remarks in 2002 about the "Axis of evil" and an American "crusade" in Afghanistan, and, President Obama's 2009 assertion in his acceptance speech of the Nobel Peace Prize that "evil" exists in the world each smack of the Divine Theory born anew.

As you can see, the divine theory of the origin of the state has, at one time or another, had wide appeal. Perhaps the time in which it enjoys the greatest prominence is during war. It would be difficult to find a warring society that was not buttressed in its martial resolve by its leaders' suggestion that God was on its side. Indeed, it is common to find that each side in a war claims for itself the divine imprimatur. Can you imagine a war in which one side or the other believed that God was on neither side or even for the adversary? Such a proposition is ludicrous. The fact that each side invariably claims that God supports its cause dramatically points up how politically powerful the concept of God is in religious societies.

Three generalizations can be drawn about the divine theory: (1) Virtually every nation has, at one time or another, seen itself as chosen above all others in the sight of God; (2) divine selection has invariably been self-recognized—the chosen people have discovered their privilege by themselves, rather than having it pointed out by less fortunate folk; (3) the discovery of such an exalted status has usually preceded activities against other people—conquest, impoverishment, genocide—which could scarcely be justified without self-proclaimed superiority.

The Divine Right of Kings Theory Inevitably, those supporting absolute monarchy and those challenging the centralization of spiritual power joined forces in the **divine right of kings theory**. This contention was put forward as a counterproposal to the ancient theory of the two swords. French thinker, Jean Bodin (1530–1597) gave this idea philosophical respectability when he developed his theories about the origin of the state and sovereignty.

Some early Christians believed in the *original donation theory*, which is somewhat compatible with the divine right of kings theory. It was contended that Adam and Eve's fall from grace and their banishment from the Garden of Eden resulted in God's granting Adam the right to rule the temporal state, and that all later kings were his heirs.

Adherents of the divine right of kings theory believed that all power came from God, but they differed from the churchmen by suggesting that God specifically chose the king and gave him absolute power (authority unrestrained by the monarch's subjects). Here, these absolutists were joined by the Protestant reformers Martin Luther (1483–1546) and John Calvin (1509–1564), who proposed the theory of *passive obedience*. The Reformation and absolutist factions agreed that political power came from God and that those who were chosen to exercise it were higher on the social scale than ordinary people. Consequently, people were duty bound to obey the prince, even though he may be a tyrant, because he was God's magistrate on earth. Presumably fortunate for these oppressed subjects, sinful kings would be held accountable by God.

This theory had a tremendous impact. Claiming legitimacy from divine authority, monarchs became extremely powerful in this religious era. Popular refusal to obey the king was seen as heresy as well as treason. The French absolute monarchy of Louis XIV was based on this theory, and the Stuart house of England was purged because of it. Indeed, the divine right of kings theory was important even in the twentieth century. Believing that his covenant with God would be violated Tsar Nicholas II (r. 1894–1917) resisted popularly imposed limitations to his power. Had the tsar been more flexible, the 1905 and 1917 Russian Revolutions might have been averted.

The Social Contract Theory The social contract, the idea that ruler and ruled agreed on their respective roles and had obligations to one another, can be traced, in one form or other, back through millennia. Interpretations of the contract varied from time to time, but, perhaps not surprisingly, the ruler generally benefited from the theory more than the subjects did. Still, the notion that the ruler governed by the consent of the governed was always implied by this theory.

Because the divine right of kings theory was used by monarchs to claim that there should be no limits on their political power, opponents of absolute monarchy needed arguments to use against this compelling theory. The social contract theory as it developed in the seventeenth and eighteenth centuries was based on the concept of **popular sovereignty,** in which the ultimate source of the legitimacy and authority of the state is the people.

The contract, it was argued, was established when the all-powerful, or sovereign, people made an agreement that created the state, legitimized the ruler, and gave him or her certain powers. Note that *the state was created by a deliberate and rational act of the people in society.* On this matter social contract theories agree, but they disagree as to the exact form of government the contract created and the limitations placed on the powers of government by the sovereign people.

The social contract theory will be discussed more fully in Chapter 4. It is now important to note, however, that this theory is a major contributor to the ideology of nationalism. Under the social contract theory, the state is created by all the individuals within it. Therefore, the state is of them, and at the same time they are part of it. This close interrelationship between the people and the state is fundamental to nationalism. The social contract theory gives the individual an important role. At the same time, it describes the combining of individuals into a whole that is different from, yet related to, its individual parts and, according to some theorists, has a greater power and justification than the simple sum of its parts.[1]

THE HISTORY OF NATIONALISM

Nationalism is a relatively new phenomenon. Although nationalism began to emerge as long ago as the twelfth century, it did not become an established political institution until much later. Developing at the same time as the Age of Enlightenment, nationalism was a political response to the growth of trade and communications accompanying the era, but it was not until the French Revolution that nationalism became an irrepressible idea.

The French Revolution is unquestionably the most important political stimulant of modern times. Its twin ideological goals, *nationalism* and *democracy*, were given substance and form during the tumultuous events beginning at the end of the eighteenth century. The reverberations of the French Revolution quickly spread across Europe, and it can be fairly argued that the revolution's impact continues to resonate throughout the world today, because nationalism and democracy have become goals of a large percentage of the world's people. The two ideas are not only historically related, but also intellectually joined, because they share similar philosophical foundations. Most particularly, each

---

[1]This refers to the organic theory already mentioned in this chapter and developed further in subsequent chapters.

is rooted in the concept of popular sovereignty. Democracy will be examined in detail later; for now, we shall focus on nationalism.

Prior to the French Revolution, political loyalties were not so much vested in abstract concepts as they were devoted to personalities. People thought of themselves more as subjects of the monarch than as members of a nation or even as citizens of a state. Inspired by the radical ideas of **Jean Jacques Rousseau,** however, the French revolutionaries rose against their king and called upon people to assert themselves as French men and women whom the government should serve, rather than the reverse. Their *leftist nationalism* impelled them to abolish social rank and titles; all men were to take the common title of *citoyen* (citizen) as a symbol of their *liberty* from monarchist oppression, their *equality* with every other person in the state, and their *fraternity* in belonging to the French nation.[2]

The Napoleonic Wars (1799–1815) saw French troops march across Europe, spreading their revolutionary ideas as they went, and soon people in every European society, in the Americas, and in Japan were infused with the ideas of national identity and self-determination. Throughout most of the remainder of the nineteenth century (called by some historians the Great Age of Nationalism), Europe's monarchs resisted the growing appeal of nationalism, viewing it as a challenge to their own power. Gradually, however, the idea of national unity began to appeal to conservatives as a useful mechanism for encouraging political stability at home and for galvanizing support for their imperialist designs abroad. Napoleon III (1852–1870) and Otto von Bismarck, the first chancellor of the German Empire (1871–1890), were two early practitioners of *rightist nationalism.*

By the close of the nineteenth century, nationalism—a pliant doctrine, as it turned out—was espoused by elements of both the left and the right. To the left, nationalism was seen as a tool that could loosen the grip on people of monarchist oppression. Liberal philosophers such as Jeremy Bentham and Giuseppi Mazzini advocated it for improving the material well-being of people in society. Free trade, universal education, and conscription were advanced as things that could foster national prosperity and strength. On the right, politicians and thinkers saw nationalism as a vehicle by which to forge stronger, more disciplined political unions and to expand the nation's economic interests through a new burst of colonialism across Africa and Asia.

World War I, early in the twentieth century, was at least partially caused by the imperialistic competition of Europe's powers motivated by rightist nationalism. The war's end saw a general disenchantment with nationalism from the right. Indeed, led by U.S. President Woodrow Wilson, the world flirted again with leftist nationalism—a concept to be tempered, curiously enough, with internationalist safeguards. Thus, Wilson's Fourteen Points included a pledge to support *national self-determination* and a proposal to

---

[2]Remember, at this time women were denied equal rights with men.

create the League of Nations. Each of these principles was present in the *Treaty of Versailles* (1919), which ended the war. Ironically, national self-determination was allowed only in Europe, where Poland, Czechoslovakia, and Yugoslavia became new states, but European colonialism in Asia and Africa was perpetuated.

Very quickly, in fact, the cooperation and positive aspects of leftist nationalism became overwhelmed by reinvigorated nationalistic impulses from the right. In the 1920s, Mussolini rose to power in Italy, truculently calling for the reincarnation of the Roman Empire. The following decade saw the emergence of militarism in Japan, Nazism in Germany, and fascism in Spain and in several East European states. Leaders of these states encouraged their people to brood about lost glory, and belligerently asserted that their particular nation was somehow better than others and should therefore subject lesser peoples to their national wills. These policies led inevitably to World War II, the destruction of vast areas of the world, and a second general rejection of rightist nationalism.

The 1945 founding of the United Nations was accompanied by renewed calls for international cooperation. Although it can fairly be said that the UN has sometimes been used as an instrument of U.S. foreign policy and at other times as a platform for anticolonialist hyperbole, the world body has also been successful at encouraging international efforts to fight disease, to tackle global environmental problems, and to maintain peace among antagonistic peoples.

Yet nationalism has never been far from the forefront in world affairs. Among the Afro-Asian colonial peoples, nationalist urges drove movements for independence that have spawned dozens of new states. In the developed world, the struggle between the ideologies of East and West masked the nationalistic impulses of many people, but the collapse of communism in the Soviet Union, Eastern Europe, and Yugoslavia has seen nationalism emerge afresh, threatening world peace. At the same time, the twin foreign policy doctrines pursued by the George W. Bush administration of *unilateralism* (the United States shall pursue its own interest, even at the expense of general global interests) and *preemptive strikes* (the United States has the right to strike first any country that supports terrorism) are each expressions anew of rightist nationalism.[3]

Although exaggerated nationalism—sometimes called *chauvinism*—can lead to fascism, more temperate forms of national unity are often espoused by less fanatical people. Indeed, nationalism has developed a broad-based political currency. Since the French Revolution, it has been adopted on a previously unprecedented scale, and today, *nationalism is the most potent political idea in the world.*

---

[3]These doctrines were each implemented by the Bush administration—unilateralism where the United States refused to sign the Kyoto Treaty, the Anti-Landmine Treaty, and the International Criminal Court Accords, each of which the United States previously helped negotiate—and the preemptive strike doctrine used in Iraq in 2003, ostensibly to defend the world against Saddam Hussein's stockpiled WMDs, which, as it turned out, did not exist. Although President Obama has repeatedly disavowed unilateralism, still, in 2009 he also refused to sign the Anti-Landmine Treaty because of unexplained national security concerns.

THE THEORY OF NATIONALISM

Nationalism is an abstraction. Rather than giving loyalty to a person such as a noble or a king, people are asked to commit to an idea, to a tradition, to a history, to a notion of fraternity. Nationalism represents the union of a political phenomenon with the identity of the human being. As a frame of reference for individuals and their societies, it dominates the modern world. This is especially true of Western civilization. Whereas Asian societies tend to see social phenomena—family, for example—as the primary institutions, we in the West are much more political in our viewpoints. People in Western societies identify very strongly with their home countries.

Governments often take assertive steps to inculcate nationalistic emotions in their citizens because these feelings usually strengthen the authority of the state. These efforts are most obvious in the education of youth. Almost everywhere, children are systematically taught that their country is the best. Simplistic and heroic stories about national leaders are told, and the history of the country is taught in the most positive tone, to the point where the lessons are at least as attitudinal as they are historical. Consider the story about George Washington confessing to his father that he cut down the cherry tree. Because this episode never actually occurred, the schools—agents of the government— are ironically attempting to teach children to be truthful by telling them an untruth. The second lesson being taught, however, is that the nation's principal founding father was a good person who should be respected and emulated.

There are also many examples of government trying to manipulate the loyalty of adults. Political speeches invoking the national honor, its self-interest, its glorious traditions, and its fallen heroes are common. But these obvious efforts are accompanied by more subtle persuaders. The ideological components of nationalism—its worldview, its vision of a better life, and its perceptions for actions to improve society—are largely implicit rather than, as in the case of most other ideologies, explicit. Nationalism focuses on the national group as the principal political unit, and it demands that the national group be served by a state—a nation-state. Nationalism can be a unifying theory in that it demands the subordination of all identities, values, and interests to those of the national group. Hence, the interests of society and the interests of the state are equated with the national interests. Differences among the genders, social classes, religious beliefs, provincial concerns, political parties, and so forth are expected to be consistent with the national interests or to be suppressed.

Nationalism is also exclusivist. It demands that each individual give loyalty to only one nation-state. Furthermore, nationalism asks people to place the national interest ahead of other concerns and ahead of the interests of other national groups. In the United States, for example, a very nationalistic society, it is not uncommon to see bumper stickers reading, or to hear people say, "Love it or leave it," or "My country right or wrong," or "Speak English or get the hell out." These slogans express deep-seated feelings of belonging to a unique national group, one that will brook no contradiction. Consider, as an example, the French "bashing" currently in vogue in the United States

Immigrants take the oath of allegiance to the United States at a citizenship swearing-in ceremony.

© Joshua Roberts/Reuters/Corbis

because the French (along with the Germans, the Russians, the Chinese, the Chileans, the Mexicans, and dozens of others) would not agree to the U.S. preemptive attack on Iraq. What the French and others counseled was first to make sure that Iraq indeed had weapons of mass destruction (WMDs) and, second, to get the support of the UN before launching the attack. As it turns out, this was indeed prescient advice since there were no WMDs, and the United States later had to ask, hat in hand, these countries and the UN to help it pay for the war and extricate it from the bloody occupation of Iraq. Even so, however, encouraged by many of its leaders, the American people have continued to vilify the French for daring to oppose a U.S. policy, regardless of its unsoundness.

As the slogans mentioned above imply, nationalism calls for unity within the national group, and the national group insists on an extraordinary degree of loyalty. "My country right or wrong," for example, goes so far as to suggest that personal morality and integrity are to be subordinated to the nation-state. It clearly argues that the state deserves support and unquestioned loyalty even when its policies may be incorrect or even morally offensive. Such sentiments, if truly felt, exhibit an uncommon degree of personal identification with the state, for there are few other things, including family and religion that people would openly support even in the face of moral contradictions. Such **patriotism** is, indeed, a fundamental and essential phenomenon in the concept of nationalism.

A second example with which many readers may identify is the caveat's opponents of the wars in Afghanistan and Iraq who often feel compelled to speak in order to assure that they are loyal to the United States. "I support our troops, but I do not support the war" or "I love our flag, but I don't want it carried to Iraq." These are the kind of statements that many feel compelled to make, as if without them, one surrenders patriotism, loyalty, and legitimacy when opposing a policy of the government. This is unfortunate, for in the words of Bill Moyers, "Sometimes it may be necessary to oppose government in order to remain loyal to the country."

A clear distinction between *nationalism* and *patriotism* depends upon recognizing the theoretical nature of nationalism as opposed to the activist nature of patriotism. Simply put, nationalism is the ideology of the modern nation-state. It is the theoretical basis for dividing the world's people into 200 political units, each claiming to be sovereign, each demanding the ultimate in loyalty from its citizens. Patriotism, on the other hand, is not a theory, but an act or gesture of loyalty or commitment to the nation-state. Nationalism describes the nation-state and offers a theoretical justification for it. Patriotism is saluting the flag or singing the national anthem; it is a feeling of commitment to the institution that is expressed by nationalism. For example, a wave of patriotism rushed over the United States in the wake of the terrorist attacks on New York's World Trade Center and the Pentagon in Washington, D.C. Members of Congress belted out "God Bless America" on the Capitol steps, people mounted flags in home windows or on their cars, and others festooned businesses with signs proclaiming "United We Stand." Bumper stickers showing American flags and announcing "These colors don't run" adorned cars and pickup trucks. Indeed, in 2001, even some Christmas decorations took on a patriotic theme.

Patriotism is to nationalism what religious worship is to theology. Patriotism is a form of secular worship of the nation-state, and, as such, it is generally considered a noble thing. As with religion, however, patriotism can be used to justify very ignoble actions, such as the 1995 deadly bombing of a federal office building in Oklahoma City by a self-described patriot. As Samuel Johnson warned us, "Patriotism is the last refuge of scoundrels."[4]

Emotional attachment to nationalism is so strong because nationalism gives the individual an identity and extends that identity to something greater than the self. Nationalism does more than simply describe a political entity. It creates a mirror in which individuals see and define themselves. It is also a prism through which individuals observe, assess, and react to events and to other people. It simplifies complex issues by clearly defining the "we" and the "they." Consequently, nationalism encourages people to identify almost

---

[4]The patriotic expressions in the wake of the tragedy of September 11, 2001, were, perhaps predictably, of the negative and defensive "Don't tread on me" type. Yet, it was not uncommon to see people parading about with flags flapping and bumper stickers proclaiming patriotism, running stop signs, violating speed limits, or in other ways contradicting the laws and values of the society, to say nothing about recklessly endangering its citizens. Presumably, the same could be said for other cases. It is likely that some of the very people professing patriotism so dramatically also cheat on their taxes or even engage in more serious crime.

There are, of course, more positive acts of patriotism: abiding by the law, showing consideration for fellow citizens, acting to protect people's civil liberties even when other citizens may wish to deny them, and even opposing a government policy that is itself contrary to the fundamental principles upon which the country is founded. Ironically, however, in the heat of the moment, this kind of behavior is seen as disloyal and unpatriotic. It should be remembered that historically, the first casualty in our society, when people feel threatened, is usually the Bill of Rights of the U.S. Constitution. Read the U.S.A. PATRIOT Act for a current example of this debilitating phenomenon, or consider the U.S. policy under President George W. Bush, and to a lesser extent, under President Barack Obama of denying *habeas corpus* (the right to be tried or else released from custody) to certain suspected terrorists and sanctioning their torture. Regrettably, there are always people, some even at the highest levels of government, who futilely attempt to defend liberty by denying it.

exclusively with the *national self-interest*—as is, we must not forget defined by the national leaders. Those things that complement the national self-interest are thought good, whereas those things that contradict it are to be resisted. Personal interests of the individual within the nation-state must never contradict national self-interest; each individual is expected to suppress any offending personal interests for the good of the state. Furthermore, *our* national self-interest is always much more just and compelling than *their* national self-interest.

Nationalism has certain transcendental qualities, evoking a sense of history and purpose for its followers. As **Edmund Burke** put it, the state "becomes a partnership not only between those who are living, but between those who are living, those who are dead, and those who are to be born." Nationalism requires that if necessary its followers sacrifice everything—family, fortune, even life itself—for the good of the nation-state.

Rich in emotional as well as intellectual content, nationalism has immense influence in the modern nation-state. Its claim on individual loyalty is profound because the nation-state and nationalism are sources of personal identification for many people, thus unifying them. It establishes a value system and provides a mechanism through which the needs of the society can be met. And as mentioned earlier, it has encouraged some people to perform extraordinary deeds.

However, just as nationalism unites some people, it also divides others, establishing artificial barriers between various national groups. This divisiveness is true even within a state if more than one national group inhabits it. In such a situation, almost inevitably, the minority national groups become infected with the same feeling of exclusivity that influences the majority national group. Thus, the Soviet Union, Yugoslavia, and Czechoslovakia disintegrated and splintered into several smaller nation-states when the opportunity for disunion presented itself. Predictably, many other minority national groups in Russia, Georgia, and Moldova are agitating for independence, as they are also doing in Canada, Spain, Britain, Iraq, Turkey, China, and elsewhere.

The complexity of nationalism's hold on the world's people can easily be seen in the Olympics. Periodically the greatest athletes from around the world gather to compete. The claim that the athletes are amateurs has finally been acknowledged as a charade and, for better or worse, now little distinction is made between athletes who are employed by boosters to compete and those paid by professional teams. Settling the economic contradiction, however, seems not to have led us much closer to facing the glaring political hypocrisy of the Olympics. For example, a good deal of the commentary accompanying the games suggests that the event rises above politics and demonstrates that athletics is a great equalizer. These contentions are confidently advanced even as the various teams parade past the cameras behind their national flags, as nation-state scores are tallied, and as the flags of the medalists' countries are raised behind the winners while the national anthem of the gold medalist's state is played. Clearly, whatever else can be said of the Olympics, it is decidedly a political, nationalistic event, and romantic protests to the contrary ignore an otherwise patently obvious reality. Indeed, if the Olympics prove anything about the matter, they prove that nationalism has overcome sports, not the reverse.

Regardless of one's willingness to admit the political nature of such events, nationalism can be inspiring. On the other hand, extreme forms of nationalism can also be negative, leading to imperialism—wherein one nation becomes dominant over others. When the national self-interest becomes the justification for government policy, it can lead to interpretations that call for the subjugation of one nation by another. Thus, the colonial powers of Western Europe built vast empires in Asia, in Africa, and in the Americas to feed their industrial appetites. More recently, fascist Italy, Nazi Germany, and militarist Japan subjected millions of people in their drives to exert their national wills over "less deserving" peoples. The United States has also used arguments of national interest to involve itself economically and militarily in Latin America, Asia, the Pacific, and the Middle East. In short, although nationalism can be a valuable unifying factor, it also encourages people to define their interests and values in terms of something less than the good of humanity as a whole.

This focus on the self-interest of the nation rather than the interests of the larger group can be troublesome for its shortsightedness. Accepted, often with little question, as justification for national policy, the ideological imperative ignores a fundamental reality of modern political life. As alluded to earlier, in a world confronted by bulging populations pressing upon declining resources, national policy principally motivated by selfish concerns must inevitably lead to conflict. Faced with the rapid proliferation of WMDs, this prospect does not bode well for the future. Clearly, a broader perspective will have to be adopted. But this transformation has yet to occur, although the European Union may be poised to evolve beyond the strict confines of nationalism.

With the end of the Cold War and the collapse of the Soviet Union, the East–West confrontation evaporated, and although some Western leaders called for a "new world order," international affairs became even more complex and contradictory than before. Nationalism has tended to become less a factor among the advanced states, with the possible exception of the United States, but more important among some less-developed societies.

Eastern Europe and the former Soviet Union are seething with nationalist separatism. Unfortunately, the nationalistic impulse has negative aspects, including racism and anti-Semitism. By contrast, the imperatives of communications and technological advances combine with economic factors to draw many of the world's leading industrial powers into closer association. The North American Free Trade Agreement among Canada, the United States, and Mexico calls for unprecedented economic cooperation. On an even wider scale, the European Community is verging on an economic and political union that would result in the merger of Europe's states into the most powerful economic unit on earth. These two developments are not continuing without nationalistic complications, however. Nationalists and provincialists in Europe loudly question the wisdom of ceding to the larger group their economic and political sovereignty. Chauvinistic elements in France, Italy, and Germany gain political stature domestically as they vehemently and even violently oppose the arrival of foreigners in their societies.

Another serious challenge to nationalism, which some critics, and supporters alike say offers the most potent threat to it, is economic rather than political in origin. Multinational corporations and globalization of trade have visited an enormous potential contradiction upon nationalism. Some multinational corporations have greater annual revenues than the gross domestic products (GDPs; an estimate of the market value of all goods produced in a country in a given year) of some of the countries in which they do business, and they dominate the politics of some of these countries. Similarly, these corporations sometimes display little loyalty to the governments in which they are headquartered. The international pursuit of profit often tends to encourage them to act independently of the foreign policies of their home countries. Our money, I am reminded, is green, not red, white, and blue.

Globalization seemingly has exacerbated these trends. The World Trade Organization (WTO) has created taxing and labor policies that have the practical force of making moot the taxes and labor policies of some individual countries. These developments may indeed constitute the greatest threat to the nation-state system as we know it. Economic change often precedes political change and it could be that the premise of national sovereignty, upon which nationalism is founded, is no longer viable, given these economic developments. If so, one may be sobered by the prospects of corporate world governance.

Finally, a new brand of internationalism may be on the horizon. Just as nationalism is now usually associated with the right but also has leftist adherents, internationalism is usually equated with the left, but this new movement is quite reactionary. Rejecting modernization—or Westernization—many in the Muslim world are calling on their co-religionists to forsake petty national differences and join in a single nation of Islam. This *Pan-Islamic movement* was given fresh impetus with the collapse of the Soviet Union. Suddenly, a vast area in Central Asia is divided into six independent Muslim states: Azerbaijan, Kazakhstan, Uzbekistan, Kyrgyzstan, Turkmenistan, and Tadzhikistan. Naturally, these new countries turned to their co-religionists for help in becoming viable independent states, since they had not before enjoyed such status in modern times. Their political fluidity and their formerly suppressed nationalism encourage some Muslim leaders to hope that these areas might eventually be folded into a larger state spanning Central Asia, the Middle East, and North Africa. Meanwhile, a terrorist group in Yemen calling itself Al Qaeda, in the Arabian Peninsula, strives to create a pan-Islamic caliphate spanning the subsumed Persian Gulf States. It is this group that claimed credit for the failed 2009 attempt by Umar Farouk Abdulmutallab to destroy an airplane in flight between the Netherlands and Detroit.

Whether the allure of Pan-Islam is strong enough to overwhelm the Sunni-Shiite split in Islam or the nationalistic loyalties in the Muslim world, or whether the industrialized world will be able to overcome its attachment to national sovereignty are, of course, questions that only time can answer. If indeed nationalist movements are overcome by uniting economic or religious imperatives, the political power of nationalism will have to be reassessed. Until then, however, the extraordinary authority nationalism exercises on people must be recognized and appreciated.

QUESTIONS FOR DISCUSSION

1. How do nationalism and the nation-state interrelate?
2. What are the various theories of the origin of the state?
3. In what ways does nationalism influence us?
4. Analyze the origins and uses of nationalism.
5. Why is nationalism so powerful, and what are its positive and negative consequences?

SUGGESTIONS FOR FURTHER READING

Anderson, Benedict R., *Imagined Communities: Reflections on the Origin and Spread of Nationalism*. New York: Verso, 2006.

Brown, Michael E., ed., *Nationalist Ethnic Conflict*. Cambridge, MA: MIT Press, 1997.

Gellner, Ernest, *Nations and Nationalism*. Ithica, NY: Cornell University Press, 2006.

Greenfield, Liah, *Nationalism: Five Roads to Modernity*. Cambridge, MA: Harvard University Press, 2007.

Joireman, Sandra Fullerton, *Nationalism and Political Identity*. New York: Continuum, 2003.

Kohn, Hans, *Nationalism: Its Meaning and History*. Princeton, NJ: Van Nostrand, 1955.

————, *The Idea of Nationalism: A Study in Its Origins and Background*. New York: Collier Books, 1967.

Smith, Anthony D., *Nationalism: Theory, Ideology, History*. Malden, MA: Polity Press, 2001.

Spencer, Philip, *Nationalism: A Critical Introduction*. London: Sage, 2002.

Tames, Richard, *Nationalism*. Chicago: Raintree, 2004.

Tamir, Yael, *Liberal Nationalism*. Ewing, NJ: Princeton University Press, 1993.

The Evolution of Democratic Theory

PREVIEW

The kernels of modern democracy took root during the Age of Enlightenment. Some contemporaries think of democracy in procedural terms only, whereas others insist that it also includes important philosophical content. The most basic idea in democracy is that people are essentially equal, and that thus each person has a right to have a say in who governs and how they do so. Legitimate political power comes from the people, and government, therefore, is legal only when the governed consent. The act of popular consent to government is explained by the theories of popular sovereignty and the social contract.

The principal social contract philosophers believed that people originally had no government, that they were equally obliged to follow the natural law, and that they were rational creatures, capable of understanding natural law and of organizing a government that served their interests better than did the state of nature. The process of organizing society and creating government was called the *social contract.*

Nevertheless, although these philosophers agreed on many points, there were also many areas in which they differed. They agreed that the individual should be free, but they disagreed on the definition of freedom. The conservative Hobbes suggested that freedom was possible only when the individuals in society subordinated themselves completely to the monarch. The liberal Locke, on the other hand, thought that freedom was greatest when the individual was left alone. The radical Rousseau believed that human freedom would be achieved only by destroying the society that oppressed the individual and creating a new one in which equality was the dominant reality.

The three philosophers also varied in their attitude toward government itself. Hobbes thought that an absolute monarchy would best suit the needs of the people. Locke favored a parliamentary republic in which the government did little except arbitrate disputes between citizens. Rousseau, adopting the most radical point of view, believed the community created an infallible general will by a direct democratic vote of all the people in the society.

Although Hobbes said little about a person's right to private property, Locke argued that private property was vital to people, yet he was clearly opposed to unlimited accumulation. Rousseau, on the other hand, opposed unequal distribution of property because that would make people unequal politically.

THE MEANING OF DEMOCRACY

The inherent features of democracy are, even today, not completely agreed upon by the experts. Some argue that democracy is simply a way of making decisions. These scholars, sometimes called **process democrats,** claim that there is no real philosophy, or theory, of democracy. They believe that democracy is nothing more than an agreement among citizens that the majority vote will carry the issue or that one branch of government will not reach too far into the functions of another branch.

The process of democracy is, of course, very important and will be discussed in Chapter 6. For now, however, let us study the ideas of a second group, the **principle democrats.** Principle democrats argue that democracy has a very important theoretical base. Although the procedure of democracy is important, they believe it is secondary to the basic intent and objectives of democracy as expressed in democratic theory. For instance, the basic principles of modern *liberal democracy* include the ideas that the individual is of major importance in the society, that each individual is basically equal to all other individuals, and that each has certain inalienable rights such as life and liberty. In the United States—a liberal democracy—we make political decisions by voting, but we use other specific legal and administrative procedures (the right not to be forced to incriminate oneself, the right to a defense, the right to a trial by jury, and so forth) to safeguard people's liberties. These procedures are called *due process of law.* Accordingly, even if a majority of the people voted to torture someone, it could not be legally done because the *process* of majority rule is subordinate to the *principle* of individual liberty and respect for the rights of the minority.

Although certainly not uninterested in process, principle democrats regard the ultimate philosophical goals of democracy as more important than the procedures used to meet those goals. At the very least, principle democrats insist that a democratic government be dedicated to improving the conditions of life for all of its people and that some mechanism exist by which the people in the society can exercise a degree of control over their leaders and express their wishes and needs.

On its face, liberal democracy would certainly seem to meet the principle democrats' standards. Assuming that freedom will make people happy, its goal is to make people as free as possible. Liberal democracy boasts a large list of freedoms, including freedom of press, speech, religion, and assembly.

Yet, democratic socialist critics (people with democratic political systems and socialist economic systems: Scandinavia, for example) of our

© Mohammed Jalil/epa/Corbis

A hopeful Iraqi couple on Election Day display their ink-stained fingers proving they voted. Sadly, democracy turned out to be more complicated and difficult to create than the George W. Bush administration anticipated.

system contend that although it allows a wide range of political liberty, liberal democracy, accompanied by a capitalist economic system, ignores the economic needs of its citizens to the point where any effort at real democracy is doomed to failure. They aver that the political liberties, while important, are sterile, unless augmented by *economic freedoms*: the right to work, a reasonable standard of living, free education and medicine, and so on. Underscoring the point, a Soviet official once told me "People who define democracy solely on the basis of being able to criticize the government have never been hungry."

Obviously we do not agree with this point: We contend that political freedoms are at the very heart of democracy. We de-emphasize the importance of economic freedom as socialists define it, preferring to equate it with individuals being able to accumulate wealth as best they can. Our system offers greater individualism and economic diversity, but it also allows much greater economic disparity.

Clearly, this dispute illustrates huge differences over what constitutes democracy. Yet, the argument is based on something much more fundamental than process. The focus of the argument revolves around the question of which principles are inherent in democracy. What is the philosophical content of democracy?

THE EARLY HISTORY OF DEMOCRACY

There are almost 200 national constitutions in the world today, and almost all of them claim to be democratic. *Democracy* is currently a very popular term, but people have not always found it attractive. For a time, the ancient Greeks practiced *direct democracy*, in which all male adult citizens voted on government policy. Gradually, however, that system evolved into a more authoritarian form, and democracy lost public acceptance. To Plato, for example, democracy threatened rule by the mob. Plato argued that there are few people of high quality in any society and that if all citizens were allowed to rule, those of low quality, who were much more numerous, would dominate the state. This group would establish a government that reflected their meanness, and the result would be a "tyranny of the majority." Further, Plato warned that democracies were usually short-lived and that the mob would soon surrender its power to a tyrant, thus destroying popular government. Consequently, Plato favored a government headed by the intellectual elite of society:[the philosopher kings he called them.]

Aristotle, whose attitude toward democracy was somewhat less negative than Plato's, still clearly preferred a different form of government. He reasoned that under certain conditions the will of the many could be equal to, or even wiser than, the judgment of a few. When the many governed for the good of all, Aristotle accepted democracy as a good form of government. To even the best democracy, however, Aristotle preferred what he called *aristocracy*, by which he meant rule of the upper class for the good of all the people in the society. The upper class contained the people of greatest refinement and quality in the society; therefore, they were best equipped to provide sound government for the society as a whole. But it should be reemphasized that Aristotle considered government best only if the few ruled for the good of all.

Eventually, the ancient Greeks abandoned democracy, and serious interest in it did not arise again until the Protestant Reformation set in motion a major challenge to the Roman Catholic Church, the authority that, following the collapse of the Roman Empire, brought order to medieval Europe.

THE SOCIAL CONTRACT

The slow progress out of the Middle Ages was accomplished largely through the use of the scientific method, leading ultimately to the development of the **Industrial Revolution** itself. You will remember, success in solving their material problems gave people the confidence to take positive steps in search of solutions to their social, political, and economic problems. This new optimism, based on science and reason, ultimately led some thinkers to the conclusion that people were equal in fundamental ways. *The presumption of human equality was a revolutionary conclusion because it led people to challenge the validity of society's institutions and customs that distribute power and wealth unequally among citizens.* If people were equal, for example, no one had a greater right to rule than another; thus, dynastic monarchy lost its relevance.

Yet, society needed governors to maintain order, and these leaders were chosen by the community as a whole. Because people were essentially equal, no person enjoyed the moral right to govern an equal without some expression of consent by the governed. Legitimate political power, therefore, came from the people; the people were the source of ultimate legal and political authority. This theory of popular sovereignty led to much speculation about democracy during the seventeenth century. The theory that resulted, involving the actual grant of power by the people to the government, is called the **social contract theory**; that is, the social contract is the act of people exercising their sovereignty and creating a government to which they consent.

LATER SOCIAL CONTRACT PHILOSOPHERS

Although there are many social contract theorists, those of particular importance to us are Thomas Hobbes, John Locke, and Jean Jacques Rousseau.[1] Each of them agreed on three things. First, unlike the ancient Greeks, they believed that government was not a natural circumstance, and that at one time people lived in a *state of nature,* a condition in which there was no government at all. Government was a deliberately and rationally conceived human invention, and the social contract was the act of people creating and empowering government. The social contract philosophers wanted to explain why government was created and what was to be its structure and powers. These explanations, it was thought, depended on how human beings living in the state of nature conducted themselves relative to one another and, therefore, how much third-party regulation they needed.

Second, the social contract philosophers believed in the existence of a **natural law:** a set of truths that are absolute, universal, and eternal, and are the measure by which human conduct should be assessed. Because the natural law is absolute and eternal, it must apply to each person equally. Therefore, all people are equally bound by the same code of moral conduct. It is not moral for anyone to make an equal unequal, so all people owe each other certain considerations, which came to be called the natural rights.

Third, the social contract philosophers agreed that all people are rational—that is, that they are generally capable of understanding their problems and of solving them through the use of reason. Thus, it was thought that government was deliberately created as a rational attempt to solve problems people encountered in the state of nature. Human nature—the way people behave toward one another naturally when unregulated—is of critical importance because that would reveal much about the social conditions in the state of nature, what social problems existed, and how they might be resolved.

[handwritten margin notes: "state of nature", "government is a solution to the state of nature", "are we good or evil?"]

[1] It must be cautioned that while the theory of popular sovereignty and the social contract eventually led to democratic theory, only the last of these three philosophers actually supported democracy. Yet, the theories of the first two men advanced in that direction, while not actually arriving there.

Thomas Hobbes

During the seventeenth century, England went through a period of serious civil disorder. Two forces competed: _absolutism_, allied with Anglican traditionalism, versus _Puritan reform_, in league with parliamentary assertiveness. James I (r. 1603–1625) the first Stuart to rise to the English throne, believed deeply in the divine right of kings and insisted God granted him absolute power. His unpopular politics were matched by an unpleasant personality, making conflict with an assertive parliament inevitable. The situation was not quieted by James's death, since his son, Charles I (r. 1625–1649), shared his father's arrogance and absolutist views and finally, a civil war broke out, ending in 1649 with his execution for treason. The execution of Charles I was an important step. Although many monarchs throughout history had been killed in palace coups, they were usually removed from power in the name of the "rightful monarch." By contrast, in this episode the _people_ of England, led by Oliver Cromwell, held the rightful king to account. Claiming it was not enough that the monarch come to power illegally, they insisted that he also exercised power legitimately.

For the next eleven years, England was ruled by Cromwell and the Puritan religious minority. Upon Cromwell's death, Parliament decided to restore the Stuart monarchy by placing Charles II, the son of the executed monarch, on the throne. **Thomas Hobbes** (1588–1679), a mathematics tutor for the exiled prince, developed his theories in part to justify the Stuart restoration to the throne.

Hobbes believed that monarchy was the best possible form of government; yet, he rejected the theory of the divine right of kings, thus incurring the enmity of fellow monarchists. Instead, he claimed the social contract was the source of legitimate royal authority. While Hobbes believed that royal power came from the consent of the people, he placed few limits on the monarch, thus also incurring the wrath of those who wished to limit the monarch's power.

Hobbes's view of people is not a happy one. He thought that people were basically self-serving. Although they were rational, they were not in control of their own destinies because they were driven by an overwhelming fear of death. This caused people to be aggressive toward one another. Hobbes, like all subsequent social contract theorists, assumed that there had been a time when government did not exist. In this state of nature people were free to act as they wished. No law governed them save natural law, and that law had no enforcement agency. Given his pessimistic views about the nature of people, it is not surprising that Hobbes believed the state of nature was a wretched condition. Unregulated by law and government, people had given in to their baser instincts and acted aggressively toward their neighbors. They committed every kind of violence and deceit in order to raise their own status.

In _Leviathan_, his major work, Hobbes eloquently described the hopeless chaos of the state of nature. In this hideous condition there was only human conflict, a constant "war of each against all." Hobbes complained that there was "no knowledge of the face of the earth; no account of time; no arts; no letters; no society; and which is worst of all, continual fear, and danger of

survival instinct

violent death; and the life of man, solitary, poor, nasty, brutish and short." Clearly, Hobbes viewed the human condition in the state of nature as chaotic, irresponsible, and devoid of freedom.

Though he viewed people as prisoners of their own avarice, Hobbes believed they were rational. As rational beings, they realized the futility of their existence and hit upon a way of creating order out of the chaos endemic to the state of nature: the social contract. In exchange for order, they agreed to surrender all their natural rights to a monarch and render to him complete obedience. Obviously, Hobbes did not consider natural rights inalienable, as did later natural law theorists, but he did assert that the sole function of the king was to keep order. As long as the monarch did so, his subjects were bound to obey his laws. However, since the social contract was an agreement among ordinary people, the king was not a party to it and need not be bound by it. Only he could make the law; and because he made the law, the king could not be bound by it; thus, the king was sovereign. Only if he failed to keep the peace could the people resist him.

Hobbes believed that freedom, though limited, was possible only if people surrendered their liberty to a monarch—hardly a democratic point of view. Since people were driven to excess by their insecurity, they could experience freedom only when they were restrained by a superior authority. Without such authoritarian checks, people would become victims once again of their own fright-induced impulses and would return to the chaos of the state of nature. Thus, human reason, according to Hobbes, was powerful enough to understand the reasons for the chaos plaguing society, and it was sufficient to devise a solution to the problem, but it was not strong enough to allow people to become part of the solution. Put differently, although people understood that their lives were in disarray because they were not able to use reason to control their sinister impulses, for the same reason they could not themselves restore order once they understood the problem. Only an all-powerful monarch could do that.

By asserting that legitimate political power comes from people rather than from God, Hobbes made an important but unintentional contribution to the development of democratic thinking. His theory led subsequent English philosophers to the concept of the separation of church and state. Yet, even though Hobbes employed concepts normally thought to be liberal (for example, popular sovereignty and the social contract), his interpretation of these ideas led him to very conservative conclusions. The next natural law philosopher we will study, however, enjoyed indisputably liberal credentials.

John Locke

Regardless of Hobbes's absolutist intentions, Charles II was forced by Parliament to accept firm limitations to his power, and he managed to avoid fatal conflict with it. His death, however, brought his brother, James II (r. 1685–1688), to the throne. Less politically wise than Charles, James insisted he was absolute by virtue of being chosen by God to rule England. Such royal ambitions were not welcome in seventeenth-century England under any circumstances, but the fact that James was a Catholic sealed his fate.

In 1688, the English rose up against the "Catholic tyranny" and James II fled with his family to France. This episode, known as the *Glorious Revolution* because dislodging the king was practically bloodless. But James was unwilling to accept his fate. Conspiring with his co-religionists in Ireland, he attempted a comeback. In 1960 in the historic Boyne Valley, just north of Dublin, the insurgent forces were decisively defeated by William of Orange, the person chosen by Parliament to succeed James II. Thus ended the long struggle between king and Parliament for dominance in England.

Before placing William of Orange and his wife Mary on the throne, Parliament adopted a document, the *Bill of Rights*, that limited the power of the English monarchy as never before. It guaranteed Parliament the right to hold free elections, to meet frequently, to petition the king, and to legislate. The king was not allowed to suspend an act of Parliament, and he was forbidden to tax or to keep a standing army in peacetime without Parliament's approval. These restrictions had to be accepted by the new monarchs as the "true, ancient, and indubitable rights of the people of this realm."

Just as Hobbes had tried to justify the restoration of the Stuart dynasty, **John Locke** (1632–1704) developed a philosophical base to the Glorious Revolution and the limitations placed on the monarch. Locke listed a series of arguments in *The Second Treatise* that, because of their simplicity and commonsense approach, captured the imagination of Locke's fellow citizens as well as people of later generations. As George H. Sabine has written, "His sincerity, his profound moral conviction, his genuine belief in liberty, in human rights, and in the dignity of human nature, united with his moderation and good sense, made him the ideal spokesman of a middle-class revolution."[2] Though his work obviously had substantial impact on British government, his philosophy found greatest application in the principles of the American Declaration of Independence and the U.S. Constitution.

Natural Law   History's leading classical liberal, Locke believed in natural law and that people could discover its principles by using reason. Natural law, according to Locke, guaranteed each individual certain *natural rights* that could not legally be taken away, or *alienated*, without due process of law. Because all people are equally subject to the natural law (the same moral strictures), each person owes every other person a degree of respect and consideration not owed to unequals. Locke summarized these inalienable rights as "life, liberty, and estate." However, he was much more explicit than this generalization suggests. He held that *individual freedom* was an essential right; indeed, its importance to his theory would be hard to exaggerate.

---

[2]George H. Sabine, *A History of Political Theory*, 3rd ed. (New York: Holt, Rinehart & Winston, 1961), p. 540.

Although Hobbes and Locke agreed on many points, they also contradicted each other. As we have seen, Hobbes was very pessimistic about human nature. He believed that people were basically evil and that they would harm each other if they were not subject to the control of an outside authority. Hence, Hobbes equated individual freedom with restraint by the government. Locke, by contrast, was very optimistic about human nature. He thought people were essentially good and that they would normally behave decently when left alone. Government restraint, therefore, was usually unnecessary and even counterproductive. Locke believed people should be free, and he suggested that freedom was found in the absence of restraint; citizens unfettered by government. The importance to Locke of individual freedom is difficult to exaggerate. People, he thought, should be free to exercise their rights as long as they did not interfere with the rights of others.

Individual equality, in Locke's view, was another right guaranteed by natural law. Locke did not claim that all people were equal in all ways. He recognized that people differed widely in intelligence, physical prowess, and so forth; but, regardless of the obvious differences among people, he argued that they all had the same natural rights because the natural law, from which the natural rights flow, applies to all people in equal measure. Thus, no one had a greater claim to liberty than anyone else. Nor did anyone have more, or less, of any other kind of natural right, including the right to "estate" (private property).

Private Property Important for many reasons, in some ways Locke's most significant contribution is that he is the first important political philosopher to integrate economics with political theory. Since the time of his writings, the importance of economics to political motivation and behavior has become increasingly accepted, especially on the left. Indeed, his ideas form the foundation upon which the theory of **economic determinism** (that people's political beliefs and behavior are preconditioned by their economic circumstances) is based. This concept is so central to contemporary leftist thinking that it can be fairly argued that Locke invented the modern left.

Of course, Locke discussed political economies within the context of his major objective: individual liberty. Like all other early English classical liberals, he believed that private property was essential to people's well-being. The high status he gave to private property rests on two major assumptions. First, he assumed that the accumulation of private property allowed people to provide for themselves and their families the necessities of life. Once freed from the pressures of survival, people could turn to the task of developing their characters. If a society is in the throes of famine, its people care little whether the sun revolves around the Earth or the Earth orbits the sun. They are not likely to create an important art form, an advanced architecture, a subtle literature, or a sophisticated governmental system. We will see later that Marx adopted this idea, calling for the liberation of people from **compulsive toil** as a major theme in his own theory.

The second assumption of the early English liberals in support of private property involved individual identity. Locke believed that property ownership was more than a simple economic fact. A person's property reflected the individual who owned it. People were identified in part by the things they owned. What they were was expressed, or even modified, by what they had. This close link between the personality and material items is a very strong feature of Western civilization; indeed, many modern commercial advertisements rely heavily on persuading consumers of this theory; thus, the existence of status symbols.

But, Locke viewed property as a means to an end, not as an end itself. He saw private property as a vital first step to an improved human race. Locke's main interest was the individual, and he hoped for a society that would free its people to perfect their characters and their human qualities. Further, the accumulation of private property by any given individual was not to occur unchecked, an admonition consistently ignored by advocates of capitalism who often try to evoke his imprimatur. Locke believed people should be allowed to accumulate only as much as they could use. He did not countenance some people amassing huge fortunes while others lived in poverty. Thus, although he favored a market economy, thinking it most conducive to individual freedom, he would almost surely object to the great disparities in property ownership that exist in today's capitalist societies.[3]

Locke developed an elaborate theory to explain the origin and value of private property. Not only did these ideas make a vital contribution to democracy, but subsequent thinkers adopted them and applied them to vastly different philosophies. Locke's influence can easily be found in the work of capitalist economists such as **Adam Smith** and **David Ricardo,** but as we will see later, it can also be found in the economic theory of **Karl Marx.**

Locke argued that all resources were originally held in common and that people could use them as needed, but he believed that common property became private property when human labor was applied to it. He believed that when people made things from natural resources, they transferred something of themselves to the items produced. The newly created product, the result of a union between human creativity and natural resources, actually became part of the worker and naturally belonged to that person. Thus, the right of private property was born. Locke also believed that the value of any item was roughly determined by the amount of labor necessary to produce it. This idea, known as the **labor theory of value,** may be seen in Marx's famous theory of **surplus value,** discussed in Chapter 8.

---

[3]Interestingly, the concentration of wealth in the hands of the few is perhaps greater in the United States than it is in any other economically advanced society. In 1960, the wealth among the top fifth of the population was thirty times that of the lowest fifth. By 2006 the wealth gap had expanded, with the wealthy owning seventy-five times more than the poorest fifth of the country. Great concern should greet this dramatic shift, especially if Louis Brandeis's echo of Locke is correct: "You can have wealth concentrated in the hands of a few, or democracy, but you cannot have both." Brandeis was one of the truly great Justices of the U.S. Supreme Court.

As we have seen, Locke assumed that there had been a time when there was no organized society. During this period people interacted with nature, creating private property. Clearly, then, Locke assumed that private property existed before society was organized. In other words, private property was not created by society; it was created instead by people interacting with commonly owned natural resources, thus co-mingling nature and their human essence. Private property is necessary to the human condition, Locke opined, because it helps people achieve liberty. Thus, private property is important, but only because it is necessary to liberty and because it has been infused with human creativity. Thus, we arrive at a crucial point: *Private property is not important for its own sake.* It is created when part of the essence of a human being has been transferred to natural resources, and it is important only because it makes human liberty possible. That Locke considered property less important than other natural rights is clear from his attitude toward the accumulation of property. Though he thought that people should normally be allowed to accumulate property without interference from outside agencies, he clearly believed that *property accumulation should be limited.* To begin with, Locke held that no person should be allowed to accumulate more property than could be used before it spoiled. This admonition is not a serious problem to modern society because, through the use of money and credit, value has been abstracted to such a degree that one can own immense amounts of wealth and run no risk at all that it will spoil.

A second restriction on property ownership is more relevant. Similar to Voltaire's later admonition about freedom of action ("Your right to swing your arm ends at my nose"), Locke argued that people should not be able to exercise their economic rights to the extent that others are denied the same rights. As private property helps people define themselves and frees people from the mundane cares of daily subsistence, no individual should accumulate so much property that others are prevented from accumulating the necessities of life. Although Locke favored a market economy, he did so on the grounds that it was most conducive to individual liberty. If, however, wealth were allowed to so concentrate in the hands of some so that others would not have that which was basic to human freedom, redress must occur. If such a restriction did not exist, it would be possible for one person, through the control of property, to deny others their identities and even their ability to be free, fulfilled human beings. On this basis, an agency of the society could interfere with an individual's accumulation of property if in so doing the right of others to accumulate property would be protected. Though Locke did not intend it in this way, this principle forms part of the bridge between classical liberalism, which is linked to capitalism, and utopian or humanitarian socialism, discussed in Chapter 8. *The roots of both capitalism and socialism spring from common intellectual soil.*

The last principle of natural law about which Locke was very specific has to do with the individuals' collective interests. Locke assumed that the basic interests of all people in a given society were the same. So, although there might be some minor variations, whatever was beneficial for society as a whole was probably ultimately beneficial for any particular individual, another belief that can also be found in socialism. This principle led Locke to look toward the majority vote as the most important feature of political decision making. His attitude toward majority rule will be discussed in more detail later; for now, it is enough to remark that although Locke considered the individual very important, he viewed people as being united by common or social interests.

One should note at this point that while Locke believed everyone should have an equal right to accumulate property and that there should be outer limits to how much people should be allowed to accumulate, he was, after all, talking about *private property*. Further, he had no problem with some holding more property than others, he just insisted there be limits on accumulation so that all could have enough. Consequently, while Locke would certainly not be a socialist, neither would he endorse the unregulated capitalism the Libertarian Party advocates.

The Social Contract   Locke and Hobbes also differed in their views about the condition of people in the state of nature. You will recall Locke rejected the proposition that people were evil and selfish by nature; thus, the human condition in the state of nature was rather pleasant. Indeed, Locke suggested that the dominant themes in the natural state were "peace, good will, mutual assistance and preservation." Those are conditions about which socialists would have no qualms, but capitalists might find the notion of mutual assistance troubling.

Yet, even though the state of nature was usually peaceful, there were two sources of unrest. Though Locke believed people were basically good, he did not think them perfect, consequently, from time to time, some people might try to take advantage of others. Moreover, even when no malice was intended, two people might come into conflict while exercising what they each consider to be their just liberties.

Conflict between people, then, could occur in the state of nature; and because there was no third party to arbitrate the dispute, individuals were forced to defend their own liberties. This clash presented a problem because people were not equal in their ability to defend their rights from attack. Consequently, injustice could occur in the state of nature because the person who manages to prevail over another may succeed only because he or she is stronger and not because he or she is right.

Believing that people were rational, Locke went on to theorize that people saw the need for an agency to dispense justice among them. This led individuals to forge a social contract among themselves, thereby creating society and removing themselves from the state of nature.

Hobbes, you will recall, insisted that the king was not a party to the contract that formed the society and thus could not be bound by it. Hobbes held that society and government were distinct elements, thus putting the power of the king above that of the individual and the society.

Locke made the same distinction as Hobbes, but for exactly the opposite reason. The people create the society through the social contract, and then government is created as an agent of the society. Consequently, government is two steps removed from the true source of its power, the individual, and is subordinate to the society, which is, in turn, obliged to the individual. Also, since government and society are not the same thing, the fall of a government need not mean the end of the community. The community could create a new government to serve it if its original government was unsatisfactory. Indeed, it is this very argument that **Thomas Jefferson,** drawing on Locke's theory, made in the Declaration of Independence.

The Nature and Function of Government   Though Locke believed that government ought to be strictly limited, he thought it performed a vital function: to serve the people. Hobbes, by contrast, thought that people should serve the government. Locke opined that some things could be done better when people were left alone and that other things were done better by society as a whole or by society's representatives. He believed that most people could act fairly and efficiently by themselves and insisted that government should not interfere with the individual in such cases. Yet, there were times when governmental activity was necessary to protect the rights of the people. Locke saw government as a passive arbitrator. Normally, it would simply let people pursue their own best interests. When, however, two or more individuals came into conflict over the extent of their liberties, government was required to step in, arbitrate the dispute, and then step out again and let people go about their business without further interference.

Whereas Hobbes believed that people could surrender most of their natural rights to government in the hope of achieving order, Locke thought these rights were unalienable and that preserving them was necessary for a free existence. The only right that Locke expected people to surrender to government was the right to decide how extensive their individual liberties would be. Even here, however, the only time government should use its power was when individuals came into conflict over the use of their rights. Any other power was denied to government and reserved for the people.

Locke was very particular about the structure and form of government. Because he assumed that what was good for society as a whole was good for the individual as well, and that people were rational and capable of knowing what was good for them, consequently, he assumed that the society could use the will of the majority as a formula for deciding correct policy. Moreover, individuals were expected to accept the decision of the majority even if they disagreed with it. If an individual could not do so, he or she would have to leave society, thus returning to the state of nature and forfeiting the protection of government.

Besides believing in majority rule, Locke thought that people should be governed by a parliament elected by citizens who owned property. Though he argued that the people were sovereign, Locke thought it best that they not rule themselves directly. He saw members of a parliament as representing their constituents, and he believed that they should vote as their constituents wanted. Accordingly, the relationship between the government and the governed remained close. Though the people did not actually make the law themselves, the law was a product of their preferences: representative government, in other words.

Locke also called for separation of the executive and legislative powers. Most important, he believed that the legislature, which was the direct agent of the people, should take precedence over the executive branch. The legislature should decide on the policy of the government and the executive should dutifully carry out the mandates of parliament.

The government's sole purpose, according to Locke, was to serve the individual in such a way as to increase individual rights and liberties. At all other times it was to stay out of the people's business. If the government ever acted otherwise—that is, if it involved itself too much in the affairs of the people, thus reducing their rights and liberties without good reason—then the people had the right to put that government out and to create one that would serve them better. Again, we see Jefferson's inspiration for the Declaration of Independence, but we also again observe Hobbes and Locke on opposite sides. Hobbes opposed popular rebellion against the king, whom he considered the sovereign, or the highest law in the land. Yet, since the king was given power by the people for the sole purpose of keeping order, the people were justified in ousting him and creating a new sovereign only if he failed to keep order. In other words, whereas Hobbes would have the people overthrow the government for failing to keep order, Locke believed such an action was justified when the government tried to regulate people too much. A glance at the spectrum of political attitudes illustrated in Figure 2.8 will show that Hobbes's concern for order and Locke's preference for individual liberty are quite consistent with the values of today's conservatives and liberals, respectively.

Liberal though Locke's ideas were for the time, they too fell short of democracy. Locke was the "spokesman of a middle-class revolution." During Locke's time, British government was controlled by the aristocracy. Yet, a large and wealthy middle class, composed of merchants, manufacturers, bankers, and professionals, emerged on the eve of the Industrial Revolution to demand a share of political power in the society. Although Locke claimed that all people were equally possessed of natural rights, he advocated that political power be devolved only far enough to embrace the middle class by giving Parliament, which the middle class controlled through the House of Commons, the right to limit the monarch's power. Only those with property were to vote. He did not advocate the masses of ordinary people be given the right to elect members of Parliament; thus, he denied them political power.

Still, his philosophy was essential to the development of liberal democracy. Although he chose not to enfranchise the poor, his justification for giving the middle class political power was equally applicable to people of lower status; indeed, his theories were so sweeping that they could logically be applied to all people. Locke was probably prevented from extending his ideas only by the unquestioned bias toward privilege endemic to his era. Thus, democracy had to await a more egalitarian era when the mass production of goods created the necessary economic and social conditions. Still, it cannot be disputed that Locke's ideas came very close to being democratic; in the next generation, contemporary democratic thought was born. The first truly democratic political theory, however, came not from English liberalism but from French radicalism. You will recall that democracy joined nationalism as twin ideas of the French Revolution, sapping the foundations of monarchy, the fortress imprisoning Europe.

Jean Jacques Rousseau

After the dramatic political events that influenced the ideas of Hobbes and Locke, England settled into a period of consolidation and France became the new center of leftist political thought. Louis XIV (1638–1715) had established an absolute monarchy and passed it on to his heirs. Despite great advances in science and literature, France's political system was harsh and unresponsive to the people, its social class structure rigid, its economic system exploitative. These conditions led to a surge of literary activity that produced some of the period's best political thinkers. But one philosopher, **Jean Jacques Rousseau** (1712–1778), made such a creative impact as to set himself apart from the others, and *he is generally considered the founder of modern radical thought.*

The Community   Like other social contract theorists, Rousseau believed that there had been a time when neither government nor society existed. But, unlike Hobbes, Rousseau believed people in the state of nature were simple, shy, innocent, and avoided conflict. Such a condition was not unpleasant. Life was peaceful in the state of nature, *but it was not fulfilled.*

Rousseau believed that while people wanted to improve themselves this could not be achieved in the state of nature because, although it was an innocent condition, it was not a moral life. Rousseau was deeply influenced by the ancient Greeks, who, you will recall from Chapter 3, regarded people as human only if they actually participated in the affairs of state. Rousseau agreed with the ancient Greeks that morals could be developed only in an environment in which people related to and interacted with one another. This relationship did not exist in the state of nature; so, he concluded that moral life was impossible in that condition. Yet, because people wanted to improve themselves, they were compelled to forge a social contract, forming a community and thus abandoning the state of nature. The community then established a moral code that made human perfection (and even *becoming* human) possible. In the state of nature, people were more animal than human. "We begin properly to become men," Rousseau wrote, "only after we have become citizens."

Nevertheless, the formation of the community does not necessarily lead to a good life; it only makes a moral life possible. Indeed, Rousseau was convinced that although people had the capacity to be good, they were more likely to become immoral as the community became more sophisticated.

Private property, which Rousseau believed developed, only after the community was formed, encouraged greed and selfishness. The most aggressive people in the community gained control of most of the property, and they set up a government to help them maintain power. Consequently, people become prisoners either to their own greed or to that of their rulers. "Man is born free," Rousseau wrote, "and everywhere he is in chains." As we will see later, Marx and other radicals developed similar ideas about the corrupting influence of private property.

The Organic Society Rousseau offered a solution to this dilemma. He could not advise a return to the state of nature because that would require people to give up the chance to live moral lives. Instead, people must build a new community structured so that a moral existence is possible. But to accomplish this, people would first have to break the social and political chains binding them, overthrowing the old order and establishing a new one based on the three cardinal foundations of a moral existence: liberty, equality, and fraternity.

With the old regime destroyed, Rousseau encouraged people to form a new society to which they would surrender themselves completely. By giving up their rights and powers to the group, they would create a new entity. The society would become an organism, *an organic society*, in which each individual contributed to the whole. By giving up their individual powers, people would gain a new kind of equality and a new kind of power. They would achieve equality because they would all become full contributors to the group. Enhanced power would also accrue to the community, the sum becoming greater than its individual parts.

This new society would actually be a person, according to Rousseau—a "public person." The public person would be directed by the general will; *the combination of the wills of all persons in society engaged in doing what was good for all.* As such, the general will could do no wrong because it would create the right. It could not be bad because it would determine what was moral (moral relativism).

The general will also made individual freedom possible. Freedom, according to Rousseau, meant doing only what one wanted to do. When people join the community, they voluntarily agree to comply with the general will of the community. If the majority creates the general will, and if the general will can do no wrong, then the minority must be wrong; and since the individual agreed to live by the general will, those who are in the minority are expected to comply with the will of the majority, thus enhancing their freedom. If those in the minority refuse to follow the general will, they are violating their own will and thus are refusing to be free.[4] People who refuse to comply with the general will, and thus with their own best interests, can be *forced to comply.* Thus, Rousseau argues that the community has the right to *force its members to be free.* As he put it, "Whoever shall refuse to obey the general will must be constrained by the whole body of his fellow citizens to do so; which is no more than to say that it may be necessary to compel a man to be free."

By asserting that the general will cannot be wrong, Rousseau completed the circle begun by Hobbes more than a century before. It will be recalled that the English philosophers separated the monarch from the agent of moral authority—the Church. Here Rousseau claims that the community, which controls the state, actually creates moral authority itself, thus rejoining moral authority and the state, this time in a secular setting. This theory gave a philosophical justification to the anticlerical features of the French Revolution. It was also used later by Mussolini in developing his notion of the totalitarian state. (See Chapter 10.)

An important lesson learned from the example of Rousseau and Hobbes is that sometimes two different ideas, carried to opposite extremes, can result in similar conclusions. Hobbes, on the right of the spectrum, would have society bound to the absolute power of a monarch. Rousseau, on the left, demanded that people subject themselves to the general will in no less absolute fashion.

Economic and Political Systems Like Locke, Rousseau gave importance to property. But Rousseau made explicit the economic negativism Locke only implied. The French radical clearly associated private property with the founding of society itself, but he identified it as an instrument of human exploitation. Considering property an expression of political power, Rousseau wrote, "The first man who after enclosing a piece of ground, bethought himself to say 'This is mine' and found people simple enough to believe him, was the real founder of society."

Thus, Rousseau was not hobbled by any romantic notions about the place of property in society. Regarding property ownership as a *social right* rather than a natural right, he asserted that no one has an unlimited right to accumulate it. Much as Marx would later argue, Rousseau thought that private property could be used to exploit people because it was a source of artificial

---

[4]Note the step toward **moral relativism** here. Moral relativism suggests that there are no absolute principles of right and wrong; rather, society determines moral values. The concept of **moral absolutism**—that there exists a set of absolute truths that humans are bound to obey but are powerless to influence—was prominent in Rousseau's time and before. Natural law is a moral absolutist principle, after all. In fact, Rousseau's belief in the natural law is testament to his own acceptance of moral absolutism. His theory of the general will, however, although it is no less absolutist than other natural law theories, does suggest that people determine, what the absolute principles are. This is an important step toward establishing the philosophical tenets justifying popularly controlled government.

inequality among individuals. Although he never actually supported the elimination of private property, Rousseau objected to an unequal distribution of it among the members of the society. Private property, he believed, should be distributed equally among the individuals in the state. He believed that property was an important source of political power, and since in a democracy all people are supposed to have equal political power, he advocated the equal distribution of property among all citizens. However, he advanced the goal of equal property distribution for political reasons alone, and not—as would socialists later—for the material well-being of people.

Rousseau was also very particular about the governmental form he thought the community should use. To begin with, he believed that each individual's will was inalienable; it could not be transferred to another. Consequently, he opposed representative government, since no one could represent another individual's will. This led him to favor a direct form of democracy, that is, one in which the citizens vote on the laws themselves instead of sending representatives to a legislature. However, because of the limited technology of his time, the direct democracy recommended by Rousseau required that the state be very small. Like the ancient Greeks of whom he was so fond, Rousseau believed that the city-state was the only political entity small enough for all citizens to meet and vote on every law or policy.

Echoing Locke, Rousseau was also very careful to distinguish between executive and legislative functions and powers. First, he insisted on complete separation of the two. He also demanded that the legislature be more powerful than the executive. The legislature was all of the people, or the community, making up the general will. Hence, it was the sovereign or all-powerful body. The executive, according to Rousseau, was merely the government. Rousseau, like Locke, carefully distinguished between the community and the government. The government only served the community. It had no special rights or privileges and, as in Locke's theories, could be changed at any time, whereas the community remained unchanged. The sole function of the executive was to carry out the wishes of the community (the general will).

Even as Rousseau established the theoretical basis for radical, or pure, democracy, more conservative thinkers were beginning to modify the ideas of Locke and others, creating a political-economic system known as *liberal democracy*. Although Rousseau's theories greatly influenced politics on the continent, the more conservative doctrines had an immense impact in England and the United States, only to be followed by the leftist modifications of democratic socialism. In Chapter 5, we will study these two variants of democratic theory.

QUESTIONS FOR DISCUSSION

1. How can the ideas of process democrats and principle democrats be compared and contrasted?
2. In what ways do the theories of popular sovereignty and the social contract relate to each other?

3. What are the political implications of John Locke's economic theories?
4. Which of Rousseau's attitudes qualify him as the founder of modern radicalism?
5. How can the ideas of Thomas Hobbes, John Locke, and Jean Jacques Rousseau be compared and contrasted?

SUGGESTIONS FOR FURTHER READING

Boucher, David, ed., *The Social Contract from Hobbes to Rawls*. Florence, KY: Routledge, 1997.

Brown, Gillian, *The Consent of the Governed: The Lockean Legacy in Early American Culture*. Cambridge, MA: Harvard University Press, 2001.

Damrosch, Leopold, *Jean-Jacques Rousseau: Relentless Genius*. Boston: Houghton Mifflin Co., 2005.

Eisenach, Eldon J., *Narrative Power and Liberal Truth: Hobbes, Locke, Bentham, and Mill*. Lanham, MD: Rowman and Littlefield, 2002.

Hobbes, Thomas, *Leviathan*, ed. Michael Oakshott. New York: Collier, 1962.

Locke, John, *The Second Treatise of Government (An Essay Concerning the True Original Extent and End of Civil Government) and a Letter Concerning Toleration*, ed. J. W. Gough. New York: Macmillan, 1956.

MacPherson, C. B., *The Real World of Democracy*. New York: Oxford University Press, 1969.

Miller, James, *Rousseau: Dreamer of Democracy*. Indianapolis: Hackett, 1995.

Nelson, William M., *On Justifying Democracy*. London: Routledge and Kegan Paul, 1980.

Ritter, Alan, and Julia Conaway Bondanella, ed., *Rousseau's Political Writings*. Trans. Julia Conaway Bondanella. New York: W. W. Norton, 1988.

Rousseau, Jean-Jacques, *Basic Writings*. Trans. and ed. Donald A. Cress. Indianapolis: Hackett, 1978.

Shaver, Robert, ed., *Hobbes*. Brookfield, VT: Ashgate, 1999.

Tilly, Charles, *Democracy*. New York: Cambridge University Press, 2007.

Weale, Albert, *Political Theory and Social Policy*. London: Macmillan, 1983.

Liberal Democracy, Capitalism, and Beyond

PREVIEW

Economics and politics are inextricably linked in modern society. Accordingly, two major variants of democracy have developed: liberal democracy and democratic socialism. Liberal democracy combines the capitalist principles developed by Adam Smith, David Ricardo, and Thomas Hobbes with the political theories of Edmund Burke, James Madison, and Thomas Jefferson. They favored an economy based on free individual commercial activity, although Jefferson was suspicious of the purpose to which private property could be put. While Burke and Madison advocated a strong central government, Jefferson advanced states' rights, but each of the three supported a relatively paternalistic representative political system.

Contemporary liberalism developed in the tradition of Jeremy Bentham, John Stuart Mill, Thomas Hill Green, and John Dewey. More collectivist and less individualist than their liberal predecessors, those of the contemporary school equate individual happiness with the happiness of society as a whole. Because private control of the means of production has been used to oppress large numbers of people, the democratic socialists favor government action to prevent oppression. Believing that people can devise institutions that will serve their needs better, they practice social engineering. The victories and defeats of such experiments can be found in the policies of the New Deal and the Great Society, the reactionary policies of Ronald Reagan, and the negligent policies of George W. Bush. Currently, Barack Obama is trying to develop liberal solutions to the huge environmental, economic, and social problems now confronting us.

CAPITALISM

Rejecting **mercantilism,** the economic system used at his time, **Adam Smith** (1723–1790), a Scottish scholar, developed the ideas that are today understood to be the rudiments of **capitalism.** In his 1776 book *The Wealth of Nations,*

Smith asserted that a nation's wealth was not determined—as had previously been thought—by the amount of gold found in its treasury. Rather, the wealth of nations is determined by their productivity.

He thought people would be most economically motivated if they were allowed to enjoy the wealth they personally created. Thus, he envisioned an economy that was largely held by private ownership and in which people were inhibited as little as possible by government interference. In this, he applied the same principle to economics as Locke had to politics, suggesting that people were most creative when left free to act as they wished. As classic liberals, Locke and Smith favored the greatest possible individual liberty.

Smith reasoned that the distribution of wealth in an economy would be most healthy if left to the abstraction of the market forces. He advocated a policy of **laissez-faire** in which the government should have no economic policy at all. Instead, the economy would be regulated by "the invisible hands of supply and demand," thus resulting in the best possible quality and quantity at the lowest possible price.

Competition was seen as the engine of the new economic system. People would array themselves against one another in a form of economic combat. Those who offered quality goods at reasonable prices would prosper, while those who did not would find themselves forced out of the market. This economic weeding-out process was later referred to as *creative destruction* by economist Joseph Schumpeter.

The net result of this uninhibited competitive process would be an economic system of unparalleled prosperity, or so Smith reasoned. This happy conclusion rested on the assumption that *the good of the whole is best served when each person pursues his or her own self-interest*. Herein lies one of the basic differences between capitalism and socialism. Whereas capitalism assumes that society's best interest is maximized when each individual is free to do that which he or she thinks is best for himself or herself, socialism, as we shall see in Chapter 8, is based on the attitude that the individual's interests are maximized when each person suppresses selfish objectives for the greater good. Socialism is **collectivist** or **organic** in character: It assesses human accomplishment by the contribution made to the group, asking people to cultivate a social consciousness. By contrast, capitalism is **atomistic** in nature. It focuses on the individual, assuming that the social good is a coincidental result of individual success.

In the early stages of the Industrial Revolution, the age during which Smith lived, confidence in the therapeutic value of pursuing self-interest may well have been justified. The national economies of the day were badly warped by arbitrary government-sanctioned monopolies, and it was thought desirable to free economic systems from governmental restraint. The "dead hand of feudalism" still dominated much of the land, even as money began to assume greater importance in society. Inventions and the application of machinery to production promised to vastly expand the availability of goods, if only people could be persuaded to invest enough capital to make use of them. Indeed, the freewheeling system Smith proposed may have been, as Marx later concluded, the very step necessary to catapult Europe into a new era of human history.

Capitalism after Smith

Smith, however, was followed by a new generation of economists who, when capitalism was put into practice, were forced to deal with its bleak side, instead of the rather pleasant aspects Smith theorized. The early Industrial Revolution and the need to accumulate capital visited terrible hardships upon the working class, forcing workers and their families to live in the most miserable and oppressive conditions.

In the early 1800s, **David Ricardo** (1772–1823) and **Thomas Malthus** (1766–1834), two English economists, became capitalism's leading intellectual lights. Although Ricardo believed in the labor theory of value (that value was created by working people applying their creativity to natural resources), he thought it was perfectly appropriate for those who controlled capital (the money necessary to buy factories, machinery, and resources), to force labor to surrender a large part of the value it created. Otherwise, additional private capital would not be forthcoming. On this assumption Ricardo developed the theory of the iron law of wages, in which he suggested that the owner of the factory and the machines would be driven by the profit motive to pay the workers only enough to bring them to the factory to work another day. Though this process might be perceived as cruel, Ricardo defended it, arguing that only in this way would enough capital be created to fund future production. Consequently, although the workers' conditions were admittedly miserable, they would degenerate even further unless additional capital was created. Thus, profound exploitation of the workers and the concentration of money into fewer and fewer hands was rationalized.

Even gloomier than Ricardo, Thomas Malthus became alarmed by the impending disaster he foresaw. He suggested that food might be expected to increase arithmetically—from quantities of one, to two, to three, to four, and so on. Population, however, could grow geometrically—from quantities of one, to two, to four, to sixteen, and so on. If such a progression were allowed to take place uninhibited, the result would soon be catastrophic. Believing that the population was most likely to increase in good times, Malthus concluded that it was prudent, and indeed more humane in the long run, to deny the masses more than the bare essentials, thus discouraging a potentially ruinous population explosion. The well-to-do welcomed Malthus's analysis because it too suggested a moral justification for wealth collecting in the hands of a very few, while the suffering among the workers, those who produced the wealth, mounted. Malthusian theory was also welcomed by the political elite, because it suggested that poverty and suffering by most of society's people resulted from natural causes. Nothing short of abstinence could do much to stem population growth. Therefore, political leaders had no responsibility to do anything about these intractable problems. Indeed, if efforts were made to improve the lives of the masses, they would only breed more people, thus exacerbating the suffering of these unfortunate wretches later on.

Then, toward the end of the nineteenth century, a new, "scientific" rationale for the possession of great wealth by a few in the face of the misery of the masses was advanced by another Englishman, Herbert Spencer (1820–1903). Loosely extrapolating Charles Darwin's theory of natural selection, Spencer applied it to a concept of social development that became known as **Social Darwinism.** Coining the phrase "survival of the fittest," a phrase often mistakenly attributed to Darwin himself, Spencer suggested that the wealthy were so favored because they were biologically superior to the poor. Thus, according to Spencer, the possession of great wealth set the owner apart as a particularly worthy individual. It also encouraged the rich to redouble their efforts to expand their fortunes, even if this involved the increased exploitation of the less fortunate, thus righteously asserting their advanced natures over the less worthy poor. The most ardent Social Darwinists averred that something positive could result even when the exploitation of the poor became fatal, since it meant that the species was being improved as its biologically inferior members were culled out. Given the somber theories of Ricardo, Malthus, and Spencer, it is of little wonder that economics is sometimes called "the dismal science."

American Capitalism

Spencer's theory became most popular in the United States, where capitalist competition and "rugged individualism" had assumed exaggerated proportions. Harkening to the pompous lectures of William Graham Sumner (1840–1910), a Yale professor and the nation's leading proponent of Social Darwinism, American moguls—the *robber barons,* as they came to be called—steeped themselves in righteous justification while they plundered the common people.

Happily, this brutal phase of capitalism was abandoned with the reforms of the Progressive Era (1901–1920), the New Deal under Franklin D. Roosevelt (1933–1941), and Lyndon B. Johnson's Great Society (1962–1968). These economic and social reforms turned government to the task of regulating the excesses of capitalism with the welfare state. Yet, the doctrine of untempered economic individualism came into vogue once again in the 1980s when Ronald Reagan became president. He limited government involvement in the economy and celebrated the "free marketplace" as the appropriate arbiter of the distribution of goods and the dispenser of social justice. Reagan presided over a reactionary revolution that saw businesses *and banks* deregulated and social programs emaciated by lack of public financial support. The freewheeling entrepreneurial system advocated by Reagan encouraged people to suppress their social consciences and urged individuals to seek their own advantage. The gap between rich and poor widened seriously, and homelessness became commonplace. Meanwhile, the stock and commodity exchanges descended into illegal and unethical practices not equaled since the 1920s, the national debt tripled, and the United States plummeted from the world's greatest creditor state to its largest debtor.

Even so, the passion for raw individualism in the 1980s ran its course without destroying the foundations of the social and economic system forged by the New Deal. Moderates like George H. W. Bush and Bill Clinton pursued centrist policies during the late 1980s and early 1990s. However, the "compassionate conservatism" promised by President George W. Bush returned the economic environment to the same individualistic avarice and corporate corruption so prominent in the 1980s. Neglect of the environment, together with the anti-labor policies, pro-business legislation, tax shelters for the wealthy, and the irresponsible refusal to regulate the financial sector shifted U.S. economic policy back to its right, with near catastrophic results.

To date, real wages have remained flat and personal debt has more than tripled since the mid-1970s, while wealth has concentrated in the hands of the well-to-do in unprecedented proportions. Meanwhile, as government regulation of business and finance decreased, major corporations—Enron, World-Com, Adelphia, and others—were disgraced in the early 2000s by exposed corrupt and unethical business practices. These expensive embarrassments were followed by the fraud and war-profiting in Iraq by American companies like Halliburton and Blackwater USA (since renamed "Xe").

Then, toward the end of the Bush administration, the desserts of its mindless laissez-faire policies caught up with us. Encouraged by irresponsible banking practices and the low interest rate policies by the Federal Reserve System, the real estate market ballooned to unsustainable levels. Borrowers were persuaded, or duped by loan agents who were paid commissions for each closed loan, to sign real estate agreements they could not afford, driving prices higher. But, the bubble burst when these unsupportable debts began to come due. People could not pay them off, or even keep them current. Suddenly, no one wanted to buy homes while everyone wanted to sell them and the real estate market collapsed, eventually taking the rest of the economy down with it to what is now being called the "Great Recession."

Ironically, it suddenly became necessary for the government to support the financial industry—the very people who created the crises. To his credit, Chairman of the Federal Reserve System, Ben Bernanke, who deserves some of the responsibility for creating the problem by perpetrating the "free market" policies of his predecessor, Alan Greenspan, finally saw the crises developing. Acting quickly, he persuaded Bush administration Secretary of the Treasury, Henry Paulson, that a massive collapse was imminent. With President Bush basically benching himself on the issue, Bernanke and Paulson assembled the leaders of Congress and told them that action had to be taken immediately. A delay of but a few days risked a financial disaster of unimaginable proportions. In a second irony, the solution rested in resurrecting long-ignored and often demonized Keynesian economic policies calling for government intervention in the economy; a bitter epiphany for these erstwhile free marketers. Even the indomitable free market advocate, Harvard economist Martin Feldstein, capitulated on the issue telling the national press "I'm a fiscal conservative who dislikes increased government spending and increased deficits, but this is a time where we need both, and they need to be really big."

Hundreds of billions of dollars were committed to stabilize the industry. The nation's largest banks, Goldman Sachs, Citigroup, Bank of America, Wells Fargo, other financial oligopolists, and insurance giant AIG, which had insured many of the reckless bank loans, were loaned immense amounts of government money. In the midst of a rapidly declining situation, the Obama administration poured even more money into the financial markets and it also financed General Motors and Chrysler Corporation to prevent their collapse.

To date the combined spending of the Bush and Obama administrations has been almost 2 trillion dollars, most of it borrowed money. These policies appear to have diverted us from the course threatening another Great Depression, and several of the banks have already repaid their government loans, with interest, but it is not yet at all certain that we have actually stabilized the economy. Millions of workers are still unemployed, meanwhile, dozens of retiring corporate executives have walked away from the economic chaos with obscene compensation packages and many more have remained to collect enormous "retention bonuses." Some critics, including a profoundly frustrated President Obama, have asked why we may wish to retain the executives who almost destroyed the largest, most productive economy in the world? On the other hand, the CEO of Goldman Sachs glibly justified the bonuses by saying the company is "doing God's work." Apart from the numerous theoretical questions regarding our economy, the implications of at least one practical question should concern us all. *Is there not something profoundly wrong with the fundamental ethics and health of our economy which must be addressed immediately?* Born of greedy, selfish, irresponsible, unethical, and illegal behavior by many in the business world, and also by the willful ignorance and pecuniary avarice of much of the general public, American capitalism is caught up in a series of recurring spasms threatening the vitality and even the continued viability of the system.

In the mid-1980s there were the insider trading shenanigans personified by Ivan Bowsky who defiantly proclaimed "greed is good," and junk bond magician, Michael Milken. Later in the decade and early in the next, the deregulation of the Savings and Loan institutions and the foolish and unethical practices of many S&L executives, led to the entire industry evaporating at a cost to the taxpayer of $130 billion to $250 billion. At the time, some authorities warned darkly that the deregulation contemplated for the banks would create a financial failure that would make the S&L crises look like child's play. And, so it did.

This financial debacle was followed by the failure of some of the country's leading corporations. Driven by incomprehensible greed, ethical lapses, serious violation of law, deregulation, and lax government oversight, Enron, Global Crossing, WorldCom, and others collapsed, devastating tens of thousands of investors, unemploying thousands, and sending shivers through people's confidence in the leadership of corporate America as about $200 billion disappeared forever. Hard on the heels of this shock came the Dot Com disaster. Looking to get rich quick by getting in on the ground floor of some high-tech fields, thousands of people invested billions in the early 2000s in companies that never showed a profit. Suddenly, investors sobered, causing a crash in high-tech stocks. Then, only a few years later, virtually the entire financial system came apart in the current crises, fostering a profound recession. Given this abysmal record, nurtured by simpleminded confidence in the "free market," one might reasonably wonder what is coming next?

While affording great opportunity to its citizens, American capitalism reserves many of its greatest advantages for those with enough wealth *to buy into the system.* The adage "It takes money to make money" is indeed prophetic. For example, the most lucrative tax advantages in our system are reserved for people who have *capital* (money not needed to live on, so it can be invested). People of modest means must spend or save all, or almost all, of their money for living expenses. On the other hand, the wealthy invest most of their money; thus, they are able to buy tax advantages others can't. The average middle-class income, because it is all spent, is subject to sales taxes, where such taxes are collected. People who invest most of their income pay a far smaller proportion of their income in sales tax, because they don't spend most of it. The middle class currently consists of those who make between $36,000 and $57,660 annually. They are required to pay 7.65 percent of their total income in Social Security and Medicare taxes. Since Social Security taxes are not collected on annual income above about $107,000, however, people who make more than that amount pay nothing on the remainder; thus, they pay a much smaller percentage of their total income to the Social Security tax than do most people. For example, someone making $107,000 a year will pay 7.65 percent of his or her total income (no deductions are allowed) in Social Security tax. By contrast, someone making $214,000 in the same year would pay 7.65 percent on the first $107,000, but nothing on the second $107,000, or only 3.83 percent of his or her total income. Thus, the person making $107,000 per year pays double the rate of personal income to the Social Security tax as someone making twice the income. The wealthy also enjoy great advantages in regards to income tax. The income tax is supposed to be progressive, and so it is, on paper. However, the wealthy don't make most of their money from wages, they make it from long-term capital gains (profits made from investments). Whereas the tax rate on money made from work is between 10 and 35 percent, the tax rate on money made from long-term capital investments is between 5 and 15 percent. Clearly, the tax system penalizes money made from work while rewarding wealthy people who have sufficient capital to be able to live from profits. Further, when most of your income comes from wages, there is very little opportunity to hide it from the tax collector. Not so for investors whose income is much less traceable.

At this point, the argument is sometimes made that people who invest their money risk losing it and thus deserve the lower tax rate. Perhaps so, but the tax system not only gives investors an advantage by taxing profits at lower rates than it does wages, investors who lose money also gain another advantage in that they are allowed to deduct their losses. The advantage is so great,

During the Great Depression of the 1930s, millions of proud but unemployed people reluctantly queued up to receive lifesaving food from charity organizations.

in fact, that often it is more profitable for investors to lose money on certain investments than to increase their income.

The advantages afforded the wealthy in our system are even more startling when one becomes aware of the tendency for wealth to accumulate in fewer and fewer hands. Remember recent statistics indicate that the nation's wealth has become more concentrated in the hands of the few than at any other time in a century. In 2006, the wealthiest 1 percent of the U.S. population owned more than the aggregate value held by the lowest 90 percent of the population.

Some people argue that the economic system is malfunctioning when it gives greater advantages to the wealthy than it gives to the poor. "The rich get richer and the poor get poorer," they grimace. In fact, however, the capitalist system is not malfunctioning when it favors the wealthy—indeed, it is doing exactly what it is supposed to do by demonstrating such bias. Capitalism depends on *private* enterprise. It must have private capital investment if it is to function adequately. The most efficient way of creating private capital is to concentrate huge amounts of money in the hands of a tiny minority of the people rather than spreading it out more equally among the masses. The fortunate few then put their amassed fortunes into capital investments, increasing productivity. The increased productivity is then divided between the wealthy, in the form of profits to be reinvested, and the masses, as improved living and working conditions. The trick is to divide the nation's productivity properly. If too much money is siphoned off into profits, as tends to be the case with **supply-side** economic policies, consumers will lack funds with which to buy, causing widespread unemployment. If, by contrast, too much productivity is diverted to the consumer, as can happen in demand-side economics, too little money will be left for capital investment, resulting in aging plants and machinery, reducing efficiency and productivity, causing inflation.

It is clear, therefore, that while a healthy economy needs to leave enough money in the hands of the consumers, capitalism depends on the existence of a tiny, enormously wealthy class, if enough capital is to foster production. Consequently, laws in capitalist societies are deliberately structured so as to funnel to the wealthy members far greater economic benefits than are enjoyed by the rest of the people. Taking advantage of these privileges, the same families are apt to remain wealthy through time. The Rockefellers, Guggenheims, Mellons, Fords, and other families of great wealth, having amassed fortunes at the early stages of our industrialization, are likely to remain wealthy because the law is tilted in favor of their doing so. So much for the fabled level playing field!

This is not to suggest that other people cannot become wealthy. The meteoric rise of Microsoft's Bill Gates from virtually nothing to a personal fortune of tens of billions of dollars is a good case in point. So is the fact that in 1996 there were just thirteen billionaires in the United States, but by 2006, just ten years later, there were over 1,000, a seventy-nine-fold increase! At the same time, the share of GDP going to wages in 2006 was lower than any previous year since 1947 and the net worth of Americans, after an increase since World War II of 142 percent, declined by 13 percent in the first ten years of this century. Furthermore, the fact remains that although about 50 percent of the adults in the United States were invested in the stock market, in 2007 over 90 percent of all the value held in stocks in the United States was owned by less than 3 percent of its people.

In short, capitalism, the economic system supposedly predicated on competition, actually depends on the monopolization of wealth, and government policies are designed to ensure that monopolization. In a reflective moment, *one might question how true to the principles of individualism and laissez-faire our system is when the government so energetically intervenes to ensure that money remains in the hands of the few.* Indeed, one might not be faulted for thinking that such interventionist policies might be more accurately viewed as a kind of socialism for the few—a circumstance that results in the economic deck being stacked against the many. In fact, the rules of the economic game are not at all the same for the middle class and the classes below it as they are for the well-to-do. Moreover, since these advantages are actively sought for themselves by the well-to-do, it could be suggested that the greatest enemies of competition are the capitalists themselves.

Nevertheless, the United States has risen from a relatively poor agrarian country to become the greatest industrial power in the world's history. Its people enjoy a wonderful standard of living; even most of its poor lead an enviable existence compared with that of most people in the Developing World. Perhaps even more remarkable, these economic successes have been achieved in a political and economic environment that remains open to personal free expression, affording its citizens a latitude of activity admired around the globe. Previous to this era, the worst excesses of individualist aggrandizement were tempered by government regulation, and the excesses of the current era are now under study in Congress and hopefully will be curtailed significantly. Further, the social welfare programs put in place by FDR, Johnson, Nixon, Clinton, and now Obama are designed to further blunt the cruelest aspects of capitalism. However, the government assuring the wealthy of their privilege and acting to mitigate the economic impact on the losers in capitalistic "competition" has deliberately introduced socialist policies. Pure capitalism insists on an unregulated market and it rewards only the people who become winners in an economic melee unbiased by government intervention for, or against, anyone. Therefore, ours is a mixed economic system.

In any event, capitalism and democracy developed coincidentally, both having been nurtured by confidence in human potential spawned by the scientific method, the Industrial Revolution, and the resulting liberal individualism. Indeed, it was very difficult to distinguish between capitalism and democracy during what one might call the neoclassical period of liberal democratic theory.

NEOCLASSICAL LIBERAL DEMOCRATIC THEORY

The group of political theorists who followed Hobbes, Locke, and Rousseau differed from them in a number of ways, though they had much in common with them as well. One of the differences is highly significant, however. The early philosophers were trying to justify an imagined political system which they hoped would become a reality. The *neoclassical liberal democratic philosophers* were trying to design governmental schemes in an environment that was *already* democratic. This single fact made their political views quite different.

Philosophers Hobbes, Locke, and Rousseau had done their jobs well. Their ideas eventually led to the adoption of early, if somewhat mutated, forms of democracy in England and the United States. Being philosophers, however, none of them found themselves in the difficult position of having to put their notions about good government into practice. Although the logical and persuasive expression of thought is no mean task, perhaps even more difficult, and certainly much messier, is the business of making theoretical concepts fit in the arena of practical politics. That task was left for the second wave of democrats, each of whom distinguished himself as a practical politician as well as a thinker.

Edmund Burke

Edmund Burke (1729–1797) became an articulate spokesman for the ideals of the English state, crown, and church. He was noted for his eloquence in Parliament, where he served for almost thirty years.

Conservative Philosophy   As mentioned in Chapter 2, Burke is the father of modern conservative philosophy. Conservative positions have always existed, to be sure, but Burke was the first to analyze the basic principles and motivations of conservatives.

Burke's attitude was Hobbesian in several respects. Social and political stability were the major goals of his theories. He believed that a good government is one that assures order in society. Although Burke was a conservative, he did not always object to change; indeed, he regarded it as a necessary feature of life. However, he felt that any change should be gradual, well thought out, and consistent with the prevailing social conditions. He opposed changes that might disrupt the society, believing that the only modifications which should be made are those that will keep things much as they are.

Examples of how Burke applied this theory are found in his positions on the revolutions in England, the United States, and France and in his attitude toward the British East India Company. Burke defended the 1688 revolution in England and the 1776 revolution in the Anglo-American colonies on grounds that each was an attempt to restore to a society constitutional principles that an oppressive king had unfairly denied. By the same token, however, Burke is famous for his passionate objection to the French Revolution. In his classic work *Reflections on the Revolution in France,* he argued that since the revolution had abruptly cut France off from its past development by replacing its monarchy with a republic, it posed a dire threat to French civilization itself.

Burke's resistance to change stemmed from his assumption that human reason is not competent to dramatically improve social or political systems. Burke believed that the institutions of any society are the products of the accumulated wisdom of centuries. No single generation has the ability to produce abrupt changes that will improve society. Indeed, by meddling with institutions that have been perfected over centuries, people may weaken them or destroy them completely. Burke viewed civilization as a fragile thing that could be ruined if it were not protected from human folly.

Burke believed that any existing institution had value; that is, an existing institution, a product of the wisdom of the ages, has proved its value by surviving and should therefore not be trifled with. If they were not useful, institutions would disappear, Burke reasoned. Any proposal for change, regardless of the soundness of the thought that produced it, could not possibly reach the level of refinement an institution develops over time. So, according to Burke, a new institution can never be as valuable as an older one.

Surprisingly, Burke on the right, like Rousseau on the left, believed that there had been a time when people existed as solitary individuals without a society as we know it. They came together; however, out of a need to interact with each other, and in so doing, they formed an institution that has become part of the definition of humanity itself. Burke believed that goodness, morality, even civilization itself became possible only when people created society. Society thus becomes the context in which people can refine their characters and develop their human traits. Moreover, society develops an organic character. It becomes a personality in its own right, a "political personality."

Although Burke did not emphasize this point as much as Rousseau, he believed that absolute power came from the society and the state. The society may be a collection of "foolish" individuals, but when those individuals join to form a society, their collective judgment becomes "wise" and "always acts right." Burke's respect for tradition and history, coupled with his assumption that society had almost mystical powers, contributed to an attitude toward society that approached religious devotion. Here, too, he not only followed Rousseau but anticipated the ideas of **Georg Hegel** (1770–1831), whose political thought we will study in Chapters 8 and 10.

Theory of Government   True to the Hobbesian tradition, Burke believed that the primary purpose of government was to keep order. He was also uneasy about the concept of popular rule. Accordingly, he made a strong defense for representative government. He argued that the proper governing agency of England was Parliament. Yet, Parliament should not necessarily be controlled by the people. Rather, it was an institution through which the minority would rule the majority, albeit in a benevolent fashion.

Burke maintained that a good ruler must meet three qualifications. *Ability* was, of course, necessary if the government was to be managed efficiently. Second, Burke echoes Locke in suggesting that only people with *property* should be allowed to govern. Whereas Locke believed that people with *property* were apt to act more responsibly than the less well-to-do, Burke, the more conservative of the two, went much further. Articulately reflecting the right's suspicion that the poor are the aggressors in society, Burke said that a few people were of substantially greater quality than others, and a just society would reflect this difference in its distribution of wealth and power. However, because people without property are never content with their status, they constantly agitate to deprive the wealthy of their property. This disruption of society could best be controlled if power was granted solely to property holders.

Not surprisingly, Burke's third qualification for government was *high birth*. Although Burke did not argue that the upper class would always rule better than other classes, he pointed out that the nobility tended to have a greater stabilizing influence than any other class, that its judgment was usually better, and that it did not suffer the more base motivations of the lower classes; thus, it should rule. Note the overriding importance given to stability, or order, in each of the last two qualifications.

Burke rejected Locke's belief that members of Parliament should be bound by the wishes of their constituents. Those wishes should be considered, of course, but members of Parliament should not let such pressure sway them from exercising their better judgment. Legislators were elected to make policy for their constituents, but they were not to be thought of as "ambassadors" who could act only on the instructions of their constituents. As Burke put it, "While a member of the legislature ought to give great weight to the wishes of his constituents, he ought never to sacrifice to them his unbiased opinion, his mature judgment, his enlightened conscience."

As must be clear by now, Burke also rejected another liberal democratic position: *the fundamental equality of people.* People, he argued, are obviously unequal. They have different abilities and intellects. Consistent with his conservative views, Burke believed that the most important distinctions among people are property and social status. He asserted that, by and large, those who have property and status have them because they are more deserving than their inferiors. By the same token, the well-to-do, being more influential than the poor, deserve more representation in government.

Burke was also a nationalist. Indeed, his ideas did much to transform the leftist ideal of nationalism into a concept that conservatives could embrace. He saw the state in transcendental terms; it was the repository of a civilization that each generation should improve but that none should dare change dramatically. Indeed, the state linked present generations with those past and those yet to come. As such, it included a faint promise of immortality.

As a nationalist, however, Burke rejected the local autonomy of federalism in the United States. He argued that when people were elected to Parliament, they were not to represent the narrow interests of their constituencies. Parliament, he believed, was a national legislature. "You choose a member, indeed," he said in a speech to his constituents, "but when you have chosen him, he is not a member of Bristol, but he is a member of Parliament."

In the best Tory tradition then, Burke saw democracy as a system in which the people choose representatives who will rule them in their best interests. This attitude stems from a pessimistic view of human potential founded on a lack of confidence in the power of human reason and on a denial of the existence of human equality.

James Madison

More moderate than Burke, **James Madison** (1751–1836) also enjoyed a long and distinguished political career. His most important political writings, like those of Burke, were responses to the dramatic political events of his day. Though still a young man in 1787, Madison was an experienced statesman by the time of the Constitutional Convention. At this meeting and a few years later, when he wrote and carried through Congress the Bill of Rights, he made his greatest contributions to government, even though he continued a brilliant career long afterwards.

Because he brought to the Constitutional Convention the fundamental structure on which the U.S. government is based, Madison is often called the Father of the Constitution. He is also one of our best sources of information about the political intent of the drafters. Sharing the authorship of a collection of essays known as *The Federalist Papers* with Alexander Hamilton and John Jay, Madison treats us to a beautifully written, well-reasoned explanation of the political theory on which the Constitution is based.

Madison's View of Politics Madison was a very complicated character whose political attitudes vacillated from right to left on the spectrum, depending on the circumstances. With regard to popular government, Madisonian philosophy is definitely conservative. His studies convinced him that when faced with a crisis, popularly controlled governments usually degenerated into mob rule, finally ending with the people giving power to a tyrant of some sort. Thus, Madison, like almost everyone present at the Constitutional Convention, had little respect for pure democracy.

Though Madison probably believed in popular sovereignty in theory, he did not trust the people themselves. In *The Federalist* (no. 10), he describes human nature in unambiguous Hobbesian terms: "So strong is this propensity of mankind to fall into mutual animosities that where no substantial occasion presents itself the most frivolous and fanciful distinctions have been sufficient to kindle their unfriendly passions and excite their most violent conflicts."

Despite his Hobbesian disposition toward people, Madison did not share the English philosopher's confidence in strong government as a remedy for human shortcomings. Quite the contrary. Like Locke, he believed that individual liberty was the main goal of a political system. Yet, unlike Locke, he was not at all confident of the individual's ability to achieve and maintain liberty in a democratic society. This conflict involved Madison in a dilemma. He believed that people ought to govern themselves in some way, but at the same time, experience taught him that popular governments soon degenerated into dictatorships.

Therefore, Madison was convinced that government was necessary, and he preferred a popularly controlled political system. Still, his studies showed that neither the people nor the government could be counted on to maintain "liberty, which is essential to political life." He had observed that government, when left unchecked, was oppressive and cruel. At the same time, however, he believed that human nature was not only aggressive and selfish but *unchangeable* as well. He therefore wanted to construct a system that would play the oppressiveness of government against the avarice of people, hoping that each would check the negative aspects of the other. This mutual negation, he speculated, would result in good government and the greatest amount of individual liberty possible. Madison explained his dilemma in *The Federalist* (no. 51) when he wrote:

> What is government but the greatest of all reflections on human nature? If men were angels, no government would be necessary. If angels were to govern men, neither external nor internal controls of government would be necessary. In framing a government which is to be administered by men over men, the greatest difficulty lies in this: You must first enable the government to control the governed; in the next place oblige it to control itself.

Madison's solution to the problem, the separation of powers and checks and balances, as you will see shortly, is at once the genius and perhaps the curse of the great statesman and of the American political system.

Madison's Political System   Madison did not fear the individual; indeed, he supported individual rights and liberties. What concerned him about politics was not solitary individuals but groups of individuals united to exert political influence. These groups he called *factions,* today we call them political parties.[1]

Madison noted that in politics people had a habit of combining into factions to pursue mutual interests. This grouping he considered unfortunate but unavoidable. *The faction about which he felt the greatest trepidation was the majority.* You will recall that he believed people were essentially selfish and that if, in a democratic system, a group was in the majority for a sustained period, it would use its power to oppress the minority.

Using the Constitution to protect minorities, *Madison's system of government is largely an attempt to divide and frustrate the majority.* Madison envisioned a political system with the broadest possible power base. For example, he rejected the common belief that a democracy could work only in a very small area, arguing instead that it could succeed in a large country like the United States. A large population spread over a huge area, he reasoned, would make it difficult to create a permanent majority. Such a society would probably divide into varied and fluctuating minority factions, making a long-lasting majority unlikely. Instead, majorities would be created out of combinations of competing minorities. Thus, any majority would be temporary, and new ones would be elusive. This system, which political scientists now term *pluralism,* will be discussed in more detail in Chapter 6.

Economic disparity was also a necessary component of Madison's scheme. Madison was something of an economic determinist. Although not as much of an extremist about it as Marx. Madison believed that economic factors inspire people to political activity more than any other stimulus. Although Madison thought that religion, culture, ideals, and geography also influenced people, he concluded that economic concerns are the most powerful force in people's lives. "A landed interest, a manufacturing interest, a mercantile interest, with many lesser interests," Madison wrote, "grow up of necessity in civilized nations, and divide them into different classes, actuated by different sentiments and views." Madison's wish for a diverse and aggressive economic system, together with his belief that people are by nature combative, led to the conclusion that capitalism is the economic system best suited to the political structure he had in mind.

Indicative of Madison's complex nature, though he tended toward the left so far as economic determinism is concerned, his attitude about democracy

---

[1]Interestingly, Madison, like most of the other authors of the Constitution, originally opposed the formation of political parties. But later, after the Constitution was ratified and implemented, Madison found himself frustrated by the conservative elements led by Alexander Hamilton, so he joined with Jefferson to establish the Republican Party, today's Democratic Party.

was, with one very important exception, almost identical to Burke's. Unlike Burke, he wanted to localize rather than nationalize politics, since this process would institutionalize tens, or even hundreds, of local factions and hopefully discourage the emergence of a permanent national majority faction. Madison was very pessimistic about the chance of a successful democratic government. His studies indicated that pure democracy is usually unsuccessful and "can admit of no cure to the mischiefs of faction." Yet he believed that the people should rule themselves, but only through elected representatives. What he called a *republic* is more accurately termed a *democratic republic* or *representative democracy*. In his view, elected officials would represent their constituents, but he also expected that they would be free to use their judgment rather than being bound to the wishes of their constituents, as Locke had expected. Reminiscent of Burke's elitist views, Madison wrote in *The Federalist* (no. 10) that a republic would

> refine and enlarge the public views by passing them through the medium of a chosen body of citizens, whose patriotism and love of justice will be least likely to sacrifice it to temporary or partial considerations. Under such a regulation it may well happen that the public voice, pronounced by the representatives of the people, will be more consonant to the public good than if pronounced by the people themselves, convened for the purpose.

Thus, Madison expected that the United States would be governed by an enlightened and benevolent elected aristocracy that would protect the *interests* of the people but would not necessarily be bound by the people's *will*.

Checks and Balances   Madison's best known and most creative contribution is the system of **separation of powers** and **checks and balances.** In developing this system, he owed a great deal to two earlier students of government, James Harrington (1611–1677) and Charles Montesquieu (1689–1755). Both of these men were interested in a democratic republic and in developing a way of limiting the power of the government over the people. Using their ideas as a base, Madison created a complex system of institutional and popular restraints.

By separating the powers of government, Madison hoped to make it impossible for any single branch of government to gain too much power and use it to dominate the others. No person could serve in more than one branch of government at a time, and each branch was given its own separate and distinct powers. The legislature, divided into two houses, was to make the law, the executive was to carry it out, and the judiciary was to adjudicate legal disputes and interpret the law. Yet, each branch was given some powers that overlapped with those of the other two branches. The legislature controlled the purse strings, and it was also allowed to ratify appointments to the executive and judicial branches. The executive appointed judges and could veto laws. The courts were expected to nullify any law or executive action that violated the Constitution.[2] These are just a few examples of the checks and balances provided for in the American system of government; there are many others, and we shall discuss them in Chapter 6.

Another way Madison diffused power was by creating *federalism.* The powers of government were divided between the state and national governments. In this way, Madison hoped to prevent either level of government from gaining too much power. Federalism also divided the people of the United States into several compartments. Madison hoped that although majorities might develop at the state level, the various majorities would check each other, thus preventing a permanent majority at the national level. Confident of his vision as he was, Madison obviously failed to foresee the emergence of national political parties. Ironically, he himself later became a leading figure in the national party movement.

The mechanisms mentioned above are the *institutional checks and balances,* but Madison reserved his ultimate impediments, the *popular checks and balances,* for the people. This effort to frustrate a permanent majority was built into the electoral system itself. To begin with, only members of the House of Representatives were elected directly by the people. Until the Seventeenth Amendment was passed in 1913, senators were elected by the state legislatures. The presidents and vice presidents were, and still are, elected by the Electoral College. Although not required by the Constitution, all electors are now elected by the voters, but the Constitution does not mandate that the electors have to vote for the presidential candidate the people favor. Judges are even more removed from popular control, since they are appointed to the bench for life. This arrangement, together with the fact that elected federal officers (members of the House, senators, and the president) serve for terms of different lengths (two years, six years, and four years respectively), was deliberately contrived to soften the effect of popular "passions" expressed by the voters.

Popular control is also reduced by the fact that the terms of office of elected officials are fixed by law and cannot be interrupted except under very unusual circumstances. The people elect many officials, but only when the law calls for election and not necessarily when the people wish to vote on a particular office.

It is clear that the American political system, as developed by Madison, is not very democratic in the participatory sense of the term. In fact, it severely limits the ways in which people actually rule themselves. The people cannot pass laws; they cannot repeal laws. They cannot legally remove a person

---

[2]While the Constitution gives the federal courts explicit instructions to set aside state law found to violate the national charter, it does not grant the power of judicial review to them, in so many words, over national law. But there is little question that the founders intended such a power to exist. In *The Federalist* (no. 78) Hamilton clearly calls on the federal courts to hold federal statutes to the limits of the Constitution.

from office before the expiration of the term.[3] Officials may be impeached, of course, but even this is not done by the people. Congress impeaches; the people have no official voice in the matter.

To cap the irony, popular sovereignty, which means that the people are the source of all law and power, is supposed to be the central feature of democracy. Yet the Constitution of the United States may not be amended directly by the people of the United States. It may be amended only through their representatives in Congress and the state legislatures; there is no direct role at all in the amendment process for the "sovereign people."

One should gather from these comments that our political system was not designed to be very democratic in the literal sense of the term. The people are allowed to formally participate in their government very rarely; their direct control over government officials is limited to Election Day. It is true that popular control and participation are much more significant than a simple statement of the people's formal powers indicates, but the fact remains that the system was not intended to be very democratic. Even so, the American political system has been liberalized considerably since the Constitution was written. However, the theoretical justifications for these changes are found more in the ideas of Thomas Jefferson than in those of James Madison.

Jefferson's Alternative

A man of reason, **Thomas Jefferson** (1743–1826) was America's Voltaire. His most famous work, the Declaration of Independence, justified the American Revolution and became a beacon, leading freedom-loving people throughout the world to their goal. America's most articulate statesman, Jefferson may be placed to the left of Burke, Madison, and Locke on the political spectrum, but he was clearly not as extreme as Rousseau. Though he generally leaned toward Locke's version of the social contract and natural law, he shared Rousseau's respect for the common people and for participatory government. More than most of the other natural law theorists, Jefferson favored revolution as a way of bringing about meaningful political change. Arguing that twenty years without a rebellion would be too long if government officials were to remain servants of the people, Jefferson glibly wrote: "The tree of liberty must be refreshed from time to time with the blood of patriots and tyrants."

Jefferson's Declaration averred that all people were created equal, that "the Laws of Nature and Nature's God" had given every person a set of rights that could not be legally alienated, and that among those rights were "Life,

---

[3]Many states allow their voters to remove state or local elected officials by a process called *recall*, but the Constitution does not recognize such a power regarding federal officials.

Liberty, and the pursuit of Happiness."[4] As a social contract theorist, he believed that government was the product of an intentional act by the people in the society. He agreed with Locke that all "just powers" of government accrue to it from the people and that the government is supposed to serve the people, not the other way around. If the government does not serve the interests of the people, its masters, Jefferson wrote in the Declaration, "it is the Right of the People to alter or abolish it, and to institute new Government, laying its foundation on such principles, and organizing its powers in such form as to them shall seem most likely to affect their Safety and Happiness."

Jefferson's faith in the common people was unshakable. Unlike Hobbes, Burke, Madison, or Hamilton, Jefferson believed that the people were the only competent guardians of their own liberties, and that as such they should be in firm control of their government. Discussing the role of the people in a republic, he wrote to Madison from France in 1787 that "they are the only sure reliance for the preservation of our liberties."

Jefferson's liberal democratic theories have acted as a counterweight to Madison's more conservative democratic ideas; indeed, the interplay between these two basic attitudes has dominated American political history. During the American Revolution and under the Articles of Confederation, Jefferson's ideology prevailed. However, for many reasons, not the least of which were the low priority given private property while the Articles were in force, and the inherent weakness of the government, the Articles failed in 1789.

James Madison, Alexander Hamilton, Benjamin Franklin, George Washington, and other delegates to the Constitutional Convention deliberately replaced the leftist Articles with a much more conservative, less democratic, and more paternalistic system of government. They created a government in

---

[4]You will recall from Chapter 2 that in drafting the Declaration of Independence, Jefferson amended Locke's phrase "life, liberty and estate" to read "Life, Liberty and the pursuit of Happiness." This distinction is important. Though Jefferson was a classical liberal theorist in the tradition of Locke, he, like Rousseau, lived a full generation after the English philosopher and saw a different reality. Locke saw private property as a means of achieving greater freedom, however, by the time of Rousseau and Jefferson, the capitalist class had moved much closer to the source of power; some capitalists were actually beginning to use their control of property to deny equality and liberty to others. Jefferson hoped to better reflect Locke's intent by substituting the vague phrase for the concept of private property. Clearly, with the ideas of Rousseau and Jefferson an important change had occurred in leftist thinking about private property. Instead of considering private property a *natural right,* they gave it secondary status as a *social right:* a right that can be defined, regulated, and limited by society as it sees fit. And so it remains today. The left generally deemphasizes the importance of private property and values it only as a contribution to the welfare of the society, whereas those toward the right of the political spectrum take a more traditionally Lockean position and equate private property with individual liberty.

One should remember, however, that even Locke opposed unlimited accumulation of private property by any individual. The American capitalists' argument in support of unlimited accumulation of private property is actually a perversion of the theories of Locke and Adam Smith rather than a true reflection of their ideas.

which power was much more centralized than it had been under the Articles of Confederation. They also severely limited popular control over the government. The Constitution, in fact, was no less than *the culmination of a conservative counterrevolution against the dominant theme of the American Revolution.*

The conservative victory was not as complete as one might think, however. Since 1789, the year the Constitution went into effect, the system has gradually been liberalized. Indeed, George Mason, Jefferson, Samuel Adams, and others insisted, in return for their support, that the conservative Constitution be amended to mention the specific rights of the people under the new law. The original document was concerned primarily with the structure and powers of the central government. Little reference was made to the rights and liberties of the people, and the leftists insisted that they be added. This addition, of course, was the *Bill of Rights.*

Ever attendant to the needs of his society, it was Madison—in a move to the left—who actually wrote the Bill of Rights, and Madison was the prime manager of its passage through Congress and ratification. Since its adoption guaranteed constitutional protection of individual rights, the country has progressed through a number of other liberalizing eras, further relaxing the restraints imposed on the people by the Constitution as originally adopted. The changing social and economic effects of industrialization demanded political democratization. In the early nineteenth century, the administrations of Thomas Jefferson (1801–1809) and Andrew Jackson (1829–1837) extended the vote to almost every adult white male citizen. And the Lincoln epoch (1861–1865) not only liberated the slaves but also brought about the Homestead Act (which made free land available to poor farmers), promoted federal aid to education, and made possible the construction of the transcontinental railroad. The Progressive Era amended the Constitution to provide for women's suffrage and for popular election of U.S. senators, enacted the progressive income tax, and established the procedures of initiative, referendum, and recall. The New Deal (1933–1941) brought Social Security, collective bargaining, and many social-welfare programs. The Great Society (1964–1969) launched a war on poverty and racial bigotry, and the past three decades have witnessed drives to liberate women and gays. Each of these eras produced great change. Nevertheless, each was followed by a period of reaction in which many of the changes were dismantled. The net result is that the liberties of individuals in the system have been gradually, if not completely, equalized and increased. Although much remains to be done, the nation has evolved to something closer to the Jeffersonian political ideal than Madison and his colleagues intended. Moreover, the passage of time and the evolution of liberal theory, as Jefferson anticipated, eventually restored democracy to the left.

THE EMERGENCE OF DEMOCRATIC SOCIALISM

During Locke's time, people had begun to think that they could use reason to improve social conditions. After all, through science, reason had improved their material existence. They speculated that if there were natural forces guiding all other creatures, there might also be natural forces guiding people. Accordingly, liberalism was born swaddled in the theory of natural law.

Jeremy Bentham (1748–1832) belonged to a later generation, however. Indeed, he was in the forefront of the second wave of English liberal thinkers. Like earlier liberals, he was a product of the scientific and technological progress achieved since the Enlightenment. He too believed that people could use reason to improve themselves, but he thought that the **natural law** theory led to a philosophical dead end. Bentham held that as long as the people in a society were confident that there was a "right conduct" that could be found through the active pursuit of "right reason," society would be dynamic and changing. However, as soon as those in power thought that they had found the answer, all the citizens would have to conform to the leader's idea of right conduct. At that point, the society would lose its vitality, becoming stagnant.

Utilitarianism and Positivist Law

Bentham did not argue that there was an absolute, eternal, and universal rule in nature (the natural law) by which people should govern their conduct. Instead, he based his liberalism on belief in the value of human self-reliance. Rejecting natural law, Bentham suggested his own measure by which to evaluate human conduct. He called it **utilitarianism.**

"Nature," Bentham wrote in *An Introduction to the Principles of Morals and Legislation,* "has placed mankind under the governance of two sovereign masters, *pain* and *pleasure.*" Human happiness would be achieved when pain was at a minimum and pleasure at a maximum. The value, or *utility* of any policy, therefore, can be measured by the amount of pleasure or pain it brings to an individual or to society as a whole. Rejecting elitism, Bentham assumed that one person's happiness is equal to the happiness of any other. Further, Bentham believed that the well-being of society would be maximized by any policy that brought "the greatest happiness to the greatest number." The principle of utility, or utilitarianism, was Bentham's major interest. Almost everything he did or wrote was a variation on that theme, and he developed a theory of law by which to implement it.

Positivist law resulted from the combination of Bentham's rejection of natural law, his utilitarianism, and his conviction that government should take *positive* steps to maximize the happiness of the society. "The business of government," he wrote, "is to promote the happiness of society." The authority of a given law, in Bentham's view, had nothing to do with any concept of eternal good or justice, as natural law theorists believed. Law was not based on an absolute, unchanging truth. It was *not* a semi-sacred thing that people should worship and never change. Law, in Bentham's view, was a tool by which the society could modify its social conditions in order to increase its happiness. Thus, Bentham's theory of positivist law took down the pedestal on which law had been placed by the early liberals. It brought law back within reach of the society by calling for change and reform.

Although Bentham viewed as valid any law that was made by the proper authority, he did not regard every valid law as good law. Instead, he distinguished between being procedurally correct and being just. To assess the wisdom of law, Bentham applied his utilitarian test; he wanted to know how many people were affected negatively and positively by the statute.

If, however, a society were to adopt a policy that gave the greatest happiness to the greatest number, it would need a way of measuring utility. To satisfy this need, Bentham developed his *hedonistic calculus*. This elaborate formula included a list of fourteen categories of human pleasure, twelve categories of pain, and seven standards of measurement. These, Bentham suggested, should be used by a *scientific legislature* to determine the wisdom of a proposed policy. Though his hedonistic calculus is impractical and even a bit ridiculous, it stems from an admirable concern for improvement and democratization of the government and the legislative process. Moreover, one should bear in mind that this formula, suggested in a time when people were enchanted with science, was a well-meant attempt to measure scientifically the justice of any policy or law, rather than leaving the question to the mercy of legislative whim or social class bias.

Bentham's contribution was important. He had the foresight to lead Western thought out of the trap inherent in the absolutist principle of natural law. In utilitarianism, he gave us a practical standard by which to measure the value of a particular policy. With these ideas he set liberalism on a new course, one that could significantly improve the condition of society. In calling for positive governmental steps to improve the society, he provided motivation for many reforms that were adopted in England between 1830 and 1850: the civil service, the secret ballot, equal popular representation in Parliament, expanded educational opportunities, humane treatment of animals, and much more. It is perhaps not too much to say that Jeremy Bentham and his followers gave England a new social conscience. In short, Bentham was the founder of contemporary liberalism (see Chapter 2).

Democratic Socialism

The introduction of utilitarianism and positivist law into democratic theory led to a whole new concept of popular government. The relationship of people to their government had changed drastically since Locke's era and even since the time of Madison. In the seventeenth and eighteenth centuries, the most likely oppressor of the people was indeed the government. Few other institutions were powerful enough to oppress the masses. Those that were strong enough, such as the church or the landowning class, almost always used government to dominate the people. Democracy itself was relatively untested at that time. What democracy there was often degenerated into mob rule and eventually turned into a dictatorship of one kind or another.

In the nineteenth century, however, democracy was more successful, and its development was accompanied by the growth of industrialization and capitalism. The new political system was praised as government by the people, yet the economic system seemed to squeeze ownership into the hands of fewer and fewer people. This process continued until a single company became the major employer in a given locale or even owned the town outright. Wages were kept low, hours of work were long, safety issues were ignored, and men, women, and children were exploited.

It became clear that people could be controlled by economic forces the way they had been controlled by government in the past. Capitalism, which had been developed by liberals, and was long supported by them, because it tended to increase individual wealth and freedom, became suspect because of its ability to exploit people. Gradually, those on the left of the political spectrum began to wonder why, if the government was supposed to be democratic and if the economic forces in the society were exploiting the people, the people did not use their control of the government to prevent tyranny by the economy. *This new emphasis revolutionized liberal democracy, making it more socially oriented and less individualistic.* Although Bentham was the first modern liberal, his thinking only prepared the way for the new attitude toward democracy. It took several later thinkers to bring these new ideas to maturity.

John Stuart Mill Although a student of Bentham, **John Stuart Mill** (1806–1873) surpassed his teacher with his scholarship, logic, and clear writing. So great were his intellectual powers that he is generally recognized as one of the most important philosophers of the nineteenth century. Like Bentham, he was a political activist, and he even spent three years in the House of Commons. From an early age, he supported contemporary movements, such as free education, trade unionism, equal apportionment of parliamentary seats, and repeal of the corn tariffs. Moreover, he was among the first male thinkers to advocate the equality of women.

Mill was interested in many areas of thought, including philosophy, logic, morals, and economics. His most important work, *On Liberty* (1859), is perhaps the most eloquent treatment of individual freedom in the English language. In it, he argued that although democracy was the preferable form of government, even democracy had a tendency to limit individual liberty. Therefore, freedom of speech and thought should be given absolute protection under the law because individual liberty was the surest way of reaching happiness.

Influenced by Bentham's ideas, Mill became a utilitarian. He reasoned that happiness is the principal objective of the society and that happiness can best be achieved when people do good for each other. The original motivation for kindness toward another person, Mill argued, was *enlightened self-interest.* That is, individuals do good deeds because they know that they themselves will ultimately benefit from such acts. However, Mill took his analysis one step further and in so doing was led toward a very different conclusion than that reached by others who supported the enlightened self-interest theory of motivation. Mill argued that, in time, people can become used to doing good and will continue to do so even if they do not expect any particular reward.

In other words, Mill came very close to arguing that people are not necessarily selfish, or that if they are, they can change or control that part of their nature. This optimism about human character is typical of leftist ideologies.

Mill's conclusions gradually led him to attack laissez-faire capitalism and made him the first liberal democratic philosopher to attack the "enslaving capacity of capitalism." Mill's arguments were so effective that few liberals have supported laissez-faire since his time. Before Mill, laissez-faire had been opposed only by the extreme left—by Marx and other socialists and radicals. Under Mill, the liberal democrats began a movement to the left that led many of them to prefer socialism over capitalism as an economic companion to democracy.

Thomas Hill Green   Professor of moral philosophy in England, **Thomas Hill Green** (1836–1882) became a leading leftist thinker. Like Mill, he was concerned with individual liberty. "We shall probably all agree," he wrote, "that freedom, rightly understood, is the greatest of blessings; that its attainment is the true end of our efforts as citizens." Green was careful, however, to point out that freedom did not mean the right to do whatever one wished without regard for others. It was not the same as the absence of restraint, as Locke had suggested. Reacting to the economic and political impediments imposed on most people by industrialization, Green defined freedom as the "liberation of the powers of all men equally for contributions to a common good." Thus, Green's call for freedom in a *positive* and *social* sense represents another major leftward shift in liberal thought.

Green suggested that individual freedom comes not from people being able to contribute to their own welfare but from people being able to contribute to the society as a whole. He argued against government playing the role Locke envisioned, that is, merely serving as a passive arbiter of disputes between individuals. Instead, he believed that government should take definite steps to increase the freedom of people. One of the elements in the society that he saw being used to restrict the individual's liberty was private property. The Industrial Revolution had seen great wealth concentrate in the hands of only a tiny group of fortunates, whereas ordinary people, driven from the land to the factories, became increasingly dependent on others: on a system of production and distribution over which they had no control. Thus, people became subject more than ever before to the power of the ownership class. Viewing these trends as undemocratic, Green urged people to use the institutions of government to protect themselves from the powerful economic forces over which they otherwise had no other control. This position, of course, is an early philosophical justification of the **welfare state.** Hence, he gave forceful support to a government that would take *positive* steps to improve the lives of the people through policies promoting free education, labor laws protecting women and children, sanitary working and living conditions, and much more.

Poverty can be a prison as confining as any penitentiary, Green believed. If this assumption is correct, and if the state is responsible for increasing the individual's freedom to the greatest possible degree, as Locke had argued, then it is clear that a government must take responsibility for the material well-being of its citizens. In short, Bentham, Mill, and Green led liberalism beyond the conviction that government had only a political obligation to its citizens. Government must not limit itself to sweeping the streets and catching burglars. On the contrary, as Locke himself had inadvertently implied, government is responsible for liberating citizens economically and socially, as well as politically and legally.

Green's ideas were of great importance to the contemporary liberal movement. They not only added to the philosophical foundations for positive governmental action to protect the citizens from powers against which they were otherwise helpless, in the tradition of Bentham and Mill; they did much more. Green's work directed liberalism away from solitary individualism toward a social conscience and collectivism. This trend will build until eventually liberals support an organic theory of society similar to but less extreme than Rousseau's. Still, Green based his liberalism on Bentham's utilitarianism and Mill's enlightened self-interest, not on any moral view of human rights. It was left to another philosopher to give liberalism the moral depth it has enjoyed in contemporary times.

John Dewey   The leading American philosopher of contemporary liberalism, or social democracy, was **John Dewey** (1859–1952). He stated its goals more clearly than anyone else, putting the final touches on the philosophical principles that find liberals trying to change political institutions for the good of society. Dewey strongly believed in the intelligence and dignity of people and in the power and wisdom of individual contributions to the collective good.

Dewey brought liberalism back to its central theme. He argued that all people were equal in their humanity. This does not mean that there are no differences among people's physical or mental attributes. Such an argument would be foolish. Yet, regardless of the differences among people, no individual is more human than the next, and each person contributes to society. Consequently, each has a right to equal political and legal treatment at the hands of the state. To deny such treatment would be an abuse of the **human rights** to which each individual has equal claim. Importantly, Dewey argued that precisely because there are physical and intellectual differences among people, equal political and legal treatment becomes necessary. Otherwise, Dewey argued, those who do not have great strength or intellect could be tyrannized by those who do: a rich insight.

Having reestablished this basic assumption, Dewey extended the logic of Bentham, Mill, and Green. Dewey agreed that the happiness of the individual is the primary goal of the society. However, he held that no definition could remain unchanged. Our understanding of all things is determined by our environment and our experiences. This empirical attitude—the attitude that lies at the foundation of *pragmatism,* which Dewey supported—tended to consider all knowledge tentative and conditional. Thus, the meaning of happiness, society,

| John Dewey (1859–1952)

and human rights, and even of the individual itself, is constantly changing as our perception of the social environment evolves: "An individual is nothing fixed, given ready-made," Dewey wrote to emphasize his *moral relativism.* "It is something achieved, and achieved not in isolation, but [with] the aid and support of conditions, cultural, and physical, including in 'cultural' economic, legal, and political institutions as well as science and art."

Yet Dewey did not suggest that we are at the mercy of the environment simply because it creates our definitions. Consistent with enduring liberal belief, he opined that people could make their lives better by applying their intelligence to the problems they faced.

Dewey's belief in the changing nature of truth and his confidence in human reasoning led him to advocate *social engineering.* Unlike conservatives, who believe that existing institutions have value in themselves and should not be meddled with, Dewey was an enthusiastic supporter of social experimentation. He encouraged people to modify and adjust institutions so as to increase the happiness of society. He rejected Burke's argument that an institution is the product of the collective wisdom of successive generations and that no single generation is competent to improve that institution by changing it dramatically. In contrast, Dewey wrote that liberalism "is as much interested in the *positive construction of favorable institutions* legal, political, and economic, as it is in the work of removing abuse and overt oppressions" (emphasis added). Consequently, not only are people able to modify institutions that oppress them, but they should go further by creating institutions that will increase their happiness.

People, Dewey asserted, should study their society and not hesitate to make institutional changes that would improve their lives. They were not to stop there, however. He encouraged them to try to mold individuals themselves, thereby improving human beings and making them more socially compatible. This concept is indeed a far cry from Madison's rather dim view that human nature is base and unchangeable. "The commitment of liberalism to experimental procedure," Dewey explained, "carries with it the idea of continuous reconstruction of the ideas of individuality and of liberty in intimate connection with changes in social relations."

This dedication to the concept of *social engineering* by the most influential American philosopher of the twentieth century had important effects. Dewey's ideas inspired liberals to create the policies of the New Deal, the Fair Deal, and the Great Society, and Obama's current efforts to reform health care, improve and expand education, repair the economic system, modernize the nation's infrastructure, and lead us to the changes in lifestyle necessary to preserve a happy environmental balance.

This chapter and Chapter 4 have dealt with the theory or principles of democracy. Yet, as indicated in Chapter 4, democracy includes specific procedures as well as principles. In Chapter 6, we shall consider the most important procedures and institutions found in contemporary democratic systems.

QUESTIONS FOR DISCUSSION

1. How can liberal democracy and democratic socialism be compared and contrasted?
2. What are the basic features, strengths, and weaknesses of capitalism?
3. How do Burke, Madison, and Jefferson compare and contrast on concepts such as the nature of people, liberty, nationalism, and economics?
4. How can the attitudes about government held by the neoclassical liberal democrats and the social democratic liberals be compared and contrasted?
5. What assumptions turned contemporary liberalism toward socialism, and why?

SUGGESTIONS FOR FURTHER READING

Bentham, Jeremy, *An Introduction to the Principles of Morals and Legislation*. New York: Harper and Row, 1952.

Dewey, John, *Liberalism and Social Action*. Amherst, NY: Prometheus Press, 1999.

Dickens, Peter, *Social Darwinism*. Philadelphia: Open University Press, 2000.

Fairfield, Roy P., ed., *The Federalist Papers: Essays by Alexander Hamilton, James Madison, and John Jay*. New York: Anchor Books, 1961.

Fishkin, James S., and Peter Laslett, eds., *Debating Deliberative Democracy*. Malden, MA: Blackwell, 2003.

Frieden, Jeffrey A., *Global Capitalism: Its Fall and Rise in the Twentieth Century*. New York: W. W. Norton, 2006.

Green, Thomas Hill, *Lectures on the Principles of Political Obligation*. Ontario, Canada: Batoche Books, 1999.

Hacker, Jacob S., *The Great Risk Shift*. New York: Oxford University Press, 2006.

Hayek, Friedrich, *The Road to Serfdom*. Chicago: University of Chicago Press, 1976.

Heilbroner, Robert L., *The Worldly Philosophers*, 5th ed. New York: Simon and Schuster, 1980.

Isbister, John, *Capitalism and Justice: Envisioning Social and Economic Fairness*. Bloomfield, CT: Kumarian Press, 2001.

Mill, John Stuart, *Principles of Political Economy*. Toronto: University of Toronto Press, 1965.

Moyers, Bill, *Moyers on Democracy*. New York: Random House, 2008.

Murphy, Robert P., *The Politically Incorrect Guide to Capitalism*. Washington, DC: Regnery Pub. Inc., 2007.

Schumpeter, Joseph, *Capitalism, Socialism, and Democracy*. New York: George Allen & Unwin, 1994.

Smith, Adam, *The Wealth of Nations*, in *Adam Smith's Moral and Political Philosophy*, ed. Herbert W. Schneider. New York: Hafner, 1948.

Spencer, Herbert, *The Man Versus the State*. Caldwell, ID: Caxton Press, 1884.

The Liberal Democratic Process

PREVIEW

Direct democracy exists when the people make the laws themselves, and when representatives make the laws for the people, the government is called a republic. Pluralism is a variant of the republican form in which interest groups are the primary link between the people and the policymakers.

Democracy must work within a governmental system. The American federal system divides power between two basic levels of government: state and national. The American government also uses the presidential-congressional system. Its most prominent features are election of legislators and the executive to unrelated, uninterruptible terms; the separation of powers; and the checks and balances.

The British unitary system concentrates all governmental power at the central level, and the central government then empowers local governments. Within the national government, power is concentrated in Parliament through the use of the parliamentary-cabinet system. The legislature, specifically the House of Commons, is at least technically superior to the executive and judicial branches and can pass any law it deems appropriate. The only popular elections held in this system are elections to Parliament. Parliament chooses its leader, who forms a government, the cabinet, which shares administrative powers and responsibility.

The United States and Britain each employ the single-member district electoral system, discouraging the existence of more than two major parties. On the other hand, the multimember district tends to encourage the existence of more than two major parties because it gives minor parties a better chance of victory; but this system usually fails to produce a majority in the legislature.

A single-party system exists when only one party has a reasonable chance of gaining control of the government. The two-party system tends to produce a majority for the winner and therefore encourages strong government, but it also benefits from having a powerful opposition party. The multiparty system tends to give voice to the various opposing points of view in a political system but can be unstable because it usually fails to produce a majority party.

Several theories about representation have been developed. The central question is, how much authority should the representatives, as opposed to the people, enjoy over policy decisions? Regardless of what form is used, democracy suffers severe criticism today. Friend and foe alike question its continued viability in a modern technological setting.

PROCESSES OF DEMOCRACY

In the preceding two chapters we studied the theoretical aspects of democracy. Before we leave the subject of democracy, we should briefly consider the practical applications of these theories: the processes of democracy. Popular government is the essence of a democratic system. Early liberal thinkers understood this principle, and they regarded the legislative process as the core of democracy. The executive and judicial branches were thought of as service agencies that carried out the laws made by the people. Accordingly, the democratic process was equated with the policy-making or legislative process, and the relationship between the people and the legislative process became the most important criterion for distinguishing among the various democratic systems.

Democracy and the Legislative Process

There are three major democratic procedures, and they are distinguishable by the relationship the people bear to the legislative, or policy-making, process. In the simplest form, called **direct democracy** or pure democracy, the people act as their own legislature. (See Figure 6.1.) There are no representatives; in other words, the people make the laws themselves by voting directly on propositions related to the issues. You will recall that Jean Jacques Rousseau favored this kind of governmental system. He argued that no one could truly represent another person's will. Thus, all the individuals in the society must represent themselves.

This form of democracy has been used by several societies. Ancient Athens practiced direct democracy, and even today one can find it in some Swiss cantons (provinces) and in some New England town meetings. Some states of the Union also use the initiative process, by which their citizens write and pass laws themselves, thus circumnavigating their state legislatures.

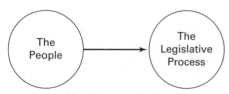

The relationship between the people and the policy-making process is direct.

FIGURE 6.1
Direct democracy.

Direct democracy is still practiced in two Swiss cantons, Appenzell Innerrhoden and Glarus. In this photo, citizens attend the Landsgemeinde (cantonal assembly) and vote directly on the laws of the canton. The swords sported by some of the older men are traditional symbols of citizenship.

Before the advent of modern technology, direct democracy was not possible in an area larger than a city-state; therefore, it has not been very popular. Today, however, it is possible for a society, using computers, television, and the telephone, to govern itself in a much more direct way than in the past. However, any society that has the technological capacity to create a direct democracy through electronics is so complex that many of the technical problems it faces may be beyond the understanding of ordinary citizens, given the limited amount of time they could reasonably be expected to devote to matters of public policy. It took Congress over a year to develop and pass the 2010 health care reform, for example. Such an accomplishment probably could not have been done by the general public. So, while no longer technologically impossible, direct democracy in its most extreme form—no representative government at all—probably remains impractical.

A second form of popular government is called *indirect democracy, representative government,* or **republic.** Each of these terms refers to the same system. However, the word *republic* originally did not necessarily refer to a democratic system. It simply meant government without a king. For example, before the Roman Empire was founded in the first century B.C.E., the Roman Republic was governed by the aristocratic class (patricians) through the Senate, but most of the citizens of Rome (plebeians) could not serve in the Senate or choose its members. Though it was certainly not a democracy, this system was a republic simply because it was not ruled by a king.

The term republic has taken on a somewhat different meaning in the United States. The word is used in the Constitution and was explained by James Madison in *The Federalist* (no. 10). Madison made it clear that *republic* referred to a government of elected representatives who were responsible to the people to some extent. Consequently, the term republic actually means *democratic republic* in American constitutional law: Republic, because representative bodies govern the state; democratic, because the voters choose the representatives.

A democratic republic is an indirect form of democracy. Instead of making the laws themselves, the people elect legislators to do it for them. Thus, the people are removed one step from the legislative process, and their relationship to the policy-making process is less direct than under the pure form of democracy. (See Figure 6.2.)

However, there is a negative correspondence between the terms *republic* and *democracy;* that is, the more republican the government, the less democratic it becomes, and vice versa. Put differently, the more a society gives its representatives to do, the less the people have to do for themselves. Conversely, the more the people participate in their political system, the less power their representatives have.

For instance, a system molded along the lines that Thomas Jefferson favored would be very democratic and only slightly republican. Jefferson thought that the popularly elected representatives should be bound to vote the way their constituents wanted. While a very republican and only slightly democratic form might be one in which the elected representatives were allowed to vote as they wished on any issue and the people defeat them in the next election only if they disagreed with the way the representatives had voted. This is the procedure desired by the neoclassic liberal democrats.

Using the definition we have just developed, one must conclude that the U.S. form of government is highly republican but only slightly democratic. U.S. citizens do not have a great deal of *formal* control over their political

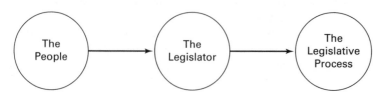

The legislator is added, making the people's relationship to the legislative process indirect.

FIGURE 6.2
Republic.

system. You will recall that Madison folded into the Constitution a number of checks, discouraging the people from having direct control over the government. He wanted the system to be controlled by the representatives—the elite—with the electorate being able to vote them out only if the people became displeased. It must also be said, however, that although the people have little direct control over the government, the political system is very responsive to indirect popular pressure. That is, the president and members of Congress are very solicitous of public opinion when they make policy. Indeed, a growing number of critics claim that the politicians are much too concerned about public opinion.

The third major form of democracy, **pluralism**, is in some respects closer to the kind of system foreseen by Madison. He assumed a country as geographically large and as economically, socially, politically, and culturally diverse as the United States could not attain a single majority on most issues. At the same time, the population of this country is so large that a single ordinary individual is powerless to affect the system. The individual's best chance to protect important interests is to support groups that are committed to advancing such interests. Labor unions, environmental organizations, trade associations, and churches are examples of such groups in a modern context.

Pluralism recognizes that the individual must join with other people to achieve his or her political goals. Consequently, in this system the *interest group* is sandwiched between the people and the legislature. (See Figure 6.3.)

However, pluralism has certain problems. To begin with, it removes the individual a step further from the policy-making process, creating important philosophical difficulties. Our political practices seem to take the decision-making process further and further from the direct control of the people—a potentially dangerous situation in that they run the risk of encouraging public dissatisfaction.

There are other difficulties with pluralism. Even if there were no contradiction between democratic theory and pluralistic practice, pluralism would be an imperfect form of representation. For instance, not all the interests in society are represented equally well. The best organized and best financed interest groups can represent their points of view most effectively. The National Rifle Association, for example, is a very well organized and amply funded group of

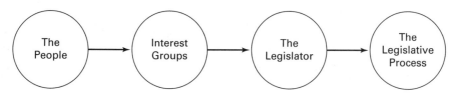

The interjection of the interest group between the people and the legislator removes the people one step further from the legislative process.

FIGURE 6.3
Pluralism.

like-minded individuals; it has been very successful in achieving many of its goals. On the other hand, farm labor, because of its migrant nature, its poverty, and its politically disaffected people, tends to be poorly represented. Moreover, even if our major interests are represented by one group or another, it is unlikely that all of our concerns are represented. Additional problems arise with pluralism stemming from the difference between the individual's interests and the interest organizations that are supposed to represent the individual. For example, although a particular problem for which an interest group exists to combat may have become moot, the staff of the interest group, because their jobs depend on the vitality of the organization, could continue to stir the political pot to artificially maintain relevance. Contract negotiations sometimes see similar conflicts of interests. The leaders of a labor union and the corporate executives with whom they are negotiating are occasionally suspected of prolonging the bargaining beyond the point where agreement could be reached. Thus, each negotiator appears to its respective constituents to be tough and indefatigable. Impressed with the apparent intractability of the issue and the tenacity of the negotiators, each client may agree to the negotiated settlement, convinced that nothing more can be gained and delighted with the efforts of its negotiator.

A final aspect of pluralism should be analyzed before we end this discussion. We have seen that the legislative process is affected by a considerable number of interest groups. When a particular issue arises, however, only a small number of groups are concerned with it. The issue of same-sex marriage is an example. Who might favor and oppose it? Some church groups and other socially conservative organizations would oppose it, of course, whereas gay groups and certain civil libertarian organizations would favor it. Although many of the members of most other interest groups (AARP, the Sierra Club, the AFL-CIO, the Chamber of Commerce) might have opinions on the issue, the interest groups themselves would probably not become involved in the policy formulation process because it is not directly relevant to the objectives of the interest group. So, let us assume that only the interest groups in Figure 6.4 with plus or minus signs are involved

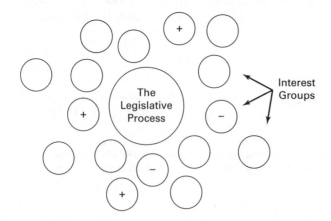

FIGURE 6.4

Interest groups in a pluralist system.

in the issue of same-sex marriage: Those with pluses favor same-sex marriage and those with minuses oppose it. The interested groups are obviously a minority of the total number of interest groups, and they probably do not represent anything near the majority of the people in the country. Yet, they will be the most influential in determining the fate of the policy.

The victorious side of any issue will not necessarily be the side with the largest following; it will be the side with the greatest power on that particular issue. In other words, pluralism has taken the "body count" out of democratic politics. No longer are issues settled by simply counting those in favor and those opposed to a question, if indeed they ever were decided that way.

Many factors besides the size of membership contribute to the power of interest groups in relation to political issues. *Money* is, of course, a major source of power for most successful interest groups. In fact, money is essential for any interest group that hopes to succeed for a sustained period of time. Yet, money is not the only, or even necessarily the most important, source of power for interest groups. Some groups are sustained by *charismatic leaders* such as Dr. Martin Luther King Jr., Ralph Nader, or Pat Robertson. Others benefit from *an efficient organizational apparatus*, the AARP, for example. The National Rifle Association derives its power from having a larger number of highly motivated members. Still others amass power by deftly *associating their issues with the dominant values of society*, as does the Sierra Club.

Of all the sources of interest group power, *knowledge* is undoubtedly the most important most of the time. Politicians often know little about the issues they must resolve and usually look for information that will help them make wise decisions. If an interest group can establish credibility on a given issue, it can do a great deal to influence policymakers. The Union of Concerned Scientists, the American Society of Civil Engineers, and the U.S. Conference of Mayors are but a few examples.

Pluralism is considered democratic, because it is assumed that the leaders of the interest groups are responding to the needs and wishes of their memberships. What if this is not the case, however?

Elite Theorism

Among the most persistent and insightful critics of the American political system are the **elite theorists**. As the name implies, these critics argue that the U.S. government is not a democracy and that pluralism is a sham. At best, they contend, the U.S. government is an *oligarchy*, a system ruled by a relatively small number of people. The rulers of this country, the elite theorists contend, are the people who control the large industrial and financial firms, the military-industrial complex, leading academic institutions, labor organizations, and other interest groups. The leaders of these groups, according to these critics, control policy making, and although they may do so in a benevolent fashion, they are not necessarily responding to their respective memberships. Consequently, the political system is far from democratic.

C. Wright Mills, the most influential of the elite theorists, wrote of a *power elite* that controls the political system. He argued that these people maintain their dominant position through economic, social, school, and family relationships. Robert Michels, another elite theorist, suggested a different dynamic when he set forth his theory of the **iron law of oligarchy**. This theory holds that in any organization only a small percentage of members will be active. Accordingly, the leadership of any body will—by default of the inactive membership—come from a tiny group of activists. Think about any group to which you might belong (the student government, the PTA, a labor union, a church group): Who really runs it? If, as Michels suggests, it is the activists, is it democratic?

The power elite, of which Mills and others have written, is composed of two strata: The primary level is a miniscule number of people who head the great families, corporations, labor unions, and socioeconomic institutions (the Ford Foundation and Harvard University, for instance). At the secondary level is a much larger group, but still a tiny percentage of the entire population. They are political leaders, jurists, military leaders, lobbyists, journalists, and so on, at the state and national level.

The elite group, while they may disagree on short-range and technical issues, find themselves in basic agreements on the fundamentals: Capitalism is beneficial; the Constitution is good, American values are admirable, and threats to them are to be resisted. This fundamental accord derives from the individuals' socialization and self-selection. The bulk of them come from similar life experiences, social classes, schools and universities, and religious training. Indeed, if a person of extraordinary talent were to wish to join the power elite, but refused to share the accepted values, he or she might find admission into this group very difficult.

How, you might wonder, do the elite theorists differ from the pluralists? Interestingly, most elite theorists and pluralists do not disagree about the basic structure of the political system. They concur that the system is responsive to interest groups. The difference between them rests in their definition of democracy. Although pluralists admit that the leadership of various interest groups has great power, they believe that the general membership has enough control over the leaders to make them responsive and therefore to make the system democratic. The elite theorists see essentially the same reality as the pluralists, but they are not satisfied that the people's power over their leaders is strong enough to qualify the system as democratic.

Conspiratorial Theories Just as the pluralists must be understood as distinct from the elite theorists, care must be taken not to confuse the elite theorists with those who espouse **conspiratorial theories**. Conspiratorialists, always present in American politics, are currently a growing phenomena, egged on by talk radio and the Internet. These people are phobic about politics. They believe that someone, usually a small group of unseen people, is secretly and diabolically controlling things from behind the scenes. Among the suspected master manipulators are communists, international bankers, Jews, Satan worshipers, and just plain *them*.

In the 1960s, the Pulitzer Prize–winning historian Richard Hofstadter analyzed the conspiratorial approach to politics, referring to it as the *paranoid style*. Although Hofstadter concedes in his book *The Paranoid Style in American Politics* that some secret planning accompanies virtually every political movement, the paranoid style imagines a plot of colossal proportions affecting millions and threatening the very nation itself. Using isolated facts together with a curious leap in imagination to prove to their own satisfaction the existence of a monumental conspiracy, persons adopting the paranoid style mentally catapult from the "undeniable to the unbelievable," as Hofstadter puts it. They are convinced that their imagined opponent is totally evil and that their own motives are pure but often misunderstood. Public rejection of their point of view is often interpreted as persecution, and so their stance becomes increasingly militant as they see their situation becoming more and more hopeless. The various **militant civilian militia** groups around the country that have come to prominence since the collapse of the Soviet Union in the early 1990s are deeply embroiled in conspiratorial suspicions. They see the federal government as a sinister culprit, constantly maneuvering to deny innocent patriots their liberties.

The suggestion that the nation, or indeed the world, is controlled by such secret and evil power is frequently found very attractive. It has become popular from time to time in the United States, and it is currently gaining popularity again in certain quarters. Its popularity derives from the convenient fact that it brushes aside the immense complexity of modern politics and substitutes for it a very simple scenario. If people can believe that they are manipulated by unknown and uncontrollable forces, they can escape any responsibility for understanding or solving social problems. For more activist conspiratorialists, it reduces politics to a very simple equation. There is a single source of our difficulties, and if only we can get at the source and root it out, all will be well.

Yet, the very simplicity of such theories makes them suspect. It stretches credulity beyond rational limits to suggest that a few masterminds could, without our knowing about it, be pulling the strings that make the rest of us dance like puppets. No less bizarre is the belief that the federal government has somehow become the tool of megalomaniacs whose mission is to enslave the hapless citizenry. To some people, however, believing in an evil force is preferable to coming to grips with the complexities of reality, and accepting such fantasies represents the ultimate abdication of the personal responsibility so necessary to a successful democracy.

Unlike the conspiratorial theorists, the elite theorists do not claim that all fateful decisions are made by a single cabal of unseen ogres. Rather, they believe that each issue generates a different elite. Those with great power on one issue—aerospace, for instance—may have relatively little impact on another, farming for instance.

Elite theorists contend that the political system is composed of thousands of elites who coalesce and dissolve alliances with each new issue. The point is not that a single group dominates every issue; rather, it is that, for better or for worse, there are several thousand extremely powerful people who comprise the elite of the country and who are able to join in temporary alliances to have their way on particular issues.

SYSTEMS OF GOVERNMENT

Democracy is a process and a philosophy about public policy-making, but these policies must be put into practice by a system of government of some sort. Let us now consider the most important systems of government.

Although a multitude of governmental systems exists, two forms are particularly important. We will focus on the United States and Great Britain because each developed political systems that are used, in modified form, in many other democratic societies.

The American System

Federalism   With the adoption of the federal Constitution, the United States invented an entirely different form of government than had previously been known. A **federal** government is one that divides powers between the state and the national levels of government. Each level is guaranteed certain rights, including the right to exist, so that states cannot legally destroy the national government or another state government, and the national government may not dissolve the states.

The states and the national government enjoy certain powers exclusive of each other while sharing other powers concurrently. Making war and peace is an example of an **exclusive power** for the national government; education and family law are exclusive to the states. Taxation is a **concurrent power** because it is exercised by both levels of government. If state and national laws contradict each other, however, the supremacy clause in the Constitution requires that state law is void and the national law stands. As you can see, federalism—or the division of powers—is complicated.

The Presidential-Congressional System   Yet another invention of the American founders is the **presidential-congressional system.** In this arrangement the legislature and the executive are elected separately. Moreover, they are elected to *fixed terms* that cannot be interrupted.

The American electoral process affects our system of government in several important ways. Since public officials are elected separately, they are not indebted to each other for their election. Also, since only the president and the vice president are chosen in a national election, they are the only officials who can claim to represent the nation as a whole.

Furthermore, the people may elect an executive from one party and a majority of the legislature from another. Although this circumstance, called *divided government,* appeals to the desire of some people for balanced government, it can also cause a serious problem. If the two-party platforms reflect definite ideological differences, members of different parties are unlikely to reach agreements readily, a condition that could lead to legislative stagnation, or "gridlock," with Congress passing bills and the president vetoing them. Even if the executive and the legislative majority are from the same party, the fact that they are elected separately to terms that can be interrupted only under extraordinary circumstances tends to diminish the need for party discipline and loyalty. The legislature cannot require the executive's resignation by a vote of no confidence; similarly, the executive cannot suspend the legislature and force elections. Thus, legislators from the president's party can oppose bills sponsored by the executive because they know that the president will not resign if the bills fail to pass. By the same token, the president does not feel compelled to appoint cabinet members from the ranks of the legislature, as the British prime minister must.

Nevertheless, the fact that elected politicians serve terms of office that are virtually uninterruptible tends to give stability to the system. That is to say, under the presidential-congressional system officials serve out their terms regardless of what happens (barring death or resignation). True, Congress can impeach officials, but impeachment is an awkward and slow process that has been used only a few times to remove federal judges from office, but it has not been successful against the two impeached presidents: Andrew Johnson and Bill Clinton.

Except under very unusual circumstances, then, our elected officials will complete their terms, come what may. As a result, the government does not change suddenly during times of crisis. Although this stability is usually considered an advantage of the presidential-congressional system, critics argue that the government seems unresponsive at times. Elections are not called when issues demand them or when the people want a change of leadership; the people get to vote only when the law provides for an election. During the constitutional crisis over the Watergate controversy in the early 1970s and during the administrations of Bill Clinton and George W. Bush, many people turned envious eyes toward the parliamentary-cabinet system because, at almost any time, unpopular officials can be removed by a parliamentary vote of no confidence or by a direct vote of the people. As appealing as the quick-turnover feature of the parliamentary-cabinet system may seem, it can cause serious instability. Times of great political stress may be the most inopportune time for governments to change frequently. Other distinctive features of the presidential-congressional system are **separation of powers** and **checks and balances**. The law specifically separates the branches of government from each other. For instance, no person may serve in more than one branch at a time. A member of Congress entering the executive branch would have to resign his or her legislative seat.

Further, the executive, legislative, and judicial branches are each given separate powers that only they may exercise. The courts are responsible for adjudicating disputes; they also are the final authority on the interpretation of the law. Only the legislature can approve expenditures, whereas the executive is solely responsible for the administration of policy and is virtually unrestrained in foreign affairs.

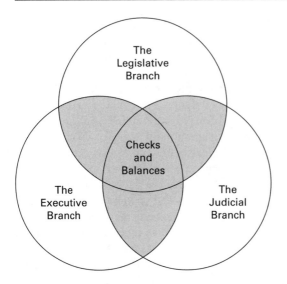

FIGURE 6.5

Separation of powers and checks and balances.

As Figure 6.5 shows, the basic powers of the three branches are indeed separate and unique; however, some of the powers of each branch overlap with those of the other two. These overlapping powers are called the *checks and balances*. They are intended to prevent any branch from becoming too powerful and dominating the others. You will recall that James Madison, who devised this system, did not trust government, so he tried to make sure that all branches were relatively equal in power and that each acted as a guardian against abuses by the other two. Yet, we should remember that Madison, like Thomas Hobbes, also had little trust in the people, so he wrote in a number of checks against the majority as well (see Chapter 5 for examples).

Most of us have a positive attitude toward the separation of powers and checks and balances. We normally share Madison's apprehension about government, although perhaps most of us are not as intense about it as he was. There are, however, some undesirable aspects of this feature in our system. By dividing and diffusing power and then causing each of the branches to compete with the others, the presidential-congressional system encourages conflict and even stagnation within the government.

This situation is aggravated by the vagueness of the Constitution. This lack of clarity sometimes results in a very combative atmosphere. When the built-in division of government is combined with the abstract wording of the Constitution, we find that each branch is encouraged to exercise its powers assertively while, at the same time, preventing the other two branches from gaining excessive influence. Such maneuvering leads to constant conflict among the three branches. Frustrated by the seemingly endless bickering between Congress and the president, people sometimes ask, "Why can't they get along?" The answer is that they are not supposed to. They are designed to be in conflict.

The British System

In many respects the British system is more responsive to the public than is the American system. On the other hand, it is also less stable during times of crisis.

Unitary Government   Britain has a **unitary** structure of government. Older than federalism, the unitary structure is used by most governments in the world. This arrangement concentrates all governmental power at the central level. Any local governments that exist are created and granted powers by the central government. Local governments, in other words, are dependent on the central government for their powers and have for themselves no direct constitutional authorizations or guarantees.

The unitary structure seems strange to us because our government uses the federal form. However, the unitary arrangement should not be unfamiliar, since it may be seen in the relationship between our state governments and local agencies. Only the relationship between the states and the national government is federal in the United States; that is, both the national government and the state governments are guaranteed by the federal Constitution. City, county, parish, township, special districts, or other agencies of local government are not mentioned in the U.S. Constitution and are therefore completely subject to the state governments. Local governments may be guaranteed by provisions of their states' constitutions, but they have no protection under the Constitution of the United States. The same relationship exists between the central and all lower governments in Britain.

The Parliamentary-Cabinet System   Although there are now many variations on the theme, the **parliamentary-cabinet system** was first developed in England, and the British government still provides a classic example of this institution. Unlike the presidential-congressional system, the parliamentary-cabinet system separates the positions of **head of state** and **head of government**. In the American system, the president performs both roles, but in Britain the monarch is head of state—the symbol of the history and political continuity of the country—and the prime minister is head of government, the country's political leader.[1] The British head of state has little real power. She or he can dismiss Parliament and call for new elections, appoint ministers, and issue proclamations, but each of these acts is performed only after a request by the prime minister. Although some constitutions, such as those of France, India, and Russia, give the head of state important powers, most give the office only a symbolic role.

The bulk of the political power in the parliamentary-cabinet system is vested in the Parliament. The modern British system, which developed out of John Locke's political theory, never adopted Madison's structural changes.

---

[1]Other countries using this system but that do not have a hereditary head of state usually elect someone to the post for a relatively long term, often seven years. Elected heads of state commonly have the title of president.

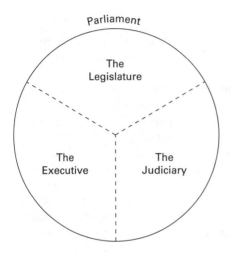
Parliament

The
Legislature

The
Executive

The
Judiciary

FIGURE 6.6
The parliamentary-cabinet system.

Hence, separation of powers and checks and balances are much less prominent in the British model than in the American system.

A major principle of the British system is *parliamentary primacy*. You will recall that the classical democratic thinkers considered the legislature the chief agency of the government, with the executive and judiciary secondary in importance. Consistent with this philosophy, the British Parliament is, at least in theory, not subject to restraint by the other two branches. No act it passes can be declared unconstitutional. Indeed, some scholars argue that the Parliament *is* the constitution.[2] On paper, then, the cabinet becomes nothing more than the executive committee of Parliament and is directly responsible to it. In practice, of course, the relationship between the cabinet and the Parliament is more complicated, but this is a matter of political practice rather than law.

The principle of parliamentary primacy makes impossible the equality of the three major branches implied in the presidential-congressional system. So, the checks and balances cannot work the way they do in the Madisonian model.

Figure 6.6 represents the parliamentary-cabinet system of government: The power of government is not distributed among three separate branches. Actually, each branch of the government is part of the same whole: Parliament is made up of the legislature, which is theoretically dominant; the executive; and the judiciary. The House of Commons, part of the legislature, is the only body actually elected by the people. Consequently, it acts as the chief agent of the people, and as such it is the major democratic institution in the system. Members of the cabinet need not resign their seats in the legislature before they enter the executive branch. On the contrary, cabinet members must usually be members of Parliament in order to be appointed to the executive body. The courts are also nominally part of Parliament: The Lords of Appeal in Ordinary, Britain's highest court, is technically a committee of the House of Lords. In practice, however, the judicial branch in Britain holds itself quite independent of the government.

---

[2]While the British Parliament is bicameral, comprised of the House of Commons and the House of Lords, the House of Commons is by far the more powerful of the two. At one time very strong, today the House of Lords is scarcely more than an advisory body to the House of Commons.

© Reuters TV/Reuters/Corbis

Prime Minister David Cameron in a heated House of Commons debate.

At the beginning of each new legislative term, the House of Commons chooses someone whose leadership the members will follow. This individual is, of course, the leader of the majority party and will be *appointed* prime minister by the head of state. Note that there is no popular election for the chief executive in the parliamentary-cabinet system. The prime minister must meet only one requirement: He or she controls the majority of Parliament and can get any bill passed that he or she recommends. If Parliament ever fails to support the recommendation of the prime minister, he or she must resign. Parliament will then either hold new elections or pick a new prime minister from the extant majority. Parliaments are elected to a maximum term of four or five years, but elections can be held at any time, thus beginning a new term. The decision as to whether or not new elections will be held is usually made by the head of state, who follows the advice of the prime minister.

The fact that Parliament actually chooses the prime minister and that the prime minister decides when elections will be held creates a unique relationship between the executive and the legislature. This relationship tends to increase party discipline and loyalty. A vote by Parliament against a policy recommended by the prime minister might do more than defeat the particular policy; it might bring down the government as well. Not wishing to help destroy their party's government and loath to stand for reelection prematurely, members of the ruling party in Parliament are encouraged to vote with their executive's policies more regularly than in the presidential-congressional system. Thus, because the House of Commons is elected by the people and actually chooses the prime minister, it appears to be very independent of the executive. But, in fact, because of the separation of powers in the United States, members of Congress are even more independent of the president.

Another important area in which the British and American systems differ is the executive branch. The presidential-congressional system has a *singular executive;* that is, the people of the United States elect only two executive officials, the president and the vice president, and the Constitution gives executive powers only to the president. All other major executive officials are appointed by the president and are given executive powers to administer. Technically, therefore, all executive powers, regardless of who exercises them, are the president's powers. The only function given to the vice president by the Constitution, besides being prepared to succeed the president, is to preside over the U.S. Senate. Ironically, this role is the most blatant contradiction of the principle of separation of powers.

The parliamentary-cabinet system, by contrast, has a *plural executive* because, like the prime minister, cabinet members are also appointed by the monarch and technically exercise his or her powers. Thus, the status of the members of the British cabinet is much closer to that of the chief executive than is true in the American system. In the United States, the president may give direct orders to cabinet members because they are appointed by the president and exercise the president's powers. In the parliamentary-cabinet system, however, the cabinet members are appointed by the same authority that appoints the prime minister: the monarch. The cabinet members are also more independent of the prime minister, because it is not the prime minister's power they are exercising but the power of the state itself. The prime minister may not give a cabinet minister a direct order because each minister is the sole head of his or her own department.

In the American system, the cabinet is a body of advisers and administrative assistants to the president. The president has the ultimate power and makes the decisions. If the president delegates this power, he or she is still responsible for policy. In the British system, the cabinet is a body of equals headed by the prime minister. The policies of the government are made by the cabinet as a whole. Instead of being flanked by subordinate advisers, the prime minister must get people appointed to the cabinet who can help hold the parliamentary majority together. Thus, at least senior cabinet members are powerful parliamentarians and are influential in party affairs in their own right; clearly, although the prime minister is the first among equals, he or she does not dominate the cabinet completely.

Not only does the prime minister not completely control the cabinet, but, due to the principle of **collective responsibility,** he or she is also not solely responsible for the policies of the government either. Under this principle a governmental decision is arrived at by a consensus of the cabinet. The decision then becomes a policy of the government, and all government ministers (that is, cabinet members) should support it. Although votes are not usually taken in cabinet meetings, a policy is not adopted until it has broad cabinet support. A policy would never be adopted if the members whose ministries were principally involved did not agree to it. Once a policy is adopted, however, any minister who still opposes it must remain silent or resign. If the prime minister or the prime minister's policies fail to receive majority support in Parliament, the entire cabinet must resign as a group.

Unlike our system, the parliamentary-cabinet system tends to centralize the power of government in the hands of Parliament. As already mentioned, the House of Commons can pass any law it chooses. It could end the monarchy, reshape the judicial branch, or suspend elections, thus ending British democracy as we know it. (In fact, in times of emergency, Parliament has done each of these things, but the original system was restored when the emergency subsided.) There is no opposing governmental power to prevent such actions, as there is in our system. Instead of encouraging competition and conflict, as does the United States model, this system depends on cooperation and self-restraint. Accordingly, if the system is to work well, citizens must be politically mature. The people's belief in democracy must be so strong that public expectation and opinion serve as the ultimate check on abuse of power.

In some ways the parliamentary-cabinet system is more responsive to the citizens, and therefore more democratic, than ours. For instance, elections can be called at any time before the end of the term if the issues require such action. Since this often occurs and Parliaments seldom remain in office for a full term, issues force elections. Accordingly, elections tend to be much more issue-oriented in the parliamentary-cabinet system than in the American model. Since American elections occur whenever scheduled (general elections are held on the first Tuesday following the first Monday in November of even years), regardless of whether or not the issues are pressing at the time, our elections are often personality contests rather than policy driven.

The parliamentary-cabinet system is not without its difficulties, however. Perhaps the greatest problem with this system is that it can be very unstable. As indicated earlier, the system tends to be weak during times of controversy. Elections can be called and governments changed very often. Just when a stable government is most needed, this system can be most volatile.

The situation is made worse if no majority party is elected. When a single party wins more than half of the seats in Parliament, there is very little trouble determining who will form the government. In some cases, however, the seats of Parliament are divided so evenly among three or more parties that no party controls the majority, as happened in the parliamentary election in England in 2010. Then a **coalition government** must be formed, as it was following the May 2010 British election, in which two or more parties join to make a majority. They agree on the government's positions on the major issues and divide the various cabinet offices between them. Note that while the parties join a single government, they do not merge into a single party.

Coalition governments tend to be very unstable. Disagreements often occur between the coalition's parties, tempers rise, and one or more parties may pull out of the coalition and turn against the government. This reversal of loyalty causes loss of confidence in the government, which must then resign. New elections are held, and if a single party does not win the majority of the seats, a new coalition must be forged—only to begin the process all over again.

ELECTIONS

Perhaps nothing is more important in a democratic system than its electoral process. Through elections the people express their will on the issues and choose their leaders. One should not be surprised to learn that elections, vital as they are, are complex, multifaceted processes.

Electoral Districts

The kind of electoral district used largely determines the way a particular political system functions. There are two basic kinds of electoral districts: the single-member district and the multimember district. The **single-member district** is used in the United States in all partisan elections. Regardless of the number of candidates running, only one person will be elected within a single-member district. It is a *winner-take-all election*. Members of Congress, for example, are elected from congressional districts, each district having only one seat. Thus, because New Mexico, for example, sends three members to the House of Representatives, the state is divided or apportioned into three districts, each electing a single individual to go to Congress.

Since each state's two U.S. senators are elected by the state as a whole, the states are actually single-member districts for Senate elections as well. The states are also single-member districts in presidential elections because *all* the state's electoral votes are awarded to the candidate who wins the most popular votes in that state. (Maine and Nebraska do it a bit differently, but their electoral systems still amount to single-member districts.) Each state, therefore, gives a single prize consisting of a certain number of electoral votes to the winner of its presidential election.

To study the impact of the single-member district, let us assume that parties A, B, and C each ran a candidate for Congress in a particular district and that the popular vote in the district was distributed as indicated in Table 6.1. Because only a **plurality** (the most votes) is necessary to win in most systems

TABLE 6.1	
Elections in Single-Member Districts	
Party	Vote Distribution
A	41%
B	39%
C	20%

TABLE 6.2

Results of the 2005 and 2010 British Parliamentary Elections

Year Seats Won	Party	Percent of Popular Votes Won	Percent of Parliamentary Seats Won
2005	Labour	35	55
	Conservative	32	31
	Liberal Democrat	22	10
	Other	10	5
2010	Conservative	36	47
	Labour	29	40
	Liberal Democrat	23	9
	Other	12	4

using single-member districts, party A's candidate is the clear winner. At first glance, awarding victory to the candidate who won the most votes—albeit not a majority—may not seem to present a problem, but upon closer scrutiny, several anomalies become apparent.

As long as there is more than one candidate for the single seat, the seats will always be distributed disproportionately to the votes cast. In our example, although party A won the largest number of votes, a majority of the voters (59 percent) voted against the winner. In other words, 41 percent of the voters won 100 percent of the representation. All those who voted for party B or C might as well have stayed home, since their votes do not count toward electing any representatives at all. Consequently, the percentage of congressional seats most parties win is probably not even approximately the same as the percentage of votes it earned. This fact can cause some serious distortions. For example, England, using single-member districts in its parliamentary elections of 2005, showed returns as indicated in Table 6.2.

The Labour Party in 2005 carried a majority in Parliament with only 35 percent of the popular vote, the lowest margin in British history to win a majority of Parliament. The Conservative Party got almost the same percentage of the electorate, but since it did not concentrate its votes well, it won far fewer Parliamentary seats. Clearly, the Liberal Democratic Party did an even poorer job of concentrating its voters in only a few constituencies (electoral districts), and went terribly underrepresented. In 2010, however, the Conservatives won the most seats in Parliament, but not a majority so they needed to form a coalition government. The Liberal Democrats actually won fewer Parliamentary seats in 2010 than in 2005, but since they joined with the Conservatives in a coalition government, they share power, albeit not equally, with the Conservatives.

The same kind of distortion can occur in American presidential elections. Vice President Al Gore won over one-half million more popular votes than

George W. Bush in the 2000 presidential election. Yet, because Gore won a few states (mostly large ones) by huge margins (he carried California by 12 percent, for example), but narrowly lost in a lot of states, Gore ended up with only 267 electoral votes to Bush's 271.

The single-member district also works to the advantage of a single-party or two-party system. Looking back at Table 6.1, we can see that although party A won the election, party B came close. Since party B needs to increase its vote by only 2 or 3 percent to win, it will probably enter candidates in future elections. The circumstances are quite different for party C. Since it has to more than double its vote in order to win, it does not have much chance of survival. Failing to get even close to victory, all but the most dedicated supporters will probably soon leave party C for party A or B, whose chances of victory are better, and the two major parties will soon find that they are the only serious contestants. American political history is replete with unsuccessful attempts by minor parties to rise to power, and the use of the single-member district is largely responsible for their failure. Ross Perot's Reform Party is a case in point. In 1992, Perot won 19 percent of the popular vote. Although this is a substantial number, since he did not win the most votes in any state, he won no electors at all. Clearly, the myth of his chance to defeat the two major parties was demolished. In 1996, Perot received only 9 percent of the popular vote, not even half of his previous tally. Since then the Reform Party has slipped into obscurity because no one is likely to give hundreds of millions of dollars to fund its next presidential bid, since it has yet to win a single elector.

The alternative to the single-member district is the **multimember district.** As the term implies, this system provides for the election of several officials from a given district. This electoral method is used in many states. Most countries using multimember districts employ a system of **proportional representation** to distribute seats on an equitable basis. For example, let us assume that there are five seats open in an electoral district, and parties A, B, and C entered candidates in the election. If the vote were distributed as indicated in Table 6.1, each party would win something. Parties A and B would win two seats each and party C would win one seat. Although it would not win dramatically, party C would gain something under this procedure and would undoubtedly remain in existence. In addition, new parties would be encouraged to form simply because the percentage of votes necessary to win is greatly reduced, as the number of parties increases. Thus, a multiparty system is likely to develop. Britain's Liberal Democrats are, of course, very keen on switching to this electoral system, since they would thus instantly become a major political player.

Political Party Structures

Political parties have several functions. Stating positions on issues, providing candidates, and holding officials responsible for their acts are only a few of their most important responsibilities. The goal of a political party is easily stated: to gain control of the government. Of course, in a democracy political parties take control of the government through the electoral process.

There are basically three kinds of political party systems. A **single-party system** exists when one party, over an extended period of time, controls the vast majority of legislative seats and its choice for the chief executive is assured. There may be any number of other parties in the country, but none of them is able to win more than a tiny fraction of the vote.

Many people equate the single-party system with dictatorship. Although dictators often try to maintain power by making opposition parties illegal, it is not true that a single-party system necessarily will produce a dictatorship. Indeed, single-party democracies are not unheard of. During the Era of Good Feelings in this country during the early nineteenth century, the Democrat-Republican Party faced no effective opposition. Yet, the period is considered to have been democratic, since leaders were still chosen by the voters and the competition that ordinarily takes place between parties occurred within a single party.

A more contemporary example of a single-party democracy can be found in India. Before the usurpation of power by Indira Gandhi between 1975 and 1977, India was a single-party democracy. The Congress Party was favored by an overwhelming majority of the people, often winning as many as two-thirds of the seats in the national parliament and the state legislatures. India, however, provides a dramatic example of the greatest problem of a single-party system. Though such a system can be used in a democracy, the opposition is so small and weak that it can do little to hinder the dominant party if the country's leaders decide to destroy the democratic process. So it was with Gandhi. Feeling her personal power threatened, she imprisoned her opposition, censored the press, intimidated the courts, and eliminated popular liberties. When she had finished, the Indian democracy lay in ruins. To her credit, however, Gandhi restored democracy to India in 1977, accepting her own parliamentary defeat in the process. Displaying amazing political resilience, she was subsequently returned to power by the people of India after the failure of the opposition government, only to be assassinated in 1984.

A **two-party system** exists when only two parties have a meaningful chance of winning control of the government. Used in several countries, including Australia and the United States, this system has the advantages of the single-party system without running the same risk of becoming a dictatorship. The greatest advantage of the single-party system is that it produces a strong government; its candidates always win with a majority of the vote. If the system has two major parties instead of only one, elected officials also usually win with a majority, yet, the dominant party is checked by a substantial opposition party. But, since there is only one important opposition party, what happens if the opposition does not oppose? Such a failure occurred in 2001 to 2002 when the Democrats, cowed by a popular president, did not mount meaningful opposition to the U.S. invasion of Iraq.

Another disadvantage of the two-party system is that it severely limits the available options and it tends to distort the complexity of politics. Having only

two significant parties, such a system implies that there are only two important sides to any issue: the establishment "in" position and the establishment
"out" alternative. In reality, there might be many different positions on each
issue. Furthermore, limiting the opposition to only one significant party tends
to mute the full range of alternatives on the issues, to say nothing of providing only two viable candidates for each office. This severe lack of alternative
candidates and views, it is suspected, is a major reason for American low voter
turnout. Europeans, most of which have multiparty systems, enjoy much more
politically engaged publics and far higher voter turnouts.

A **multiparty system** exists when several parties have a significant number
of seats in the legislature. Although it best reflects the various minority arguments on the issues, making politics more interesting, the multiparty system
tends to divide the people into so many different factions that the majority is
completely lost, leaving only a set of competing minorities. More and more
minority parties develop as the willingness or ability to compromise is lost,
and the parties tend to state their differences in very specific terms. The proliferation of alternatives and the specificity of debate in this system are admirable, to be sure. However, the lack of compromise as well as the inability to
produce a majority party makes this otherwise attractive system less appealing
than it might be.

The multiparty system can function reasonably well in a parliamentary-
cabinet form of government; it is less compatible with the presidential-
congressional system, however. No party that fails to carry a majority of the
seats in a parliament can govern without forming a coalition of minority parties that agree on policy and on selections for the various cabinet positions.
Coalition governments, as you already know, are notoriously unstable.

Volatile as this procedure may be, the parliamentary-cabinet system can accommodate it because in this system terms of office are not fixed by law. Not so
in the presidential-congressional system. Even if there is no majority in the legislature, the executive and legislative officials must serve uninterruptible terms
of several years. Long periods of governmental stagnation or worse may result.

Perhaps the most poignant example of the dangers of combining incompatible governmental and political party systems may be found in the events
that ended the Allende government in Chile in 1973. Salvador Allende won the
plurality of the popular vote, but not the majority in the presidential election
of 1970, so the election was thrown into the Congress. As a Marxist, Allende
was a very controversial figure; the Congress hesitated to elect him. Finally, after much negotiation, an agreement, or coalition, was established and Allende
was elected president. But after Allende's inauguration, controversy developed
over his policies. Eventually the various parties in the coalition withdrew their
support, denying Allende a majority of the Congress. Faced with the prospect
of a deadlock that would last for years until his fixed term expired, Allende
began to rule by decree, issuing administrative orders that were fiercely opposed by some elements in the country. Economic hardship set in; boycotts,
strikes, and demonstrations followed. Finally, for the first time in almost half

a century the Chilean army, with the support of the U.S. government, staged a coup. Allende was reported to have committed suicide, the army, led by General Augusto Pinochet, suspended civil liberties, executed thousands, and imprisoned many more.

Appealing as the multiparty system might look to people who are frustrated by the seeming lack of difference between the two major American parties, we should be very cautious about opting for the more diverse system. The lack of compromise inherent in the multiparty system bodes ill for a form of government that, like our own, requires fixed terms of office. The lack of a majority government also tends to make the multiparty system less than desirable; in fact, as we have seen, it is basically incompatible with the presidential-congressional system.

REPRESENTATION

The subject of representation in a democracy is almost as complex as the question of elections. Assuming that the system is not a direct democracy, as Rousseau preferred, the student of politics immediately confronts the question of what the basis of representation should be. Because ours is a democratic society, our natural inclination is to insist that population be the basis of representation. Further, we would probably agree that all people should enjoy equal representation. Yet, there are several foundations on which to base representation besides population. In fact, the U.S. system does not favor people as much as we may assume it does.

Another basis for representation is territory. In the United States, each state—regardless of its population—is represented by two senators. As a result, California, the nation's most populous state, with a population well over 38 million, has the same representation in the Senate as states one-fortieth its size. This is not very democratic.[3]

Another dilemma is the question of whether public officials should represent the national interest, as Edmund Burke argued, or should reflect the interests of a more local area, as James Madison recommended. If the national interest receives the greatest attention, an unfeeling central bureaucracy can mandate policies that seem to make little sense to local areas. On the other hand, when local interests become paramount, policy tends to become provincial and narrow, working to the disadvantage of a modern state.

Of all the arguments concerning representation in a democracy, none is more controversial than the dispute over whether public officials should represent the people's *will* or their *interests*. This quandary returns us to the question of how democratic a republic should be. If the system is to be highly democratic,

---

[3]As we have seen from the health reform bills of 2009–2010, the Senate is undemocratic in a second important respect. It gives the minority power to obstruct legislation the majority favors through the filibuster.

the representatives should make every effort to vote as their constituents wish. The most republican attitude, as you'll remember Burke advised, is that the representative should seriously consider the wishes of constituents, but "he ought never to sacrifice them to his unbiased opinion, his mature judgment, his enlightened conscience." Accordingly, the representative should ignore the will of the people, if it contradicts what he or she perceives to be in their best interest.

Theories of Representation

The question of how the people should be represented is as old as democracy itself. Many political theorists have grappled with the problem, but none has been persuasive enough to dominate the argument. This brief review of the various theories of representation will demonstrate how vital and how complicated this question is.

The **reactionary theory of representation,** supported by Thomas Hobbes and Alexander Hamilton, is based on the need for order and authority. The executive, preferably a monarch, and the parliament serve the public interest as they perceive it. Although they should be open to popular input, being of superior knowledge, breeding, and judgment they should not be hindered by popular sentiment. The people, for their part, must support the state and accept the government's policies willingly in the confidence that the politicians have acted in the public's best interest.

This elitist position provides for no popular control. Indeed, many people might reject this theory as undemocratic; its only popular aspect is the assumption that the rulers are protecting and benefiting the public interest.

Less extreme is the **conservative theory of representation,** supported by Edmund Burke and James Madison. Conservatives grant popular control without encouraging public participation in the governing process. In this variant the people choose those who are to govern them; they choose their *trustees.* Yet, the people do not have the right to compel their representatives to vote or behave in a particular way. If, however, the officials do not satisfy them, the people may replace them with other members of the elite at the next election. The government of the United States is based on this model.

John Locke and Thomas Jefferson subscribed to the **liberal theory of representation,** the most democratic of all the republican theories. According to this theory, all people are essentially equal and all are therefore equally capable of ruling. This mass-oriented theory requires that the representative act as a messenger, or a *delegate,* for his or her constituents rather than as a policymaker. Public officials are obliged to vote the way their constituents want them to.

The **radical theory of representation,** advanced by Jean Jacques Rousseau and the New Left of the 1960s, calls for the greatest amount of popular input. Rejecting representative government altogether, this theory holds that only the people themselves are capable of representing their own views, at least on the important issues. Thus, this theory claims that pure or direct democracy is the most desirable form of government; indeed, it is the only truly democratic form.

SOME CRITICISMS OF DEMOCRACY

Democracy has many critics at every point on the political spectrum. It is attacked by the far left as well as by the far right. Some of the most biting criticisms, however, come from supporters of democracy itself.

Some critics argue that democracy is a hopelessly visionary idea based on a number of impossible principles that can never really work because they are too idealistic. They claim that ideas such as human equality or the actual practice of self-government are futile dreams that can never be carried out. At best, they say, it is really the elite who rule in a "democracy." The fact that the general public believes it is running the system proves that the subtleties of government are beyond the understanding of ordinary people.

Another criticism of democracy is based on the belief that the majority of the people have only average intelligence and creativity. Therefore, a government controlled by the majority would probably be biased in favor of the average or the mediocre. Prejudice against the innovative, the unusual, or the excellent would dominate such a system; laws would be passed to move the society toward the lowest common denominator. The truly superior individuals would suffer as ordinary people imposed their will on the country. Summing up this position, Russell Kirk, a leading conservative, writes: "Aye, men are created different; and a government which ignores this law becomes an unjust government, for it sacrifices nobility for mediocrity; it pulls down the aspiring natures to gratify the inferior natures."[4]

Democracy is also attacked as being slow and inefficient. The mechanism for decision making, which we have just studied, is awkward, unable to make the speedy decisions necessary in a digitally-driven society. These critics also point out that although democracy might have been possible during a simpler era, our technology has complicated society to such an extent that popular government is no longer possible. Ordinary people with everyday concerns are simply not equipped to handle the complexities facing policymakers in the modern state. Our society has evolved faster than we have been able to adjust, and one of the casualties of this development must be democracy itself.

These are just a few criticisms of democracy. Many more specific criticisms could be made, but a catalog of these is unnecessary. The general comments made here should be considered carefully, however, because they are supported by some of our most brilliant thinkers. To think of democracy as the best possible form of government is not to make it so. Questioning the continued viability and usefulness of democracy is a healthy exercise in which all citizens should engage, if for no other reason than to better understand it and thus improve our application of it.

---

[4]Russell Kirk, "Prescription, Authority, and Ordered Freedom," in *What Is Conservatism?* ed. Frank S. Meyer (New York: Holt, Rinehart & Winston, 1964), p. 34.

QUESTIONS FOR DISCUSSION

1. What are the fundamental assumptions necessary in a democracy, and how do pure democracy, democratic republic, and pluralism complement and/or detract from these assumptions?
2. Distinguish between pluralism, elite theorism, and conspiratorialism.
3. How can the American and British systems of government be compared and contrasted? What are the strengths and weaknesses of each?
4. How are political party systems influenced by electoral districts?
5. What are the advantages and disadvantages of the various kinds of political party systems?
6. What are the basic kinds of representation, and what assumptions underlie them?

SUGGESTIONS FOR FURTHER READING

Bugliosi, Vincent, *The Betrayal of America: How the Supreme Court Undermined the Constitution and Chose Our President.* New York: Thunder's Month Press/National Books, 2001.

Connolly, William E., *Pluralism.* Durham, NC: Duke University Press, 2005.

Dahl, Robert, *Who Governs?* New Haven, CT: Yale University Press, 1961.

Diamond, Larry, and Richard Gunther, *Political Parties and Democracy.* Baltimore, MD: Johns Hopkins University Press, 2001.

Flathman, Richard, *Pluralism and Liberal Democracy.* Baltimore, MD: Johns Hopkins University Press, 2005.

Hofstadter, Richard, *The Paranoid Style in American Politics.* New York: Knopf, 1965.

Mill, John Stuart, *On Liberty,* ed. Elizabeth Rapaport. Indianapolis, IN: Hackett, 1978.

Mills, C. Wright, *The Power Elite,* New York: Oxford University Press, 1956.

Rosenthal, Alan, et al., *Republic on Trial: The Case for Representative Democracy.* Washington, DC: CQ Press, 2003.

Tocqueville, Alexis de, *Democracy in America,* trans. George Lawrence. New York: Anchor Books, 1969.

Zolo, Danilo, *Democracy and Complexity: A Realist Approach.* University Park: Pennsylvania State University Press, 1992.

Anarchism

PREVIEW

Arising from a reaction to the growing power of government and the increasing influence of capitalism, anarchism developed among a small but highly motivated number of people. Poorly understood in our society, anarchism is the purest expression of individualism in political thought. Anarchists of all sorts see institutional government as an impediment to human progress and wish to eliminate it in part or even completely. Agreeing that government should be limited, anarchists tend to disagree on matters of substance and on tactics. Social anarchists—those on the left—wish to free individuals from governmental restraint so that individuals can do the greatest good possible for society as a whole. By contrast, individualist anarchists—those on the right of the political spectrum—seek to limit government so that individuals can accomplish the greatest good for themselves alone.

Anarchists can be left-wingers or right-wingers, pacifistic or violent, devout or atheistic, socialist or capitalist. Indeed, except for the reduction or elimination of institutional government, there are few things on which anarchists agree. Currently, anarchism is becoming fashionable among certain elements in the American public and others. The militant civilian militias threaten insurrection in defense of their supposed individual liberties, and some leftists are drawn to anarchism in an effort to combat what they regard as the emergence of supergovernment controlled by international corporations.

DEVELOPMENT OF ANARCHISM

Even as the imperatives of the Industrial Revolution motivated some people to seek more popular participation in government, others agitated for social organization without institutional government. As Europe industrialized, wealth was increasingly concentrated in the hands of the few, and power was centralized in the state. Feelings of impotence and helplessness overcame workers who saw their skills made obsolete by machines and who consequently were put to mindless, repetitive production tasks. Where once they had produced whole products, they now found themselves paid a pittance on assembly lines doing jobs that required little skill. The simple life of the peasant evaporated as people were forced to live in squalid ghettoes surrounding the smoke-belching factories. The government, once remote, began to play an increasing role in the lives of individuals, promulgating restrictions, issuing regulations, giving orders, and making demands. Ironically, as the institution of government became more pervasive, the people in government became almost anonymous. Growing with its new tasks, a faceless bureaucracy confronted the common people, imposing its will with vigor, even as it became abstract and ambiguous in form.

Although opposition to organized government can be traced as far back as ancient Greece, anarchism as an ideology and as a political movement did not take shape until the early nineteenth century, with the rise of the Industrial Revolution. It was then that the means of social control were complete enough and political power adequately centralized to impose the weight of property and government to the extent that they were perceived as impediments to human development.

DEFINITION OF ANARCHISM

Woefully misunderstood in the United States, **anarchism** continues to hold a strong attraction for some people in the world. Indeed, anarchist ideals have recently also become popular in the United States among some right-wing extremists and survivalists and among a growing number of left-wing extremists who fear that economic globalization is overwhelming our society.

Anarchism is often equated with *anarchy*. This is an understandable mistake, but it results in an unfortunate misapprehension. Anarchy implies chaos, disorder, and confusion resulting from the absence of government. Few, if any, anarchists advocate such a state of affairs. Indeed, they contend that the opposite will result from the elimination of government. Essentially, anarchists believe that human beings have outgrown the need for government—if, indeed, they ever needed it in the first place. Government, it is assumed, was created to facilitate human development, but instead it actually impedes people from fulfilling their potential. Thus, believing that people will unilaterally conduct themselves appropriately without outside power systems enforcing conformist behavior, all anarchists want to see government reduced. Because of its reliance on human self-government, *anarchism is the purest form of democracy.*

However, no anarchist wants to eliminate government entirely. The most extreme anarchists do want to end all forms of *institutional government,* but they do not advocate anarchy, because they believe that the most important kind of government will remain: *individual self-government.* Less fervent anarchists support the existence of local governments (villages, communes, syndicates), but they would greatly reduce, or eliminate entirely, national governmental systems.

More expansive than simple antagonism toward government, anarchism also opposes institutions that buttress the state, helping it to impose restrictions on human behavior and development. Social class distinctions are rejected as an artificial and contrived barrier by which a society's power elite denies others privilege. Racism is a similar device. Private property is criticized, since it is often viewed as an institution denying people freedom. According to some anarchists—Pierre Joseph Proudhon being the most articulate on this point—property is used to dignify the few and belittle the many, thus becoming an instrument of oppression. Similarly, religion is sometimes condemned because it is seen as a tool used by the power elite to control the masses. Although most anarchists are atheists, denying the very existence of God, some, like Leo Tolstoy, remained devout but abandoned established religion for less exploitative interpretation of Christianity.

Many anarchists resist any institution which tends to demand that people conform to "accepted" behavior. Consequently, schools are often seen as instruments of regimentation and oppression. All societies use education to socialize their young. Not only do schools teach traditional subjects like reading, mathematics, and music, but they also teach appropriate social behavior. For example, anarchists view teaching elementary students to line up before entering the classroom as an abomination. Such regimentation, anarchists believe, deforms children, squeezing from them their natural spontaneity and robbing them of creativity. Such discipline denies people freedom, forcing them to surrender their individuality and creating slavish automatons out of once unspoiled creatures. But schools are only one example. Anarchists view most of society's institutions similarly, including labor unions, scouting, the law, peer group pressure, etiquette, manners, and so forth. All of these institutions are, in the broadest sense, government. The anarchist chafes at its authority, feeling that government places undue restrictions on people, crippling them and denying them the freedom inherent in the human spirit. Put differently, rather than helping people fulfill their human potential, government—and other authoritative institutions—*dehumanizes them.*

As the globalization of capitalism accelerated following the collapse of the Soviet Union, a new dimension of control and regimentation is evolving, according to some critics. The argument is focused on organizations facilitating economic globalization, like the World Trade Organization (WTO), the World Economic Forum, and the Group-8 (the world's leading industrial countries and Russia). Opponents of these efforts believe that economic development is making former political structures obsolete and that huge international corporations are cooperating to form a supergovernment which they control through these organizations. According to its critics, this new economic entity, impervious to popular control, is an antidemocratic, profit-driven behemoth that is dwarfing the individual and is engaging in ruthless, unchecked worldwide labor exploitation.

With the emergence of this perceived threat, new life has perhaps been breathed into anarchism. The most dramatic confrontations to date between the left and the new economic world order occurred in 1999, at the WTO meeting in Seattle, Washington, and at the 2001 meeting in Genoa, Italy, of the G-8. The 1999 protest turned violent as the police overreacted to the provocations of the demonstrators. Dubbed "the Battle in Seattle," it was reminiscent of the labor violence common a century before, when leftists struggled against the suffocating influence of the emerging great trusts. During that last great period of labor unrest, anarchists distinguished themselves as they joined with organized labor, intellectuals, socialists, and other leftists to oppose the new form of monopolization.

In Genoa, anarchists from throughout Europe joined tens of thousands of protesters, but this time they came prepared to fight, provoking street riots and even causing some peaceful sympathizers to abandon the city. Unlike the anarchists in Seattle, these leftists resorted to violence as an offensive rather than a defensive technique. Since then, however, the world's governments' preoccupation with international terrorism, combined with the wish to defend against further radical violence, has caused increased stringent security measures. Dignitaries at these economic summits now meet behind barricades erected to separate them from the public at meeting sites that take on the look of armed camps. Indeed, even the United Nations Climate Change Conference in Copenhagen in 2009 became a scene of street violence in which anarchists and other extremists demonstrated for measures that would ameliorate the conditions contributing to global warming.

Meanwhile, more subtle anarchist movements are taking root in less advanced countries. The Zapatista movement in Mexico protests age-old exploitation of the peasants as well as the newer economic consequences of the North America Free Trade Association (NAFTA). This populist movement has taken effective control of several areas in the south and has encouraged locals to form "Good Government Councils." These spontaneously formed groups basically ignore the official government. Similarly, with the virtual collapse of the Argentine government in 2002, workers and peasants organized numerous economic and local political units run by ordinary workers and citizens. More recently, anarchists continue to resist developments in world trade. They played leading parts in resisting WHO meetings and even the 2009 Group-20 economic summit in Pittsburgh, Pennsylvania.

These developments are still only in their formative stages, however. Whether anarchism will be able to find its political legs in this era is yet to be seen. What is interesting, though, is that anarchism still seems to find a following even in an age of unprecedented economic centralization and electronic wizardry. As a matter of fact, current technological advancements are actually fostering and encouraging certain types of anarchism. The Internet, for example, is indeed a kind of technological anarchism. No one actually owns it, itself an astonishing fact in this era of exaggerated private ownership. People can contribute to it and participate in it as they wish, with little or no regulation imposed. Ironically, as political and economic systems become more and more subject to central control, in some respects, technology has afforded ordinary people increased freedom from that control.[1] Fascinating!

In general terms, anarchists want to maximize human liberty. They view government and its supporting institutions as antithetical to freedom and deleterious to human development. Instead of being useful institutions that facilitate human progress, governments block its path. Viewed from this perspective, anarchism is perhaps not startling to some people. Indeed, although few of us are actually anarchists, many of us harbor some anarchist tendencies. Many of us see some elements of government as detrimental rather than helpful to our interests. Standing in line for hours to have a driver's license renewed, trying to have college transcripts forwarded, paying hard-earned money in exorbitant taxes to support impersonal bureaucracies whose regulations prevent us from doing as we wish, finding government more responsive to economic interests than to individual needs, and dozens of other frustrating experiences can kindle within each of us the desire to see elements of the government reduced or eliminated.

But, while all anarchists oppose government to some extent, few other generalizations can be accurately applied to them as a group. There are, in fact, several misconceptions about the ideology; for example, in the United States, anarchism is seen as a necessarily violent movement. This error is understandable because so much violence was attributed to anarchists in this country at the turn of the twentieth century. The Haymarket Riot of 1886, the assassination of President William McKinley in 1901, the Great Red Scare of 1919, and the Sacco-Vanzetti hysteria of the mid-1920s were but a few dramatic episodes in which real or alleged anarchistic violence was blamed for the turmoil characterizing the era.

Although anarchism certainly does not deserve the full blame ascribed to it in these events, many immigrants to the United States who came from Southern and Eastern Europe at the time were adherents of the violent anarchist theories of Mikhail Bakunin. Beyond what anarchists actually did to deserve their violent reputations, a concerted effort by European and United States governments to sully their reputations was also implemented.[2] Thus,

---

[1]There, of course, have been efforts by governments to regulate use of the Internet. In Chapter 9 we shall examine the issue relative to China. At the moment it is worth discussing the Swedish matter. There, the government passed several laws protecting copyrights of music and film which people were pirating from cyberspace. Beginning in 2006, a large number of people—mostly young people—organized a political party essentially devoted to the absolute free use of the Internet. In only four years the *Pirate Party* attracted the third-largest party membership in Sweden, and motivated the organization of similar parties in twenty other European countries. It has won two seats on the Swedish delegation to the European Union and it is preparing for upcoming parliamentary elections. Its stated objective is to create "a free and open society for everyone." Despite its rapid success, the Pirate Party has yet to make inroads in the government's attempt to protect copyrights, but even its limited success is virtually unparalleled among single-issue parties.

[2]For a contemporary study of the concerted negative propaganda campaign, see Alex Butterworth, *The World That Never Was*, (New York, N.Y. Pantheon, 2010).

the impression developed that all anarchists were bomb-throwing malcontents who should be suppressed for the good of society.

In fact, however, anarchism can be violent or pacifist, depending on the particular theory advocated. Indeed, the earliest anarchists eschewed violence and opposed government on grounds that it was itself the greatest perpetrator of violence in society.

Another misapprehension about anarchism is that it is solely a leftist ideology. In reality, anarchism can be found on either the far right or the far left of the political spectrum. All anarchists would see government reduced or eliminated, leaving the individual free to pursue his or her best interests. To this extent all anarchists are the same. However, a critical distinction among them is revealed when we investigate exactly why they wish the individual to be freed from governmental restraint. What, in other words, is the individual's relationship to society?

Leftists of all persuasions view the individual in relation to the collection of all other people. Anarchists on the left, the **social anarchists,** wish to free people from governmental control because they believe that government prevents individuals from making the greatest possible contribution to society as a whole. The state, they believe, is a tool of mass oppression and should be eliminated if humanity is to advance freely to its fullest potential. The state is used by the ruling class to dominate the governed, thus unfairly and artificially restricting the progress of others. For example, laws giving one social class more economic and political rights than others are often found in stratified societies, and these rules invariably benefit those who make them—the ruling class.

The social anarchists would reduce or eliminate the offending governmental institutions, stripping away the artificial restraints on individual freedom, thus allowing each person, regardless of social class, to make his or her greatest contribution to the society as a whole. Counted among the social anarchists are William Godwin, Pierre Joseph Proudhon, Mikhail Bakunin, Peter Kropotkin, Leo Tolstoy, and Emma Goldman. Some of these social anarchists (Bakunin, Kropotkin, and Goldman) advocated the use of violence, whereas others (Godwin, Proudhon, and Tolstoy) denounced such practices as immoral or at least counterproductive.

Social anarchism is perhaps the best known form of anarchism because of the prolific literature produced by its adherents and because of their dramatic deeds for the cause. Yet, the anarchists of the far right are probably the most numerous, at least in the United States. Instead of favoring a society in which all individuals advance together, one in which the material differences between individuals are kept to a minimum, the anarchists of the right—**individualist anarchists**—envision a kind of Social Darwinism in which the society will advance best when each individual is encouraged to achieve what he or she can for himself or herself. This principle of "ownness," as Max Stirner called it, suggests that humanity is best served when people advance or fall back in relation to their individual abilities.

Individualist anarchists resist government policies such as minimum wage laws, welfare programs, affirmative action policies, and progressive income taxes, arguing that these policies protect the weak at the expense of the strong. Such policies artificially warp society, retarding progress, and should be eliminated. Individualist anarchist theories have been expressed by celebrated people such as Max Stirner, Henry David Thoreau, Josiah Warren, and S. E. Parker. The militant civilian militia movement, currently so popular in some quarters of the United States, is heavily laced with individualist anarchist objectives.

PARTICULAR THEORIES OF ANARCHISM

Anarchism has a large number of variations. Some anarchist theories have heralded freewheeling individualistic societies, whereas others have advocated communist structures. Some anarchists have made atheism an objective; others have called for people to forsake government for societies based on religious unions. Violence has often been seen as the vehicle for instituting anarchism, but pacifism has also been counseled. Government has been faulted as the tool of oppressors, and it has also been challenged for impeding the strong while artificially protecting the weak. Because of the diverse views of anarchists, it is difficult to construct generalizations that accurately describe this theory. Anarchism is, indeed, *the purest expression of individualism in politics.* Consequently, rather than generalizing any further, it will be useful to briefly examine the basic ideas of history's leading anarchist thinkers.

The Pacifists

William Godwin (1756–1836) is generally credited with founding modern anarchism. The son of stern Calvinist parents, Godwin followed many of his ancestors into the ministry. Yet, his considerable familiarity with French and English rationalism persuaded him to leave the church to pursue a literary career instead. Godwin was truly a product of his era. Like his contemporary, Thomas Paine, he had been schooled in the nonconformist philosophies of radical Protestantism and came to believe in the virtues of human individualism, seeing the church and later the state as conspiracies to benefit a few at the expense of many.

Godwin was devoted to the concept of human equality. In this vein, he became the first philosopher in modern times to advocate gender equality as well as social equality. Indeed, he married **Mary Wollstonecraft** (1759–1797),[3] generally recognized as history's first feminist.

In 1793 Godwin published his most important work, *The Enquiry Concerning Political Justice,* which immediately established him as a leading social critic. Basically, he suggested that all people are fundamentally equal and rational. If left to their own impulses, people would naturally create a harmonious society in which all would benefit and none would suffer at the hands of

---

[3]Their daughter, Mary, became the wife of the English poet Percy Bysshe Shelley, and it was she who authored the story of Frankenstein.

others. Unfortunately, however, society had evolved institutions that subdued the natural human impulse, creating a biased and exploitative society.

As you have already learned, these libertarian ideas[4] were not unique to Godwin; Rousseau and other leftists shared this view. However, the English philosopher not only condemned the national government and its centralized institutions but also lashed out at schools, organized religion, the family, and other local institutions as purveyors of the biases that threatened individual goodness and accomplishment.

Godwin opposed most laws and institutional restraints imposed upon the individual. In their place he would see the creation of a society that he vaguely described as a community without rules, founded upon the belief that individuals, left to their own inclinations, would conduct themselves with mutual respect and compassion. Those who used social and political institutions for their own advantage—the "imposters," as he called them—were to be "reeducated" to change their values and attitudes.

Incorporating most of Godwin's moralistic objections to the state and its institutions, **Pierre Joseph Proudhon** (1809–1865) gave anarchism the philosophical depth and economic perspective that made it a viable political ideology in the modern world. Largely self-educated, this son of a laborer endeared himself to the French public for his modest lifestyle and his sincere devotion to humanitarian principles.

Proudhon professed the **labor theory of value** (the theory that the value of any object is determined by the amount of labor needed to produce it) and used it to answer the question posed in the title of his best-known book *What Is Property?*: "Property is theft," he responded on the first page. By this he meant that all unearned property (rent, interest, profits) was stolen from the workers who produced it.

Proudhon, the first person to call himself an anarchist, demanded the elimination of government and other institutions, which he claimed unduly denied the people earned property and human rights so that the governing class might flourish. Denouncing the established order, he advocated restructuring society into voluntary associations of workers. These institutions—*syndicates,* they were called—would dispense the necessary services usually provided by government. Thus, *anarcho-syndicalism* was born; it remains to this day a potent influence in the labor movement of France as well as of many other countries. Indeed, the industrial unions—the United Mine Workers, the United Auto Workers, and many others—in this country are organized on a syndical (industry-wide) basis as opposed to the skilled-crafts, or guild, model.

Syndicalism, Proudhon believed, should be voluntary and should be created at the expense of the state. It should liberate the worker from the twin masters of capitalism and government. Frustrated by the growing complexity of modern bureaucracy and decrying the lack of morality in state policy,

---

[4]The term *libertarian* used in this context is meant to mean "liberty-loving." It does not refer to the ideas of the Libertarian Party of the United States.

Proudhon condemned authority as corrupt and decadent. Traditional political authority, he claimed, exists solely to "maintain *order* in society, by consecrating and sanctifying obedience of the citizen to the state, subordination of the poor to the rich, of the common people to the upper class, of the worker to the idler, of the layman to the priest." Since he thought the state exploitative and without moral justification, Proudhon would see it eliminated and replaced by an institution that more accurately reflected the economic and political rights of the people.

Still, however, Proudhon did not call for violent overthrow of the state. Instead, he would have the workers take it upon themselves to ignore traditional authority and organize the syndicates. Thus denied the support of the productive elements in society, the state would collapse, leaving only the voluntary associations of workers or syndicates. Having been influenced himself by his friend, the utopian socialist **Charles Fourier,** Proudhon was recognized as "the master of us all" by Mikhail Bakunin, and his thought dominated the French trade union movement for better than a half century after his death.

Leo Tolstoy (1828–1910), Russian noble and literary master, was another noted anarchist. Following a frivolous youth, Tolstoy became troubled by the suffering of Russia's peasants. Equally disturbing to him was the realization that the peasants' plight resulted from deliberate policies of the Russian Orthodox Church and the tsarist regime.

Tolstoy developed a great admiration and respect for the individual and particularly for Russia's peasants. He saw the peasants confronted with the tremendous power of the state that brutalized them. His sympathy for the peasants deepened when he saw them suffering so desperately, even as they were encouraged to bear exploitation by the church, which Tolstoy felt manipulated the scriptures to serve the state and its ruling class. The great writer's compassion and admiration for the peasants were expressed as early as 1869 in his magnum opus *War and Peace.* In this exquisite novel about the 1812 Napoleonic invasion of Russia, Tolstoy develops the thesis that the hated aggressor was

© Bettmann/Corbis

I Leo Tolstoy (1828–1910)

not turned back by tsars and generals. Rather, Napoleon was defeated by the dedication, suffering, and sacrifice of millions of lowly individuals who stood in the defense of Mother Russia.

Tolstoy's anarchism stemmed from two fundamental and closely related convictions: his interpretation of Christianity and his commitment to pacifism. These ideas were most explicitly put forth in *The Kingdom of God Is Within You* (1894). Echoing the force theory of the origin of the state, Tolstoy believed that the state resulted from nothing more than the imposition of power by the strong over the weak. Physical violence, he contended, was the basis of political power. A devout Christian who was convinced that Christianity demanded peace and human justice, Tolstoy considered the state illegitimate on the basis of its presumed method of development: the use of force. Yet, beyond this conclusion, the state continued its offense by perpetuating violence. Indeed, Tolstoy saw the state as the principal source of violence in society.

On the pretext of having to protect society from aggressive neighbors, the state organized armies. However, in Tolstoy's experience, the armies were actually turned against the people they purported to protect. In other words, the state perpetrated violence against its own people. Why did the state use violence against its own citizens? To exploit them, to squeeze the last measure of energy and production from them while denying them the desserts of their labor. The state, then, in Tolstoy's view, was illegitimate from its beginnings and continued to assault the individual with orchestrated violence and exploitation. In short, the state was evil and invalid.

To those who argued that the state was the context in which civilization developed, Tolstoy refused to concede the point. But, he argued, even if the state might have been necessary at one time to create the atmosphere in which religion, education, culture, and communication could develop, society clearly had evolved beyond its previous dependence. Asserting that modern people are quite capable of creating and maintaining civilized institutions without the state, Tolstoy indicted the state, charging that it actually hindered rather than encouraged civilized society.

Having thus challenged the legitimacy of this monstrous evil, Tolstoy called on the Russian people to destroy the state itself. Yet, he cautioned against the use of revolution for the cause. Instead, he encouraged people to abandon their commitment to the Russian Orthodox Church, which he viewed as the handmaiden of the state. Tolstoy rejected the ceremony, vestments, and clergy as irrelevant trappings of the true faith (he was excommunicated for these beliefs). Rather, he called on each individual to be dedicated to the principles of Christian peace and human fraternity.

He called on people to recognize only one law, the law of God; to be bound only by the dictates of their own consciences; and to ignore any other pretensions to authority. True Christians, he said, could not give their allegiance to the state, for that would mean abandoning their own consciences and the law of God. Christians, he said, are independent of the state because they recognize the law of God as the only true law. Further, they are bound by their faith to follow their own consciences relative to those laws, ignoring other mandates; if they do otherwise, they jeopardize their immortal souls. "Man," Tolstoy wrote, "cannot serve two masters."

The proper response to government, Tolstoy asserted, was simply to ignore it. When the state issues an order, the people should drop their hands and walk away. Tolstoy believed this technique, today called *passive resistance,* would spell the doom of government. Government's ultimate tool for ensuring compliance is force, but force is acceptable only when it is combating violence. Beating people who will not raise their hands in anger is simply reprehensible and indefensible. Indeed, in the end, it makes the government look absurd. When official violence is met only by persistent nonviolence, the absurdity of government force quickly becomes evident, and government itself loses any moral justification.

The power of Tolstoy's doctrine of passive resistance as a political tool has been appreciated by many people over the years, but no one understood its potential as well as India's great leader Mohandas (great soul) Gandhi. With unshakable resolve, Gandhi entreated his people to resist the British colonial government, not with barricades and bullets, but with quiet, firm, nonviolent disobedience.

Gandhi's tactics were very effective in the long run. After much pain proceeding from their refusal to answer violence with violence, his followers used stubborn but peaceful protest to demonstrate dramatically the immorality of using force. Eventually unable to justify the use of force against a pacifist adversary, the British finally relented and India became independent. As powerful a tool as it may be, passive resistance will not necessarily always reward its advocates. Suggesting that the British government bent before a moral imperative that would have left Hitler or Stalin unmoved, someone once quipped that Gandhi was very clever in his choice of opponents. American leaders, among them Henry David Thoreau, Dr. Martin Luther King Jr., and Cesar Chavez, also became skilled in passive resistance while pursuing their causes.

The Revolutionaries

Russia, Europe's most oppressive state, produced several other important anarchists besides Tolstoy. However, his passive resistance approach was not seen by many of his compatriots as a viable method for changing the system.

Perhaps history's best-known anarchist is **Mikhail Bakunin** (1814–1876), a Russian aristocrat. Preceding Tolstoy, he also resisted the church and the state as exploitative and oppressive institutions. Unlike the venerable author, however, Bakunin also advocated atheism and violence. Indeed, he is credited with being the founder of violent anarchism. Condemning the state as humankind's greatest obstacle to attaining liberty, Bakunin advocated terrorism, revolution, and destruction. More radical even than Marx, who at least called for revolution by honest working people, Bakunin contended that a successful revolution would come about by arming the underworld of society—its vagabonds, pimps, thieves, murderers—the **lumpenproletariat.**

Alternating between long periods of revolutionary activity, imprisonment, and exile, Bakunin was unable to reduce his ideas to systematic presentations until the last decade of his life. By then he had gained international notoriety as a revolutionary, and so his reputation remains today. Basically, Bakunin rejected all forms of human conformity. He regarded most of society's institutions as devices to enslave the human spirit, denying it the freedom for which it was destined. For example, he rejected religion and belief in God. To believe in a superhuman power necessarily meant the abdication of the free human spirit and the enslavement of people to a supposed divine spirit. Placing total emphasis on human freedom, he challenged God to liberate people. "If God existed," he wrote, "only in one way could he serve human liberty—by ceasing to exist."

Bakunin had been strongly influenced by the Russian **Narodnik** (Populist) movement, which lionized the Russian peasant. The perfect social arrangement, he opined, would be composed of rural communes in which each citizen freely and voluntarily agreed to work. Unlike Rousseau, however, Bakunin would have nothing to do with the principle of majority rule. Seeing each individual as a free spirit, owing no debt to anyone else, he envisioned that each person in society would remain free either to give or to withhold consent from the norms of the group. Thus maximizing individual freedom, Bakunin hoped to liberate people from societal restraints, expecting that they would then be able to make their contributions to the whole as free and willing participants rather than as slaves to the opinion makers of the community.

Although Bakunin failed to depose a government during his lifetime, he is indisputably the most influential anarchist history offers. His ideas are credited with inciting assassinations, terrorism, and rebellion in many countries. His philosophy had a great impact on subsequent anarchists and other radicals; it was particularly popular among the peasants of Italy, Ukraine, and Spain. Indeed, Ukraine in 1917 and Spain in 1936–1939 hosted the only sustained anarchistic experiments, and both were based on Bakuninist theory.

Much less the activist and more the scholarly writer was Prince **Peter Kropotkin** (1842–1921). Like his Russian compatriots Tolstoy and Bakunin, Kropotkin was a noble who profited from the privilege his society afforded that status. Trained as a scientist, Kropotkin made a number of important contributions to the geographical studies of the Russian Far East and Scandinavia. Ironically, between 1862 and 1867 he served as an aide to Tsar Alexander II, but eventually he became captivated by the revolutionary energy of Bakunin. Kropotkin became an activist in the 1870s but returned to the scholarly life after being imprisoned for his political activities. From the mid-1880s until 1917 he resided in London, occupying himself with scholarly and philosophical writing.

Kropotkin's scientific background encouraged him to dispute the then popular doctrine of **Social Darwinism,** as put forth by **Herbert Spencer.** He was convinced that higher animals, and man in particular, had met with the greatest success when acting cooperatively rather than aggressively.

Government, according to Kropotkin, tended to divide person against person, class against class, country against country, and was therefore destructive of human tranquility and progress. It was the "personification of injustice, oppression, and monopoly" in his view and must therefore be eliminated and replaced by an anarchist society based upon communist principles and voluntary mutual aid among free individuals.

Kropotkin believed that people were essentially social beings and that the state tended to make them antisocial. With its elimination, he believed that people could be educated to accept a noncoercive political stance and an economy based on mutual work, cooperation, and sharing. Thus, a positive rather than negative atmosphere would evolve and would accrue to the ultimate benefit of all in the society.

Kropotkin's attitude toward revolution was ambivalent. An avowed Bakuninist during his early years, he did engage in revolutionary activities, but he later questioned whether revolution was the most effective method by which to transform society. Although he certainly never became a pacifist, Kropotkin tended to lean increasingly toward the belief that, nourished by the increasing capacity of industrialization to sustain a communist society, anarchism would evolve naturally from the human desire to be free, thus no provocative leadership was necessary.

With the tsar's overthrow in 1917, he returned from England to Moscow after forty years in exile. Declining offers of official positions in the government, at seventy-five years of age, he preferred retirement. However, apparently anticipating the authoritarian policies of the Bolsheviks, when they came to power at the end of 1917 he told a friend, "This buries the Revolution."

Closely associated with Kropotkin was an Italian, **Enrico Malatesta** (1853–1932). An implacable revolutionary organizer and a spirited speaker, he remained a devoted activist for over fifty years. Becoming convinced that only revolution would bring about the new world of human harmony, he demanded that leftists forsake the salons and drawing rooms where politics was debated and go into the streets with demands for change. "Propaganda by the deed" became his slogan as he urged followers to foster insurgency through assassinations of political leaders and other politically disruptive behavior. Widely traveled in Europe and the Americas during his long career, Malatesta found himself banished from several countries. He spent more than a decade in jail and escaped the death penalty on three different occasions. Having deeply influenced anarchist movements in Italy, Egypt, France, Belgium, Argentina, Rumania, Spain, and the United States, it is perhaps ironic that he should have spent the last decade of his life in retirement in his native Italy, which was then ruled by Mussolini, an unabashed statist.

Emma Goldman (1869–1940), influenced by Malatesta, became the most important anarchist in U.S. history. Fleeing tsarist Russia, she came to America in 1886, only to be brutalized in the sweatshops of the garment industry in Rochester, New York. Disillusioned by the harsh economic conditions as well as by the prejudices of the moral strictures of American society, she became increasingly radical. Alexander Berkman, who became her lifelong lover, introduced her to Bakunin, Malatesta, and other anarchist thinkers, as well as to the tiny American anarchist movement.

Emma Goldman delivers one of her stem-winding speeches.

© Corbis

Soon Goldman became a leading voice advocating radical causes ranging from atheism to the use of contraceptives by women. A fiery speaker, she often brought crowds to their feet and the police to her door. Arrested time and again for leftist agitation, Goldman came to be known as "Red Emma."

During most of her career, Goldman was an activist. She led protests, addressed rallies, advocated strikes, published the anarchist journal *Mother Earth,* and even sold her body to get enough money to buy the pistol with which Berkman tried to assassinate the industrialist Henry Clay Frick. As World War I approached she became a leading opponent of the "capitalist's war," again finding herself in jail and finally deported to the Soviet Union. Her initial enthusiasm for the Soviet regime was soon transformed into bitter disappointment; however, causing her to support the Russian navy's brief anti-Bolshevik rebellion on the island of Kronstadt in 1921 and ultimately inducing her to leave the country for London.

Continuing her radical activities throughout the 1920s and 1930s, Goldman became a vociferous opponent of fascism and Nazism. She joined the anarchists in Spain resisting the reactionary rebellion of Francisco Franco and ultimately died of a stroke in Canada while trying to raise money for the anarchist cause.

Advocating Malatesta's "propaganda by the deed" early in her career, Goldman, like Kropotkin before her, gradually came to question the violent acts of her youth. Time found her increasingly drawn to temperate approaches and away from the terrorist methods of Bakunin. In the end, Emma Goldman advocated the elimination of government, to be replaced by a network of communes based on mutual trust and consideration among individuals who remained free to think and act as they chose.

Although Bakunin inspired the relatively mild Kropotkin and the activists Malatesta and Goldman, history's most extreme anarchist movement also owes a great deal to him. Unlike their revolutionary mentor, the **Nihilist** remained in Russia. Resisting the pressure for change in the nineteenth century, the tsarist regime responded to demands for reform and modernization with reaction and brutal repression. The government's obstinate intransigence frustrated the radicals and encouraged them to resort to increasingly extreme activities, eventually including conspiracy, terrorism, and assassination.

The Nihilists were the most frustrated group of radicals, abandoning all hope of reform and coming to believe that society itself had to be brought down. The term *Nihilists* was first introduced in *Fathers and Sons,* a novel by Ivan Turgenev. Developing the most chaotic, violent, and destructive variant of anarchist theories, the Nihilists were prominent between the 1860s and 1880s. Inspired by Bakunin's observation that "The passion for destruction is also a creative passion," Nihilist philosophy contended that government was so rotten, so corrupt, so decayed that it was beyond repair. The only constructive act possible, in the minds of these unhappy people, was the destruction of society. Anything that survived the violent onslaught would perhaps be worth saving. In a single sentence, Nihilist Dmitri Pisarev (1840–1918) captured the philosophy of these tortured radicals: "Here is the ultimatum of our camp: What can be smashed, should be smashed; what will stand the blow is good; what will fly into smithereens is rubbish; at any rate, hit out right and left— there will and can be no harm from it."

The most notorious Nihilist was *Sergi Nechayev* (1847–1882). A protégé of Bakunin, Nechayev schemed and plotted unscrupulously. Devoted to only one idea, the destruction of the state, he lied, cheated, and even murdered his own coconspirators. Proclaiming his Nihilist convictions, he wrote: "We must devote ourselves wholly to destruction, constant, ceaseless, relentless, until there is nothing left of existing institutions." Though in practice the Nihilists were amateurish and bungling and were eventually wiped out, their blatant violence terrorized the Russian government and caused it some loss of esteem, since its brutal policies had so obviously produced Nihilist extremism.

Individualist Anarchists

The people thus far discussed, whether violent or not, religious or not, socialist or not, were social anarchists (anarchism on the left); they opposed government because they believed that it limited people's freedom. However, they were not interested in individual freedom solely for the individual's own sake. Each of the social anarchists recognized that individuals within society are directly related to each other and are somehow responsible to each other. Such is not the case with the individualist anarchists (anarchists on the right). Easily the most solitary anarchist approach, this ideology recognizes only the individual, denying any obligation or even much value to interrelationships among people. Exceeding the confines of what is usually understood as *individualism,* these anarchists promote a concept that might better be termed *individualistism.* Contrary to the social anarchists, these anarchists would free individuals to make the greatest contribution to themselves. They see the state policies such as social welfare programs, minimum wage laws, affirmative action policies, and progressive taxes as artificial protections of the weak, wrongfully inhibiting success of the strong.

The founder of individualist anarchism is **Max Stirner** (1806–1856), a German philosopher and social critic. Stirner led a relatively undistinguished life except for a brief moment of notoriety in the late 1840s, when his most successful work *The Ego and His Own* was published. The book attracted both positive and negative attention. For the latter cause, no less a light than Karl Marx rose to take issue with its contentions. Within its pages Stirner portrays humanity as a completely *atomistic* group of individuals who owe no true responsibility to anyone save themselves.

According to Stirner, society's institutions, including government and religion, are artificial props wrongfully forcing the strong to sacrifice in support of the weak. Stirner suggests that all acts, though usually rationalized as being for the greater good, are actually committed out of selfish motives. Thus, he argues that contrary to what people say, they do not worship God for God's sake, but for their own benefit. The worship of God is a protective device intended by the worshipers to save their souls. Yet they piously represent it as an unselfish act. Stirner sees this pretense as a self-deception preventing people from openly and efficiently acting in their own interests.

Stirner demands that people abandon their feeble attempts at mutual responsibility and concentrate on themselves alone. Defiantly proclaiming his thesis of "ownness," Stirner wrote: "*My own* I am at all times and under all circumstances, if I know how to have myself and do not throw myself away on others.*" In another place in *The Ego and His Own* he restates the point even more bluntly: "I am everything to myself and I do everything on my own account."

Thus establishing to his satisfaction "*the sovereignty of the individual,*" Stirner encourages each person to act without regard to the society as a whole. People are justified in taking what they wish simply because they desire it. The social good is a hoax created to limit the power of the strong. When society protects the weak, it destroys individual freedom. Stirner calls upon people to refuse recognition of their supposed obligation to others, thus liberating themselves from the artificial fetters unrightfully imposed upon them. Exalting in his own presumed freedom, he exclaimed, "The *people* are dead. Up with *me!*"

A much more threatening figure is Theodore Kaczynski: the Unabomber. In his *Manifesto,* published just before and actually leading to his capture in 1996, this 30,000 word document reminds one of Hitler's *Mein Kampf* in its venomous sweeping statements and erratic presentation. In it, Kaczynski lambasts what he calls modern leftism for its collectivists principles and its "betrayal" of individualism; he blames the Industrial Revolution whose technology transformed peoples' lives into a slavery to large organizations; he rues the modern power structure which he sees as making the masses of people utterly powerless; he asserts that people should aspire to a society simplified by a preindustrial economy; and he calls for a revolution to accomplish this goal. By forsaking modern social, economic, and political structures and returning to a more individualistic "natural" (read primitive) environment, individuals, he contends, will find themselves empowered. Large groups, he wrote, deny people their liberty, so at best, individuals should limit their association to small groups. (Exact sizes are not specified.) Modern society, he writes in his *Manifesto*, "makes an individual's life easier for him in innumerable ways, but in doing so it deprives him of control over his own fate."

Proclaiming himself an anarchist, Kaczynski calls for the destruction of the industrial society he sees as the culprit. To replace it, he writes vaguely,

> Whatever kind of society may exist after the demise of the industrial system, it is certain that most people will live close to nature, because in the absence of advanced technology there is no other way that people CAN live. To feed themselves they must be peasants or herdsmen or fishermen or hunters, and so on. And generally speaking, local autonomy should tend to increase, because lack of advanced technology and rapid communications will limit the capacity of government or other large organizations to control communities.[5]

Dismissing the trauma and privation that might accompany such a transformation, Kaczynski cavalierly suggests, "As for the negative consequences of eliminating industrial society—well, you can't eat your cake and have it too. To gain one thing you have to sacrifice another."

At its greatest extreme, individualist anarchism can lead to an attitude of complete self-reliance and a frightening exclusivity. It can become reminiscent of Thomas Hobbes's vision of the natural state: "A war of each against all." Stirner's "ownness" and Kaczynski's ideas can become a kind of "one, true, and only meism" in which only the self counts. It can isolate people from one another—indeed it seeks to do so—more than any other political theory.

Anarchistic Tendencies in the American Political Character

Although Ayn Rand is usually associated with libertarianism, her theories are rich with anarchistic implications. One of this country's most popular contemporary writers, *Ayn Rand* (1905–1982), a Russian-born thinker, advocated *objectivism* in novels and journals. This theory lionizes individualism and relegates collectivism to irrelevance. Reminiscent of Stirner, Rand claims that selfishness is good and altruism is decadent. She encourages her followers to focus on their own narrow interests in the belief that the only worthwhile accomplishment is one perpetrated by an individual purely motivated by selfish interests. Rand's popularity in the United States stems from her laissez-faire economic ideas, but also because her atomistic approach is deeply rooted in the fabric of American society. Perhaps stemming from the frontier ethic under which people relied on themselves to carve a life out of the wilderness, the mystique of *rugged individualism* has enjoyed particular popularity in the United States. The tendency toward an atomistic society in which the individual comes first and society is secondary—almost incidental—has certainly been an important force in our history.

Because many of their beliefs are similar to fascism and so they will be studied again in Chapter 10, the antigovernment beliefs of people associated with the

---

[5]Kaczynski, Theodore, /Industrial Society and its Future/(Wikisource, 2007)

militant civilian militias in this country have clear anarchistic tendencies. The 1995 explosive destruction of the federal building in Oklahoma City, this country's most deadly act of terrorism to that time, was perpetrated by American "patriots." While not actually members of a militia, the bombers espoused ideas similar to those of the militant civilian militias. Suddenly public attention was riveted on this previously little-noticed movement of *governmentphobes* whose fear of the motivation and intent of government policy stretched credulity beyond reasonable limits.

"I love my country, but I don't trust its government" is a slogan often voiced by these disgruntled people. While large differences separate many of these groups, certain similarities among them are clear. Profoundly conspiratorialist, they see government as being the captive of evil forces that are bent on enslaving them and abolishing their personal liberties. Their reading of the Second Amendment to the U.S. Constitution incorrectly assures them of the "right" to keep arms without government interference.[6] Finally, violent confrontation is romantically viewed as imminent between the government and those who feel they must righteously defend their individual liberties against the encroachment of federal laws and law enforcers.

Virtually every unpleasant policy or activity of the government is twisted and reshaped by these antigovernment crusaders until it is recast as evidence of the plot to deny the American people their liberties. Gun control laws; the North American Free Trade Agreement (NAFTA); the General Agreement on Trade and Tariffs (GATT); the Federal Reserve Board; agents of the Federal Bureau of Investigation (FBI), the Internal Revenue Service (IRS), the Alcohol, Tobacco, and Firearms Agency (ATF); and so on are seen as conspirators bent on robbing Americans of their freedom.

Militia movement leaders variously claim that the federal government, which is secretly controlled by sinister forces, is plotting to cooperate with a UN invasion of the United States; that it planted a bomb in Oklahoma City itself in order to discredit the militia movement; that it deliberately murdered innocent people who were trying to defend their just liberties at Ruby Ridge, Idaho, in 1992 and at Waco, Texas,[7] in 1993. Warning that a violent confrontation is imminent between thousands of armed citizens of the United States and their government, militia leaders threatened U.S. senators in congressional testimony, warned that 15,000 Gurkha troops were hiding in the Michigan hills awaiting orders to swoop down on the unsuspecting Midwest, claimed that the backs of

---

[6]The U.S. Supreme Court has recently ruled that people may keep guns in their homes for self-protection, but, it was careful to indicate that state and local authorities may legislate reasonable regulation of people's use of firearms.

[7]Following an investigation of the Ruby Ridge encounter, the federal government agreed to give a large payment to Randy Weaver for the wrongful deaths of his wife and his fourteen-year-old son, but no responsible authority has claimed that the government deliberately assassinated the two Weavers. A later investigation headed by former senator John Danforth of Missouri found no untoward government behavior associated with the tragic deaths of David Koresh and his cult followers in Waco, Texas.

road signs were marked with coded instructions to guide UN invading columns, and announced that the federal government was controlled by satanic forces.

The paranoiac ramblings of these extremists and the rather comical specter of aging militia members becoming America's defenders of liberty should not distract us from the fact that several thousand people find these images compelling. In a nation like our own, which has had a long romance with individualism, such ideas can be very appealing to certain groups of people, especially when threatened and insecure. For example, the membership of the militia groups briefly actually increased significantly after the Oklahoma bombing.

QUESTIONS FOR DISCUSSION

1. What social and economic conditions led to the development of anarchism?
2. In what ways do anarchists disagree with one another and on what do they agree?
3. How can individualist and social anarchism be compared and contrasted?
4. What are the fundamental ideas of nihilism, and to what historical era does it belong?
5. How does the modern American militant civilian militia movement relate to anarchism?

SUGGESTIONS FOR FURTHER READING

Adem, Seifudein, *Anarchy, Order and Power in World Politics: A Comparative Analysis.* Hampshire, England: Ashgate, 2002.

Arvich, Paul, *Anarchist Voices: An Oral History of Anarchism in America.* Princeton, NJ: Princeton University Press, 1996.

Butterworth, Alex, *The World That Never Was.* New York, Pantheon, 2010.

Call, Lewis, *Postmodern Anarchism.* Lanham, MD: Lexington Books, 2002.

Chomsky, Noam, and Barry Pateman, *Chomsky on Anarchism.* Oakland, CA: AK Press, 2005.

Godwin, William, *Enquiry Concerning Political Justice.* Middlesex, UK: Penguin Classics, 1985.

Goldman, Emma, *Anarchism and Other Essays.* New York: Dover, 1969.

Guerin, Daniel, *No Gods, No Masters: An Anthology of Anarchism,* trans. Paul Sharkey. Oakland, CA: AK Press, 2005.

Kropotkin, Peter, *Mutual Aid: A Factor in Evolution.* New York: New York University Press, 1972.

Marsh, Margaret S., *Anarchist Women, 1870–1920.* Philadelphia, PA: Temple University Press, 1981.

Stirner, Max (Johann Kaspar Schmidt), *The Ego and His Own,* trans. S. T. Bylington. London: Rebel Press, 1993.

Woodcock, George, *Anarchism and Anarchists.* Chicago: LPC Books, 1995.

Socialist Theory

PREVIEW

Socialism arose as a protest against the inhumanity of unregulated, raw capitalism. Decrying private property, individualism, and selfishness, socialism is founded on three principles: public ownership of production, the welfare state, and improving the human condition by eliminating poverty.

While socialism's origins reach back to the French Revolution, the ideology is rooted in the Industrial Revolution. It gradually evolved two great branches, humanitarian socialism and "scientific socialism." The Utopians—early humanitarian socialists—though well-meaning, discredited socialism with their impractical idealism and their failed social experiments. Their failure left the field open to Karl Marx's "scientific" approach.

Believing he had discovered the formula by which human history could be understood, Marx thought that people's ideas are conditioned by their economic environment and that economic change fosters a dialectic conflict between those ruling and those ruled in society. Eventually, the social class controlling the new dominant means of production will win the struggle to create political and social conditions beneficial to it. According to Marx, the final conflict will find the capitalist and proletarian classes engaged in a struggle that the proletariat will win because, although the capitalist system is productive, it is also exploitative and parasitic. When the proletariat class comes to power, it will establish a dictatorship, which, in turn, will create a socialist economy and eliminate all nonproletarian classes. This development will lead to greater productivity and the elimination of poverty. As each country becomes socialist in its turn, national boundaries will disappear and eventually a single utopia will replace the divided, exploitative, and cruel world of capitalism.

THE DEVELOPMENT OF SOCIALISM

Socialism began to emerge as an ideology just before the turn of the eighteenth century. It developed as a protest against the harsh exploitation of workers and of other ordinary people that was common to capitalism. The Industrial Revolution had given people a new framework for thought. It also brought mechanized production and replaced human or animal energy with steam. Yet, as machines and energy sources became more sophisticated, the costs of mass production exceeded the resources of the individual. Consequently, cottage industries were replaced by the factory system. Family ownership of industry was eventually displaced by stock market investors and professional managers. Each of these developments removed ownership from production and estranged the owners from the workers.

This new economic system allowed people with money to buy up the machinery and factories needed to produce goods. People who had been self-employed, or who at least had worked closely with their employers, found themselves forced into huge factories, mills, and mines. The resulting depersonalization of labor was increased by the new machinery, which tended to make old skills obsolete. Workers were put behind machines to perform monotonous and menial tasks requiring no skills beyond those needed to keep the machines functioning properly, even as wages were suppressed because skilled jobs disappeared.

The factory system brought with it a whole new way of life. People were herded into the cities, where housing was cramped and squalid. Sanitation facilities were so woefully inadequate that people were forced to live in filth. The factories themselves were dark, damp, and poorly ventilated, and workers found themselves isolated from anything that might reduce their productivity. Thousands died of asthma and tuberculosis because the air they breathed was contaminated by smoke, steam, dust, and filth. Many people toiled as long as sixteen hours a day in the summer and thirteen and a half hours in the winter, sometimes seven days a week. At times workers could not even leave the factories and were forced to sleep beneath the machines to which they were enslaved.

Women and children were the most desirable laborers because they could be paid less and were least likely to resist the harsh discipline imposed on them. The family unit disintegrated. A working mother might seldom see her children unless they also worked in the factory. Small children were left completely unattended for long periods. Men, usually the first to be fired, sometimes had to depend on the earnings of their wives and children for subsistence. The disgrace and humiliation of these circumstances often drove men to leave home, to dissipate in drunkenness, to perpetrate cruelties on their families, or even to commit suicide.

The owners were often indifferent to the suffering in their factories. Some capitalists rationalized the wretched conditions of the laborers by claiming that industry saved these people from idleness, the greatest sin of all. Others used Social Darwinist arguments, claiming that the laborers were obviously inferior to the owners and *should* be worked hard. They resolved that eventually the inferiors would die out, leaving a more wholesome and intelligent race. (Who would then do the mundane, repetitive tasks of industrialized production was not offered by these pseudo-scientists.) The owners imposed heavy fines and even corporal punishment for whistling or talking at work, for working too slowly, or for being late. The law gave the workers no protection and demanded a heavy penalty for theft. When a woman was put on trial for stealing a few coins to feed her starving children, Thomas Hood, a poet of the time, wrote in anguish, "Oh God, that bread should be so dear and flesh and blood so cheap!" Charles Dickens, however, is probably the best-known author inspired by the plight of the worker. Just a glance at *David Copperfield, Hard Times,* or *Oliver Twist* impresses the reader with the hopeless circumstances of the poor during this era. Decrying the imposed misery, reformers demanded exploitation be replaced by a system that treated people justly and humanely: socialism.

Communism and Socialism

The confusion of communism and socialism should be examined. **Communism** is an ancient concept extending back to prehistory. Indeed, there is evidence suggesting that communism was the first mode of human social existence; virtually all primitive people practiced some form of communal existence. Communistic societies are composed of four essential properties: they are *collective* (people work and own in common); they are *rural* (although some experiments in urban communism now exist, before the closing years of the nineteenth century communism was usually not associated with urban areas); their economic base is *agrarian,* or agricultural; and they are *local in their orientation.* That is to say, the people who live on communes—the "communists"—usually have abandoned the societies in which they found themselves and fled to a communal farm. Rejecting the values and regulations of society, they create their own universe. The commune becomes the entire world for its occupants as they ignore the environment surrounding them. So it was historically, and communes are largely so today.

Communism has also become associated with applied Marxism: the "Communist Bloc" or "Communist China." This newer application of the term, you will soon learn, is because Karl Marx sometimes used the word *communism* but, as you will soon see, the world he envisioned was not rural, agrarian, and locally oriented.

Socialism, by contrast, is a relatively recent phenomenon. Socialism advocates the application of collectivist principles, not to a single agricultural enterprise but to the entire national economy. Since the transportation, communications, and bureaucratic capacities to administer such a national economy did not exist until the 1800s, little serious thought was given to this idea until then, although both Plato's *Republic* and Sir Thomas More's *Utopia* speculate about systems that could be considered socialist.

Socialism also has four fundamental properties. It shares *collectivism* with communism; however, rather than being local in orientation, socialism proposes applying collectivist principles to a national economy. Its base is *industrial* rather than agricultural, meaning that it is largely *urban,* and not rural, as is communism. Socialism has, of course, been tried in rural societies, but it has not been very successful there. Rural societies seldom produce sufficient wealth to feed, house, and clothe everyone in the society adequately; so when the wealth is equalized, it improves people's lives only marginally. Indeed, *the greatest irony of socialism is that it is most successful in highly productive societies; yet, people in those societies are already relatively wealthy and are not interested in socialism.* Put differently, socialism is most attractive to societies that cannot afford to apply it successfully. This is a fundamental dilemma. Whether this contradiction will be overcome in the rural societies in which socialism is currently being tried is impossible to tell, but the odds seem long indeed.

THE COMPONENTS OF SOCIALISM

Socialism is a complex idea system, one that is often misunderstood in this society. It is not only an economic system, it is also a social, political, and moral philosophy. Often wrongly equated with communism in the United States, socialism is a buzzword sometimes used to discredit otherwise legitimate ideas and proposals. Opponents of the 1994 proposals for a national health system in the United States, for example, dismissed it as "socialized medicine," as if to suggest that if an institution is associated with socialism it is wrong on its face. Fortunately, much of the debate in 2009–2010 regarding adopting a national health care system was more somewhat focused on substantive issues.

Socialism, as distinct from communism, can be described in terms of three basic components. Two of them, *ownership of production* and establishment of the *welfare state,* are mechanical and are not necessarily related to each other. The third, however, belief in the **socialist intent,** is the most fundamental aspect of socialism and must be present together with one or both of the mechanical features; otherwise, true socialism does not exist.

Ownership of Production

The concept of public ownership and control of the major means of production, distribution, and finance is a fundamental principle of socialism. The traditional way to socialize an economy is by **nationalization.** Nationalization exists when government expropriates and operates an industry. In Western societies, nationalized industries are usually managed by boards or commissions appointed by government officials and may be removed only by parliamentary vote. Some good examples of this kind of arrangement are the British Broadcasting Corporation, the Tennessee Valley Authority in the United States, France's Renault Automobile, and the Indian Railway. In the few remaining communist countries (the People's Republic of China, Cuba, North Korea, and Vietnam, for example), a government-owned industry is more likely to be closely connected to the society's political leaders than is true in noncommunist countries. Although it is the traditional method of socializing the economy, nationalization has gradually lost favor in Western countries. Following the Scandinavian model, socialists in the advanced Western states have increasingly turned to **cooperatives** as a means of socializing the economy.

Attempting to combine the virtues of private motivation with the benefits of collective ownership, cooperative enterprises are composed of individuals who collectively own them and who share in the work, the risk, and the profits. Usually they elect a board of directors to manage the enterprise. Such cooperatives can become quite extensive. For instance, a village that owned a fleet of fishing boats could expand by buying a cannery, which would become part of the cooperative's assets. With part of the profits from these two *productive coops,* the village could buy large quantities of groceries, clothing, and hardware and create its own *consumer cooperative,* making the best possible price available to its members by buying in volume. Almost any kind of enterprise can be collectivized in this way; there are even cooperative banks similar to our own credit unions.

Cooperatives were developed because serious problems with nationalization became apparent as various enterprises were expropriated by the state. To begin with, not all enterprises can be operated as well under a nationalized structure as in a less centralized system. The size and remoteness of the central government are major drawbacks. No matter how well intentioned it may be, the bureaucracy necessary to run a nationalized enterprise tends to be insensitive to consumers' needs and to the dynamics of the market itself.

The Indian Railway is one of the largest rail transportation systems in the world. It is owned and operated by the Indian government.

The political limitations of nationalization are perhaps even greater than its economic problems. When a large part of society's production, exchange, distribution, and employment is controlled by the government, the latter's involvement in the lives of individuals is greatly increased. Totalitarian states can be born of such enormous power. Any free society must be very cautious of centralized power. In addition, free people must be wary of placing all their productivity in the hands of government. To whom would they turn for settlement of economic disputes if all enterprises were owned by the state?

When socialization has been used, however, the cooperative has worked best with the middle to light industries. Retail sales, appliance manufacturing and servicing, and housing construction are examples of industries that have succeeded in a cooperative setting. Heavy industry and certain nationwide services are usually better socialized by the nationalization process. Basic industries such as weapons production, utilities, transportation, and communication are too vital and perhaps too big to work well under the cooperative structure. Some other industries, such as automobile manufacture, energy production, insurance, and metal production, may also be best suited to nationalization.

Socialist countries not only differ on the method of socializing the economy but also vary greatly in the degree to which their economies are socialized. Of all the socialist societies, only the communists saw total socialization as the ultimate goal. In the past three decades, however, even the communist states have begun to experiment with some limited forms of market economics. The country most resistant to change is North Korea, but now even it has been compelled by severe economic problems to modify some economic policies, if only slightly so far. In all other socialist countries, regardless of how long socialist governments have held power, large portions of the economy remain under private ownership. Non-Marxist socialists long ago concluded that some enterprises work poorly when they are not privately owned. Thus, they support socializing only those industries that function best under collective management, leaving the rest to the private sector. During the 1980s and 1990s several European economies denationalized many industries. With the advent of the "Great Recession," however, there may be a retreat from privatization. We must wait to see.

In most noncommunist socialist societies, as well as in capitalist countries, an important half-step is employed to protect the public against the excesses endemic in private enterprise. An economy principally motivated by private gain tends to encourage cutting corners. Increasingly, profits at the expense of decent wages and benefits, or at the expense of safe, well-made products, is virtually unavoidable in capitalist systems unless government oversight inhibits them. Thus, all modern economic systems regulate the economic behavior of capitalists. Minimum wage laws, industrial safety regulations, government inspection of food, workers' rights, fair competition practices, truth-in-advertising requirements, and so on, are standard features. There are always arguments about the exact nature of these laws and protections, but few question the wisdom of the existence of such safeguards. And, as we saw in Chapter 5, failing to adequately regulate important industries can be ruinous.

The Welfare State

Production, however, is not the central economic focus of socialist thinking. Much more important to the socialist is the distribution of the goods and services produced in the society.

To the capitalist, private property is the reward for individual effort and economic achievement. Consequently, wealthy people are treated with respect, implying that somehow they have accomplished something particularly virtuous. A value system that puts wealth on a pedestal is not likely to look on poverty with much understanding. The stigma of being poor or even only unemployed was very real during the 1920s, when unregulated capitalism was at its height. However, also during that decade, government economic policies were extraordinarily favorable to big business, and government regulation of the marketplace was virtually nonexistent. The result was catastrophic. The Great Depression of the 1930s saw a quarter of the workforce without jobs, long lines at soup kitchens, lives ruined, fortunes evaporated, families devastated, and futures truncated.

Dazed and disoriented, the American people were slow to realize that they were victims of an irresponsible economic system captained by people not necessarily devoted to the public interest but rather motivated by personal benefit. Once the blinders of the laissez-faire myth were lifted, the public viewed society in a more realistic way and capitalism was modified, becoming more sensitive to economic diversity.[1]

In the 1930s, President Franklin Delano Roosevelt (FDR) employed Keynesian economics techniques, introducing the **New Deal,** a massive reform program that injected enough socialism into the system to give capitalism a human face. Although the New Dealers stopped short of nationalizing more than a handful of industries, they vigorously regulated business and encouraged workers to organize unions and bargain collectively for better wages and benefits. The greatest attention, however, was given to creating the **welfare state** so that wealth might be more equitably distributed throughout society and individual suffering reduced. Following Europe, which had already developed the welfare state, FDR introduced programs in the United States in the 1930s that have become commonplace: Social Security, government price supports for agriculture, unemployment and workers' compensation, welfare programs, federal guarantees for housing loans, government insured savings deposits. Since the 1930s, the welfare state in this country has been expanded to include public health plans, job training, federal aid to education, public funding for small business opportunities, and so on.

---

[1]The "Great Recession" beginning in 2007, while not nearly as severe, was in many ways very similar to the Great Depression in that the public was lulled by a false belief that the market was self-correcting and could not become too badly distorted, and by the fact that unregulated businesspeople led us to disaster through incredibly irresponsible behavior. Yet, perhaps because the debacle in this century was not as severe as it was in the 1930s, the American people don't seem to have learned the lesson quite as well as their predecessors.

Although the United States is still far from a socialist country, the lessons of the Great Depression led the government to adopt some socialist policies in order to prevent a recurrence of the suffering encountered during the 1930s.[2] We were not alone in this attempt, however. Indeed, many countries preceded us and went far beyond the United States in developing policies that would redistribute wealth within the society. The communist countries tried to invoke total socialism, but their efforts have largely failed. More successful are the Western European countries, which have socialized banks, utilities, transportation, and some manufacturing while also developing extensive social welfare policies. Although programs vary from country to country, virtually every Western European country spends almost twice as much of its economic output as the United States on its social programs. Western European countries and Japan provide far more generous housing subsidies, parental leave plans, prenatal care, grants to the poor, public health protections, and unemployment benefits, as well as a plethora of other programs.

It should be noted here that the generally held American belief that capitalism is more efficient and cost effective than socialist welfare programs is far from universally true. Medicine is a good case in point. While the medical care in the United States is among the most advanced in the world, the system it uses to deliver medical care is by some important measures the worst among advanced economies. In 2005, the United States spent $5,267 per capita on health care, far higher than any other industrial country, each of which has national health programs.[3] (Switzerland, the next highest spender, paid $1,821 per capita.) Yet, as profits for private insurance companies, pharmaceutical corporations, and even hospitals have increased sharply, the United States, as compared with other industrial countries, has a higher infant mortality rate, the lowest rating for its children's health (it ranks forty-seventh in the world for deaths of children below five years old and the rate of women dying in childbirth has actually increased over the past twenty years), a shorter average life span for its citizens, and higher health care inflation (an 81 percent increase between 2000 and 2005). Furthermore, over 49 million people in the United States had no health insurance at all in 2010,[4] a circumstance duplicated in no other industrial society. (Incidentally, the United States also ranks at the bottom among industrial countries in safety and economic well-being of its children, according to a 2007 UN report.)

Regardless of the specific programs used, socialism is not always completely egalitarian. It tends to narrow the gap between the haves and the have-nots.

---

[2]Regrettably, some of these bitter lessons were ignored in the past decade, resulting in the Great Recession beginning in the United States in 2007 and sweeping across the world's economies.

[3]In 2010, Rush Limbaugh threatened he would move out of the United States if Obama's health care reform passed. Since every other advanced society enjoys a far more extensive national health care system than ours, one wonders where he intends to flee: Zaire?

[4]Even with Obama's health care plan, passed in 2010, millions of people are still expected to be without coverage in 2018, when it kicks in fully.

TABLE 8.1

Total Tax as % of Gross Domestic Product, 2008

Denmark	50.0%	Spain	37.3%
Sweden	49.7%	Portugal	37.0%
Belgium	46.8%	Russia	36.9%
France	46.1%	New Zealand	36.5%
Norway	43.6%	Luxembourg	36.4%
Austria	43.4%	Ireland	34.0%
Italy	42.6%	Canada	33.4%
Germany	40.6%	Australia	30.5%
Netherlands	39.5%	US	28.2%
UK	39.0%	Japan	27.4%

Source: Heritage Foundation

Yet, only the most extreme socialist wants to eliminate all differences in material status. Most socialists recognize that people are different: Some are more talented or hard-working than others and should be rewarded for their extra contributions. Still, they believe that all people have a right to a reasonably comfortable life. Consequently, they want to eliminate poverty. Extreme wealth is not necessarily incompatible with socialist ideals, however. Indeed, people with great wealth may be found in almost every socialist society.

Although Western Europe has successfully reduced poverty and its accompanying social anxiety, these gains have not been achieved without great costs. The tax rates in these societies are extremely high. Indeed, the United States, largely because it spends relatively little on social welfare programs, has the lowest tax rate as a percentage of gross domestic product of all industrial countries except Japan. (See Table 8.1.) Also, many European states are experiencing serious economic difficulties in maintaining their generous social welfare benefits and have trimmed them. No advanced society is likely to retrench enough to fall to the low level of benefits provided in the United States, however. The growing disparity in wealth among the citizens of nonsocialist states is simply not attractive to any, save societies like the United States that are wedded to notions of individualism and to the market system ideal.

The Socialist Intent

As explained earlier, the first two basic features of socialism (ownership of production and the welfare state) are mechanical in nature and are not necessarily related to each other. It is conceivable that a society could socialize many, or even all, of its major means of production and still avoid creating a welfare state. Although no state has yet adopted such a policy, it is theoretically possible. It is also possible for a government to establish a welfare state without, at the same time, socializing production. In fact, the United States has generally followed this policy since the Great Depression.

A third basic feature of socialism, the **socialist intent,** unlike the first two, is essential if the system is to be truly socialist. This is the goal of *setting people free from the condition of material dependence* that has held them captive since the beginning of time. It is the wish to liberate people from the fetters of poverty and to make resources available to all people with which they can improve themselves individually and collectively advance civilization. In short, the main focus of socialism is economic: improving the material well-being of most people in society because that will better the human condition.

Socialists look forward to a time when the productivity of society will have been increased to the point at which there is abundance for all. It is hoped that this happy state of affairs, impossible in earlier times, will bring about profound changes in people's conduct, attitudes, and beliefs. In previous eras, scarcity made it necessary for people to compete with one another. In the competition for goods, they treated each other inhumanely in order to survive. Forced into conflict with each other in order to make a living, people became trapped in a pattern of conduct that not only was harmful to them but also prevented them from developing their nobler aspects.

Now, however, for the first time, technology has created a condition in which people can produce enough to satisfy all their basic needs. As the general material conditions of society improve, the specific differences in material status among individuals will decrease. Since there will be plenty for all, traditional property values such as private ownership, the use of money, and the accumulation of luxuries by one class while others live in squalor will disappear. A new society will emerge, one in which citizens are on an equal footing with one another reducing class strife. Of course, only Marxist socialists argue that all conflict is caused by class differences. Yet, all socialists are convinced that materialism is a major feature in social and political relationships. Removing the cause of material anxieties, therefore, greatly improves social relationships.

Economic equalization is central to socialism and it will lead to democracy, socialists believe. Socialism is inherent in democracy, since it is to the individual economically what democracy is to the individual politically. The venerable British socialist and political scientist Harold Laski wrote, "Socialism is the logical conclusion of democracy." Taking an even more extreme stance, some socialists claim that democracy is *impossible* without socialism. Money, they reason, is a major source of political power. Thus, as Rousseau argued, economic systems that distribute wealth unevenly make political equality—democracy's most fundamental predicate—impossible.

By this time, the perceptive reader is probably wondering about the classification of such obviously undemocratic (in the sense of liberal democracy) systems as those of fascist, national socialist, or communist states. Clearly, these systems use socialist economic techniques such as nationalizing industries and creating the welfare state. Yet, each of these systems, in practice if not in theory, reduces human equality rather than increasing it. In each of these systems the society is highly stratified and popular government is barely a pretense, let alone a realistic goal. In fact, these systems appear to be socialist because they have some collectivist institutions, yet they fail the test because they do not aspire to socialism's essential component: the socialist intent. Rather than encouraging equality and democracy, these systems oppose the development of these concepts. They often claim to have egalitarian goals, but in fact, they are simply trying to replace old ruling classes with new ones, denying basic human equality in the process. They are, as Michael Harrington wrote, *antisocialist socialisms*. By contrast, the socialist intent asks individuals to produce as much as they can and, in the spirit of social consciousness, to share their product with the society at large. By this means, it is assumed, each will get the greatest benefit, thereby creating the best possible life for all.

THE HISTORY OF SOCIALISM

From the French Revolution to Marx

The stirrings of socialism began shortly before the French Revolution. Jean Jacques Rousseau, although not a socialist, developed several ideas that became the foundation of the new ideology. Rousseau's concept of the **organic state** is basic to the ideology of socialism. Rousseau viewed people as individual parts of a holistic society. So complete was the union of individuals with the group that the value of their accomplishments would be measured by the amount of benefit the society derived from them.

Rousseau's ideas deeply influenced history's first socialist, **François-Noël Babeuf** (1760–1797), who lived during the early stages of the French Revolution. A visionary, Babeuf recognized that the revolution would fall short of its radical goals of "Liberty, Equality, and Fraternity" (a phrase taken from Rousseau's writing). Accordingly, Babeuf called for yet another revolution, one that would create social justice for the common person. Babeuf, however, did not live long enough to make more than a momentary impact on the left wing of the French revolutionaries. Falling afoul of less radical leaders in France, he went to the guillotine in 1797 at the age of thirty-seven.

After Babeuf, socialism can be divided into two basic types. **Humanitarian socialism** (the Utopians, Revisionists, and Fabians) is the older of the two. It is based on the conviction that human morality demands that people share in the work and in consuming the fruits of labor. It is thought perverse to allow some people to prosper while others suffer in a society that produces enough for all. Helen Keller, the remarkable deaf mute who, with the help of the resources of a well-to-do family, overcame her limitations, wrote in her memoirs this poignant statement reflecting humanitarian socialism:

I had once believed that we were all masters of our fate—that we could mould our lives into any form we pleased. . . . I had overcome deafness and blindness sufficiently to be happy, and I supposed that anyone could come out victorious if he threw himself valiantly into life's struggle. But as I went more and more about the country I learned that I had spoken with assurance on a subject I knew little about. I forgot that I owed my success partly to the advantages of my birth and environment. . . . Now, however, I learned that the power to rise in the world is not within the reach of everyone.[5]

"Scientific" socialism,[6] by contrast, is founded on the Marxist notion that human social evolution (history) is governed by certain objective laws that are inexorably leading humankind to socialism. (See Figure 8.1.)

Utopian Socialism[7]   After Babeuf's death the violent approach to socialism he developed became dormant, awaiting a new generation of leftist thinkers. As the time line in Figure 8.1 illustrates, the momentum passed to a far less radical group. The **utopian socialist** movement developed from a sincere desire for equity within society and from genuine compassion for the masses at the bottom of the social structure. Members of this movement were among the first to appreciate the social implications of the Industrial Revolution. For the first time, they concluded, society would be able to produce enough for *all* to have enough. This fortunate circumstance confronted them with a moral dilemma, however. "If it is possible to feed, house, and clothe everyone, thus satisfying the most basic human needs, is it moral not to do so?" Predictably, they argued that lavishing wealth on a few while most others languished in squalor was, indeed, immoral. Furthermore, holding that people were both rational and moral creatures by nature, the utopians believed that people would, with some encouragement, come to understand that socialism was the only moral socioeconomic system. For the moment, however, the value of egalitarianism was obscure to most people, they thought, because no example of an egalitarian society existed to prove how productive and blissful such an arrangement could be. Consequently, the utopians decided to create small local communal colonies, believing such settlements would become prototypes of the new social order.

Much more important to the socialist movement than the communal experiments was that the utopians were the first to mobilize the working class. Asserting the **labor theory of value**, they claimed that only workers create

---

[5]Helen Keller, *Midstream: My Later Life* (New York: Greenwood, 1968), p. 156.

[6]The term *scientific* is used here in the nineteenth-century sense of the word. Today we have a very rigorous notion about what science is, but until the twentieth century, this was not the case. Before then, almost anything that relied on an empirical rather than metaphysical base was considered scientific. For example, in the eighteenth century, clock makers, because their field depended on numbers and calibrations, were accepted as members in the British Academy of Sciences.

[7]The word *utopia* is taken from Sir Thomas More's philosophical romance *Utopia,* written in 1514–1516. Grounded in the philosophy of Plato and the romantic accounts of travelers like Amerigo Vespucci, More's work featured an ideal state where private property was abolished.

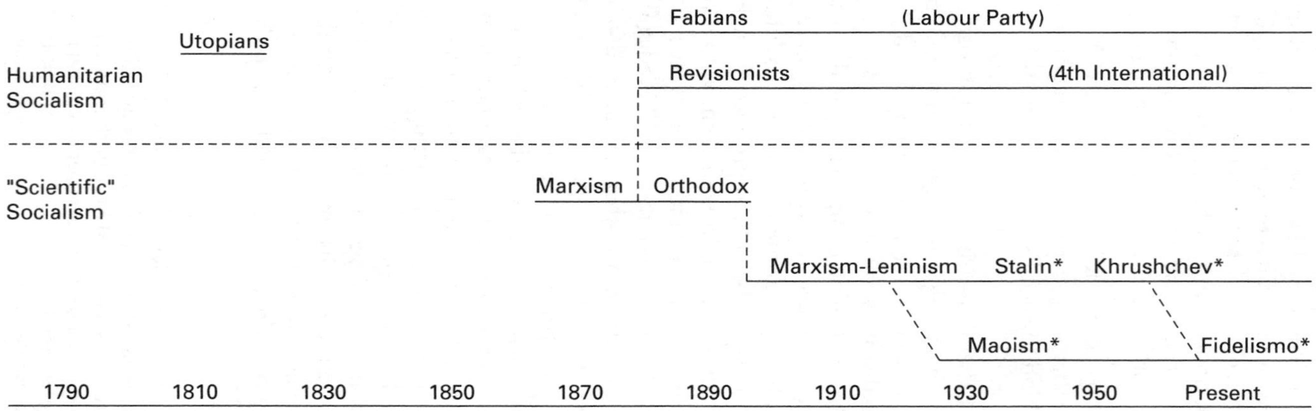

FIGURE 8.1

Time line of the socialist movement. Dates are approximate.

* To be discussed in Chapter 9.

Utopians

Humanitarian
Socialism

"Scientific"
Socialism

Marxism | Orthodox

Fabians   (Labour Party)

Revisionists   (4th International)

Marxism-Leninism   Stalin*   Khrushchev*

Maoism*

Fidelismo*

1790 1810 1830 1850 1870 1890 1910 1930 1950 Present

wealth; therefore, society should adjust its social, economic, and political systems to prevent unequal distribution of wealth. Utopian support of the worker against the owner gave an important boost to the development of trade unionism by giving it an economic doctrine and moral justification.

The utopian socialist movement originated with the help of two unlikely, almost unwilling, founders and a third who was more deliberate: Saint-Simon, Owen, and Fourier. Ignoring Babeuf, some people consider **Claude Henri Saint-Simon** (1760–1825) the founder of French socialism. A soldier in the French Army sent to help the fledgling United States in its war for independence from England and, later, a successful banker, Saint-Simon is perhaps more socialist in the reading than in the writing. His followers read into his works a socialist intent that he may not have meant to convey. Besides his wish for mutual human kindness and compassion, Saint-Simon's strongest socialist arguments were his criticisms of capitalism. Capitalism, he concluded, was wasteful because it pitted people against each other and imposed poverty on many to produce wealth for a few. Moreover, he contended that capitalists made profits far beyond their own productivity, a fact Saint-Simon despised, thereby making himself popular with the French working class.

As a partial solution for the evils he saw in the capitalist system, Saint-Simon proposed a centralized banking system that would make social investments. He also called for the elimination of property inheritance and supported universal education. His ideas did not become generally known until after this desperately unhappy eccentric's suicide, however, when a cult of admiring followers lionized him and probably credited him with beliefs he did not actually hold.

An equally enigmatic figure is the second founder of utopian socialism, **Robert Owen** (1771–1858). A self-made industrialist, Owen was basically a conservative man who ardently supported Britain's social, political, and economic institutions. A talented administrator, he had risen from the position of clerk to that of owner of a textile mill by his mid-twenties. He, however, was concerned about the wretched condition of his employees and became associated with **Jeremy Bentham** and other social reformers of the day.

Owen was strongly opposed to "dole" programs in which people were simply given money by the government or by charities. However, he realized that capitalism had to be tempered by concern for the basic humanity of people and that it could destroy human dignity when left unchecked. Further, he was convinced that exploitation of the worker was ultimately unprofitable and that everyone would be better off if the working environment were improved.

Acting on these convictions, Owen reformed the management policies of his New Lanark, England mill. By raising wages, encouraging trade unionism, rejecting the exploitation of women and children, encouraging universal education, and creating a company store where employees could buy goods at reduced rates, he achieved remarkable results. In less than five years, production at New Lanark had risen markedly, the workers at the mill were far better off than workers anywhere else in England, and Owen had made a fortune. This happy circumstance proved, to Owen's satisfaction, that, as Marx was later to contend, character was conditioned by the economic and social environment. Bad working conditions were not only immoral but simply bad business, unnecessarily depressing the workers and lowering profits as well.

Encouraged by his early success, Owen retired from his business enterprises at the age of fifty-eight and dedicated himself to popularizing and testing his controversial ideas. Traveling widely on speaking tours, he was even well received by the U.S. Congress. He opposed the imposition of *socialism* (a term he coined) on people by government and warned that people themselves had to be prepared to adopt it before it could be successful. However, he believed the worst excesses of capitalism had to be curbed so that the worker would not be exploited. Owen also opposed nationalization of industries, though he favored producer cooperatives.

Like Saint-Simon, Owen was perhaps more a liberal capitalist than a true socialist. Still, he is considered the founder of British socialism, and his moderate approach set the tone for many of England's social reforms. Like most other utopian socialists, Owen was convinced that communal living was the wave of the future and that a few successful examples would prove the attractiveness of this lifestyle. So convinced was he that he invested several years of effort and his entire fortune in unsuccessful attempts to establish communes. Most noted was the effort at New Harmony, Indiana (1825–1828). A third influential utopian socialist, **Charles Fourier** (1772–1837), was not only a critic of capitalist economics, but he also became a vocal opponent of traditional institutions such as religion, marriage, and the family. Perhaps his most important criticism centered on the structure of society under capitalism. Objecting to the nation-state, Fourier envisioned a society broken up into thousands of small, politically independent, self-sustaining communal entities. These communities might associate with one another in a type of confederacy in which the fundamental independence of each unit remained unchanged. The government of the communes was to be democratic, the labor and its products being shared equally by all the members. In such a simple setting, Fourier believed, life would be pleasant and work would become an enjoyable activity in which all would take part willingly.

Fourier's influence was significant. Several communes based on his model were started, but each failed and was abandoned. Still, Fourier's thought influenced many well-known socialists: Charles Dana, Horace Greeley, Nathaniel Hawthorne, and George Ripley were among his American disciples. Fourier also impressed later thinkers such as Proudhon and Marx, and his theories influenced the collectivization of farms in the Soviet Union.

Because it was a new country when utopianism became popular, the United States was often the scene of communal experiments. Interestingly, America was regarded as the land of opportunity and hope by socialists as well as capitalists. Here, it was thought, a new society could be founded, one that was insulated from the stratification and prejudices of the old world. Although these communal experiments failed, several attained an importance beyond their role as socialist experiments. Intellectual leaders were often drawn to these societies. Important literary, technological, and scientific works were sometimes inspired by them, especially by Brook Farm in Massachusetts and by Owen's New Harmony. Similarly, the experimental commune at Oneida, New York, became the site of America's largest flatware producer after the commune collapsed. Even so, the failure of the communes led to a general disillusionment with the theories on which they were based, and popular attention soon turned from utopianism to more practical approaches.

MARXISM

Important as the utopians were to the development of socialism, their influence is largely limited to their own and the following generation. Far more important to socialist theory was **Karl Marx** (1818–1883). Prior to Marx, though socialist theories differed greatly in details and structure, the basis of the proposed socialist societies had been the humanitarian hope that people would treat each other better as their material conditions improved. Furthermore, the development of socialism in any particular society was not seen as inevitable. Rather, socialism was a practice that had to be chosen by the people it was to serve. Though Marx was a compassionate person and certainly not an opponent of free choice, his conclusions were not based on a humanitarian desire for a better life. His theory postulates certain "laws" of human motivation and conduct that can be scientifically understood, and that make socialism an inevitable product of human historical development. Though his theory was a radical departure from the views of his predecessors, his intellect and scholarship were so superior to theirs that he captivated the socialist movement until his death in 1883.

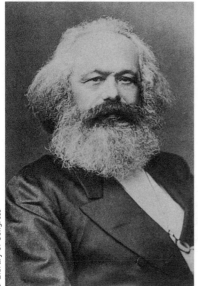

By Marx's time, the naiveté of utopianism had discredited socialism in the minds of most Europeans. Significantly, his theories rescued it from oblivion, transforming it into an idea that captivated the imaginations of millions of people. Marx was also responsible for adding to the meaning of communism. In his introduction to the *Communist Manifesto*, A. J. P. Taylor tells us that Marx used the word *communism* not as a descriptive term but as a polemic intended to arouse people. It excited some and frightened others. Utopian idealism, on the other hand, had led Europeans to regard *socialism* with indifference, because

I Karl Marx (1818-1883)

it was impossibly visionary and idealistic. Consequently, although Marx espoused *socialism,* that is, a national collectivized economy, he used the word *communist* for the title of his call to revolution, hoping that the substitute term would inflame the political passions of his audience. For that reason, "communism" has come to be associated with Marxist socialism.

Born in Trier, Germany, to prosperous Jewish parents in 1818, Marx earned his Ph.D. in philosophy at the University of Jena. Following his graduation, however, his radical political ideas frightened Europe's governments during this reactionary, post-Napoleonic era, resulting in his being forced out of one European country after another between 1844 and 1848. Along the way, he befriended **Friedrich Engels** (1820–1895), the son of a wealthy Prussian industrialist family. Engels became Marx's lifelong collaborator and benefactor.

Meanwhile, the political situation in Europe became more repressive as various leftist groups demanded political reforms of the intransigent ruling monarchies. Finally, rebellions broke out across the continent in 1848. Thinking that the proletarian revolution they awaited was at hand, Marx and other socialists belonging to the Communist League feared that the opportunity might be wasted for want of a doctrine directing the revolutionaries. Accordingly, Marx wrote the *Communist Manifesto* in Belgium, a brief essay setting forth the ideology of the impending revolution. It contains a brief sketch of Marx's ideas and includes several important thoughts that Marx adapted from the work of his friend Engels.

As the rebellions were suppressed one after the other, Marx took refuge in England in 1849. There he settled into a scholarly life, spending most of his time in the British Museum researching and writing his major work, *Das Kapital.* Much more the scholar than the practical politician, Marx brooded over the years as the proletarian conflagration he anticipated failed to materialize. Yet, he remained confident of the acuity of his theory, and his intellectual prowess was so great that he dominated the socialist movement throughout his life. It was only after his death that major variations of his thought attracted substantial followings among socialists.

MARX AND CAPITALISM

Whatever the ultimate validity of his theories, Marx has been shown by history to have erred in a number of important respects. Our understanding of Marx will be enhanced if we consider a few of his greatest mistakes before studying his theories.

Marx firmly believed that his generation came at the very end of the capitalist era, and he fully expected the socialist revolution to occur at any moment. Given the despicable conditions of the working class during his life, Marx can be forgiven for expecting that the masses would rise up to cast off their chains should things continue to deteriorate. Perhaps they would have done so had capitalists been as blind and insensitive as Marx imagined. He was quite wrong, however, in his estimation of both the productivity of capitalism and of its capacity to adapt to threatening conditions. In fact, industrialization organized by capitalism far outproduced even the wildest expectations of its nineteenth-century enthusiasts and the Western capitalists grudgingly responded to proletarian demands with policies that shared with the worker enough of the newly created wealth to put off a disastrous conflagration.

As it turned out, Marx was witnessing the beginning of the capitalist era rather than its end. Premechanized economies are usually incapable of producing enough to satisfy all the economic needs of their people. Thus, productivity usually falls below the level we shall call *subsistence*. In these conditions, scarcity is a fact of life, causing anxiety. To escape depravity, a few people in such societies manage to become wealthy by accumulating enough, or more than enough, to satisfy their needs, thus leaving even less to be consumed by the already hard-pressed masses. Thus, the portion of production left for ordinary people to consume falls even farther below subsistence, aggravating the suffering of the majority.

Industrialization of an economy can eventually increase productivity, but first money must be found to buy the factories, resources, and machines. Where does the money come from? Some undoubtedly comes from the coffers of the wealthy, but history knows of no wealthy class impoverishing *itself* to increase production. Instead the wealthy have consistently demanded sacrifices from the poor to pay for most technological advances. So, wages are suppressed and working conditions decline, thus creating capital to invest in mechanization. Consequently, if the masses are already suffering because they must consume at less than the subsistence level and are required to sacrifice even more to create enough capital for industrialization, their conditions of life and work must be terrible indeed.

Such sacrifices do not come voluntarily. To enforce these deficits for the workers, the owners of production used the powers of government, forcing workers to toil for meager wages under terrible conditions. Labor unions were suppressed; strikes were broken by thugs, the police, or the army; and social welfare benefits were nonexistent. Blatant collusion between government and the owners of production occurred in every society that industrialized, including England and the United States. Brutal force had to be used to induce the already suffering workers to make the additional sacrifices they would not otherwise make voluntarily. It can be taken as a rule that, in the earliest stages of industrialization, the living conditions of ordinary people decline dramatically as capital is squeezed from the worker.

This stage of the Industrial Revolution—its most exploitative period—was witnessed by Marx and by Dickens. Marx's error was not in decrying these conditions but rather in concluding that the workers' circumstances would continue to degenerate rather than eventually improve. What actually did occur is, with the forced increase of capital, production began to climb. Marx anticipated that, driven by the need to increase profits, capitalists would intensify exploitation of the workers until the latter could no longer stand their misery: Revolution would then erupt. This bleak prediction has not come to pass in the West. Industrial productivity grew to such an extent that it brought huge profits to the owners and, at the same time, vastly improved living and working conditions for the common people. Perhaps sensing that Marx was indeed correct in predicting their doom if they did not provide improved conditions for the workers, the capitalists have slowly accepted collective bargaining, fringe-benefit packages, wage increases, and social protection programs. Each of these benefits, however, followed great struggles by workers for their rights. Interestingly, with the recent decline of the labor unions and the rise of conservativism, American workers are again experiencing a severe reduction in real wages and debilitating loss of benefits, even as corporate profits climb and executive compensation reaches obscene levels.

Yet, contrary to Marx's predictions, capitalism has not engineered its own doom. Industrialization is hugely more productive than Marx, or anyone else in the nineteenth century, could predict. Furthermore, capitalism was far more flexible and pragmatic than Marx anticipated, thus far surviving long beyond the centennial of his death. Although it has received some very serious blows, the worst of which were the rise of fascism and the Great Depression, capitalism continues, albeit in modified form, while lately, socialism has been in retreat. But, one might ponder the continued efficacy of American capitalism should the recent trends of wealth concentrating in the hands of the very few while the middle class emaciates and the multitudes experience increasing impoverishment. However, even if Marx's prediction of capitalism burning itself out is ultimately to be prescient, his confidence that socialism must ultimately follow remains suspect since his arguments for the inevitability of socialism's succession are far less compelling.

THE BASIC PRINCIPLES OF MARXISM

The ideas of Karl Marx were fostered by three major factors characterizing nineteenth-century Europe. First, the Industrial Revolution had created previously unimagined levels of production, even as the methods of producing and distributing wealth saw a tiny number of people enjoying sumptuous lives while the vast majority of people toiled and lived in inhumane conditions. Workers left their poor but relatively wholesome lives in the countryside only to find themselves confronted by the humiliation of depersonalized sweatshops surrounded by utterly squalid urban slums.

Second, with the 1815 defeat of Napoleon, Europe's monarchs, hoping to preserve their antiquated privileges, inflicted on their subjects the most repressive political conditions experienced up to that time. They tried to return Europe to control of the ancient regimes, ignoring the popular goals of the French Revolution. Third, previous advances in science fostered in the nineteenth century's intellectuals an exaggerated confidence that science would lead to the solution of all human problems. Sir Isaac Newton (1642–1727) and Charles Darwin (1809–1882) had developed explanations of the laws governing the physical universe and biological development, thus giving rational explanations for things that previously could be explained only by fables, myths, and fairy tales. Reveling in this liberation from the darkness of ignorance, many nineteenth-century thinkers, including Jeremy Bentham, Herbert Spencer, and Sigmund Freud, sought to discover the laws governing human behavior, and to use that knowledge to improve political and social conditions. Karl Marx, chafing under the heavy heel of reactionary monarchical oppression, and bitterly offended by the greed and exploitation he saw in capitalism, became a leading figure among these "social scientists."

Wretched as the social and political conditions had become, Marx was still optimistic about the future of humanity. He saw people in historical terms. Individuals, he believed, were destined for freedom and creativity but had been prevented from developing completely because they were slaves to their own basic needs. Before the Industrial Revolution, human productivity had not been great enough to provide a sufficient supply of the necessities of life to free people from **compulsive toil** (a term coined by Marx to express Locke's concept of the necessity to work incessantly just to survive). With the emergence of industrialization, people became—for the first time—productive enough to provide an abundance of goods. They could now devote more time to the development of their own humanity. Yet capitalism, the economic system used to industrialize Europe, failed to distribute its abundance fairly. Indeed, Marx saw that it tended to take away from the workers more and more of the products they created, giving them instead to the capitalist, a non-worker who exploited the toilers.

The irony of the dilemma Marx witnessed is clear: For the first time in history, humanity had created means to produce enough for all people, potentially liberating them from compulsive toil, so that they might now enjoy the spare time necessary to refine their humanity—to be free, in other words. Yet, what nature had denied people for millennia was now being withheld from them by human-made economic, social, and political institutions. Clearly, in Marx's view, capitalism was to be appreciated for its productivity, but it was also to be despised for its oppression, and must be abandoned for a more equitable system.

Marxist Theory of Social Structure

A major assumption in Marxism is **economic determinism.** On this premise Marx built the rest of his theory. Economic determinism suggests that the primary human motivation is economic. "It is not the consciousness of men that determines their existence," Marx argues, "but their social existence that determines their consciousness"; that is, what we value and what we do politically is determined by our economic circumstances. It stands to reason, therefore, that people in similar economic circumstances will have much in common.

This idea is not unique to Marx. The political effects of economics were widely understood among the intellectual community. Even James Madison proceeded from a similar assumption about human motivation. Consider this statement from *The Federalist* (no. 10):

> But the most common and durable source of factions (political adversaries) has been the various and unequal distribution of property. Those who hold and those who are without property have ever formed distinct interests in society. Those who are creditors and those who are debtors, fall under a like discrimination. A landed interest, a manufacturing interest, a monied interest, with many lesser interests, grow up of necessity in civilized nations, and divide them into different *classes, actuated by different sentiments and views.* (Emphasis added.)

As a matter of fact, economic determinism has gained general currency in the world today, with most people believing that economics plays an important part in determining political behavior. In this respect at least, Glenn Tinder posits that we are all now Marxists.[8]

Marx saw all societies as composed of two basic parts: the **foundation** and the **superstructure**. The foundation of any society, according to this theory, is material. In other words, the economic system is at the base of the society. Marx further divided the economy into two basic factors: the means of production and the relations of production. The *means of production* are the resources and technology at the disposal of a particular society, and their interrelationship determines the kind of economic system the society enjoys. The *relations of production* (or social classes) are determined by the affiliation between human beings in the society and the means of production. The owners of the means of production enjoy the most beneficial position in the economy and thus become members of the most influential social group—the ruling class. (The acuity of this part of Marx's proposition becomes clear if one tries to imagine a wealthy class that does not have great influence in society.) Thus, in a pastoral society the ruling group would be those who own the most livestock; in an agrarian society the greatest landowners would dominate; and in an industrial society the capitalist class rules.

The foundation of society (the economic and social class systems) determines the nature of society's superstructure, which rests upon the foundation. The superstructure is composed of all nonmaterial institutions in the society, and each is arranged in a way that suits the ruling class. Included in the superstructure are values, ideology, government, education, law, religion, art, and so forth. (See Figure 8.2.) *The function of the superstructure is to assure the rulers continued dominance and to keep the ruled in their place.*

Marx conceived of government as a tool of class oppression that manipulated all the cultural elements in the society to the advantage of those who controlled the economy. "Political power, properly so called," he wrote, "is merely organized power of one class for oppressing another." Marx called religion "the opiate of the people" because he believed that it drugged them, numbing their senses and disposing them to put up with their wretched

---

[8]Glenn Tinder, *Political Thinking*, 4th ed. (Boston: Little Brown, 1986), p. 184.

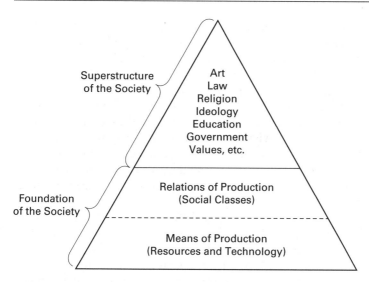

FIGURE 8.2
Marxian abstract of society's structure.

existence on earth so that they would be rewarded in a "mythical" afterlife. The aphorism "That's the cross I have to bear" illustrates the attitude to which Marx objected. He wanted people to abandon the rationalizations with which they had been programmed by their rulers. When they did, they would become aware of their plight, and take the first step toward revolution and freedom.

Extrapolating, the principles of economic determinism, Marx suggested that two societies with similar economic systems would develop similar superstructures (similar political and social systems). For example, societies with feudal economic bases (that is, agrarian societies in which the land is owned by a tiny elite and the bulk of the population works the land of the great nobles) will develop similar social and political institutions in their superstructures. Their political systems include monarchies supported by a powerful aristocratic class of landowners. The values, laws, ideologies, and educational systems tend to justify these political and economic systems. The dominant religion tends to be structured in a hierarchical fashion similar to the structure of the Catholic Church, and the Church also acts to support the system.

On the other hand, according to Marx, capitalistic systems (those whose economies are based on money and industrial production controlled by a small elite) evolve different institutions in their superstructures. Representative democracies give the illusion of popular control, but the governments are actually captained by the moguls who own the means of production. The values, laws, ideologies, and educational systems encourage sympathetic public attitudes toward these political and economic systems. Protestantism advanced individualistic and egalitarian doctrines, and it was free of the Catholic bias against usury and commerce. Further, espousing the ethic that hard work and frugality result in individual progress, social good, and even (perhaps) eternal reward, Protestantism anointed moneymaking with moral justifications and would therefore replace Catholicism as the dominant creed during the capitalist era.

Although it is certainly not difficult to find circumstances that contradict Marx's views about how economics predisposes society, one would be remiss not to recognize that indeed there is much to be learned from this analysis. It is true, for example, that the areas which developed extensive capitalist systems—England, Holland, Switzerland, northern Germany, Scandinavia, and the United States—also accepted Protestantism as the dominant religious form. Even in Catholic France, which also built a substantial industrial base, the Huguenots (French Protestants) own a disproportionately large percentage of the capital wealth.

It is also true that societies make concerted efforts to socialize their citizens. That is, they take great pains to inculcate in their people the dominant values and norms of society and these attitudes invariably accrue to the benefit of the people who control the system. In the United States, for example, American Government is a required course in most states at the elementary, high school, and college levels. Why is this subject thought to be so important? Other than creating jobs for political scientists (your author included), society assumes democracy depends on a well-informed citizenry; thus the requirement. Yet, these courses (especially in the lower grades) do more than simply inform students. Great effort is expended to develop a positive attitude among students about their system of government thus illustrating a conscious attempt by society's leaders to instill in each generation the values that society espouses.

Marxist Historical Theory

One need not be a Marxist to believe in economic determinism. Indeed, as Tinder tells us, all modern people do, to one extent or another, though few rely on it to the extent Marx did. However, one must believe in economic determinism to be a Marxist since it is fundamental to the ideology. However, **dialectic materialism** is even more fundamental to Marxism; indeed, it *is* Marxism. Consequently, anyone who accepts dialectic materialism is, by definition, a Marxist. It is a theory of history and it is the basis for the belief by his followers that Marx created a "scientific" theory of socialism.

The Dialectic   The concept of the **dialectic** progress reaches back to the ancient Greeks. This belief suggests that progress is achieved by the tension created by competing phenomena. This creative tension results in improvement, or so the theory goes. The application of the dialectic dynamic to historical progress was first made by **Georg Hegel** (1770–1831), one of the most influential political philosophers of modern times. Hegel developed a theory of history in which change, which he believed was motivated by dialectic conflict, was the central theme. He suggested that any reality is two things. It is itself, and it is part of what it is becoming. Thus, the only consistency Hegel saw was change itself.

Hegel thought in this process of change brought on by struggle, no truth was ever lost, since today's reality would become part of a more perfect truth tomorrow.

To better understand Hegel's theory, let us consider the following example. We will call the existing state of affairs the *thesis*. Eventually, any thesis will be challenged by a new idea, which we will call the *antithesis*. A conflict between the thesis and the antithesis will follow; the *dialectic process*. The result of this conflict will, according to Hegel, be a *synthesis* of all the good parts of the theses and of the antitheses. Then the synthesis becomes the new thesis to which another antithesis eventually develops. Struggle between them ensues, and a new synthesis, and eventually a new thesis evolve, and the process begins again. The negative aspects of the thesis and antithesis are destroyed in the dialectic process. This, Hegel called the "negation of the negative." Thus, Hegel saw history as inevitably progressive, with each new era an improvement over the last. And he expected the dialectic to continue refining and improving human institutions until the society reached perfection. (See Figure 8.3.)

Dialectic Materialism   Marx agreed with Hegel that humanity would eventually reach the end of the process of change. In other words, both Hegel and Marx were idealists, each believing that people could develop a perfect social and political existence. However, Marx did not accept Hegel's version of the dialectic but changed it to suit his own view of historical progress. Hegel had argued that the dialectic, or the struggle between the thesis and the antithesis, was actually guided by the will of God and resulted in spiritually inspired changes in the earthly social or political environment. Marx, it is said, stood Hegelianism on its head by suggesting the opposite. Citing economic determinism, Marx claimed that the dialectic was a conflict among worldly interests—social classes, to be

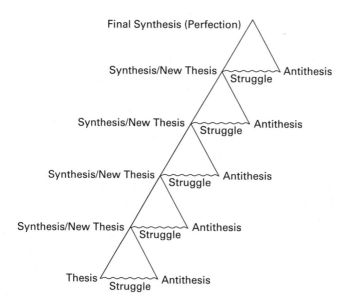

Final Synthesis (Perfection)

Synthesis/New Thesis — Antithesis
Struggle

Synthesis/New Thesis — Antithesis
Struggle

Synthesis/New Thesis — Antithesis
Struggle

Synthesis/New Thesis — Antithesis
Struggle

Thesis — Antithesis
Struggle

FIGURE 8.3
Hegelian dialectic.

exact. *Materialism,* not *spiritualism,* inspired the dialectic, according to Marx. You will recall that in Marxist theory society's superstructures are designed to keep things unchanged, thus serving best the interests of the ruling/ownership class. Yet, Marx pointed out that society's foundation inexorably changes, albeit gradually, eventually causing transformation of the economic system and the social class structure. As a new economy evolves, it becomes dominated by those who own it. Inevitably, according to Marx, the newly emerged dominant class serves as an antithesis or challenge to society's old dominant class. Struggle between these antagonistic classes—the dialectic—motivates historical change and progress.

Marx, therefore, believed that human conflict was caused by social class differences. In addition, he held that the struggle occurring at the end of one historical era and leading to the dawn of a new one was a struggle between opposing social classes. Further, he believed that humanity had passed through four historical stages and was about to enter its fifth and final era. Each historical era was characterized by a unique economic system, leading to a specific political system (superstructure).

The first era of human history, Marx believed, was based on *primitive communism.* People were unorganized and unsophisticated during this age. There was no occupational specialization or division of labor. Every person worked at producing, and people necessarily shared their produce with one another in order to survive. The antithesis to this system developed as people began to specialize in the production of certain goods. This **division of labor** resulted in more abundant and better-quality goods, but it also caused a major division within society. As people focused on producing their specialty, the original collectivism of society was lost. The spears an artisan produced became his spears, and he traded them for products that other people produced. Thus, in Lockean fashion, *private property* was born, but with it the nemeses of humankind. Society tended to value various objects differently, and the value of the individual became equated with the things he or she owned. This fateful differentiation resulted in the beginnings of a class structure that created strife within the society. This strife led to a new era. As the members of a tribe began to differentiate among themselves, they also began to develop prejudices against other tribes. Eventually, after much strife, a new order was born because one tribe, or group of people, came to dominate others. The dominant people forced the dominated people into servitude. Hence, *slavery* became the basis of the economic system in the next era.

Empire, one nation of people governing another, became the dominant political system based on a foundation of slavery. The antithesis to the era of slavery and empire was the challenge from the barbarian hordes. When the barbarians finally prevailed over the empire, a new political-economic system emerged, called *feudalism.* Feudalism was a system in which a landed aristocracy provided police and military protection to the peasants, who soon became *serfs* (people legally bound to the land—"land slaves") and farmed the nobles' lands. Since feudalism depended on a large number of self-sufficient manors, trade was almost completely stopped for a time. Gradually, the stability provided by the nobles and the demand for luxury items stimulated a rebirth of trade. The aristocrats, however, usually looked down on commerce, so trade and its profits were left to a new class, the **bourgeoisie**.[9]

The bourgeoisie antithesis grew in strength until it finally toppled the feudal aristocracies in a series of revolutions; the English Revolution in the 1640s and the American and French upheavals of the late eighteenth century are among the earliest and best-known examples. The new era initiated by those revolutions featured capitalism as its economic system. Marx called the new political systems *bourgeois democracies*. The term *democracy* was given to these political systems because, as Marx explained, there was a pretense of popular government through legislative representation; in reality, however, the capitalists always controlled the system.

Capitalism fostered factory workers, the **proletariat** (or "wage slaves"), a class that would act as the antithesis in the fourth historical era. Marx believed that the tension between the two classes would intensify into a new, and this time final, dialectic struggle. Capitalism had increased human productivity to the point at which all basic material needs could be satisfied. Nevertheless, it was exploitative in nature, so that the goods produced were not equally distributed; in fact, the reverse was true. Marx assumed that the victory of the proletariat was inevitable; it would be a victory of the exploited over the exploiter. He also believed that the proletariat itself would not be exploitative because it would have evolved a socialist mentality. If all other classes were eliminated, the source of all human strife would disappear and a new, classless society holding its goods in common would emerge. In this socialist society all people would find peace and happiness. (See Figure 8.4.)

Marx, however, spent most of his time analyzing capitalism rather than discussing socialism; consequently, his theory is very hazy in places. For instance, he never described the communist utopia in detail. He did say that it was to be democratic, but, as we have already learned, that could mean any number of things. Practically the only specific he mentioned about the utopia was that its economic system would be totally socialist. In other words, in the new society there would be absolutely no private property except for personal effects. Marx is also vague about what part he expected the peasantry to play in the final revolution. This question is vital to students of Marxism because they note that, without exception, the countries that developed Marxist systems as a result of indigenous political movements (for example, Russia, Yugoslavia, China, North Korea, Vietnam, and Cuba) had populations consisting largely

---

[9]*Bourgeoisie* is a French term translated as "middle class" in English, but care must be taken not to think of the middle class as being between the rich and poor. Marx meant the word as it is defined in French: the educated, professionals, wealthy merchants, and tradespersons who developed as commerce increased.

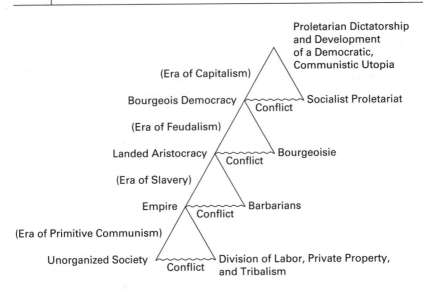

FIGURE 8.4
Marxian dialectic.

of peasants.[10] Vladimir Lenin and Mao Zedong, as we will see in Chapter 9, filled in some of the details of peasant participation in the building of socialism. They also answered many other crucial questions about the practical application of Marxist theory.

Marxist Economic Theory

Marx studied capitalism and the ideas of Locke, Smith, Ricardo, Malthus, and others very carefully, analyzing them perceptively in *Das Kapital*. In this work, he concludes that "capitalism has within it the seeds of its own destruction." In short, Marx believed that the fall of capitalism was inevitable and that it would lead to socialism.

The Theory of Work Marx, like John Locke, believed that work could be the way in which people might express their creativity. Indeed, both men believed that work is the process through which people develop their humanity and fulfill themselves. By interacting with nature in what is termed labor, individuals develop and change their own character. The essence of human beings,

---

[10]You will remember the socialist dilemma: *socialism is actually a rich man's sport.* Only wealthy countries produce enough so that, if shared adequately, the majority will see a marked improvement in their material lives. The rub comes from the fact that in wealthy countries the standard of living of most people is sufficiently high to make socialism unattractive. Thus, it is usually only in poor countries that the notion of equalizing the wealth enjoys much currency. Yet, to spread the wealth equally in an underdeveloped country is only to make everyone equally poor.

therefore, becomes closely related to their work. To Marx work was a form of "self-creation." Describing the laboring process, Marx wrote, "Man is constantly developing and changing—creating his own nature." In other words, the product of our labor is part of us, and something of us is in the things we produce through work. This attitude might appear naive at first glance, yet which of us has not felt great satisfaction and a closer relationship with objects we have made ourselves?

The Theory of Self-Alienation Marx's theory of work and his attitude toward capitalism led him to his theory of human **self-alienation**. He believed that workers became alienated from themselves because of three exploitative features of capitalism. First, since work can be a form of "self-creativity," it should be enjoyable, Marx reasoned. Yet, because the capitalists squeeze every possible cent of profit from the workers, they make the conditions of work intolerable. Consequently, instead of enjoying work or the act of self-creation, the members of the proletariat grow to hate the very process by which they could refine their own natures. Consequently, they become alienated from a part of their own selves. Second, Marx believed that capitalists *must* exploit the workers in order to produce a profit. The capitalists force the workers to sell the product of their labor and then use that product against the workers to exploit them further. This, Marx claimed, forces the workers to regard their own product, something that is actually part of them, as alien and even harmful to them; thus, it becomes another cause for self-alienation. Third, and here Marx is truly paradoxical, the capitalist is criticized for mechanizing production because this process robs laborers of their skills and reduces them to little more than feeders of machines. All the creativity is taken out of work, making it impossible for people ever to develop their humanity fully: This is the ultimate alienation. Marx is curiously contradictory at this point. Clearly, he saw himself as a prophet of the future. He claimed that socialism was the coming economic system and that it would become even more productive than capitalism. Yet, in this theory, he is resentful of mechanization and even appears to look back nostalgically to an earlier era. In a passage from *Das Kapital,* Marx, often a laborious writer, displayed unusual eloquence while discussing human self-alienation.

> Within the capitalist system all methods for raising the social productiveness of labor are brought about at the cost of the individual laborer; all means for the development of production transform themselves into means of domination over, and exploitation of, the producers; they mutilate the laborer into a fragment of a man, *degrade him to the level of an appendage of a machine, destroy every remnant of charm in his work and turn it into a hated toil;* they estrange from him the intellectual potentialities of the labor-process in the same proportion as science is incorporated in it as an independent power; they distort the conditions under which he works, subject him during the labor-process to a despotism the more hateful for its meanness; they transform his lifetime into working-time and drag his wife and child beneath the wheels of the Juggernaut of capital. (Emphasis added.)

The Labor Theory of Value The **labor theory of value** was not created by Marx. It was generally accepted during the eighteenth and nineteenth centuries; in fact, it was openly supported by the great classical economists Adam Smith, John Locke, and David Ricardo. Living as he did at the end of the period dominated by classical economists, Marx is probably the last major economist to support the labor theory of value. In fact, Marx was once called "a Ricardo turned socialist" because he shared so many assumptions with the great capitalist economist yet adapted them to different conclusions.

The labor theory of value is concerned with the *intrinsic worth* of an object. Value is a complex concept. The value most modern economists are concerned with is the *exchange value* of items, that is, the amount of money one can get for items on the market. *Sentimental value* is another measure. Though the market value of one's dog may be high, one may not wish to sell the dog because its sentimental value is greater than anything anyone will offer for it. *Use value* is a third expression of worth. Though the sentimental value one attaches to an old car used to drive back and forth to work may be low and the exchange value little higher, the usefulness of the car might be quite high since it adequately performs a needed function. *Esthetic value* is yet another assessment. The grace of an old building may far exceed its commercial value or its usefulness.

By contrast, the labor theory of value is concerned with establishing a standard for measuring intrinsic value. In other words, what is a given item worth by objective measure? What is it *really* worth? This concept assumes that two kinds of value are brought to the production process. Resources, machinery, and finance are termed *constant value;* that is, these factors, when applied to the production of an item, cannot add any value to the item greater than their own intrinsic worth. Only labor is a *variable value* because only labor produces something of greater worth than itself.

Here Marx pays tribute to the genius of human creativity. The materials necessary to produce a watch, for example, can be placed next to the tools and machines used in watch making; nevertheless, a watch will not be produced until human creativity—*labor*—is applied. Similarly, the components of an unassembled building have an aggregate value, but when they are combined through labor to become a house, something new has been produced, and its value far exceeds the sum of its individual parts.

The intrinsic value of any object, Marx assumed, is therefore determined by the amount of labor—human creativity—needed to produce it. The *price* of the object, the amount of money it will fetch on the market at any given time, is determined by supply and demand. However, the *value* of the object is determined by the labor time needed for its production.

The Theory of Surplus Value The **theory of surplus value,** according to Engels, is Marx's most important discovery. Marx observed that capitalists held a monopoly on the means of production—resources, factories, and machinery. Ordinary people must work to survive, but because the capitalists control the means of production the workers must sell their labor at whatever price the capitalist will pay. Marx accepted Ricardo's **iron law of wages,** which you will recall, suggested that capitalists, driven by the need to make profits and capital, will pay their workers only subsistence wages—enough to feed themselves and their families—because that much is necessary to bring them back to work the next day. Therefore the workers are enslaved to the masters who pay them only the most meager wages, regardless of how much value they produce.

According to this theory, the workers' intrinsic value is the money needed to feed themselves and their families. Anything they produce above the subsistence level is *surplus value.* Since under Ricardo's iron law of wages the capitalists pay only a subsistence wage, barest amount necessary to bring the worker back the next day, Marx concluded they keep the surplus value produced by the workers as their profit. For example, let us say that it takes six hours of work to produce the necessities of life for a laborer and his or her family. If the employer forces the laborer to work for thirteen hours, yet only pays a subsistence wage, the capitalist has forced the laborer to surrender seven hours of surplus value. Because the surplus value can be produced only by labor, Marx goes on to argue, it belongs to the laborer by right. Accordingly, any profit the capitalists make from the labor of their employees is ill-gotten and exploitative. The capitalist is, therefore, a villain, a parasite who lives by sucking the economic lifeblood of the proletariat, and must be erased from society when the proletariat takes over. Needless to say, Ricardo, the capitalist economist, would not have agreed with this conclusion. Ricardo believed that the capitalists' control of property distinguished them from other people and justified their exploitation of the worker, for such exploitation creates capital, thus assuring further productivity. The difference between Ricardo and Marx on this point is not so much a question of economics; rather it is a dispute about what is moral.

At this point you might be wondering how Marx expected capital to develop if profits, or surplus value, were not allowed. The answer is simple: Marx did not oppose capital per se; *he rejected the capitalist.* He did not condemn profit; he opposed private profit. The German scholar knew that capital was necessary for production, but he rejected the notion that it should be controlled by private individuals. Capital, he suggested, was created by all and should be owned by all. Marx certainly did not oppose creating surplus value to be used to invest in increased productivity. What he objected to was that private citizens should be allowed to monopolize the means of production and use that power to force workers—the creators of value—to surrender their goods in order to survive. Put differently, no one should be allowed to profit from the labor of another.

Marxist Theory of Revolution

Marx vacillated over whether violence was necessary to achieve socialist goals. During the early part of his professional life, he clearly suggested that one could not hope for a change from a capitalist system to a socialist one without violence. Gradually, however, he began to weaken this position until finally he admitted that certain systems (such as those in England, Holland, and perhaps the United States) might be responsive enough to adopt socialism by nonviolent means. Violence was still necessary elsewhere, however. Later, Lenin would again insist that no meaningful change could occur without violence.

The basis of Marx's argument for violence was his perception of the dialectic process. He believed that technological change cannot be stopped: Resources will become depleted, and new means of production will inevitably evolve, resulting in economic change. When the economy changes, economic determinism dictates that the entire foundation of the society must be transformed, compelling a change in its superstructure as well. In other words, economic change cannot be prevented. Economic change forces social change, which, in turn, drives political change. Violence is necessary in this process because the rulers who control the economy feel their economic and political power threatened by the uncontrollable changes taking place in the means of production. Vainly trying to resist the inevitable, they use their governmental power to keep themselves in control. However, they are resisting the progress of history. History is therefore propelled from one era to another. A series of revolutions punctuate the dialectic dynamic; each new era is born in the victory of those who control the new dominant means of production. In the final struggle the proletariat will confront their capitalist exploiters. The capitalists will use force, but their resistance is doomed to defeat at the hands of the irresistible pressure of history.

More specifically, Marx predicted the demise of capitalism. Competition, he argued, would force the capitalists to buy more machinery. Yet, only human labor can produce a surplus value; thus, the capitalists' profits would decline as they employed fewer people. At the same time, unemployment would increase among the proletariat as competition forced increasing numbers of former capitalists into the proletarian ranks. On the one hand, the size of the proletariat and the depth of its misery would increase; on the other, the wealth in the society would be held by fewer people. Marx predicted that every capitalist society would be subject to increasingly frequent and ever more serious economic convulsions. Eventually, the misery of the proletariat would increase to a point that could no longer be endured and a revolution would erupt, bringing the system to its knees. "The knell of capitalist private property sounds," Marx wrote, savoring the irony, "The expropriators are expropriated."

Using the French Revolution as his model, Marx envisioned a spontaneous uprising of the workers. Conditions for the common people in prerevolutionary France had degenerated to miserable levels. Yet, little was done in the way of advance planning for a popular revolt prior to its eruption in Paris in 1789. The precise cause of the French Revolution remains a mystery, but what is clear is that after centuries of aristocratic abuse, the people of France had quietly reached the breaking point; on a hot day—July 14, 1789—some seemingly trivial event sparked public fury that culminated in a frightful period of social and political chaos, and the world was changed forever. Just as the French had vanquished their aristocratic oppressors with little prodding, so too did Marx expect the proletariat to dislodge their bourgeois masters.

The principle of class consciousness is critical here. Marx assumed that the workers had not yet fully comprehended that they were a group completely separate and distinct from the bourgeoisie. When the proletariat became fully aware of its unique situation in society—when it developed *class consciousness*—it would realize the full extent of its oppression and the parasitic nature of its rulers. It would then spontaneously rise up in revolution.

Helping to develop class consciousness is the role Marx saw for himself and his revolutionary colleagues. Calling his followers the **vanguard of the proletariat,** Marx advised that their function was to do what they could to instill in the worker an understanding of the true nature of their class-riven society. Importantly, Marx did not advocate that revolutionaries should organize and lead the revolution. He saw their function as more educative than combative. Once fully aware of their circumstances, the proletariat would initiate the revolution themselves. Marx's attitude toward revolution and revolutionaries is particularly important because, as we shall see in Chapter 9, Lenin, who was supposedly a disciple of the German master, abandoned this rather passive role for a more activist one.

The Marxist Political System

Of all the subjects on which he wrote, Marx is probably least clear in discussing the political system that would exist after the revolution. Basically he conceived of the proletarian state as developing in two steps. First, he expected that the proletariat would create a dictatorship. The purpose of the **dictatorship of the proletariat** would be to eliminate all but a single proletarian class. Since all human strife emanated from social class differences, according to Marx, human harmony was possible only if class differences were eradicated. This goal could be achieved through a process of reeducation.

Although the purpose of the dictatorship of the proletariat is quite clear, the exact nature of the institution remains shrouded in ambiguity and has been the subject of considerable debate. Lenin, who took an elitist attitude, insisted that the dictatorship should be *over* the proletariat as well as superior to all other elements in the society. He argued that not only should the Communist Party (the Bolsheviks) lead the revolution, but that it should also become the dictator of the proletariat.

Since Marx insisted on a democratic format in all other things and since he never attempted to form a communist party, as Lenin later did, it is highly unlikely that he meant to imply the model Lenin employed. Indeed, Michael Harrington, a noted American socialist scholar, suggested that Marx actually intended something approaching a democracy when he called for the "dictatorship of the proletariat." Marx expected that the overwhelming number of people in society would be among the proletariat when the revolution occurred. If he meant that the dictatorship was to be *by* the proletariat, the situation would indeed be different. The huge majority of people—the proletariat—would impose its egalitarian policies on the tiny corps of remaining capitalists. In numerical terms, at least, such a system would be more democratic than that which Lenin ultimately put in place.

In any event, as the dictatorship succeeded in redirecting the society toward the socialist utopia, more and more people would adopt the **socialist ethic,** meaning willingness to work to one's capacity and to share the fruits of labor with the rest of society. This concept is clearly the most revolutionary aspect of Marx's thought. Like all leftists, he believed people could change, redirecting their lives and actions toward more desirable goals. To this end, Marx expected the dictatorship to encourage people to abandon their selfish, atomistic ways, adopting collective, or organic, values that accrue to the good of society as a whole. The new society would operate on the principle "From each according to his ability, to each according to his needs."

If people could be encouraged to enjoy their labor, they would become more productive than was possible in a capitalist system. If the productivity was shared equally by all, social anxieties and frustrations would most probably abate, creating a happy, contented populace. Thus, crime, war, and human turmoil would disappear. As strife and anxiety declined, a gradual change in society's foundations would lead to the second Marxist state. The need for the dictatorship would disappear. Eventually, when the last of the nonproletariat was gone, the state would have "withered away": The police state would have ceased to exist. Then, all the individuals in society would be "free" to *govern themselves* responsibly for the good of all, and the system would have evolved into a *democratic utopia* similar to that desired by many anarchists. Only a skeletal shell of the former state would be left, and it would simply administer the economy. As Engels put it, "In the final stage of communism, the government of men will change to the administration of things."

Internationalism

Since Marx believed that dialectic materialism was a law of historical development, he expected that socialism would be adopted in every country in the world sooner or later. The exact schedule for the adoption of socialism in any country depended on its economic development. Though he made no specific predictions, Marx clearly expected that the most industrialized nations of his day (England, Germany, France, Belgium, and Holland) were on the verge of the proletarian revolution. Ironically, the first successful Marxist revolution occurred after his death in Russia, an agrarian, deeply religious country.

During Marx's lifetime, the nation-state system was an important political fact, as it is today. Indeed, since the nation-state system had developed along with capitalism, Marx believed that it was part of the capitalist superstructure. He argued that nation-states were organized by the capitalists to keep people who really had a great deal in common separated from one another. People of the same social class from different countries, he reasoned, actually had more in common with each other than did people of different classes within the same country. National boundaries were only artificial separations designed to reinforce the capitalist system. Indeed, Marx declared that "workingmen have no country." Consequently, he believed that as various countries became socialist, they would recognize the divisiveness of national boundaries and would erase the lines that separated them until finally all national boundaries would have "withered away" and the entire world would be a single socialist utopia.

Because humanitarian socialism had been discredited by the utopians, and because of Marx's intellectual preeminence, he dominated socialism throughout his life. Almost immediately after his death, however, humanitarian socialism revived with new vigor, even as Marxism was transformed from theoretical speculation to practical political action. We shall now consider these developments in the following chapter.

QUESTIONS FOR DISCUSSION

1. Compare and contrast the major features of communism and socialism.
2. How do humanitarian socialism and "scientific" socialism differ historically and ideologically?
3. What are the major components of Marxism?
4. How do economic determinism and dialectic materialism relate to each other?
5. In what ways was Marx perceptive about his world and in what ways did he err?

SUGGESTIONS FOR FURTHER READING

A' Amato, Paul, *The Meaning of Marxism*. Chicago, IL: Haymarket Books, 2006.
Bernstein, Edward, *Evolutionary Socialism,* trans. E. C. Harvey. New York: B. W. Heubsch, 1909.
Harrington, Michael, *Socialism*. New York: Bantam Books, 1972.
Hegel, Georg Wilhelm Friedrich, *Reason and History,* trans. Robert S. Hartman. New York: Liberal Arts Press, 1953.
Hook, Sydney, *From Hegel to Marx: Studies in the Intellectual Development of Karl Marx*. New York: Columbia University Press, 1994.
Howard, Michael W., ed., *Socialism*. Amherst, NY: Humanity Books, 2001.
Jarnow, Jesse, *Socialism: A Primary Source Analysis*. New York: Rosen, 2004.
Jennings, Jeremy, ed., *Socialism: Critical Concepts in Political Science*. London: Routledge, 2003.
Marx, Karl, and Friedrich Engels, *The Communist Manifesto*. Baltimore: Penguin Books, 1967.
McLellan, David, *Karl Marx: His Life and Thought*. New York: Harper and Row, 1973.
Miliband, Ralph, *Marxism and Politics*. Oxford: Oxford University Press, 2003.
Mongar, Thomas, *The Death of Communism and the Rebirth of Original Marxism*. Lewistown, NY: Edwin Mellen Press, 1994.
Taylor, Keith, *The Political Ideas of the Utopian Socialists*. London: Frank Cass, 1982.

Applied Socialism

PREVIEW

After Marx's death, the socialist movement shattered into separate components: the orthodox Marxists, the revisionists and Fabians, and the Marxist-Leninists. Orthodox Marxism soon collapsed, a victim of its own inadaptability. Insisting on a gradual, nonviolent achievement of socialism, the revisionists and Fabians have had a great impact on virtually every non-Marxist socialist movement in the world. For his part, Lenin significantly modified Marxism, transforming it into a practical though elitist movement. He reinfused Marxism with violent impulses, and he made Marxism a political reality. Most importantly, he modernized Marxist theory and created a practical template by which to implement it. Succeeding Lenin, Stalin created an intractable totalitarian model and transformed the ideology from an internationalist theory to a nationalist doctrine. However, Stalin's passing from the scene made increasingly clear the limited utility of the model he bequeathed. Successive efforts at reform, alternating with ostrich-like retrenchment proved unsuccessful in forestalling the inevitable, and ultimately, the Soviet behemoth collapsed of its own dead weight.

China, adopting a populist variant of Marxism, has been more able to adapt itself to current economic and social imperatives. Even so, although the Communist Party of China remains in control of the society, ideological commitment has become very weak, and the loss of faith, combined with widespread corruption, raises serious doubts about the future of communist rule.

Although Cuba continues to resist political change, it too has had to bend to demands for economic and social liberalization. So too with North Korea and the Indo-China peninsula. A common thread running through the ideologies of China, Cuba, North Korea, Vietnam, Laos, and Cambodia is their committed resistance to Western domination. This essentially nationalistic commitment is not dissimilar to the ideologies of other developing former colonial countries. Additionally, it tends to give resilience to these regimes that they might not otherwise enjoy.

Meanwhile, although largely discredited in the early 1990s, socialism is gradually, if tentatively, regaining popularity in some of the countries of the former Soviet Union and Eastern Europe. However, the most enthusiastic socialist movements are found in Latin America. Indeed, its adherents have all but swept the region. But whether these poor, agrarian societies can sustain it is far from certain. Finally, there has been a new socialist surge in the United States, but probably this is only a momentary episode as the society attempts to grapple with the Great Recession. Whatever its current condition, socialism enjoys innate qualities that almost certainly guarantee its continued existence.

SOCIALISM AFTER MARX

When Marx died, the socialist movement no longer enjoyed the guidance of a single dominant thinker. Yet, the resulting ambiguity encouraged creativity, and eventually three distinct socialist doctrines emerged: orthodox Marxism, revisionism, and Marxism-Leninism.

Orthodox Marxism

Guided at first by Engels himself, the **orthodox Marxists** were led by **Karl Kautsky** (1854–1938) after Engels's death in 1895. Kautsky was a distinguished scholar, but his political acumen did not match his academic skills and he led his followers into a hopeless dilemma.

As the name implies, the orthodox Marxists clung rigidly to Marxist theory and resisted change to it. Such single-minded devotion to a set of ideas stifled imaginative thinking, ultimately spelling its doom among intellectuals and practical politicians alike. Looking forward to the revolution that would end the capitalist state forever, Kautsky refused to cooperate in social reform with nonsocialist governments. This attitude badly weakened the orthodox position. Depending on the workers for support, the Kautskyists brought on their own failure by opposing programs that would improve the proletariat's lot. Desperately needing legislation on maximum hours, minimum wages, working safety, and social insurance, workers abandoned the orthodox Marxists for more practical political parties. Forced by the pressure of events to retreat inch by inch from his inflexible position, toward the end of his life, Kautsky finally supported liberal reforms and admitted that revolution might not be necessary after all.

Revisionism

Eduard Bernstein (1850–1932) is the founder of the **revisionist** school of socialist theory. Finding that several Marxist predictions did not match actual historical developments, Bernstein began to devise a revised, more moderate socialist paradigm. He was aided in this effort by the brilliant French socialist **Jean Jaurès** (1859–1914). Perhaps the most significant characteristic of the revisionist doctrine is that it represents the return of socialism to its original humanitarian motivations, rescuing it from the moral sterility of Marx's "scientific" socialism.

Bernstein and Jaurès were not unappreciative of Marx's contribution to socialist thinking, but they felt compelled to challenge almost every major Marxist principle. Of course, no socialist could deny the importance of economic determinism, but the revisionists believed that Marx had given it too great a role

© Bettmann/Corbis

Eduard Bernstein (1850–1932)

as a political stimulant. Economics, they argued, is an important motivator, but it is not the only one, nor is its impact on human motives constant, since it tends to decrease as people satisfy their most basic needs.

Noting that Marx had misjudged the development of capitalism, Bernstein pointed out that the capitalist class was increasing in size rather than decreasing. Literally millions of people were entering the capitalist class by buying stocks. Further, as more and more governments bowed to the demands of organized labor and other social reformers, wealth was becoming more evenly spread within society, and the lot of the proletariat was improving instead of growing worse. It was obvious to the revisionists that rather than racing toward inevitable self-destruction, capitalism was evolving and adjusting to new circumstances. It was becoming less exploitative and more generous to the workers in the distribution of goods. Since Marx had not anticipated this development, Bernstein reasoned it proper for socialism to modify its strategy.

Revolutionary socialism began to seem inappropriate as a way of ending the evils of capitalism. Would it not be far better to develop *evolutionary* ways of achieving socialism? This speculation led Bernstein, Jaurès, and their followers to conclude that their cause would be better served by abandoning dogmatic theories and supporting pragmatic political policies designed to achieve socialism peacefully and gradually through existing European political systems—by winning elections. This adjustment introduced a very successful political movement. Nearly every non-Marxist socialist movement owes its origins to these practical political thinkers. They founded the modern *democratic socialist movement*.

Bernstein's influence did not stop at Europe. Though the Americans Daniel De Leon and Big Bill Haywood proposed militant socialism in their Socialist Labor Party, their efforts met with little success. But Eugene V. Debs and Norman Thomas carried socialism to modest popularity with the revisionist approach of their Socialist Party in the United States.

Although not precisely revisionist, a second development in contemporary humanitarian nonviolent socialism developed in England during the late 1800s.

Founded in the tradition of **John Stuart Mill** in 1884, the year after Marx's death, the **Fabian Society** was dedicated to bringing socialism to England.

Like Robert Owen twenty years earlier, the Fabians rejected the policy of forcing socialism on society. They argued that socialism must be accepted from the bottom up rather than imposed from the top down. Yet, they were confident that socialism would be adopted by all freedom-loving people because they were convinced that only socialism was compatible with democracy. Money, they reasoned, is such an important source of power that any political system truly devoted to political equality could not realistically countenance an economic system that did not equalize the distribution of wealth. Consequently, socialism in England was inevitable.

Largely consisting of literary figures, including George Bernard Shaw, H. G. Wells, and Sidney and Beatrice Webb, the Fabian Society was particularly well suited to its task. It usually avoided direct political activity and concentrated on convincing the English people that socialism was the only logical economic system for the British nation. The Fabians carried their message to the people in pamphlets, in articles written for journals and newspapers, and in their novels and short stories. Adapted as it was to the British style and temperament, Fabianism was very successful. Today's British Labour Party claims descent from the Fabian movement, but for the past two decades it has shed many of the usual socialist trappings.

Marxism-Leninism

Vladimir Ilyich Ulyanov Lenin (1870–1924) became a revolutionary early in life and found himself exiled from Russia to Switzerland in 1900. There he fell in with a small but fractious cabal of Russian Marxists. The major question dividing them was how best to bring about the workers' revolution. Lenin became the leader of the Bolsheviks, who contrary to Marx's prediction, believed the revolution would not happen on its own. Being more politically realistic than Marx had been, Lenin found it necessary to develop significant changes to the German scholar's theories, if the fundamentals of Marxism were ever to be brought to Russia.

Theories of Revolution and Revolutionaries   Although originally believing that socialism could be born only through violent revolution, Marx later held out hope that it might evolve peacefully in certain liberal societies. Lenin, on the other hand, never wavered in his belief that force was necessary if socialism was to replace a capitalistic or feudalistic society.

Marx taught that the revolution would take place when the workers had developed a clear awareness of the exploitation of their station. Galvanized by their hopeless misery, they would become a unified political force. Relying on the trade unions and other agitators to teach the workers about the grinding oppression they endured—what Marx called *class consciousness*—he expected that the proletarian revolution would eventually erupt automatically, ending the bourgeois state and bringing the workers to power.

© Bettmann/Corbis

Vladimir Ilyich Ulyanov Lenin
(1870–1924)

Lenin also contradicted Marx on this point. He argued that the proletariat would not develop class consciousness without the intervention of a revolutionary group. Thinking labor unions too easily controlled by capitalists, Lenin believed that a different group was needed to ignite the revolution. To justify this concept, he expanded on Marx's rather unimportant theory of the **vanguard of the proletariat.** Unlike Marx, who gave the vanguard of the proletariat no other task than teaching class consciousness, Lenin, the more skilled political strategist, envisioned the vanguard itself as a small, disciplined, totally dedicated group. It would be the principal revolutionary agent that would overthrow the government and establish a socialist state before the proletariat itself fully developed class consciousness. This disagreement is what lies behind an important difference in expectations between Marx and Lenin. Because Marx thought that a class-conscious proletariat would spontaneously rise up against capitalist exploitation, he expected that the **dictatorship of the proletariat** would exist for a relatively brief period during which the small number of remaining nonproletarians would be reeducated, creating a classless society.

In Lenin's plan, by contrast, the vanguard would trigger a revolution long before the conditions that Marx anticipated actually developed. In this case, socialism would be imposed on the society by a minority instead of being forced on the governing elite by the majority. Although Lenin's model would bring the revolution on sooner, the dictatorship of the proletariat would have to last much longer than Marx anticipated because such a huge percentage of the population would have to be transformed into a socialist proletariat before the ideal society could be realized.

Marx was vague about the vanguard of the proletariat. One cannot be sure whether he intended the proletariat to assume the role of dictator itself until only one class existed or if a dictator was to govern all, including the proletariat. Lenin, on the other hand, was quite specific on this subject. The vanguard of the proletariat (the **Bolshevik Party,** renamed the Communist Party in 1918) was to become a collective dictatorship. In other words, the Bolshevik

Party would carry out the revolution and then impose a dictatorship on the entire society until it was prepared to enter the utopian stage. Thus, as Lenin saw it, the dictatorship of the proletariat was not to be a dictatorship *by* the proletariat but a dictatorship of Bolsheviks *over* the proletariat.

Lenin also created a structure for the vanguard of the proletariat at the international level. After taking power in Russia, he created the International Communist Movement (the **Comintern**) in 1919. It was supposed to spread revolution and socialism throughout the world. Meeting with only mixed results, the Comintern was eventually transformed by Stalin after Lenin's death. Instead of a revolutionary catalyst, it became a mere appendage of Soviet foreign policy. *Thus, socialist internationalism was overwhelmed by Russian nationalism.*

In the short run, the efficacy of Lenin's activist and *elitist* tactics seemed borne out by the 1917 revolution in Russia. However, non-Leninist Marxists argue that the collapse of the Soviet Union proves that Marx was correct in the long run. A successful Marxist society cannot be created by an elite group that imposes such a society on unwilling masses from the top down. Rather, they aver, it can only be successful, as Marx insisted, when the people are fully prepared to accept it.

Imperialism   As the twentieth century began, the pressure from critics of Marxist theory became intense. Marxism was not only attacked by capitalists and conservatives but also questioned by a growing number of socialists. The core of the theory, dialectic materialism, promised a proletarian revolution that never occurred. Indeed, as the revisionists pointed out, the conditions of labor were improving in the industrial countries, making the revolution appear to be a myth. Lenin was hard pressed to explain this seeming contradiction, but his conclusion was a clever analysis that went far beyond a simple rationalization of Marx's error.

Since Marx's death, a new kind of capitalism had developed. As he predicted, firms became larger, though less numerous, their financial needs growing along with their size. But, needing vast amounts of capital to sustain these huge enterprises, the corporations became increasingly dependent on banks for financing until the bankers themselves gained control of the monopolies. Marx had not foreseen this new phenomenon, which Lenin called *finance capitalism.*

Finance capitalism marked a new, much more exploitative stage than the previous condition of *industrial capitalism.* Under these new conditions, the owners of the means of production were bankers and financiers, not industrialists. For example, J. P. Morgan, a noted financier, created the Northern Securities Trust in the late 1800s, tying up all the major railroad trunk lines in the United States. He also put together the world's first billion-dollar corporation, United States Steel, in 1901. Morgan and his associates knew nothing at all about the railroad or steel business. Yet, by manipulating capital, they gained control of two basic U.S. industries. Ignoring Morgan and other capitalists' genius for mobilizing capital and applying it to production, Lenin argued that they contributed nothing to the productivity of those two industries, thus according to the **labor theory of value,** the fantastic profits of these "robber barons" were stolen from the rightful owners, the proletariat.

In addition, the very fact that the national economies were monopolizing industry was having a profound effect on the international scene. The centralization of ownership was occurring because it was becoming harder to profit from domestic markets. New markets had to be found. At the same time, Lenin believed that the ownership class had begun to realize the truth in the Marxist prediction of a revolution by a proletariat whose misery could no longer be borne. This led the owners to find new sources of cheap labor and resources. Thus, they began to *export their exploitation* through colonialism.

Capitalist exploitation of foreign lands began in earnest in the 1880s—too late, Lenin later wrote, for Marx, who died in 1883, to assess. The new colonialism, which Lenin called, *imperialist capitalism,* also delayed the proletarian revolution. Driven to increase profits, yet needing to protect themselves against a rebellion by their domestic proletariat, the capitalists began to exploit the labor of the colonial people. Then, to relax the tensions created by their previous domestic exploitation, the capitalists shared some of their new profits with their domestic workers. Not only was the domestic proletariat's revolutionary tension reduced by this improvement in living standards, but their virtue was corrupted. Allowing themselves to be "bought off" by profits stolen from the colonial proletariat, the domestic workers became partners in the capitalist exploitation of the unfortunate colonial people. This economic prostitution disgusted Lenin, who saw it as yet another evil policy of the capitalist enemy. How ironic, he mused bitterly, that capitalism could so corrupt the working class.

Capitalist imperialism, however, was ultimately self-destructive, Lenin thought. Eventually, all the colonial resources would be consumed by the various capitalist states. With no more colonies to subdue, the profit-hungry imperialist nations would begin to feed off each other, causing strife and conflict that would end in a general confrontation among the capitalist imperialist powers. **Imperialism,** Lenin declared in 1916, *is the final stage of capitalism.* It will ultimately lead to a conflict in which the capitalists will destroy each other. Thus, Lenin concluded that World War I was a giant struggle in which the imperialist nations hoped to finally settle their colonial conflicts, and that socialists should take advantage of this conflict and confusion by seizing control of Western governments after the capitalists had exhausted themselves in futile fraternal warfare.[1]

---

[1]Lenin's theory of imperialism has had several important results. It not only can be seen, as he did, as a cause for World War I, but at least a partial cause of World War II as well, given Hitler's insistence of *Anschluss* (claiming that Germany had a right to expand its control throughout Europe in order to feed the superior German nation). Imperial Japanese expansionism in Asia and the problems it caused with the United States' own economic interests should also be considered. Quite apart from these, Lenin's theory of imperialism has also done much to awaken the consciousness of people subjected to capitalistic colonialism throughout the developing world, and must be counted among the causes of the current desperation felt by Islamic fundamentalists, some of whom have been driven to embrace terrorism.

Although Lenin's theory of imperialism explained why the Marxist revolution had not yet occurred among the advanced industrial states in the West, there was still no answer to the question of why it had occurred in a tenth-rate industrial country such as Russia. Fruitful thinker that he was, Lenin again turned to imperialism for an explanation. Expounding his theory of the **weakest link,** he argued that colonialism gave the advanced industrial countries a tremendous competitive advantage over the less-developed, non-colonialist capitalist states. If the latter were to compete against the cheap labor and raw materials available to their imperialist opponents, they would have to exploit their own labor force even more. The increased exploitation suffered by the workers in the less-advanced countries would naturally push them toward revolution at the very moment when the proletariat of the advanced capitalist countries was being bought off with a share of the colonialist spoils. Russia, Lenin concluded, was the weakest link in the capitalist chain. The terrible repression of the Tsarist state combined with the revolutionary skill, organization, and dedication of the Bolsheviks, Lenin suggested, made it logical that the Marxist revolution would occur there rather than happen first in the advanced capitalist states.

Achieving the Utopia Completing his blueprint for the practical application of Marx's sometimes vague theories, Lenin outlined the economic and political development of the future workers' paradise. The economic system to be used by the Bolshevik dictatorship of the proletariat was what Lenin called state socialism. According to this theory, the state was to control all elements of the economy. The workers—employees of the state—would produce a profit, and the profit, or surplus value, would then be returned to the society by way of investments to increase productivity, social and governmental programs to aid and protect the citizens, and consumer goods to benefit the society.

The maxim Lenin articulated for distribution of goods to citizens paraphrases Marx's famous statement: "From each according to his ability, to each according to his needs." Instead, Lenin said: "*From each according to his ability, to each according to his work.*" (Emphasis added.) This formula is even more practical than it appears at first glance. Marx had seen the dictatorship creating a single proletarian class imbued with the socialist ethic by one of two methods: educating the masses to convince them of the wisdom of socialism or simply removing the intransigent from the society. Here, Lenin introduced a third technique for achieving the single-class utopia. He authorized forcing people into submission to the socialist leaders by withholding from dissidents the necessities of life: starving them into submission to the dictatorship of the proletariat.

More practical than Marx, Lenin contradicted the German master in several important respects. More an activist than a philosopher, he was always concerned with the workability of a process, often leaving theoretical inconsistencies to sort themselves out. He ignored the democratic spirit of Marx's theory in favor of an elitist revolution, claiming that its utopian ends justified its extreme means. "One cannot make an omelet without breaking eggs" he is reported to have said. He violated the dialectic by demanding an early revolution, which he followed with an elitist dictatorship that Marx almost surely never intended. He used his theory of imperialism to describe a stage of capitalism not foreseen by Marx; he then used it to explain why the revolution happened first in Russia and failed to take place in the highly industrialized countries. Finally, along with state socialism, Lenin proposed a new kind of labor exploitation about which Marx would have had serious qualms. Yet, with all their twists and turns, these modifications and amendments were always intended to bring to fruition the Marxist ideal: a society at peace with itself in a world characterized by human harmony.

THE SOVIET UNION AND RUSSIA

Commenting toward the end of his life on the variety of ways his friend's theories had been interpreted, Friedrich Engels reportedly said: "Marx would not be a Marxist if he were alive today." Yet, varied as the interpretations were, even greater changes were made in the original theory when it later was applied to practical political situations.

Lenin's and Stalin's Policies

Lenin came to power in 1917. Moving quickly, he withdrew Russia from World War I in 1918 by making peace with Germany. Immediately afterward, Lenin had to turn his efforts to defeating the counterrevolutionary White Armies that surrounded him during the Russian Civil War (1918–1921). Meanwhile, the Western Allies, including the United States, invaded Russia in 1919, trying to bring the Communist regime down. In the midst of this conflict and confusion, Lenin also tried to create a socialist state at one fell swoop. But his efforts to expropriate factories and farms failed miserably. Production collapsed and famine ravaged the land until a rebellion against the government erupted among once loyal Soviet sailors just as the Civil War was won.

Moving decisively, Lenin brutally suppressed the rebellion of his former allies, but at the same time, he retreated from efforts to socialize the whole economy all at once. Under the **New Economic Policy (NEP)** that was adopted, the entire economy, except heavy industry, finance, communications, and transportation, was returned to private hands. The NEP was to be used to increase production to prewar levels, and then a new effort to create socialism was to be launched.

Even as Lenin relaxed his grip on the economy, however, he began to tighten his political control over the society. Opposition parties were outlawed and destroyed. The trade unions were brought under state control. The national boundaries began to take shape as the Ukraine, Armenia, Georgia, and Azerbaijan were brought into the Union. More important, the party gradually became bureaucratically oriented instead of revolutionary in focus. As the Communist Party consolidated power, the NEP increased productivity, until, by Lenin's death in 1924, the great revolutionary could take solace in the knowledge that his political creation would survive him.

Lenin's death was followed by a leadership struggle during which **Joseph Stalin** (1876–1953) ruthlessly outmaneuvered his adversaries, one by one. Giving vent to his paranoia, Stalin warned of a *capitalist encirclement* of the Soviet Union that could be broken only by resorting to nationalism. Stalin entreated his followers to *build socialism in one country*, making it impregnable against its capitalist enemies. Stalin advocated this strategy in opposition to the proposal of his archrival, **Leon Trotsky** (1879–1940), to engage in **permanent revolution** against capitalism until worldwide socialism was achieved. Stalin's conservative nationalistic appeal, however, struck a chord with his war-weary compatriots, and he gained their support in his struggle for dominance.

The policy of building socialism in one country is also of the greatest ideological significance. It effectively *subjects Marxism-Leninism to the dictates of Russian nationalist goals,* a result both Marx and Lenin would certainly have abhorred. This policy is of particular importance, for nationalism is the most powerful political idea of our era. Under Stalin the strongest internationalist ideology in recent history was completely overwhelmed by the irresistible onslaught of nationalism. Though Stalin was the first to adapt Marxism-Leninism to nationalism, later varieties of Marxism only underscore the grip in which nationalism holds it.

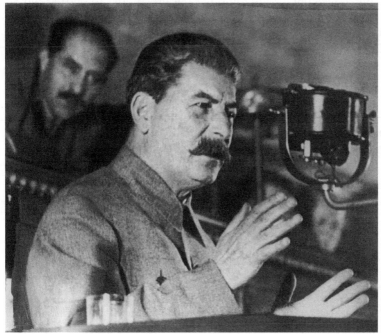

© Sovfoto/Eastfoto

❚ Joseph Stalin (1879–1953)

In 1929, with Trotsky out of the way, Stalin decided it was time to abandon Lenin's NEP and resocialize the economy completely. Thus, he initiated the first of the *five-year plans,* a crash program to modernize, industrialize, and centralize the country in the 1930s. These programs called for the nationalization of all industries, trades, and occupations and included the collectivization of the farms. They also forced the Soviet people to make enormous sacrifices so that resources could be diverted from the production of consumer goods to the military and heavy industry. The forced collectivization of the farms and the sacrifice of consumer goods caused incredible misery and millions of deaths. These ruthless policies were not without success, however. Compressing into ten years the economic advances other states stretched out over several decades, the first two five-year economic plans, while certainly not as productive as Stalin claimed, catapulted the Soviet Union to the status of a major industrial power.[2]

In the process of industrializing the Soviet Union, Stalin created a *cult of personality* portraying him as the infallible, omnipotent leader. At the center of a *totalitarian state,* Stalin used *terrorism* as a governing tool. Purging his enemies, real or imagined, he saw millions die of famine, in remote forced labor camps, or at the shooting wall.

The next decade brought World War II. Absorbing the devastating Nazi invasion in 1941, Soviet troops gradually pushed the Germans back to their homeland by 1944. Retreating into Germany, the Nazi armies abandoned Eastern Europe. One country after another fell under Soviet control, only to find that their liberation from the Nazis was simply the first step in the imposition of a new, equally severe regime. Reeling from the ruthless Nazi slaughter and pillage that caused the deaths of 27 million Soviets and destroyed a quarter of the national wealth, Stalin brutally suppressed the Eastern European countries, some of which (Bulgaria, Hungary, and Rumania) had, before, willingly helped Hitler despoil the Soviet Union.

Soviet Atrophy

The long dark rule of Stalin finally ended with his death in 1953. Victorious in the power struggle occasioned by Stalin's passing, **Nikita Khrushchev** (1894–1971) brought an end to the worst excesses of Stalin's terrorism through his *de-Stalinization* program. However, in Eastern Europe, the de-Stalinization

---

[2]The five-year plans were expressions of the "planned economy," as opposed to the West's "demand economies," based on market forces. They sought to provide for and control production and distribution of everything in the economy. Remarkably successful at creating targeted economic growth, the Soviet economy bifurcated, with its heavy industry and military production reaching impressive heights, while its production of consumer goods faltered badly. Modern equipment removed the snow from streets in fall and winter, yet babushkas swept them clear with twig brooms in spring and summer. Doctors were abundant, but even simple medication like aspirin could be hard to find. And so it remained: The Soviet economy ultimately became the second most productive in the world, but embarrassing anomalies persisted.

campaign led to uprisings that were brutally suppressed, thus making it clear that Khrushchev's liberalization policies had definite limits.

In relations with the West, however, Khrushchev pursued a liberalization strategy that met with shortsighted rejection. Realizing that nuclear weapons made a general war between East and West unthinkable, Khrushchev invited the capitalists to engage in **peaceful coexistence,** thus contradicting the Marxist-Leninist doctrine of permanent revolution with its assumption that capitalism and socialism are fatally incompatible. Perhaps taken in by its own anti-Soviet propaganda, the United States refused to take Khrushchev's overtures seriously and the Cold War continued apace, coming breathtakingly close to a disastrous nuclear showdown during the Cuban Missile Crisis of 1962.

Although Khrushchev successfully managed to end the Stalinist terror, his attempt to reform Stalin's planned economy failed miserably. The Soviet economic plans were tightly controlled by a ponderous, stifling bureaucracy. This antiquated system caused productivity to flag, and Khrushchev was sure that economic decentralization was needed to get things moving again. The problem was that the only people who could successfully carry out the decentralizing reforms were the very people who benefited most from keeping things unchanged—the bureaucrats. Accordingly, Khrushchev's increasingly frantic schemes to reform the system ended in repeated failures. Ultimately, they cost him his job. In 1964, Khrushchev was removed from office by a profoundly conservative cabal led by *Leonid Brezhnev* (1906–1982).

Repelled by Khrushchev's incessant and seemingly ill-conceived reforms, the Kremlin leaders became consumed with creating stability. Stability soon became political and economic stagnation, however. Job security was almost absolute from top to bottom in the society. Party members lost their idealism, government officials became corrupt, workers were even less conscientious than before. Absenteeism, alcoholism, shoddy workmanship, breakage, and waste rose to serious proportions. Squeezed by low productivity and an enormous defense budget, the Soviets tried desperately to equal the United States' military capacity while shortages of staples as well as luxuries became permanent problems. Shortages in state stores encouraged people to satisfy their needs illegally as the black market became pervasive throughout the society.

A spiritual malaise set in, and ideological conviction declined abruptly during the Brezhnev years. The decline of popular resolve in response to corruption and scarcity was exacerbated by the growing gerontocracy governing the country. Few of the aging bureaucrats left their powerful positions, and the system was sapped of the vitality it had previously enjoyed. Hope for reform dimmed as one aging, infirm leader after another followed Brezhnev to power.

Finally, in 1985, **Mikhail S. Gorbachev** (born in 1931) was named General Secretary of the Communist Party. Well educated, energetic, and progressive, Gorbachev believed that the moribund Soviet Union had to change if it was to survive. Beginning cautiously at first, but then quickly expanding his program, Gorbachev launched an astonishing series of economic, cultural, and political reforms. He demanded greater labor discipline, encouraged limited free expression, and even attempted to reduce the stultifying power the Communist Party exercised over the government.

Like Khrushchev, Gorbachev failed. Resisted by bureaucrats who resented the loss of power his reforms threatened, by economic managers who were wary about the amount of personal responsibility they would have to bear for production, and by the workers themselves, who refused to cooperate with a policy that called upon them to work harder with no concrete assurance that their lives would improve, the economic reforms stalled. However, grasping the opportunity to use reform to loosen the Soviet grip, many minority national groups within the Soviet Union and peoples of Eastern Europe organized separatist movements that ultimately destroyed the Soviet Union.

Trying to stop the inevitable, hard-liners within the Soviet Communist Party arrested Gorbachev in an attempted coup. This too failed, however. Gorbachev was freed, but its constituent parts (the Ukraine, Lithuania, Moldova, Kazakhstan, and so on), led by Russia, declared their independence, one by one, and the Soviet Union simply melted away.

Russia was led to independence by President **Boris Yeltsin** (1931–2007). Unfortunately, his courageous political acts were not matched by governmental integrity. Russia's effort to modernize and privatize its economy became immersed in intrigue and corruption. Productivity plummeted even as a dozen or so ruthless businesspersons (the "oligarchs"), encouraged by U.S. policy, used political bribery, economic chicanery, and other nefarious techniques and contacts to buy up vast portions of the Russian economy. Finally, Yeltsin, little more than a hapless alcoholic by 1999, stepped aside in favor of the hand-picked **Vladimir Putin** (born in 1952), whose heavy-handed governing style vaguely reminded some observers of the Soviet methodology.

While his stint as president could not be extended beyond 2008 because of constitutional term limits, he chose faithful supporter Dmitry Medvedev to succeed him while he ostensibly moved down to become prime minister. Yet, all indications are that Putin is still in firm control of the state. He has even spoken out forcefully on foreign policy matters, a jurisdiction which is constitutionally given to the president. His foreign policy pronouncements have expressed increasing wariness about the United States' intentions in Europe and he has tried to play upon the same emotions experienced by many Europeans who were repelled by the belligerent and unilateral policies of George W. Bush.

CHINA

Imperial China, one of history's most successful political systems, was based on the principles of Confucianism. Confucianism, once reviled by Mao but now enjoying new official approval in China, is as much a political theory as a code of moral conduct. Indeed, in this ancient philosophy, moral conduct and a well-ordered state are equated. Confucius taught that all people should know their place and should accept it, thus maintaining a harmonious society, the most desirable state of affairs. The law, rooted in Confucian teaching, provided that the scholarly mandarins, and other elites, would rule and the peasantry would obey. This sociopolitical arrangement served the Chinese remarkably well for centuries. The Chinese people enjoyed the benefits of an advanced civilization and an orderly society while the West foundered in the ignorance and social disorder of the medieval period.

Yet the West took the initiative during the fourteenth and fifteenth centuries, while China, Japan, and Korea placed a premium on tradition, ultimately rejecting new ideas as harmful. Accordingly, Asia turned inward and isolated itself from foreign influences.

As a result, the West surpassed the East in developing modern technology and political doctrines that accommodated the changes brought about by the new economic order. As the East's resistance was worn down by the pressure of the West's technological superiority, the philosophies of the ancient regimes began to appear less viable, and Western ideologies, such as nationalism and later Marxism, and currently unregulated capitalism, became more appealing. Though these Western ideas were modified somewhat, the fact remains that the East has been captivated by Western institutions, economic styles, and political idea systems.

The Belligerent Stage of the Revolution

Though its political tradition became antiquated, the imperial system survived foreign occupation and domestic rebellion until early in the twentieth century. The inevitable could not be forestalled indefinitely, however, and the Chinese Revolution began in 1911, with its belligerent phase continuing until 1949.

In 1911, the Manchu Dynasty collapsed before the onslaught of republican forces led by an unimposing, idealistic man, **Sun Yi Xian** (Sun Yat-sen)[3] (1866–1925). His ideology was a somewhat confused mixture of Western political theories, mild socialist economic ideas, and Eastern traditions. He was too idealistic and naïve to understand completely the forces he had helped unleash, however, and China's needs were far too complex for his simplistic solutions. In the end, he was outmaneuvered by the Machiavellians surrounding him, and he spent the rest of his life struggling with autocratic elements for control of China. At the same time, the Communist Party of China (CPC) was founded with Soviet help in 1921. Attending the first party congress was a radical young schoolteacher, **Mao Zedong** (Mao Tse-tung) (1893–1976).

Meanwhile, because he was perceived as a socialist, Sun's appeals to the West for aid in his struggle were repeatedly rebuffed. Finally, he turned to the Soviet Union, which was quick to appreciate the potential for revolution in China. The Soviets not only aided the founding of the CPC but also helped Sun organize his own party, the **Kuomintang.**

---

[3]Before 1970, Chinese words in English were commonly spelled using the Wade-Giles system of transliteration. In 1970, the People's Republic of China adopted the *pinyin* system, and most English publications have since adopted that format. To keep confusion to a minimum, I have included the Wade-Giles spelling of historical names once in parentheses following the *pinyin* spelling.

The country had fallen into chaos, with its far-flung provinces governed by tyrannical and petty warlords. A Soviet-encouraged alliance between the Kuomintang and the CPC lasted from 1924 to 1927, but Sun's death in 1925 brought to power his lieutenant, *Jiang Jieshi* (Chiang Kai-shek) (1887–1975). Jiang, a military man, turned the Kuomintang to the right, and suddenly attacked the communists in 1927. Thousands of communists were slaughtered by Jiang's army. The CPC escaped utter annihilation only by fleeing the cities for the safety of the countryside.

The Ruralization of Chinese Communism   Two years before, Mao had returned to his native Hunan province in southeastern China and studied the peasantry as a revolutionary force. In Hunan, Mao produced his first significant work, *Report on the Hunan Peasant Movement,* which called on communists to abandon the cities for the countryside because the peasants, not the proletariat, were China's true revolutionaries. With this document, he laid the foundation of Maoist thought, a brand of Marxism distinct from the Soviet version.

The Long March   Meanwhile, gaining an almost decisive military advantage over the communists in 1934, the Kuomintang army surrounded them in the south and threatened their destruction. To avoid annihilation, the communists broke out of the encirclement—leaving their southern base behind—and

© Bettmann/Corbis

| Mao Tse-tung (1893–1976)

fled to safety in northern China. This epic 6,000-mile retreat, called the **Long March,** was more a running battle than a march, scarcely 35,000 of the original 100,000 communists survived. The Long March also precipitated a leadership struggle within the CPC, and Mao gained the top position in the party—a position he would hold until his death.

The march finally ended in Shensi province in north-central China, where a new base was established in 1936. Hostilities between the communists and the Kuomintang were interrupted by the Japanese invasion of China. The two Chinese adversaries joined in a second alliance (1936–1945) until Japan's defeat. The cruelty and corruption of Jiang's government cost it critical support in China. Mao, on the other hand, enjoyed great popular support in the north and considerable appeal in the south. A series of stunning defeats saw Jiang giving ground until finally, in 1949, all was lost. Accordingly, he and his supporters fled to the Chinese island-province of Taiwan and established a government there that endures to this day. For his part, Mao established the People's Republic of China on the mainland, and the two states have endured an uneasy truce since 1949, although the People's Republic insists that Taiwan remains a wayward territory which must, someday, be returned to China proper.

The Political Stage of the Revolution

The communist regime in China has been marked by a series of important, sometimes traumatic, events. Mao Zedong remained a radical force in Chinese politics, often plunging China into tumultuous programs aimed at achieving great goals for his people. When they failed, the reforms were followed by periods of consolidation that evolved into the staging grounds for the next set of Mao's radical reforms.

Declaring that "women hold up half the sky," he demanded that they be freed from traditional male domination. On the economic front, he forcefully divested the absentee landlords of their farmland, temporarily turning it over to the peasants; the farms were eventually collectivized as part of the plan. He also tried to use the Soviet five-year-plan model to industrialize. The economic and social dislocation caused by these policies engendered violent resistance, and often deadly force was used to accomplish the government's goals.

By 1957, although many of the plan's goals had been achieved, the CPC leadership increasingly felt that Mao's radicalism was becoming counterproductive. Thus, a movement developed to maneuver him into retirement. Mao responded with another sudden lurch leftward.

The Re-revolutionized Revolution In 1957, Mao embarked on a series of "rectification campaigns," hurling China into political and social convulsions that dominated its development for decades. Wishing to mobilize the people to demand change from the bureaucracy, he asked for public criticism of the system. But quickly the public complaints about the system threatened to escape his control, so after only two months he brutally suppressed his own *Hundred Flowers Campaign.*

Smarting from this failure, Mao took the initiative again, desperately trying to recover his fading influence. A **Great Leap Forward** was announced, based on the twin pillars of Mao's ideology: conquering material want by applying superior willpower (a very un-Marxist idea) and overcoming technological problems by organizing China's vast population. His program attempted to vastly increase industrial output by taking industry to the people in the villages, and he tried to increase agricultural production by converting farms to agrarian factories. But, by 1960 the reforms had failed miserably. Production had fallen drastically, and famine threatened the stability of the regime. Mao retreated into semiretirement and the Great Leap Forward was forsaken. Unwilling to surrender the revolution to the moderates, in 1966, Mao ramped up another radical reform. Calling for a **Great Cultural Revolution,** he inspired youthful radicals to form units called the *Red Guard.* Demanding a return to basics, Mao unleashed the Red Guard on bureaucrats and intellectuals, punishing them for "counterrevolutionary" offenses. By 1969, the situation had become so bad that even Mao admitted that things had gone too far. The army was turned on the Red Guard and order was finally restored. When the dust settled, China found itself radicalized, but bruised and bleeding as well. Productivity had plummeted again, and the government and the party were in disarray. Thousands of pragmatic moderate party members and government officials were purged and replaced by radical zealots.

The moderates' fortunes, at low ebb in 1969, began to recover gradually in the early 1970s, as people, tired of radical-imposed disruption and sacrifice, began to demand a better standard of living for their families. While Mao lived, the radicals—led by the infamous *Gang of Four,* of which Mao's wife, Jiang Quing, was the central figure—were able to remain dominant. On Mao's death in 1976, however, the radicals were quickly purged, and the moderates, led by **Deng Xiaoping** (1904–1997), plunged into a number of reforms bringing China back from the brink of self-destruction and setting it on a course of phenomenal economic development, which has been continued by Deng's successors. Reminiscent of the Soviet NEP, China's leadership returned about 75 percent of the economy to private hands and to the market forces, retaining most heavy industry, transportation, and communications in the hands of the state. The Chinese now refer to their economy as *market socialism.* Responding to critics who complained that the reforms were not socialist, Deng, a pragmatic moderate, is said to have quipped, "It does not matter if the cat is black or white as long as it catches mice."

Despite several attempted reforms of the land ownership laws, party hardliners have so far been able to foil efforts to remand farmland to private ownership. Only able to lease land for a stated number of years, peasants have little incentive to invest in long-term land improvements or expensive equipment. Still, now that farmers are able to sell much of their produce on the open market, production has increased markedly and China has become a food exporter rather than an importer. Yet, Chinese agriculture stands at an impasse with further large increases in production awaiting necessary reforms.

For their part, private entrepreneurs organize small family businesses, inefficient state enterprises are allowed to go bankrupt, and state workers are paid on the basis of productivity rather than according to Mao's egalitarian policies. As a result, China's industrial productivity has dramatically increased, fostering an economic growth rate that is among the world's highest. Indeed, China now has the world's third largest GDPs, after the U.S. and Japan, and following an economic slowdown in 2008, it has come roaring back out of the Great Recession. Indeed, it is often regarded hopefully as the engine of worldwide economic recovery. China's stunning economic success over the past thirty years has led to several important changes. Further, China has begun to flex its economic muscles. Now the United States' largest creditor, China has used its dollars to build one of the world's largest financial reserves, to invest in many Western enterprises, including trying to buy U.S. energy companies and other large enterprises—it even flirted with the idea of buying General Motors and did buy the Volvo Cars unit from Ford Motor Co. in 2010[4]—and lavishing foreign aid on several developing countries, thus increasing its global political clout. At the same time, however, high-ranking Chinese officials have expressed concern about the continued economic viability of the dollar and even suggested that perhaps world trade should move away from its use and adopt a global currency instead. These economic moves have been accompanied by efforts to modernize China's military as well.

However, China's economic successes have been accompanied by many social problems. The explosion of individual economic liberty and its benefits are accompanied by rising levels of vagrancy, vice, corruption, juvenile delinquency, mass murders of school children, and crime of all sorts. Moreover, inflation has pushed formerly fixed prices to unprecedented heights and is currently threatening a housing bubble similar to that which brought low the U.S. economy. Many people have witnessed a distinct improvement in their lives, and a budding middle class—a bourgeoisie, if you will—has developed. But others, especially in the rural areas, remain poor. Thus, the gap between rich and poor is growing very large, very rapidly, in a society that has recently developed crass materialistic aspirations, a potentially explosive development. China's "floating population," perhaps numbering 100 million people, wander the country looking for work. This search has caused millions of young adults to leave the farms for the cities, leaving their children behind to be cared for by grandparents. These "left behind children," often suffer depression born of feelings of abandonment, displacement, and loneliness. Despite recent attention to health, public health services have recently declined as the state's socialist medical care has retreated before the growth of the market economy. Concomitantly, industries powered by coal, together with a significant increase in the number of automobiles on the road, have combined to foul the air. The UN now ranks China as among the world's most polluted countries.

---

[4]In 2009, China became the world's largest market for new automobiles, selling 14 million cars. It also is the world's leading energy consumer having more than doubled its use of energy between 2000 and 2009. Still, per capita energy consumption in the United States is five times greater than in China.

The nation's emotional health is also jeopardized, as evidenced by the fact that suicides are reaching epidemic proportions. Three reasons for this development appear to be central. First, the increased stress experienced by people from the growing insecurity incumbent in the market system is clearly a major contribution. Second, the seeming hopelessness of a growing number of women is an important cause. China is the only country where suicides by women are greater than those by men. This, in a country where the male population is much greater than the female.

Third, is China's population problem. The one child only policy adopted more than three decades ago means that few Chinese today enjoy the benefit of having siblings, aunts, or uncles. An estimated 400 million fewer births have occurred since the one child policy began.[5] While this reduction has helped China deal with an insupportable population growth, it has brought about other serious problems. Today there are over 32 million more males than females under the age of twenty years. (Cultural and economic factors encourage the Chinese to prefer male children. Tragically, gender-based abortions and even infanticide have reduced the number of female children.) Obviously there will be too few wives for the number of bachelors looking for mates. Besides encouraging prostitution and divorce, the huge dearth of wives is likely to create widespread frustration and anxiety among young adult males. Furthermore, the declining birthrate, together with the increased longevity of the Chinese people due to better nutrition and health care, means that the percentage of older people is increasing even as the percentage of young people declines. Thus, there will soon be fewer taxpayers and caretakers for a growing older generation. In a land where there are scant social security programs for aged peasants, this deficit is critical. Furthermore, there will also be a serious decline in the advantage upon which China has built its economy: a large, inexpensive workforce. Obviously, China has looming problems.

When Deng died in 1997, he was succeeded by Jiang Zemin who presided over the most successful period of economic growth in China's history. Bowing to term limits for China's leaders earlier put in place by Deng, Jiang stepped aside and was replaced in 2002 by **Hu Jintao** (born in 1942) as General Secretary of the CPC and president of the country.[6] Unlike Jiang, who is associated with policies encouraging economic development at almost any price, Hu has made more populist appeals calling for reforms to redress the imbalance of wealth and other policies to create a social safety net for the poor. Although Hu's intentions may be sincere, to date little else of significance has been provided the poor and the aged.

Official corruption, dating back through all of Chinese history, has become an urgent problem for Hu, since it is increasingly difficult for the party to persuade

---

[5]The current fertility rate in China is 1.8 children per woman of childbearing age. This is less than the percentage needed for replacement.

[6]Experts regard the elevation late in 2010 of Xi Jinping to vice chairman of the Central Military Commission as a signal that Xi will replace Hu when his second term expires in 2012.

people of its legitimacy while its members are deeply involved in shady deals. Yet, the turpitude is spreading rapidly and deeply within the society. Making money and enjoying material luxury has become extremely fashionable, and the people best positioned to exploit lucrative commercial opportunities are political leaders at virtually every level of the society. Accordingly, China is plagued by illegal schemes to divert vast amounts of construction funds to the pockets of high-ranking political officials. Local authorities bilk peasants out of the land their families have farmed for centuries, while ranking military leaders embezzle government funds and accept bribes. Party officials buy and sell official posts, and judges sell "justice." Chinese officials have sanctioned shoddy workmanship, adulterated drugs, toxic building material and toys, tainted food products, and even defective knockoff condoms, leading to unwanted pregnancies and births, and spreading disease.[7] The extent of corruption throughout the economy is not known for sure. Estimates of the percent of the economy kept under-the-table run from 3 percent to 15 percent. Seemingly, someone needs to be paid off to compete any but the most basic transactions. Consequently, it may be impossible to remain honest in China. Indeed, flagship American firms like IBM, McDonald's, and Whirlpool have allegedly been involved in Chinese bribery. Teachers and school officials demand money to pass students, surgeons do better work with an extra "consideration," drivers' tests can be passed easier if a little something is forked over. Even children are caught up in the corruption; there are cases of child enslavement and of other children being kidnapped and sold to adoption agencies. Presumably some of these children are adopted by Western parents. Sixty thousand Chinese children have been adopted by American families, for example.

Then there are the "black jails" in which, according to a 2009 report by Human Rights Watch, ordinary citizens who wish to report local official misconduct to higher authority can be illegally detained by hired thugs, or even police. Held for weeks, they can be brutalized, molested, and intimidated in makeshift lockups in hotels, nursing homes, and psychiatric centers. Captors hope plaintiffs will get the message and return home without squealing on their local officials.

Hu has railed against corruption and pledged severe measures against violators. Some observers, however, question the government's sincerity about coming down hard on corruption. In 2008, they posit, a 7.9 earthquake shook Sichuan province to its bedrock. Following a brief but seemingly sincere effort by the government to bring aid and comfort to the stricken, the government suddenly became uncooperative. Reliable figures of the death toll have not yet been released and the government refuses to answer questions from the parents

---

[7]Many of these products went out to the international market as well, including to the United States. As a result, Chinese manufacture is held in such low esteem that the government hired an American public relations firm to burnish its commercial image. But, foreign public opinion is not all China needs to worry about. The Chinese people, particularly in rural areas, are so burdened by official corruption and abuse that they are becoming increasingly resentful; protesting and demonstrating against mistreatment by local officials. Indeed, it has become so bad that there are several recent cases of people who killed malevolent officials, becoming heroes among the local peasants.

of the estimated 5,000 children killed as their school building collapsed on them. Local activists have been jailed for demanding to know why so many schools dissolved into fatal rubble while party headquarters buildings survived the quake. Similarly, two government officials who were "punished" for allowing baby formula tainted with the chemical melamine to reach consumers, causing the deaths of six children and the serious illness of 300,000 more, were reinstated in government positions within a year.

Whatever the case regarding Hu's commitment to containing corruption, he has shown no inclination to liberalize the political system. In spite of announced "action plans" to encourage human liberties, in actuality these seem to be little better than "eyewash." Chinese authorities clamped down hard on dissent just prior to the 2008 Beijing Olympics, arresting dozens of critics of the regime. Since then, pressure on the remaining dissidents has only mounted with the arrest or firing of critical journalists, editors and bloggers, political activists, religious reformers, environmentalists, legal scholars, and human rights advocates.

Tellingly, running up to the twentieth anniversary (June 4, 2009) of the brutal government crackdown on protesting students in **Tiananmen Square,** a new round of arrests sent even more critics and activists to prison in an effort to silence new protests. Western newspapers reported that the square on that day held many more security personnel than visitors. While there has been an increasing number of protests and riots over local issues like illegal land expropriation and other corruption, there is little apparent danger of another Tiananmen-type protest any time soon. A 2009 Pew Research Center poll found 86 percent of Chinese basically satisfied with their country and its government, and the younger the person the stronger the support. Discussions with teenagers about Tiananmen draw either shrugs or protestations of ignorance from the youth. "This is the stupid generation" one Tiananmen protester who saw hundreds of his co-protesters killed is reported to have said of them.

Reminiscent of Ford and General Motors' cooperation with Hitler by using forced labor in their European factories during World War II, China has enlisted the aid of Microsoft, Google, Yahoo, and others in trying to control Internet use. Claiming they are only following the laws of the host country, these firms have given the government names of cyber dissidents and aided in the state's efforts to censor and control Internet use. Furthermore, Cisco has sold China equipment it uses to control its Internet-using populace.[8]

---

[8]In a 2007 congressional hearing, then House Foreign Affairs Committee Chairman, Tom Lantos, himself once a refugee from persecution in Communist Hungary, excoriated Yahoo for cooperating with Chinese authorities, ending in the imprisonment of a Chinese journalist who did no more than use the Internet to forward to an international human rights group a government memo with news coverage of the Tiananmen Square student protest of 1989. "While technological and financial giants," Lantos told Yahoo's CEO, "morally you are pygmies." Then, early in 2010, Google, professing its wish to divorce itself from those unethical practices, but suspected by critics of being motivated by self-defense against Chinese cyber espionage and other by business calculations instead, withdrew its search engine from China proper, but maintained an uncensored facility in Hong Kong.

Once available only to the elite, today Internet use is spreading throughout the society. In early 2010 it was estimated that China had almost 400 million—more people than live in the U.S.—Internet users. Internet cafes are now ubiquitous in cities and towns. Indeed, "Internet addiction" is a growing problem among the youth. Largely used for social purposes by youngsters, many parents worry that their children, fixated on the computer, are neglecting their education and other responsibilities. To combat the problem doctors have prescribed antidepressants, over 300 rectification camps try to reform the afflicted, and a reported 3,000 youths have even been subjected to electric shock therapy to break them of their addiction.

Meanwhile, social liberalization is progressing apace. The once-puritanical society has abandoned the drab Mao suits for more colorful and fashionable clothing. Foreign films and other products are commonplace. Sexual love, once a forbidden topic, is now among the most popular themes in literature, music, and film. Even nightclubs and disco dancing are enjoyed by those who can afford them. Sex shops, now relatively commonplace in the cities, sell everything from pornographic videos to supposed aphrodisiacs. And, some female university students enhance their life styles by providing "escort services" to wealthy patrons. AIDS has accompanied sexual liberation. When it first manifested in the West, the Chinese government scoffed, charging it was a foreigner's and capitalist disease. After some time, however, it spread rapidly even as the government continued to ignore the issue. Communicated largely by prostitutes and migrant workers, the disease is now a significant problem about which the public is abysmally ignorant. A recent poll of 6,000 people found 48 percent believed the disease was transmitted by mosquitoes. Hence, for the past few years the government has tried desperately to inform the public through television, pamphlets, neighborhood meetings, and as on. Government programs now encourage sex education in the schools and the use of condoms, a laudable policy, except that Chinese-manufactured knockoff condoms are of such poor quality that they are suspected of often bursting or leaking, passing on the disease.

China's pattern of insisting on economic reform and political orthodoxy has been consistently applied. Hong Kong was returned to China by the British in 1997, and Macao was returned in 1999. In each case, these former colonies have been allowed to continue their capitalistic economic practices, but political tightening is occurring at the same time. Tibet, formerly an independent country but now a dissident territory of the People's Republic of China, suffers from severe political and cultural repression. Indeed, its culture and national identity are in danger of becoming extinct. A similar fate may await the Uighur (pronounced we-ger) people. Native to the Xinjiang Autonomous Region, China's largest (three times the size of Texas) but sparsely populated territory, this Turkic-Muslim people straddle the ancient Silk Road, the major trading route between Asia and Europe until the sixteenth century. Enjoying benign neglect because of their remote location until the Soviet Union collapsed and its former Muslim regions bordering Xinjiang became independent states,

China began to worry that the Uighur might develop separatist aspirations. Before long, the Uighurs began to see their land inundated by Han (ethnic Chinese). In 1949, the Uighurs comprised 76 percent of the population of Xinjiang, but now it is only 46 percent. Resentful of being crowded out of their own homeland and wincing at the economic and cultural persecution they felt at the hands of the Han—and also angered by the United States, which held several of their brethren at Guantanamo for years, even though the government admitted it had no reason to detain them—the Uighurs became understandably distraught. Suddenly, in September of 2009, three days of violence broke out in Xinjiang's capital of Urumqi. Intended to be a nonviolent protest of a Uighur man's murder in China proper, the demonstration was broken up by police, and a riot erupted. More violent than the ethnic riot in Lhasa—the capital of Tibet—occurring just days before the Beijing Olympics, which took 120 lives,[9] the Urumqi riot was the worst ethnic violence in China in years with 197 people killed and 1,600 injured. China does not only have problems with its ethnic minorities. Taiwan, largely populated with Han escapees from Communist rule, remains independent. But China is bringing more and more pressure on the island state to re-unify with its continental parent.

On the mainland, various other dissident movements have been suppressed. Fledgling opposition parties have been broken up. The religious movement *Falun Gong,* whose doctrine is critical of the current regime, has been actively repressed. Other religious activities that the state views as politically motivated have met with persecution. Nor has the CPC ignored the political potential of new technology. The Internet alarms Chinese authorities who see it as a "runaway" information system and a dangerous public opinion molder. Consequently, as you know, the government has responded with political restraints and attempts to control what can be seen and what can be conveyed on the Internet. (We should not forget that some of these intrusive policies have been facilitated by American corporations.)

The travails of Liu Xiaobo are dramatic examples of the political threat Chinese authorities see posed by the Internet and other forms of open communications. A long-time dissident who played a leading part in the Tiananmen Square protests of 1989, Liu has found himself serving repeated prison terms for his efforts to use the Internet and other vehicles to demand democratic reform in China.

In 2008, he participated in writing the *Charter 08* which demanded democratic reforms and was signed by about 300 other dissidents. For his effort, Liu has been vilified and imprisoned for an eleven year sentence, and his wife was placed under house arrest. But he was also awarded the 2010 Nobel Peace Prize, a matter of considerable embarrassment for the Chinese government, and a group of Nobel Peace Prize laureates signed a letter demanding Liu's

---

[9]In 2010 another series of riots spread from Tibet to Beijing by Tibetan students protesting the new government policy to make Chinese the main language in Tibetan schools.

release and encouraging international leaders to pressure China for his release while attending the November 2010 Group 20 Meeting.

Perhaps moved by growing pressure for democratic reforms, more than 400 aged leaders of China, including Mao Zedong's former private secretary, have signed another open letter demanding reform. Also, Wen Jiabao, China's current Premier, has begun publically calling for political liberalization. Yet, to the present, the government appears unmoved.

Meanwhile, China's economic reforms are modernizing the country and, together with the current Russian experience, may be posing a dilemma for the West, more subtle but perhaps more profound than simple economic or even military competition. It has become mantra in the West that a capitalist economy must inevitably lead its users toward developing liberal democracy. Yet, neither Russia nor China has yet forsaken their authoritarian governments, even though they have adopted many capitalist traits. This is most particularly true of China. Could we be witnessing the emergence of a new political-economic model: open-market authoritarianism? Such a system, should it continue to evolve, might be very attractive to the elites of many developing countries, thus giving China new appeal for its political system as well as for its economic development. Something to ponder.

However, it would also be a mistake to assume that China's return to Mao's extremism is impossible, for Chinese history teaches that no enemy is ever completely and finally defeated. With this in mind, let us now examine Maoist thought.

The Principles of Maoism

Currently, Mao's reputation in China—like Stalin's in Russia—is undergoing a major rejuvenation. Whatever the case, during his lifetime, **Maoism** (*Maoist thought*) made important contributions to Marxism-Leninism. He adjusted it to fit Asian culture and he molded it in such a way as to make it relevant to former colonial countries; those societies which, as we have learned, are among the most apt to be drawn to socialism. To accomplish this goal, he made certain modifications to the theory itself, focusing on the central concept of social class. An agrarian country lacking even the small industrial base available to Russia in 1917, China was overwhelmingly rural, so Mao turned to the peasants for political strength.

Populism   Mao and others realized that the future of the Chinese Revolution was in the hands of the peasantry. The problem of reconciling this practical reality with Marxism, a theory that sees the proletariat as central, inspired him to develop a unique variation on the Marxist theme: **populism.** Taking a page from earlier populists' book, Mao gave the peasants a leading position in the society. Of course, the peasants would eventually have to be proletarianized, but in the meantime, their virtues were announced to the world in Maoist literature. Mao believed that the peasants' simple, pure character, unblemished by the evil influences of urbanity, was the bulwark of Chinese strength. Later, during the Cultural Revolution, he called on Chinese sophisticates to "learn from the people," as millions of scholars, students, managers, public officials, and townspeople were forced to the farm to relearn basic values through hard manual labor, disrupting their lives for a decade or more.

Perhaps demonstrating that the current Chinese leadership is not so far removed from Maoism as might be wished, it exacted the same punishment on the students after the Tiananmen debacle, Thousands of students were forced to serve time on the farms, learning about the roots of China (no pun intended) before being allowed to return to their studies. China's current political dissidents are usually given the same "educational" experience.

Populism poses an ideological dilemma. If the peasants are the true foundation of Chinese society, how are they to be proletarianized without destroying their positive features? Mao solved this problem by resorting to a typically Chinese but very un-Marxist idea. Much less an economic determinist than Marx, Mao argued that ideological purity was more important than economic training and that the proletarian mentality could be developed through educational as well as economic experience. Thus, he maintained that the peasants might be proletarianized by being taught the socialist ethic, but that they need never leave the farm to complete the transformation.

Permanent Revolution Easily the most radical major form of Marxism, Maoism's principle of permanent revolution theoretically makes the development of a conservative status quo impossible. Both Marx and Lenin made vague references to the concept of permanent revolution, and Leon Trotsky adopted it as a major theme. Mao, however, took the notion even beyond Trotsky's position. He argued that revolution was a means by which people achieved their goals. The road to socialism, he claimed, must be constantly punctuated with violence. Conflict, after all, is the essence of the dialectic. Great progress, born of turmoil and social disruption, is an inevitable fact of life.

The same holds for socialists' relations with capitalist societies. There can never be true peace or permanent accommodation with capitalism because the two systems are diametrically contradictory of each other. Violent struggle between these two antagonistic systems is therefore unavoidable and can be interrupted only by brief periods of mutual restraint. Specifically taking issue with Khrushchev's doctrine, Mao contended that peaceful coexistence is a fantasy that can be pursued only at the risk of betraying the revolution itself.

The Mass Line Having witnessed the stultification of the Bolshevik Revolution by cadre turned functionaries, Mao feared above all that the Chinese Revolution might fall prey to self-oriented careerism, deadly institutionalization, and bureaucratic inertia. Combining his theories of populism and permanent revolution, Mao rejected Lenin's elitist reliance on the party to lead the revolution. Mao maintained that the people are "intrinsically red" and that given the proper ideological direction, they can be trusted to strive for revolutionary goals. Accordingly, Mao resorted to the **mass line,** calling for the mobilization of the masses again and again, thus visiting a series of sociopolitical thunderbolts on the land. The antilandlord campaign (1949–1952), the first five-year plan (1953–1957), the Hundred Flowers Campaign (1957), the Great Leap Forward (1958–1960), and the Great Cultural Revolution (1966–1976) were major events in which the people were mobilized to accomplish the goals of the revolution. Besides these epic movements, literally hundreds of campaigns were initiated, and indeed are still being invoked, to reach desired goals: Anti-insect and antirodent campaigns, anticorruption movements, sanitary campaigns, tree planting campaigns, and AIDS awareness campaigns are examples of the frequent phenomena of Chinese life that entreat citizens to produce more, conduct themselves properly, and stamp out hazards to health. China's great resource, and its great curse at the same time, is its immense population. The mass-line technique represents Mao's attempt to turn a disadvantage into an advantage.

The Bourgeoisie When the communists came to power in 1948–1949, the economy was in a sorry state, having been battered by almost four decades of war and revolution. Notwithstanding Marxist doctrine, Lenin's experience taught that immediate socialization of an economy could be dangerous. Though merchants and industrialists were not a large percentage of the population, Mao and his advisors knew that they were critical for the economic stability of China; consequently, he decided that, at least for a time, some members of the bourgeois class had to be tolerated in China.

Such a rationalization for maintaining capitalism has implications far beyond a simple pragmatic accommodation. In Mao's theory of *nonantagonistic contradictions,* China was seen to be made up of four harmonious classes: the proletariat, the peasantry, the petty bourgeoisie (intellectuals, artisans, and managers), and the national bourgeoisie (patriotic merchants and business owners). These diverse classes could coexist in peace because, although different, their interests were not necessarily in conflict.

By contrast, the evil elements in society were those that exploited the Chinese people: the landlords and the **imperialist capitalists** (capitalists with foreign ties). In this theory, Mao took a stance that is more typical of leaders of formerly colonial countries than Marxists. The question of class differences, the feature of utmost importance to Marx, was played down, and foreign exploitation, or imperialism, was stressed. Imperialism is a major theme in Maoist thought, as in Lenin's, though their definitions and emphasis differ. To combat the evils of imperialism, *Mao, like Stalin, turned to nationalism.* Accordingly, although never greatly appreciated, Chinese capitalists who had no foreign dealings were tolerated, whereas those with foreign connections were severely persecuted. Nonetheless, when the communists thought they had learned enough to run the privately owned enterprises themselves, even the national bourgeoisie was eliminated and the enterprises were nationalized. Interestingly enough, many divested capitalists were kept on to run the plants they formerly owned. A few even lived long enough to regain ownership of their factories during the reforms of Deng and Jiang, and for the past decade, capitalists have even been welcomed into the CPC.

Guerrilla Warfare   Perhaps the Maoist idea most widely applied is the theory of guerrilla warfare. Both Marx and Lenin believed that power could be seized at a single stroke and that the violent portion of a Marxist revolution would be very short. The two differed only on tactics, Marx believing that the revolution would happen by itself, Lenin supporting a conspiratorial approach. Mao, by contrast, argued that revolutions in less-developed countries would have to be protracted over a long period. He set down the principles of the doctrine in his famous work *Yu Chi Chan (Guerrilla Warfare)*. In this book, Mao divides guerrilla warfare into two basic parts: *military* and *political.*

Mao saw the military part of a guerrilla war as having three distinct phases. During the first phase, the soldiers concentrate on building secure bases, or *safe zones,* in which to rest, refit, and train troops. The second phase involves numerous small groups attacking the enemy by means of ambush and other guerrilla activities. The final phase begins only after victory is certain and consists of large troop maneuvers and battles similar to those of a conventional war.

As Mao saw it, the only real objective of guerrilla warfare is to destroy the fighting capacity of the opponent. He admonished his followers to pick their fights wisely, engaging the enemy only when they were certain of victory. Territory, he averred, must never be a major goal. Indeed, only the safe zones should be defended. Any area given up to a superior force will, with cunning and patience, be regained later. This clever strategy is most clearly expressed in Mao's famous dictum, "When guerrillas engage a stronger enemy, they withdraw when he advances; harass him when he stops; strike when he is weary, pursue him when he withdraws." Of greatest importance is the guerrillas' constant field position, from which they always put pressure on the enemy. Never destroyed, always there, the guerrillas give an appearance of invincibility, humiliating the enemy, who in the eyes of the people cannot defeat a ragtag band of jungle fighters.

More important to Mao than military operations were the political activities of the guerrilla force. Mao fully expected every soldier to do more teaching than fighting. The war would be won by convincing the peasants of the rightness of the cause rather than by defeating the enemy militarily. This emphasis on converting the people is in reality another expression of the peasant-centeredness of Mao's thought, and it is indicative of his belief that people can be persuaded to the cause if educated properly. His strategy, to "surround the cities with the countryside," had little to do with actually holding territory. Rather, it was based on a desire to win the support of the peasants, thus isolating the enemy in the cities and making its defeat inevitable.

Mao was very explicit about the methods that should be used in converting the peasants. First, the soldiers must set a good example. Mao therefore banned the use of opium in the army and insisted that the troops treat the local people with respect. He also commanded that officers live no better than their troops.

When a guerrilla unit first occupied an area, it was to gain the confidence of the peasants by helping them create local governments. This would weaken their political loyalty to the enemy. Moreover, local councils would serve as a base of local resistance if the area ever had to be left to the enemy. Next, the land was to be redistributed—taken from the landlords and given to the people who farmed it—thus giving the peasants an economic stake in the guerrilla cause. Also, the guerrilla soldiers would devote a good deal of time to rebuilding the villages in order to put the peasants on an equal and friendly footing with the soldiers as they shared their labor. During this process, the guerrillas would constantly teach the peasants the goals of the revolution, pointing out its benefits and reminding them of the enemy's evil policies.

By such means, Mao believed, the guerrilla force would build an invincible base of support. As peasant support grew, supplies, recruits, and information about the enemy would increase, strengthening the guerrilla units. At the same time, the enemy would grow increasingly isolated and weak as the ring around the cities became tighter and tighter, eventually stifling the enemy's initiative and sapping its power. In time, the pressure would become unendurable and would bring about the enemy's collapse.

Successful not only in China, Mao's ideas on guerrilla warfare were applied throughout the Developing World, including Vietnam, where the United States was defeated by a force with inferior firepower but superior strategy and commitment. Adopting Mao's military ideas to Latin American conditions, Fidel Castro seized power in Cuba and there developed another unique variant of Marxism.

CUBA

In many ways, Cuba is unique among Marxist-Leninist states, whereas in other ways, its experience was anticipated in other lands, especially China.

The Cuban Revolution

In 1898, Cuba was on the verge of overthrowing its Spanish colonialist rulers of four centuries when the United States intervened and, from the Cuban perspective, snatched victory from their grasp. At the end of the Spanish American War, Cuba was enveloped in the new American external empire. Ostensibly giving it independence in 1901, Washington anointed Cuba's first president, Tomas Estrada Palma, a Cuban-born U.S. citizen, whose salary was paid by the United States. Cuba was further held in check by the overwhelming American economic grasp and by the Platt Amendment, which essentially made Cuba a dependent of the United States. Petty dictator after petty dictator pillaged Cuba but enjoyed U.S. support, as long as American economic interests were not disturbed. Soon, American economic concerns, led by the United Fruit Company, came to own most of Cuba's sugar fields and refineries, cattle ranches, mining companies, public utilities, and more. In the 1920s, American mobsters also moved into this lucrative but hapless country, providing prostitution, drugs, and gambling for international vacationers even as the domestic population was made to feel like street-corner pimps. Meanwhile, Fulgencio Batista (1901–1973), an army sergeant who rose through the ranks, eventually became the dictator of Cuba. By the 1950s, Cuba was mortified to find itself dominated by a powerful triumvirate: Batista, the American mob, and the U.S. government.

Born in 1927, the son of a Spanish immigrant who became a wealthy Cuban landowner, **Fidel Ruiz Castro** was well on his way to joining the tiny Cuban elite as a charismatic lawyer, but his leftist politics led him to the opposition instead. As a young man, he chafed at the humiliation to which Cuba was subjected by government corruption, Meyer Lansky's thugs, and U.S. economic and political power. In 1953, Castro organized a resistance movement that ultimately drove Batista into exile in 1959.

Unquestionably a leftist, Castro was almost certainly not a Marxist during his days in the mountains. Indeed, the Cuban Communist Party, which Castro ignored until after he took power, had held two seats in an early Batista government and actually opposed Castro's guerrilla war. Finally, when Castro's victory became apparent, the Communist Party, along with almost all other opposition groups, hailed the Commandante. Yet, Castro was clearly influenced early on by a few committed Marxists, not the least of whom were the Argentine physician-turned revolutionary Ernesto "Che" Guevara (1928–1967) and Fidel's brother, **Raoul Castro** (born 1931).

Relations between Washington and Cuba's revolutionary government were strained from the outset. Castro feared that the United States might send troops to unseat him, and the Eisenhower government, persuaded that Castro was a communist, was equally suspicious of Cuba. In response to Cuban social and economic problems and in defiance of U.S. demands that American interests be left to conduct their Cuban business as usual, Castro began to expropriate, without remuneration, non-Cuban-owned land. The Eisenhower administration responded with economic pressures of its own, triggering the Cuban nationalization of all U.S.-owned properties in Cuba. The Kennedy administration was even more truculent, imposing an embargo on Cuban trade, backing the Bay of Pigs invasion, supporting acts of terrorism in Cuba, and engaging in numerous attempts on Castro's life. Castro responded by aligning Cuba with the Soviet Union, allowing Soviet missiles on Cuban soil, and proclaiming himself a Marxist-Leninist.

His conversion to Marxism-Leninism after coming to power makes Castro unique. Cuba is the only country to become communist as a result of a movement in which the revolution was not carried out by a cadre of dedicated party members. In fact, the party has only recently showed signs of developing a life and importance separate from its association with Fidel, and its dependence on the personality of the leader stands in contrast to the centrality of the party in other communist states.

Whether Castro would have created a communist system on his own is, of course, impossible to say. Certainly, Cuba would have been a socialist state.

However, the hostility of the U.S. government toward Castro was certainly a critical determinant in the events that transpired.

Once associated with the Marxist camp, Castro embarked on a number of Soviet-type but ill-conceived policies. Centralizing government control over the economy, Castro's failed economic policies, together with low sugar prices and frequent poor weather, and the impact of the U.S. embargo, combined to deny Cuba the prosperity it sought. The Soviet Union subsidized Cuba heavily, but this economic crutch served only to temporarily mask fundamental economic flaws.

For its part, the United States laid down an economic embargo in the early 1960s that continues to this day. Over the years U.S. policy toward Cuba has relaxed somewhat during Democratic administrations but tightened under Republican governments, but the embargo, reviled across the globe, remains. Not content with just applying economic pressure, however, the United States has covertly supported cabals to oust Castro, acts of terrorism against Cuba, and repeated assassination attempts against Fidel. The aggressive American stance gave Castro cause, *or cover*, to militarize the society, denying the Cuban people many human liberties, and drove Cuba to even greater reliance on the Soviet Union. However, with the 1991 collapse of the Soviet Union, Cuba has had to fend for itself, even as the United States continues its punitive policies.

The loss of Soviet support aggravated an already serious economic situation. During the 1990s, which Castro called the "special period," consumer goods and food disappeared from the markets, motor transport was abandoned, and electrical blackouts were endured. Never before fond of vegetables, Cubans suddenly planted gardens with which the people fed themselves.

As the states in the Soviet bloc abandoned socialism, many in the United States expected that Castro would also fall. Surprisingly, such was not to be the case. Castro survived; his regime continued in power. By the end of the 1990s, however, his health began to fail. Finally, on July 31, 2006, he "temporarily" relinquished power to his brother Raoul so that he could undergo intestinal surgery for diverticulitis, almost dying on the table. Finally, in February of 2008, he resigned the presidency permanently in favor of Raoul after being the leader of Cuba since January 1959. Although Fidel resigned from formal office he continues to exercise influence from backstage through publishing articles in the press, the frequency of which has grown as his health improves. He has even begun again to deliver public speeches, warning of the aggressive policies of the United States and of the potential for nuclear war between the United States and Iran.

It is not possible at this distance to know the relationship the two brothers have now that the leading and supporting roles have reversed. However, it certainly does not appear to be antagonistic. Fidel continues to enjoy broad popular support and he seems to be able to dramatically influence policy, even as he signals full support for Raoul's leadership. For his part, Raoul appears to be in full control of day-to-day government management, but insisting that "Fidel is still Fidel," he seems content to recognize the irreplaceability of his brother.

Meanwhile, the Cuban government, much to the deep surprise of some observers who expected it to collapse in Castro's absence, seems to have taken the leadership change in stride.

The leadership switch was greeted by the people with mixed emotions, of course the dissidents were happy to see Fidel go, but they announced no great confidence that Raoul would seriously reform the system. The bulk of the population appeared to be generally concerned for Fidel's health and understandably anxious about what was in store for Cuba without his hand guiding it. On the other hand, there was no expression of panic; after all, Fidel's health had been failing for some years. Rather, they seemed confident the society would weather the transformation. Himself serving in high posts of the government since 1959, and buttressed with the confidence of, as Minister of Defense, having a major part in leading Cuba through the "special period" of the 1990s, Raoul took administrative control with little apparent problem, and he embarked on several important, although not yet transformative, reforms.

When Raoul took over, Fidel was in the process of rescinding several of the policies which privatized many local businesses (auto repair shops, small restaurants, beauty shops, and the like). Indeed, Raoul, as the person most responsible for bringing Cuba back from the privations of the "special period" had actually overseen the implementation of these reforms.

Reacting to the current global recession, Raoul has initiated several liberalizing policies. These include making available to people idle government

© Alejandro Ernesto/epa/Corbis

Fidel and Raul Castro consult at an early meeting of the Cuban parliament, the National Assembly.

land on which to raise meat, vegetables, and fruit and vend them on the open market; and allowing people to gain title to their homes, thus allowing them to pass it on to their heirs or to sell it back to the government. (Selling or renting property to other private individuals is still not legal.) He also revoked former wage limits, thus allowing employers to pay more to good workers. Restraints were relaxed on "exotic" consumer goods, thus facilitating the private purchase of computers, cell phones, DVD players, motorbikes, and so on. And, Raoul has carried through with a previously planned modernization of Cuba's antiquated public transportation system, which alone will aid future important economic development. Most significantly, however, in 2010 Raoul began a policy of laying off half a million government workers claiming they are no longer needed in government employment and inviting them to gravitate to private sector jobs. This is a politically risky but economically necessary reform.

Not content to stop at economic development alone, Raoul called upon citizens to point out shortcomings of officials in the society. He commuted the sentences of all prisoners on death row except for three convicted terrorists and released several political prisoners, he has continued Fidel's relaxed policy toward religious worship, he commissioned a study of relaxing the government's foreign travel policies (Cuba is one of the few remaining countries requiring exit visas of its citizens), and he has begun to end the government's prohibition of using the Internet. Yet, Cuba's violations of human rights remain a serious problem and occasioned strong international condemnation when a political prisoner died in 2010.

The global recession hit Cuba hard, and Raoul has been relatively forthright about its consequences. With an aging workforce, he has presided over a five-year lengthening of the retirement age to 65 for men and 60 for women. Furthermore, in a July 2008 speech, he cautioned that citizens had to prepare for "realistic" socialism and that the usual government subsidies may have to be curtailed.

During his campaign for the U.S. presidency, Barack Obama expressed a keen interest in improved relations with Cuba. Typically, however, Obama has taken cautious, thoughtful, measured steps toward this. However, a December 2008 poll that showed for the first time that a large majority (65 percent) of Cuban Americans polled in South Florida support normalization of relations with Cuba and 55 percent want the U.S. embargo lifted may soon speed up Obama's effort at amelioration.

Taking care to assess the Cuban response at each stage, Obama has begun several initiatives, each small by itself, but representing a substantial offer in the aggregate. He signed an order to close the prison at the U.S. Navy base at Guantanamo Bay, Cuba, although this goal will not be soon achieved. He relaxed travel and money transfer restrictions for the 1.5 million Cuban Americans to visit relatives. He loosened the restrictions on the export of certain goods to Cuba and he is allowing Cuban Americans to pay for Cuban relatives' cell phones. He initiated resumed talks on immigration issues and re-established direct mail service between the two countries. Cuba has responded

with an invitation to cooperate with the United States in fighting drug trafficking and terrorism, and in hurricane disaster preparedness. Obama has also
reversed long-standing U.S. policy of opposing Cuba's readmission to The Organization of American States.

Perhaps playing good cop-bad cop, Raoul has been pragmatic and cooperative while Fidel has been skeptical about Obama's overtures. The remaining
outstanding issues obstructing the normalization of relations as expressed by
the two respective sides are, for the United States, Cuba must develop more
democratic institutions, including allowing freedom of speech, and it must free
its political prisoners.[10] While Cuba demands that the United States stops meddling in its affairs; that it abandons its "wet-foot dry-foot" policy which returns Cuban refugees who do not set foot on American soil, while allowing to
stay those who do; apologizes for the U.S. part in the Bay of Pigs invasion; and
eliminates the embargo.

When the possible rapprochement of Cuba and the United States is examined carefully, positive steps by Cuba since 2007 and those taken by the United
States since 2008 are quite impressive, considering that the two were at logger-
heads only a short time ago. If each party is sincere about repairing relations,
nothing on the list of demands on either side is beyond negotiating successfully. The American position seems the most certain. Immigration difficulties
will probably be ironed out at the negotiations table. And, the embargo seems
less and less supportable with each passing month. It has no support interna-
tionally, a majority of the U.S. public—including now the Cuban Americans—
favor ending it, and Congress could probably even rustle up enough votes to
repeal it.

Matters are more complicated on the Cuban side. For example, it is a fact
that the Castros have long used the embargo as an excuse for the Cuban economy doing so poorly. If it is no more, responsibility for failure will probably settle where the lion's share of it belongs: on the Cuban leadership. For that reason
it is strongly suspected that each time the United States draws close to repealing
the embargo, Cuba deliberately does something to anger the United States, thus
scotching the deal: President Carter was put off by Cuba sending troops to aid
leftist rebels in Africa, and during the Clinton administration a private airplane

---

[10]Interestingly, in December 2006 the Cuban Commission on Human Rights and National Rec-
onciliation, an illegal organization in Cuba, but grudgingly tolerated by the government, listed
283 confirmed political prisoners held by the Castro regime, while the United States held about
400 "enemy combatants" at its naval base at Guantanamo Bay, Cuba. Ironically, the United
States held far more political prisoners in Cuba than did the Cuban government.

Causing further embarrassment to the United States' record of protecting human rights,
and even in combating terrorism, the Bush administration actively frustrated efforts to bring Luis
Posada Carriles to justice. Posada, a Cuban exile and former covert CIA operative, is wanted in
Cuba and Venezuela for a 20-year spree of airline and hotel bombings, resulting in the death of
dozens of people. Posada remains at liberty while awaiting trial for entering the United States
illegally, as this disgraceful episode tarnishes with hypocrisy the United States' commitment to
the war on terrorism.

carrying Cuban exiles was shot down over international waters. (Whether the pilot was doing something illegal by entering Cuban air space before being shot down remains a matter of dispute.) So there is a legitimate question as to whether the Cuban government actually wants an end to the embargo.

That issue aside, there is a leadership problem in Cuba. In early 2009, two high-ranking government reformers, each widely seen as possible post-Castro leaders, were purged from their government and party offices and replaced by septuagenarian generals. This move clearly boosted the military's influence at the top level of power, but it also clouded the succession issue. Fidel will probably not resume power and Raoul is likely to leave the scene before too long. Significantly, there seems to be no one from the younger generation positioned to rise to power; this vacuum could set the stage for a succession struggle Cuba has not experienced in modern times.

During a recent visit to Cuba, I had occasion to engage in conversation with government officials, party members, academics, and ordinary citizens. In both private and public conversations, I asked how Cuba had weathered the "special period"; why did it not collapse, as had other Soviet bloc governments, and as many U.S. authorities had predicted. The answers were varied and often complex, but three universal, although certainly not unanimously held, themes emerged. If Cuba compares itself to the advanced countries, it does not look too good; but among Central American societies, it compares very favorably. For example, a college professor said to me, "Look, I am my father's dream for me. I have a good education, my family and I are not hungry, we enjoy good health. There are things I'd like to see changed, of course, but why would I want all of this thrown out?"

A second reason often given had to do with Fidel's popularity. Although it is certainly not unanimous, the Cuban people generally support him. The level of support was obviously greater among the rural populations because Castro's policies have benefited the *compesinos* most. Whatever the case, Castro is admired for risking his privileged status to drive out a government of "bandits"; for the return of Cuban self-respect and self-reliance he engendered; for his defiance of the "Colossus of the North," the United States; and for the many advancements his government has brought to the ordinary people.

A third belief seemed even more broadly held than the previous two. People at all levels of society expressed concern that had the system collapsed, conditions would have returned to the pre-Castro era: The old white elite would come back to power from exile in Florida, and—with U.S. support—the bulk of the Cuban people would be returned to conditions of blatant racism, abject poverty, malnutrition, illiteracy, political and economic subjugation, and national humiliation. Indeed, it is often persuasively argued that U.S. policy, which supports Cuba's old oppressors and which threatens the social progress of the revolution, is among the main reasons the Castros are able to remain in power. A fourth reason was given by some of the ordinary people, although certainly not by party or government personnel. Some people asserted that Castro's own police-state tactics may have helped keep him in power as other communist governments collapsed.

Despite Castro's economic failures, his policies achieved some important social objectives. Illiteracy has been eliminated and free education is provided to all, a rare benefit in the region. No other countries in the region enjoys Cuba's standard of medical care. Indeed, the per capita number of Cuban physicians is higher than the American ratio, the infant mortality rate is actually lower than in the United States, and the average life expectancy is about the same. While shortages stubbornly persist, housing construction has moved masses of people from hovels to sparse but adequate apartments. Full employment was achieved, and the wretched poverty of prerevolutionary times has been eradicated. Hunger, except during the "special period," is a thing of the past, and racial equality is significantly enhanced. These accomplishments, together with Cuba's successful recovery from the economic depression during the "special period" have been important. Seemingly more self-confident and certainly more self-reliant, the Cuban people appear optimistic about the future.

In general, however, the Cuban economy remains a basket case. This is primarily due to bad management, failure to modernize, serious draught, repeated hurricane damage, the American economic embargo, and collapsing sugar prices which have all taken their toll. While the worst ravages seen during the "special period" of the 1990s have not reappeared, Cuba is still plagued with severe shortages in consumer goods, rationing of staples as well as luxuries, and crumbling housing.

Raoul, though clearly a Marxist well before his older brother, has shown a greater pragmatic ability to moderate and change with the times. In the early years, he was instrumental in forging the Cuban-Soviet alliance and in the radicalization of Cuban politics. Yet, in the 1990s he recognized the need to change Cuba's economic structure, encouraging tourism and privatizing certain low levels of the retail and service segments. Since becoming the president, Raoul has quietly encouraged further liberalization of the economy. However, lacking his brother's charisma, Raoul has always been content to remain in the background. And, so too with his current position. While he now is supposed to have supreme authority, he attends a minimum of ceremonial events, his speeches are brief, and he shies away from interviews. What the future holds for Cuba and its current government is impossible to say, of course, but it is clear that for the moment, the transition has been peaceful and the society remains calm, if somewhat concerned for what is to follow.

Fidelismo

Similar to Mao, Castro's ideological appeal of **fidelismo** is replete with nationalistic sentiments born of anticolonialism. Mao said on the day the People's Republic of China was founded, "From today on the Chinese people have stood up. Never again will foreigners be able to trample us." Castro's speeches and writing defiantly proclaim Cuba a socialist country and vitriolicly attack capitalist imperialism, putting special emphasis on the United States. In his radical early years, Castro tried to ignite revolutions against "Yankee imperialism" throughout the Americas, but these moves failed, and Castro was, for a time, rejected and isolated by his Latin American colleagues. The discovery of Soviet missiles on Cuban bases discredited him further in their eyes. After the 1960s, Castro increasingly portrayed himself as a leader of the "establishment" communist world. Far from being a placid leader, he sent Cuban troops and aid to revolutions in South Africa, Namibia, and Angola and is still esteemed for this help. Yet, his demeanor is considerably less truculent than in his early years.

Politically, the Cuban regime is unique among communist states in two related ways. First, because Castro became a Marxist-Leninist only after he had come to power, the Communist Party was organized as an instrument of state control only after the revolution and seems to have had little identity than that which it takes from Castro himself. Although its members head the various public groups, such as the press, the trade unions, and the social services, the party may not yet have established itself as legitimate in its own right. Accordingly, popular commitment to the party as an instrument of power is not as keen as in other communist countries. Yet, for the moment at least, it seems to be maintaining order and no great movement for its ouster has arisen.

Second, although Cuba's current problems have to some extent diminished public support for Fidel, he continues to enjoy more profound popular commitment—even in illness—than any contemporary communist leader. He is, after all, the last living person in the pantheon of revolutionaries who bought communism. Not unlike Lenin, Josip Broz Tito of Yugoslavia, Kim Il Sung of North Korea, Ho Chi Minh of North Vietnam, and Mao, Castro is seen as the personification of a popular revolution. Similar to his predecessors, Castro has immense charisma that assures him of a great personal following. Indeed, his personal popularity is so central to governing Cuba that *personalismo,* his personal decision-making approach and his governing style, are central to *Fidelismo.*[11]

Obviously, Cuba's fate after the Castros is a matter of some concern in Cuba. Fidel's *personalismo*, together with the aggressiveness of some Miami-based Cuban Americans toward their homeland, makes it less than certain Raoul or the Communist Party will be able to fill Castro's shoes without considerable difficulty. This is not to imply, however, that the Cuban people will completely forsake socialism when the Castros no longer dominate the scene. The social progress and the independence achieved by Cuba since 1959 will not be lightly abandoned. On the other hand, the hope among many Cubans that the younger generation of leaders would be more pragmatic than the old revolutionaries has been dashed with their removal from office. But the Cuban people are heartened by the knowledge that the most extreme anti-Castro Cuban Americans are dying out and the younger Cuban Americans are not as keen as their parents about returning to power in Cuba.

---

[11]Unlike Stalin, Mao, or North Korea's Kim Il Sung, however, Castro seems to remain personally popular without any personality cult. In fifteen days traveling throughout Cuba, I saw almost no political signs glorifying Castro. Indeed, many more pictures and statues of Jose Marti and Che Guevara than of Castro were evident.

Meanwhile, faced with harsh reality, Fidel Castro was forced to change his stance. His policies have led to mixed results. They have achieved admirable social advances, but they have also led to official corruption, stubborn economic failures, and serious human rights abuses. Once seen as the *infant terrible* of the socialist world, Castro evolved to a lonely defender of Marxist orthodoxy in the early 1990s and to a more pragmatic stance at present. Cuba, not unlike China, seems to be trying to retain as much socialism as possible while adopting as much capitalism as necessary.

Whether the Castros or their communist successors are able to adjust to the looming future sufficiently to remain relevant we shall have to see. But whatever the challenges, the Cuban people, at least for now, are firmly resolved that the island will not return to the tyranny of a tiny elite or to the humiliation of U.S. colonialism.

THE RE-EMERGENCE OF SOCIALISM

When, at the beginning of the 1990s, the edifices of communism collapsed, some people in the West predicted that socialism was doomed forever. They expected that Marxism-Leninism in China and Cuba and Stalinism in North Korea would inevitably follow the examples of the Soviet Union and Eastern Europe.

Indeed, these predictions may still come to pass. Vietnam, Laos, Cambodia, and China have made significant progress in reforming their systems and improving their relations with the West. None, however, seems destined to either collapse or to completely abandon socialism for capitalism. Still, their economies and their political systems are far less dogmatic than before. Cuba has also changed, albeit more slowly, but the age of its leaders and its proximity to the United States and to the Cuban Americans make its future more precarious. North Korea has been forced by its self-induced wretched economic circumstances to very grudgingly turn a blind eye toward some market-driven farm production and retail activities. But its 2010 currency devaluation has been such a disaster that it threatens to return the society to the devastating economic conditions of the mid-1990s. An ailing Kim Jong-il has designated his youngest son, Kim Jong-Un, his successor, as North Korea seems poised for further changes.

At the same time, however, some societies that attempted to abandon socialism have recently reversed course somewhat. Socialist governments have been returned to power in many countries that spun off from the Soviet Union. Most of these are moderate when compared with the Soviet system, but some—in Belarus, Uzbekistan, Tadzhikistan, and Turkmenistan—appear to be quite Stalinist in texture. Socialism is also resurgent in parts of Eastern Europe, and communist governments have recently won elections in Cyprus and briefly in Nepal.

Perhaps surprisingly, the strongest movement toward the left is currently taking place in Latin America. Beginning in the 1980s, Latin America began to shed its strongman, right-wing, military dictatorships and gravitate toward experiments with democracy and capitalism. Since the mid-1990s, however, disillusionment with the market forces began largely in response to perceived rising exploitation built into globalization and growing suspicion about the intentions of the United States, especially those of the George W. Bush administration. The current rules of globalization tend to favor two opposites: those states with capital (who, after all, developed and impose the rules) and those who enjoy a very cheap labor force but a relatively well-educated people. These two ends, the capitalist countries and on the lower end China, India, South Korea, Taiwan, and Brazil, see their GDPs rising. Those societies caught in the middle, with little capital and few labor skills, find themselves unable to advance economically, and, at least in Latin America, they are turning to the left for a solution.

Even the drift leftward in Latin America is not without variegation. In 2009, Chile replaced popular, but termed-out socialist president Michelle Bachelet, with a center-right aspirant, and Argentina, Brazil, and Uruguay are served by moderate leftists. Generally, their mild economic policies have been relatively successful in addressing, although far from solving, their peoples' social and economic problems.

Much more radical are the populist-socialists in Venezuela, Bolivia, Ecuador, and Nicaragua. Led by Venezuela's Hugo Chavez, these radicals have proclaimed socialist intentions and to greater or lesser extent, have deliberately defied the United States. Like Castro, playing on popular antipathy toward the United States, they have blamed it for their country's most intractable problems.

Daniel Ortega, elected president of Nicaragua in January 2007, led a rebellion in the 1980s against the United States-supported dictatorship there and he found himself fiercely opposed by the Reagan administration. Perhaps because he was elected president with only a minority of the popular vote, Ortega is reluctant to appear too radical just now. The leaders of Venezuela, Bolivia, and Ecuador, however, mince no words and few actions.

Hugo Chavez seems genuinely interested in redistributing Venezuela's wealth in favor of the nation's poor. Fortified by billions when oil revenues were high (Venezuela is the fourth largest oil exporter to the U.S. market), he has invoked his "popular economy" complete with social welfare, housing, and food distribution programs that made him very popular among the vast number of poor in his country. He has also begun to nationalize Venezuela's major industries including oil, electricity, telecommunications, and sugar. The wrenching change he has fostered, together with ubiquitous corruption, bureaucratic mismanagement, and now diminished oil revenues from a recessed market have now reduced his popularity somewhat, yet in 2010 he managed to maintain a reduced majority in Venezuela's national legislative after muscling through a constitutional amendment in 2009 that eliminates term limits, an unsettling development. Since then, Chavez has begun to silence some of his most powerful critics. Furthermore, his relations with the United States have cooled further as he expropriates foreign companies and agreed with Russia to cooperate in building a nuclear power capacity in Venezuela.

Meanwhile, Bolivia elected South America's first full-blooded Indian president: Evo Morales. He has nationalized Bolivia's oil and gas industries, most of its public utilities, other industries, and initiated broad-based agrarian reforms to protect the cocoa farmers from whence he came. Then in 2009, Morales, like Chavez, also won a constitutional amendment eliminating presidential term limits.

Rafael Correa, elected president of Ecuador in 2007, is also a committed socialist. Earning a Ph.D. from the University of Illinois, Correa has been consumed with addressing Ecuador's massive foreign debt. In doing so, he has crossed sabers with the World Bank, the International Monetary Fund, and the United States, actually defaulting on loans at one point. While he has not yet fully implemented his ambitious plans for agrarian reform, he was re-elected in 2009, the first time in thirty years an Ecuadorian president has been returned to office. Suspicious of U.S. military intentions, Correa forced the United States to leave Ecuador's Manta Air Base in 2009. Despite this friction, however, American officials have been consistent in their praise for Correa's efforts to combat the drug trafficking in his region. And, in 2010 Correa overcame an attempted police force mutiny an episode displaying both his political strength and weakness.

The successful efforts by Chavez and Morales to eliminate constitutionally imposed term limits worry some authorities who suspect it may be first steps toward creating dictatorships. Other problems could arise because, not enjoying Venezuela's economic bounty, Nicaragua, Bolivia, and Ecuador may be in danger of encountering the same economic "Catch 22" other rural-based socialist states have. In other words, while socialism is most attractive to poor states, it is least likely to work for them because there is not enough production to meaningfully improve the lives of the masses when spread out among them. Thus, the best that can happen is that everyone becomes equally poor.

Recently, four other socialists were elected to head Latin American governments: Mauricio Funes, an avowed Marxist, in El Salvador; Fernando Lugo, a former Roman Catholic Bishop, in Paraguay; Alvaro Colom of Guatemala; and former guerrilla leader José Mujica of Uruguay. They have served too little time in office to assess their policies. Since each leads a society suffering long experience with reactionary military regimes, these new leaders will be cautious about instituting needed reform. Especially given the fact that a fellow leftist president in Honduras, Manuel Zelaya, was abruptly removed from power in June of 2009 by a military coup. Unfortunately, the inexplicably tepid reactions of the Obama administration to this undemocratic act may signal that the United States cannot be counted upon to oppose military coups in the hemisphere, thus perhaps encouraging more.

American Socialism

As you learned in Chapter 5, largely because of incredibly irresponsible business practices and lax government regulation, the American financial markets came within days of collapse, and would almost certainly have caused a worldwide depression at least as severe as that of the 1930s. To forestall the crisis, the American government under George W. Bush and then under Barack Obama moved decisively. The government loaned money and bought stock in financial institutions and in crippled industries, thus infusing enough money to check, and ultimately reverse, their decline. Thus, the government became a major stockholder in the largest financial houses, the insurance giant American International Group (AIG), General Motors, Chrysler, and others.

Additional parts of the Obama response to the country's economic woes were to legislate a $784 billion multiyear economic stimulus program, which is designed to help small businesses survive the Great Recession and create jobs and other policies to help state and local governments and individuals weather the recession. Finally, the Obama administration, claiming that while the United States has the finest medicine in the world, it also has a very inefficient medical delivery system, created a national health system.

Obviously, in an individualistic society as ours, these programs were denounced by conservatives as "socialist," and, were embellished with hyperbole, predicting the ruination of the land and the end of freedom as we know it. These programs unquestionably have the government intervening more directly in the economy than before, and to that extent they are certainly socialist. But they are surely not unprecedented, nor do they imply the surrender of liberty, indeed a strong argument could be made for the reverse. Precedent for these programs can be found no further back in our history than the economic policies of Franklin D. Roosevelt, which all but the most entrenched free marketer agrees served to strengthen and prolong capitalism by injecting into it enough socialism to make the system humane. But Roosevelt was not the only interventionist. In the 1960s Lyndon Johnson's War on Poverty introduced the first single-payer national health plan with Medicare—now, along with Social Security—the country's most popular social program. (In fact the three most popular medical delivery systems in the United States are all single-payer government programs: Medicare, Veterans Hospitals, and Medicaid. Richard Nixon tried to cool inflation with a wage-price freeze in the 1970s; in the 1980s, Ronald Reagan oversaw the removal of eleven board members of the nation's eighth largest bank, Continental Illinois Bank of Chicago; and George W. Bush's administration actually started the massive government bailouts of corporate America. Indeed, while we are on the subject, isn't "corporate socialism" (tax breaks to encourage business, lucrative government contracts, free government research given to corporations, and subsidies—flat grants of money—to business) interventionist and a government interruption in the free market? Regardless how hard one listens, one is not likely to hear corporate CEOs or shareholders refuse these government gifts.

While Obama fully expects his universal health care program to join Medicare as a permanent fixture, he has given every assurance that the TARP and his stimulus package are temporary fixes in an emergency situation. Indeed, almost all of the largest financial institutions, except AIG, have already repaid their government loans, together with dividends and interest, as has General Motors.

Whether socialism, in whatever form, and whether free market capitalism are intrinsically good or bad is beyond the scope of this book and the wisdom of its author. But, just as the reverse can be shown, it can be demonstrated empirically that an unbridled free market is economically and socially dangerous and that mild socialist policies have been used to mitigate some of capitalism's sharp edges.

Will Socialism Disappear?

Regardless of the immediate fate of socialism in this country or in any other, it will almost certainly endure as a major social and political objective. There are several reasons for this inevitability. To begin with, few societies are as well suited, by tradition and temperament, as the United States to the insecurities of individualism. After having enjoyed the certainty of free education, universal medical care, and social protection against the ravages of old age, it is unlikely that many societies will willingly give them up. And if economic imperatives for a time force a society to forgo these amenities, they will almost certainly be reinstituted when they can be afforded.

Marxism-Leninism and other forms of radical socialism may be discredited, but socialism, the proposition that all people have the right to a decent human life and to be protected by society from the aggressions of those more economically powerful than themselves, is not likely to be extinguished. Whether socialism's most idealistic promises are achievable, the fact is that government can do things that no individual can duplicate with comparable effects. It has the power to regulate private firms, thus preventing their profit-driven excesses and even ensuring competition itself. The government can inspect food, certify safe drugs and implements, protect labor, clean the environment, manage finance, and perform a panoply of other services for society that might otherwise be ignored or, perhaps worse, be monopolized by profit-driven economic concerns.

Quite apart from these important but mundane chores, the welfare state and the socialist ethic are too attractive to be long ignored. In fact, if socialism did not already exist, it would certainly soon be invented, because it offers, realistically or not, a life to which almost everyone aspires: plenty for all, an end to suffering. Whether socialism is the result of the inexorable forces of history or the imperatives of human morality, whether society's plenty is to be produced and distributed by a centrally controlled bureaucracy or by some other means, the **socialist intent** endures as an ideal, and certain human beings will seek a social and political formula to ensure that each person shall have and that none shall have not.

At the same time, while socialism's highest principles speak to the best in humanity, it can also be used by opportunists. What entrepreneur, while genuflecting at the shrine of laissez-faire, will not seek government policy to enrich the corporation? What politician, steeped in the creed of individualism, can long neglect the temptation to buy popularity and votes by offering state-supported material security to the public or state-paid subsidies to business?

Even more cynically, socialism can be used as a means to politically control the public, as was true in Nazi Germany, Fascist Italy, the Soviet Union, and China. Furthermore, it can be used as an instrument of foreign policy. Currently, Russian leader Putin has nationalized much of his country's oil and natural gas production. He uses it to increase Russia's power in foreign affairs. With large reserves of gas and oil, he has made Russia essential to the continued prosperity of energy-hungry Europe. New wealth from energy sales and the leverage from European dependence have enormously increased Russia's presence on the international stage.

A new reason for socialism's continued existence seems to be emerging. The sheer expense of individualism and the raw free market may no longer be sustainable. Government control of dwindling resources and how they are used may become necessary if there is to be enough for all, and if the worst ravages of new threats like global warming are to be avoided, or at least, successfully combated. Thus, it is not unreasonable to expect national governments to move to control the exploitation and use of vital resources, or at least to heavily regulate them, if the private sector does not suitably respond to the economic and environmental challenges emerging in the twenty-first century.

Beyond the inherent attractions of socialism, its recent rise in popularity seems also driven by the prominence to which economic globalization has risen. The current growth of powerful multinational corporations is being met with public reactions that are similar to those of the earliest stage of industrialization. Feeling powerless and dehumanized, many people have reawakened to the warnings sounded from the left. Trade unionism, socialism, and even anarchism have enjoyed new popularity as a result, and some people are once again, at least for the moment, searching for movements and institutions that will protect them from what they regard as depersonalization and exploitation.

The economics of mutual protection seem less in question than its politics. Although communism has presented a formidable yet unsuccessful challenge to liberal democratic systems, a second major assault on liberal democracy, this time from the reactionary side of the spectrum, threatens. It is now time to look at the challenge from the right.

QUESTIONS FOR DISCUSSION

1. In what ways did the revisionists challenge Marxism?
2. What are the major ideological and practical innovations that Lenin made to Marxist thought?
3. How did Mao modify Marxism?
4. Why has Cuba failed to collapse along with the rest of the Soviet bloc?
5. Why is socialism, in some form, likely to remain a viable ideology?

SUGGESTIONS FOR FURTHER READING

Griffith, Samuel B., *Mao Tse-tung: On Guerrilla Warfare*. New York: Praeger, 1961.

Horowitz, Irving Louis, and Jaime Suchlick eds., *Cuban Communism*, 11th ed. New Brunswick, NJ: Transaction, 2003.

Kynge, James, *China Shakes the World: A Titan's Breakneck Rise and Troubled Future and the Challenge for America*. Boston: Houghton Mifflin, 2006.

Libowitz, Michael A., *Build It Now: Socialism for the Twenty-First Century*. New York: Monthly Review Press, 2006.

Miller, Debra A., ed., *North Korea*. San Diego, CA: Greenhaven Press, 2004.

Saney, Isaac, *Cuba: A Revolution in Motion*. New York: Zed Books, 2004.

Service, Robert, *Russia: Experiment with a People*. Cambridge, MA: Harvard University Press, 2003.

Staten, Clifford L., *The History of Cuba*. Westport, CT: Greenwood Press, 2003.

Trotsky, Leon, *The Permanent Revolution*, trans. Max Shachtman. New York: Pioneer, 1931.

Wang, Hui, *China's New Order: Society, Politics, and Economy in Transition*, ed. Theodore Hater. Cambridge, MA: Harvard University Press, 2003.

Yan Sun, *The Chinese Reassessment of Socialism*. Ewing, NJ: Princeton University Press, 1995.

Fascism and National Socialism

PREVIEW

The social stress created by rapid industrialization and urbanization, together with the economic and political turmoil at the end of World War I, caused the collapse of capitalism and the rejection of democracy in both Italy and Germany. The resulting political vacuum was filled by charlatans whose ideas constituted reactionary rejections of modern institutions and values. Mussolini and Hitler called upon their people to forsake reason and prudence and to follow them with unquestioned obedience toward mystical, irrational, and inevitably disastrous goals.

Under fascism and National Socialism the shattered economies of Italy and Germany were revitalized and committed to rejuvenating their military establishments, which had been humiliated during World War I. Once built anew, the martial institutions became the principal instruments of domestic control, of international conquest, and imperialism, subjecting weaker states to the role of satellites—servants of their political masters. The conquered people were impressed into slave labor for the good of the fatherland, and when their usefulness was exhausted, they were exterminated by the millions.

Mussolini's fascism and Hitler's National Socialism were actually reactionary movements because they rejected the values and aspirations that had developed in Western civilization over the millennia. In their place, warrior states substituted practices that denied human dignity and justified unspeakable horrors. To make matters worse, these primitive impulses were exemplified by leaders who brooked no contradiction.

Fascism and Nazism each developed as ideologies in response to practical political questions faced by Mussolini and Hitler. They differ somewhat, but they are closely related. Each features a preference for irrationalism, totalitarianism, elitism, imperialism, and militarism. Racism was a central feature in Hitler's theories while statism was Mussolini's prime objective.

Reactionary extremism did not die in 1945 with Hitler and Mussolini; it has reemerged from time to time, most recently in Europe and the United States. Foreign immigration, economic uncertainty, and the demise of the Soviet Union as the focus of reactionary angst have contributed to this phenomenon, as have racism, Christian fundamentalist fanaticism, and phobic and paranoiac attitudes about government. These groups expound violent, xenophobic, and antigovernment ideas, and they blatantly threaten to immerse society in a bloody race war.

THE FAILURE OF DEMOCRACY AND CAPITALISM

It has been said that the rise of fascism and Nazism occurred because liberal democracy and capitalism failed to meet the needs of the people in some industrial states. If democracy did fail, it obviously did not fail everywhere, nor was the failure fatal. Yet the fact remains that millions of people found that democracy did not provide the solutions so desperately needed in the troubled 1920s and 1930s. Instead, they turned to fascism and National Socialism. Indeed, these ideas still resonate with a disturbingly large number of people, not only abroad, but also in the United States. Accordingly, we must study these reactionary ideologies to better understand their causes so that they can be avoided in the future.

The Development of Fascism and National Socialism

Though the historical and philosophical roots of fascism and Nazism can be traced to ancient times, the conditions in which they finally emerged were created by two contemporary events: the Industrial Revolution and the *Great War,* as World War I was then called. The full impact of industrialization was first felt during the Great War. Warfare, once the business of kings and mercenary armies, was democratized as citizens on each side were mobilized for a total war effort. Millions of people were marched to the front, armed with new weapons of unequaled killing capacity. Hideous slaughter ensued as each nation applied the full weight of its technology, energies, resources, and inventiveness to the war.

Expecting a short war, each side was surprised to find that a stalemate had been reached. Their initial surprise evolved into disappointment and eventually into bitterness as the cruel reality of their situation became clear. Favoring the doctrine of attack, *élan vital,* generals carelessly hurled troops at defenders, whose withering machine-gun and artillery fire cut them down as they became entangled in barbed wire. Thinking that victory would go to the side that pressed the attack, but confronted with invincible defenses, command tacticians squandered human life in senseless battles such as the one at Verdun, where almost 1 million men fell in a battle that lasted for five months.

The folly of the Great War was made all the more painful by its irony. Industrialization had created a plenty never before possible, promising to eliminate poverty, and yet, the world's most advanced nations poured their treasure into a European bloodbath. Similarly, as technology made possible a new mobility that freed people from their provincial bonds, the civilized world found itself engaged in a horrifying stationary slaughter. While the world's youth was dying in the rat-infested trenches of France, large numbers of people came to the realization that science and technology, long considered the solution to all human difficulties, often created at least as many new problems as they solved.

These disillusioned people emerged from the Great War, entering the 1920s confused and cynical about their previous beliefs, and the postwar world did little to restore their confidence. Though the war had marked the end of monarchy as an important political institution, replacing it with democracy, conditions in Europe seemed even more uncertain than they had been under the previous order. Though industrialization had greatly increased productivity, it also tended to centralize wealth. Economic instability increased: Inflation was made worse by unemployment, and personal security disappeared. Millions of people felt defenseless against forces they had never known before and over which they had no control. Enticed from the farms to the cities by jobs that soon evaporated, they found themselves trapped in situations they did not understand and from which they were powerless to free themselves.

Equally confused by the chaos surrounding them, the parliamentary leaders also lacked solutions. Some politicians desperately tried to restore order and prosperity, whereas others simply looked for scapegoats. Regardless of their motives, they all became involved in endless debating, bickering, buck-passing, name-calling, and irresponsible procrastination. Popular faith in democracy collapsed as people lost confidence in themselves and in the concept of self-government. Many, having abandoned religion for the new god, science, had been encouraged to support democratic government as a result. Now, however, science was discredited, as was the idea of self-government, and it seemed to this confused and bitter generation that there was no truth left. Is it any wonder that many people put their last faith in the reactionary "flimflam men"—men who promised everything to everyone, who simplified life's bewildering complexity by focusing all the blame on a single cause (such as another race or an opposing ideology)? Is it hard to understand why societies that had tried to find rational solutions and failed would willingly abandon thought and blindly attach themselves to people who claimed that they alone knew the truth? In an era when morality had been assaulted by war, poverty, national humiliation, and defeat; when rural values had been destroyed by urbanization; when people were so overwhelmed by the complexity of industrialized living that they began to question even their own worth, is it so unlikely that millions of people could become convinced that right and wrong were meaningless and that action was the only true value? Plausible or not, this is exactly what happened—and the world paid an enormous price for its mistake.

Mussolini

Italy, which suffered from almost all the conditions described above, was a prime candidate for fascism. A poor country, Italy joined the war in 1915 on the side of the Allies. But the strain of maintaining a total war effort was too great for this weak kingdom. Massive social and economic dislocation plagued the country, causing serious political problems.

© Bettmann/Corbis

Benito Musolini
(1883–1945)

The war's end found Italy in a desperate circumstance. Embarrassed by a poor military showing and by political weakness, the Italians looked for those responsible for their disgrace. As the veterans returned home, they found few jobs awaiting them, their meager benefits consumed by inflation, and their families displaced. Angry and disgruntled, they became increasingly hostile. With a wary eye on the Soviet Union, where the Bolsheviks were expropriating private property, and anxious about the veterans' discontent, wealthy industrialists and landowners began to fear that a Marxist revolution was brewing, especially since socialism was already popular with Italian labor.

Into this tumultuous situation stepped the unprincipled opportunist **Benito Mussolini** (1883–1945). Mussolini was influenced by the grinding poverty he experienced as a child and by his father's leftist politics. He gravitated to the extreme left wing of the Socialist Party and set out to become its leader. Since he was always able to convince himself of the rightness of his position, Mussolini's socialism was probably sincere enough until it became a political liability. He campaigned actively against militarism and condemned nationalism as a relic of a bygone era that should be replaced by internationalism.

Though a socialist, Mussolini consistently rejected egalitarianism as far as leadership was concerned. Heavily influenced by the works of the French philosopher **Georges Sorel** (1847–1922), Mussolini believed that great historical events were set in motion by the initiative and leadership of a small number of people. Although the masses were expected to progress to new historical eras, they could do so only if they were led by people who were more visionary and daring than they. Even after he had abandoned the left, elitism remained a major principle of Mussolini's fascism.

Rising to the editorship of *Avanti,* a leading socialist newspaper, Mussolini tried to use it to increase the popularity of his cause. Yet the elections of 1913, the year immediately preceding the beginning of World War I, denied the socialists a majority in parliament. Its disappointing showing in the elections contributed to Mussolini's growing suspicion that socialism was incapable of unifying his people. Further, since he was personally defeated, Mussolini came to regard elections as an absurd way to choose leadership. Accordingly, with the outbreak of World War I in August 1914, Mussolini carefully observed the political trends as they developed.

Although at first Mussolini energetically adhered to the traditional socialist policy of opposing Italy's entrance into the war, advocating internationalism and peace instead, he became impressed by the virulent nationalism spreading among the public, which was leading to demands that Italy join the war. Suddenly, Mussolini reversed course. In October 1914, after only two months of war, Mussolini stunned his newspaper's readers by completely contradicting his previous stand and demanding that Italy enter the war. This reversal cost him the editorship of *Avanti* and his party membership.

Easily finding wealthy interests to support his newfound militarist and imperialist views, Mussolini moved to the far right. Abruptly interrupted by being drafted, he returned to civilian life toward the war's end, after having been wounded at the front. Once out of uniform, he quickly exploited Italian discontent with the peace conditions. Founding the Fascist Party, he decried the "humiliation" Italy suffered by being on the winning side but failing to receive the territorial concessions it sought from vanquished Austria. He also plunged into domestic issues, offering something to everyone in an attempt to attract veterans, labor, and the middle class. Yet, his new party failed to win a single seat in parliament in the 1919 elections.

Twice humiliated at the polls, *Il Duce* (the leader), as his followers were now calling him, focused his appeal on the right-wing issues so popular among Italy's wealthy classes, hoping that he could increase his strength through ample funding rather than by appealing to the unresponsive lower classes. By advocating laissez-faire and opposing the rash of strikes that had swept the land, he drew increasing numbers of wealthy industrialists to his side. Though he publicly condemned anarchy, he used money from his new friends to outfit gangs of thugs who attacked other street gangs supporting republican or communist ideologies. These *Black Shirts* vandalized, terrorized, and bullied, occasionally taking control of municipal governments by force. Paralyzed by this violence, the government did little to combat the fascists. Sympathetic police either ignored the Black Shirts' provoking street fights with rivals, or often, the police even came to the fascists' aid during their violent encounters.

In the elections of 1921, the fascist fortunes improved slightly when it won thirty-five seats in parliament. Still, this was far from a parliamentary majority. With this third defeat, Mussolini began to openly belittle the electoral process. Claiming that the vote was too insignificant to legitimize government, he suggested that only force could put a true leader into power. What the fascists lacked in votes they made up for in brute strength, and he predicted that belligerent tactics would compel the government to cede him control.

Finally, sensing opportunity in the chaos he himself had done so much to create, on October 27, 1922, Mussolini launched his **march on Rome.** Ordered to seize power, his supporters took over local governments, communication and transportation centers, and other strategic points as 8,000 to 30,000 supporters (estimates vary widely) converged on the capital to demand a fascist government. Briefly emerging from its dithering, the government finally decided to restore order by deploying the army, but King Victor Emmanuel, hoping to save his throne, refused to sign the order to call out the troops. Poorly organized and led, the fascists could easily have been stopped at this point. However, because a fainthearted king tried to preserve his obsolete crown, the fascists prevailed. Two days after the march began, Mussolini received an invitation from the king to form a government. Accordingly, *Il Duce* assumed power, though he later admitted that he actually had no specific plans or solutions for the country's woes at that point.

Thus, fascism was not created as a coherent, logical theory of government. It was, instead, a collection of rationalizations for policies adopted in reaction to various political problems as they arose. The motivation for these reactions was almost always to increase the personal power of the leader within the state. Almost never positive, the method used to increase the leader's power usually played on the fears and hatreds of the masses, focusing their attention on real or, more often, imagined evils in the society and encouraging them to vent their anxieties in cruel and ignoble ways.

Hitler

At the end of World War I, Germany was in even worse shape than Italy. The **Treaty of Versailles** imposed a harsh peace settlement on defeated Germany, unjustly assigning it total blame for the war. Consequently, Germany was forced to give up large amounts of territory to the victorious Allies, who also required ridiculously high war reparation payments amounting to over twice the amount of monetary gold extant at that time. Fearing a revival of German military power, the Allies also imposed severe limits on German armament.

The turmoil, which followed on the heels of defeat, plunged Germany into a five-year period of economic and political chaos. Unemployment rose to over one-third of the workforce and inflation was rampant. Treated as international pariahs and bewildered by their economic plight, the German people began to turn to extreme political movements, the tiny Nazi Party among them.

© AP Images

Adolph Hitler, in power for less than two years, reviewed columns of marching troops. The man at the far left of the picture is Hermann Goering, a World War I ace pilot for Germany and later the head of the German air force under Hitler. Goering committed suicide rather than face sentencing at the Nuremberg trials of 1945–1946.

The moderate **Weimar Republic** found coping with the tumultuous social, economic, and political problems very difficult. Its efforts to stabilize the situation collapsed in the early 1930s with the Great Depression. This sad state of affairs played directly into the hands of an evil genius, **Adolf Hitler** (1889–1945).

The son of a minor customs official, Hitler had an undistinguished childhood during which he apparently developed an exaggerated sense of German nationalism. An untalented and frustrated artist in Vienna during early adulthood, he was humiliated by having to become a house painter to get by. During his Viennese period, Hitler was influenced by the anti-Semitism widespread there at the time. Throughout European history, the Jewish diaspora, hoping to preserve its culture, distinguished itself by dressing differently, worshiping as it chose, keeping its own laws, and otherwise resisting assimilation with the societies of their European hosts. Thus, the Jews became an easy target for unreasoned hatred. That Jesus, a Jew after all, had been executed in the Jewish homeland, albeit by the Romans, deeply exacerbated European distrust and loathing of them, causing them to be blamed by Christians for every conceivable misfortune. Anti-Semitism was, and is, broad-based in the Christian world, and it was particularly virulent in Austria during Hitler's youth and beyond.[1]

---

[1]The number of Austrians commanding Nazi concentration camps during World War II is surprising. Moreover, some of Austria's highest political elite were active Nazis. Consider Kurt Waldheim (1918–2007), former Secretary General of the United Nations (1972–1981), who served as president of Austria (1986–1992), in spite of, or perhaps because of, his involvement in the deportation of Jews to the death camps during World War II.

Welcoming World War I, Hitler joined the German army in 1914. Fighting with distinction, he was severely wounded by poison gas, was decorated, and spent the last months of the war convalescing. Not having witnessed Germany's domestic turmoil or the collapse of the army at the front, Hitler readily joined the large number of people who claimed that the war was not actually lost, that Imperial Germany was instead betrayed by the "Jew-democrats."

In Munich at war's end, Hitler easily became the leader of an organization, numbering only seven people, calling itself the **National Socialist German Workers (Nazi) Party**. Appealing to the dissatisfied elements of Bavarian society, Hitler soon built a following and attracted some important military people to his cause. Seeing Mussolini rise to power in Italy and the Weimar government at a low ebb, he prematurely attempted to seize the Munich government in 1923, planning to march from there to Berlin and bring down the Republic. But the attempted coup, known as the "Beer Hall Putsch," was easily put down; it ended in Hitler's arrest and trial.

Highly placed friends saw to it that Hitler spent less than a year in prison and that he was comfortable there. While there, he wrote *Mein Kampf (My Struggle)*, setting forth the basic principles of Nazi ideology several years before he came to power and even before Mussolini had developed his own ideology completely. A rambling tirade full of irrational outbursts, torrential and racist invective, it is nevertheless a reliable guide to the Nazi policies that extended over the next two decades. Unfortunately, few people took the book seriously, discounting it as the rantings of a malcontent ne'er-do-well. Yet, fantastic as it seemed at the time, we now know that Hitler not only meant what he wrote but was also able to make it happen.

When Hitler emerged from prison in 1924, he worked tirelessly to build the Nazi Party and to exploit the public discontentment born of hard times. He spoke out against the "treacherous Jewish democrats and communists." Passions flared on all sides; armed thugs were sent into the streets to do battle with each other. Hitler's force, patterned on Mussolini's Black Shirts, called itself the *Storm Troopers (SA) or brown shirts.*

Meanwhile, the Nazi Party, heavily financed by wealthy industrialists, made significant gains at the polls. In the election of 1932, Hitler's party increased its seats in the Reichstag (Parliament) to 230 from 7. Although its share was not a majority of the 608-seat body, it was the largest number of seats held by any party. Meanwhile, political chaos mounted, and government indecision became chronic as street violence increased. Finally, thinking they could control Hitler, the conservatives in the government persuaded President Paul von Hindenburg, a heroic World War I general, to appoint the Nazi leader chancellor (head of government) in 1933.

Having badly underestimated their new chancellor, the conservatives were overwhelmed by Hitler's audacity, outmaneuvering his rivals in a series of swift, decisive acts. He stirred the people, persuading them that the communists and Jews were preparing to usurp power. His plan succeeded completely: Hitler won a clear majority of the Reichstag in the elections of 1933.

After this move, Hitler quickly consolidated power. The Reichstag all but voted itself out of existence by giving legislative authority to Hitler's handpicked cabinet. Opposition parties, strikes, and demonstrations were outlawed. Von Hindenburg died the following year, and the *Führer* (leader) assumed the office of president as well as chancellor and required all military personnel to take an oath of personal allegiance to him. Thus, his power was complete. Adolf Hitler had become the totalitarian dictator of the Third Reich scarcely a decade after Mussolini's success in Italy.

FASCIST AND NAZI IDEOLOGIES

Although Hitler articulated his ideology in *Mein Kampf* before he came to power, whereas Mussolini fashioned his after taking control, neither theory was developed into a logical whole. Rather, their principles evolved from pragmatic responses to various issues the leaders faced, guided by reactionary rejection of the most fundamental principles current in Western civilization: human equality, human dignity, the right to freedom, rationalism, objective truth, and the desirability of peace in human relationships.

National Socialism and fascism are, beyond question, closely related; indeed, they share such concepts as irrationalism, totalitarianism, elitism, militarism, and imperialism. Yet they differ in several important respects. Because of their philosophical and intellectual traditions, the German people were prepared for a much more complete acceptance of reactionary irrationalism than the Italian people were. Italian fascism[2] employed the corporate state economy, a phenomenon never fully developed in Germany. And perhaps most important, Hitler focused on racism, whereas Mussolini emphasized the more abstract theory of the state. Although in 1938 Mussolini belatedly tried to incorporate racism into his ideology in an effort to ingratiate himself with the *Führer,* it never really gained much importance among Italians.

Irrationalism

Fascism and National Socialism are reactionary ideologies because they reject the most fundamental contemporary features of Western civilization, hearkening back to values that prevailed in former eras. Since the Enlightenment, as we have already learned, Western civilization has been based on the assumption that

---

[2]Besides fascist Italy and Nazi Germany, various authorities have listed the following as fascist states: Japan during the 1930s and 1940s, Spain under Francisco Franco, Portugal under Antonio Salazar, Argentina under Juan Perón (1946–1955), Greece during the late 1960s, Uganda under Idi Amin, Chile under Augusto Pinochet, and South Africa during the time of apartheid. Because *fascism* is a very unpopular term, such regimes did not openly claim to be fascist. For this reason, and because of the vagueness of the ideology itself, it is hard to say with certainty that all of these states qualify as fascist regimes. Without question, however, these countries and several others, including Nationalist China, South Korea, and Paraguay, demonstrated fascist tendencies during important times in their recent histories.

people are intelligent beings who can use reason to improve their lives. Indeed, reason is a major characteristic that distinguishes human beings from lower forms of life. The upshot of this emphasis on rationalism was the development of science and technology. Though science has brought us many advantages, perhaps its greatest benefit is the ability to determine objective truth. The scientific method has given us a way to discover the secrets of the universe and better understand the physical world, revealing facts that can be proved.

Fascism and National Socialism reject objective science and reason. Life is so complex and so unpredictable, they argue, it cannot be understood by ordinary people. Objective truth is either a hoax or unimportant because the really important truths defy rational understanding, being random facts with no logical relationship to one another. Those who believe in reason, therefore, delude themselves and grasp at false reality. Reason, Mussolini said, is "barren intellectualism," lacking true meaning. The ordinary mind is not fertile; it is a wasteland full of mirages that give only illusions of reality.

These ideologies claim that truth is a subjective quality, available only to a few gifted people whose *will,* or spirit, or personality is greater than that of any other person in society. Those with superior will perceive a higher truth than others. They *instinctively* realize the right, and those who are not so gifted should listen to them, having faith in their leaders' *intuitions* and following their orders. Not even the specially gifted people in society realize truth through their intellect or through any other controllable ability, and certainly not through human reason. Instead, the source of the higher truth is instinct. The gifted ones simply *know* the truth, acting as neutral conveyers of the righteous energy from its source to society.

To support their irrationalist ideas, Mussolini and Hitler used *the theory of the myth,* which they had taken from Georges Sorel. Truth, Sorel said, is unimportant to the leader. What counts is that the masses be given a great objective. For his part, Mussolini demanded that his audience have faith in the Italian myths, abandoning other loyalties for this higher reality. "We have created our myth," he shouted. "The myth is a faith, it is passion. It is not necessary that it be a reality. It is reality by the fact that it is a goal, a hope, a faith. . . ." Myth, therefore, though it could not be scientifically or objectively proved, was true simply because it existed and served a purpose.

The purpose of myth was to mobilize the masses and channel them into a course of action. Again relying on irrationalism for support, Mussolini argued that the goal of an action was really unimportant. Meaning came from the action itself rather than from its goal. Action, he said, is its own justification; the struggle is as important as the truth or myth that motivated the masses.

Accordingly, Mussolini admitted that the main goal of his movement was simply to stir the people up and set them on a course of action that might have no provable value. Contemptuous of intellectual conviction, he demanded emotional commitment. "Feel, don't think" was his command to followers. Desiring only emotional responses, both he and Hitler used every available technique to ignite emotional outbursts among their people.

Largely ignoring the written word, Mussolini and Hitler much preferred live speeches in which they could use their considerable rhetorical talents, never giving their audience time to think about the true significance of their inflammatory words. The microphone, it is said, became the technology of fascism. It brought the words of the fanatic leaders instantaneously to previously unparalleled numbers of people. Encouraged to let their emotions outstrip rational restraints, the crowds would be brought to a frenzy, crying, shouting, chanting, applauding on cue. Such was the hysterical substance of two societies that tried to rule the world.

German Mythology Strong as irrationalism became in Italian fascism, long traditions of mythology and philosophy made it far more potent in Germany. Mythology, or folklore, has always played an important part in the German culture. Tales of the glorious Teutonic peoples have long been the subject matter of storybooks, serious drama, and family entertainment. The theme most often portrayed in German myth is that of the *volk* and its mystical powers. The concept of *volk* has no exact equivalent in English. More than just people or folk, *volk* refers to an inner quality or power residing in the German people. The **volkish essence** is a power possessed by the German people, yet one that goes beyond them as well. It is a spirit, an invincible, invisible force that is constantly engaged in conflict but emerges victorious after each battle.

Though the volkish essence is part of the German people, it can also be considered part of the German geography. In a mystical communion, the people draw strength and courage from nature. Implying that the country is blessed with mysterious powers, German mythology gives particular attention to the deep forest and heavy mist. Perhaps most vital of all, however, is the soil. Giver of life, mother of plenty, the soil has unmatched mystical properties that nourish and enliven the German people and their volkish essence.

Mythology and reality thus were never completely separated in the German mind. When in the nineteenth century some philosophers and artists began to lionize mythological figures as *the* source of reality, many people were quick to take up the theme. The philosopher Friedrich von Schilling (1775–1854) managed to attract a following among the early German romanticists, including the famed author Johann Wolfgang von Goethe. Von Schilling argued that there was a direct relationship between people and their myths—that mythology unified people, creating a social and political unit out of otherwise separate and diverse persons. "A nation," Schilling wrote, "comes into existence with its mythology." Mythology was a "collective philosophy" that expressed the national ethic.

Richard Wagner (1813–1883), a master of the epic drama, gave myth added respectability when he brought it to life in his spectacular operas. Leading a group of artists and scholars in what amounted to a Teutonic fetish, Wagner established an intellectual community at Bayreuth (just north and east of Nuremberg) that idealized the Germanic people by romanticizing their history and dramatizing their myths. Ancient heroes such as Brünhilde,

Hegan, and Kriemhild were immortalized on the German operatic stage. Most important of all was **Siegfried,** the big blond warrior who rose above mortal standards of right or wrong and triumphed in his effort to dominate. Hitler later became ecstatic when he heard Wagnerian music and made Siegfried the central hero of the Nazi state. Claiming that the *Führer* was actually the embodiment of the Teutonic essence and was destined to lead Germany to greatness, Hitler forged a link between himself and the ancient German myth. How he, short, slight, and dark haired, was able to inculcate this imagery in the German people is a measure of how effective his person and his rhetoric were.

Besides teaching the glory of struggle and the destiny of Germany to surpass all other nations, this flirtation with mythology encouraged a turn toward barbarism and a renunciation of deep-seated Western values. Physical strength was prized, as was glorious death. In addition, the exaltation of Teutons or *Aryans* was soon turned into a justification for unbelievably barbaric racism.

German Irrationalist Philosophical Tradition Unlike the Italians, who were forced to rely largely on foreign philosophical traditions for the irrationalism supporting fascism, the Nazis drew from a rich store of irrationalist theory, which had accumulated in Germany during the nineteenth century. This was not limited to mythology. A number of German thinkers began to seek explanations of life and nature in areas quite beyond the reach of human reason. However, it is important to note that many of these philosophers' theories were deliberately distorted by the Nazis to give an aura of philosophical respectability to their beliefs.

Johann Fichte (1762–1814), an early German nationalist, wanted to see the numerous German principalities united into a single, powerful Teutonic state. Fichte argued that the German people were destined for greatness. Led by a small elite, they would eventually dominate the globe because theirs was a superior race. They would establish a new and more perfect order in which the Germans would rule the lesser races while the leadership elite stood above ordinary morality, tolerating no opposition.

Heinrich von Treitschke (1834–1896), an otherwise obscure writer, was rescued from oblivion by Nazi theorists because, like Fichte, his reactionary ideas suited their cause. Following Fichte's theme, he claimed that the Germans were a superior race. He also adopted philosopher Georg Hegel's nationalist idea that the state was the platform on which the human drama, the dialectic of history, was played out. Yet, von Treitschke went far beyond Hegel, claiming that people were merely servants to the state and must obey the orders of their political superiors without hesitation. Thinking, he believed, was a futile waste of the ordinary person's time. The leaders supplied the thought while less gifted people simply followed directions.

Important as these philosophers were to the Nazis, two others were even more central to Hitler's ideology. **Arthur Schopenhauer** (1788–1860) expressed irrationalist philosophy perhaps more starkly than any other major philosopher. To Schopenhauer, life was the product of uncontrollable, inexplicable impulse, and it was therefore incomprehensible. He called the mysterious energy randomly motivating history the *will*. The will, Schopenhauer argued, had no purpose or cause and was unbounded by space or time. It was a blind, erratic, unpredictable force that manifested itself in the physical world but could not be analyzed rationally.

Beyond the reach of human reason, the will, which produced all physical and intellectual reality, made life meaningless. Finding no meaning or rational pattern in life, people were fools to try to resist the will. Any rational explanation of life was artificial, since the will is a senseless fury, a force with no justification. Because their source cannot be understood, the conditions of life cannot be improved by human effort. Life is only a meaningless struggle, and resistance is pointless. Faced with such uncontrollable and incomprehensible power, people have no alternative but to submit and let the will have its way.

Most important of all philosophers to the Third Reich was **Friedrich Nietzsche** (1844–1900). At the outset, it must be noted that Nietzsche would certainly not have been a follower of Hitler. Though he was neither a German chauvinist nor an anti-Semite, his theories were misinterpreted to serve the Nazi cause. Greatly influenced by both Schopenhauer and Wagner, Nietzsche wrote about a race of supermen who would someday rule the earth. Nietzsche used the word *übermensch*, which may be translated as "over-man." By this he meant a race of people who were stronger and more righteous than the human beings of his generation.

Nietzsche argued that Schopenhauer was mistaken when he said that life was a meaningless struggle. The meaning of life was actually to be found in the struggle itself. Conflict purified humanity because it strengthened the survivors and destroyed the weak, parasitic members of the society. Rather than being a meaningless force, Schopenhauer's will was purposeful. It was a **will to power**, a force that demanded that people fight and seek to dominate. Human domination, the will to power, therefore becomes the highest moral expression in life. Accordingly, any attempt to protect the weak or the helpless is immoral. Not surprisingly, Nietzsche found his society corrupted by schemes and plots to protect the weak and the unfit. Especially corrupt, in his mind, were Christianity and democracy. Christianity wrongly shielded the weak from their superiors; democracy favored mediocrity and penalized the excellent. Rather than freeing people, these two institutions created an enslaving pseudo-morality. Consequently, Nietzsche proposed a "transvaluation" of societal norms. In place of the Christian values of peace, humility, charity, and compassion, Nietzsche demanded eternal struggle, hubris, selfishness, and ruthlessness. Instead of the democratic virtues of equality, fairness, and happiness, he insisted on an autocracy of strength, deceit, and pain. Anticipating the end of a world dominated by Christian values, Nietzsche confidently proclaimed, "God is dead."

Such a change, he believed, would produce a new race of supermen, "magnificent blond brutes" who would eventually replace the weaker human specimens common in his time. Admiring the Spartan life, Nietzsche argued that people should be hard on themselves as well as ruthless toward others. Pain should not be avoided but rather sought out because it toughened people and strengthened them for the battle. Power, Nietzsche said, was its own justification: "Might makes right." When those with the greatest will to power dominated all others, the most perfect possible existence would have been achieved.

Hitler's attraction to Nietzsche's belief that the strong should be free to dominate the weak became clear very early in his career. In 1926, he said,

> It is evident that the stronger has the right before God and the world to enforce his will. History shows that the right as such does not mean a thing, unless it is backed up by great power. If one does not have the power to enforce his right that right alone will profit him absolutely nothing. The stronger have always been victorious. The whole of nature is a continuous struggle between strength and weakness, an eternal victory of the strong over the weak. All nature would be full of decay if it were otherwise.

He returned to this theme when he said,

> The fundamental motif through all the centuries has been the principle that force and power are the determining factors. All development is struggle. Only force rules. Force is the first law. A struggle has already taken place between original man and his primeval world. Only through struggle have states and the world become great. If one should ask whether this struggle is gruesome, then the only answer could be: For the weak, yes, for humanity as a whole, no.
>
> World history proves that in the struggle between nations, that race has always won out whose drive for self-preservation was the more pronounced, the stronger. . . . Unfortunately, the contemporary world stresses internationalism instead of the innate values of race, democracy and the majority instead of the worth of the great leader. Instead of everlasting struggle the world preaches cowardly pacifism, and everlasting peace. These three things, considered in the light of their ultimate consequences, are the causes of the downfall of all humanity. The practical result of conciliation among nations is the renunciation of a people's own strength and their voluntary enslavement.

Racism

Although racism is not an important factor in fascism, nothing is more central to Nazism. Anti-Semitism stretches far back into German history, but before the twentieth century it was no more virulent in Germany than in France, Russia, Spain, and most other European countries. It is true that German myth and philosophy had long stressed the virtues of Germanic peoples as compared with other groups. Yet this history of ethnocentrism was not the source of Nazi anti-Semitism. Strange as it may seem, Hitler based his racial theories on the works of a Frenchman and an Englishman. In the nineteenth century, the study of linguistics and anthropology had revealed that the languages of many people in Europe and Central Asia were related. Though the evidence at the time was sparse, scientists assumed that these related languages had a common origin, and many scholars began referring to these supposed people—people who have not even yet been proved to exist—as **Aryans.** These discoveries sparked several theories about the histories of the various peoples in Europe. One of the strangest of all was developed by a French count, **Arthur de Gobineau (1816–1882).** This intellectual nobleman, who had served as secretary to the brilliant commentator on early American life, Alexis de Tocqueville, was eventually sent to Germany as a diplomat. Greatly influenced by the German people, Gobineau developed a theory of racial superiority that was to have a profound impact on German history.

Basically, Gobineau argued that the Aryans had been a nomadic people superior to all other races. At various times, they had imposed their will on "inferior" peoples and had established new civilizations. The Aryans tended to intermarry with these peoples, supposedly causing the decline of each civilization as Aryan purity became corrupted.

The blond, blue-eyed Aryans had at one time wandered from the north across Europe and Central Asia. Gobineau claimed that by the nineteenth century, miscegenation had caused most of their descendants to lose their "superiority." There was only one area left in which the Aryan blood was pure enough to offer hope for a revival of human civilization. Extending across northwestern Europe, Gobineau's Aryan heaven included Ireland, England, northern France (Gobineau's home), the Benelux countries, and Scandinavia. Yet the purest strain of all, Gobineau said, was the German people. Though none of the remaining Aryans could claim to have no trace of "inferior" blood, the German people were the least mixed racially. Gobineau thought this genetic purity gave them an advantage over all other people in fostering the next advanced civilization. This would be possible, however, only if the Germans and other Aryan peoples protected their racial purity against further interbreeding. Not surprisingly, these ideas were ignored throughout most of Europe, but they became very popular in Germany.

Among the Germans who were deeply affected by these theories was the great composer Richard Wagner. Wagner's importance in popularizing and dramatizing German myth has already been mentioned, but his contribution to Nazi ideology is far more significant. In Wagner, three of the major foundations of Nazi ideology—mythology, irrationalism, and racism—are brought together. Wagner had known and admired Schopenhauer and had been briefly associated with Nietzsche. In addition, the German composer had met Gobineau and had been deeply influenced by his ideas. Under Wagner's leadership, the artistic and intellectual colony at Bayreuth became the center of German irrationalism and racism. The site was made a national shrine when Hitler came to power.

The Bayreuth ethic was carried into the next generation by a Germanized Englishman, **Houston Stewart Chamberlain (1855–1927).** The son of a British admiral, this troubled intellectual was attracted to Bayreuth and attached himself to the Wagner household. Chamberlain combined Teutonic mythology, German philosophical irrationalism, and Gobineau's racial theories, trying to achieve in literature what Wagner had accomplished in music. He argued that the Aryan race had created all the world's civilizations, but that each of these advances had been lost as a result of the impurity produced by miscegenation. Chamberlain believed that all races were impure and mixed except the Germans, who were Aryan and good, and the Jews, who were completely evil. History was simply a struggle between the Aryan good and the Jewish evil.

Chamberlain believed this struggle revealed that the German people had to protect and increase their racial purity and avoid interbreeding with Jews at all costs. This purification, he suggested, would be accomplished when a great leader emerged among the Germans to show them the way. Having set out on a course of deliberate racial purification, the German Aryans would save humanity and prove their superiority by conquering the world.

These ideas were an instant success in Germany. Kaiser Wilhelm II became an enthusiastic admirer of Chamberlain, and the two men were soon close friends. During World War I, Chamberlain supported the German war effort in the hope that it would lead to the Teutonic conquest of the world. After Germany's defeat, Chamberlain's fortunes declined, but his belief that a leader would arise to guide a racially pure Germany to world domination never dimmed. So it was that in 1923, when Adolf Hitler was still an obscure politician, Chamberlain proclaimed Hitler's destiny and predicted that Germany would soon find its true master. Thus, the tradition begun in prehistory was passed through Gobineau, Wagner, and Chamberlain and was finally adopted by Hitler as the basis of his political theory. Following Chamberlain's theories closely, Hitler claimed that history was simply a struggle for domination among the various races. The villain portrayed in this drama was the Jew. Hitler used the Jews to his own political advantage, blaming all of Germany's problems on them. His hatred and contempt for the Jews are frightening. "The Jew," he said,

> is a maggot in a rotting corpse; he is a plague worse than the Black Death of former times; a germ carrier of the worst sort; mankind's eternal germ of disunion; the drone which insinuates its way into the rest of mankind; the spider that slowly sucks people's blood out of its pores; . . . the typical parasite; a sponger who like a harmful bacillus, continues to spread; the eternal bloodsucker; . . . the people's vampire.

Hitler divided the people of the world into three racial categories. The *culture-creating* race was, of course, the Aryans. This group included the English, Dutch, and Scandinavians, but these peoples were less pure than, thus inferior to, the German people. These Aryan people, he claimed, were responsible for creating every civilization in the history of the world. Specifically, he contended that the civilizations of India, Persia, Egypt, Greece, and Rome were Aryan creations. Since all cultural achievements were supposedly the products of Aryan peoples, and since Hitler believed that the Germans were the purest Aryans, he saw them as the only hope for humanity. "Man," he said, "owes everything that is of any importance to the principle of struggle and to one race which has carried itself forward successfully. Take away the Nordic Germans and nothing remains but the dance of apes."

Below the Aryans Hitler placed the *culture-bearing* races such as the Asians, Latins, and Slavs. These peoples were deemed racially inferior; they could not spawn a new culture, but they could maintain a civilization as long as they did not allow their blood to be corrupted by inbreeding with the "lower" forms of humanity. The last group, called the *culture-destroying* races, included blacks, Romanies ("gypsies"), and Jews. Because of their supposedly destructive tendencies, these people were thought to be subhuman. They alone were allegedly responsible for the decline of the great civilizations.

Race, the dominant feature of national socialist ideology, was used to explain all aspects of the society. The *volk,* cradled in German soil, was united in a common destiny: to win the struggle against the evils of the world. Because Aryan blood was thought the strongest, the impurities among the German people would be eliminated by strictly avoiding miscegenation. A nation of supermen—of Siegfrieds, if you will—would be created by breeding racially pure people, thus producing Nietzsche's "magnificent blond brutes." To this end, the Nazis encouraged young adults with strong Aryan features to have children together. Not content with domestic production, and in obvious contradiction of their own views of racial purity, the Nazis encouraged their soldiers to impregnate Aryan-looking women in conquered countries and to bring the children, along with other Aryan-looking children, to the Fatherland to be raised as good Nazis. Hitler insisted that everything bend to the imperative of racial superiority. The "inferior" people of the world had to be made to understand and accept their subordination to the master race. If they resisted, they had to be crushed and forced to comply, for such was the destiny of the world. "Jewish institutions" such as communism and democracy had to be destroyed because they protected the weak, thus encouraging decay. Objective science also fell victim to racism. "We think with our blood" was the proud, irrationalist slogan of the Third Reich. Hitler and his colleagues rejected any knowledge that did not prove Teutonic racial superiority. "Science," he said, "like every other human product, is racial and conditioned by blood." Accordingly, a new German culture—art, biology, architecture, anthropology, history, genetics, religion—sprang up, all based on Germanic strength and superiority. Even food raised on German soil was considered superior in taste and nutrition. If others failed to recognize the truth of German supremacy, it was because non-Germans did not have the superior understanding of the world enjoyed by Teutonic peoples.

Much of this would be laughable if German racism had not been taken to other, more pathological extremes. Eugenics (a grossly perverted extrapolation from Darwinian thought which held that humanity could be improved by eliminating the genetic pool of the weak and infirmed) and Nazi ideas about race were used as excuses for sterilizing thousands of people who were mentally or physically impaired. Ghastly "scientific" experiments were performed on "subhuman" people to satisfy morbid Nazi curiosity. Millions were marched into forced labor and often were literally worked to death, and others were executed for political and racial crimes, or just because they were either too sick, too young, or too old to work.

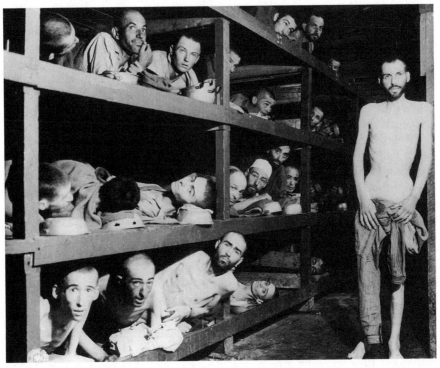

| Jewish prisoners in a Nazi death camp.

In the final days of the war, when all was lost, Nazi fanatics hoped to empty the death camps before Allied troops could liberate them. Hundreds of thousands of people were forced into death marches from the extremities of the empire back toward Nazi-held territories in Germany. In this final expression of unreasoned hatred, starving internees were marched from camp to camp, stragglers were shot, bayoneted, strangled, and beaten to death. Most horrifying of all, 9 million people, two-thirds of them Jewish, were systematically murdered in the extermination camps dotting the landscape of Hitler's empire. The stench of rotting flesh and burning bodies filled the air as Hitler pursued his hideous "final solution" to the Jewish question.

Totalitarianism

A totalitarian state is a dictatorship in which the political leaders control every institution in the society and use them for political purposes as well as for the functions for which they are ostensibly designed. Accordingly, a totalitarian dictator dominates not only the government and political parties, but also the economy, labor unions, churches, media, education, social institutions, and cultural and artistic displays. All aspects of society controlled by the state are used as mechanisms of political manipulation.

The term *totalitarianism* was coined by Mussolini, and he also developed most completely the philosophical justification for it. Even so, his inability to subject the Catholic Church to his will—he was only able to force the Church into an uneasy stalemate with his regime—prevented him from exercising totalitarian power in Italy. On the other hand, Hitler was able to do in practice what Mussolini could complete only in theory.

Theory of the State   Although Mussolini failed to create a completely totalitarian state, he cannot be accused of failing to try. To justify the accumulation of such a huge amount of power in the hands of the state, Mussolini turned to the German philosopher **Georg Hegel,** who was introduced in Chapter 8. Hegel believed that the state was the format within which history could be best understood. He called upon people to commit themselves to the state and to accept it as the principal institution from which they derive identity. Like Rousseau, Hegel argued that people derive meaning only through service to the state and that they become free only when they become subject to it. Yet Hegel did not propose a totalitarian state. Instead, he believed that there were many human pursuits that were not political and that although people should dedicate themselves to the state in political matters, the state should not interfere in nonpolitical affairs.

Selecting the parts of Hegel's theory that suited him and ignoring the rest, Mussolini transformed it into what is today called **statism.** The state had mystical properties; it was at the center of life, with incomparable purpose and meaning. Speaking to Italians, Mussolini used a vocabulary with which a Catholic society could easily identify. Only the state gave human beings their identity, he claimed, and only through it could they reach the "higher life," a condition he never specifically described.

Making use of the **organic theory of the state,** Mussolini argued that although the state was made up of individuals, it took on an importance that was much greater than the sum of its individual parts. Just as the cells of the body each contribute to a life far greater than their own, the state becomes a living being with an importance far beyond that of its individual members. Just as each individual has a personality and a will, the state draws from each, developing a personality and a will of its own. Having the greater will, the state rightfully dominates the individuals within it. The **will of the state** has such power over the society that it actually becomes the measure of all value, virtue, and wisdom. It is the "will of wills," the "good of goods," and the "soul of souls."

Faced with such horrendous power, the individual would be foolish to resist the will of the state. People must conform completely if they are to fulfill themselves. The state can make any demand, give any order, require any sacrifice, and the individual must obey. The power of the state is total, and the loyalty and commitment of the individual must be total. As Mussolini put it, "Everything for the state; nothing against the state; nothing outside the state."

Being the "creator of right" and the "good of goods," the state can tolerate no resistance. Conceiving of a society in which all people had functions—some great, some modest—Mussolini believed that all persons must perform to their maximum for the state. Those who did not meet their obligations were of little value to the society and could be removed. Such total subordination of people and human rights to a nonhuman institution flies in the face of the advances of humanity over the past several hundred years and is another reason for fascism's reputation as a reactionary ideology. Yet, the reward for compliance with the will of the state was great indeed. The "higher life" offered the purest, the most "heroic" existence possible, even promising immortality in an indirect way. Echoing Edmund Burke, Mussolini wrote, "The State is not only present, it is also past, and above all future."

Unlike fascism, Nazi ideology gave the state only secondary importance. It was not seen as the central object in Germany; rather, racial purity was most important. The state was only the arena in which the race built its strength and identified its leadership. In foreign affairs, the state was the vehicle through which the superior race governed its inferiors. The combination of absolute political power with modern technology produced a totalitarian Nazi state. Structurally, the Nazi government was very similar to the Italian regime, but unlike Mussolini, Hitler was able to carry the totalitarian ideal to fruition. To augment the power of his governmental institutions, Hitler mounted one of the most extensive propaganda campaigns in the history of the world. With the help of his propaganda minister, Joseph Goebbels, Hitler converted every possible medium into a political tool. He used every available technique to get his message across. He destroyed books and films that opposed his views; he politicized every textbook, newspaper, magazine, novel, movie, radio program, and musical score. Manipulating all the information that reached the people, he followed the formula he had set forth in *Mein Kampf:* Keep the message simple, with little regard to its veracity, and repeat it again and again. A master showman, he manipulated people through extravagant, carefully orchestrated mass rallies, using symbols, insignia, regalia, color, emotional outbursts, and patriotic passion to induce collective hysteria. Thus, he spurred the German people to levels of barbarity and fanaticism seldom, if ever, matched in modern times.

Elitism

Again referring to Hegel, who argued that people are not equal, and that the leaders of society are its heroes and therefore not subject to ordinary moral restraints, Mussolini and Hitler developed theories of *elitism.* People, they argued, are quite obviously unequal: Some are more intelligent, some are stronger, some are more talented, some are more attractive. To act as though people are equal is to ignore the obvious and to fatally deny a basic fact of nature.

Although people vary greatly, they all have an obligation to perform: To serve the state in Italy or the *volk* in Germany. Yet, being unequal, they cannot each make the same level of contribution—some are able to contribute more and some less—and citizens cannot rightfully expect to be rewarded equally for unequal contributions. Therefore, those who give the greatest service deserve the greatest benefit.

Both Mussolini and Hitler envisioned a highly stratified society with each person making his or her maximum contribution. Those who failed to fulfill their potential would be done away with. By the same token, if all did what they were best suited for, the best possible society would result. If, for example, the most able carpenters were allowed to build and the most talented bankers could bank and the most gifted teachers were assigned to the classroom, the society would profit from the best possible construction, finance, and education.

The same logic was applied to society's most important endeavor: government. Rejecting democracy as a sham founded on the false premise of human equality, Mussolini and Hitler were contemptuous of the masses—each referring to the people as "the herd." Political power must be left to the elite in society if it is to enjoy excellent government. Democracy, it was suggested, reduced government to the lowest common denominator.

Obviously referring to the Fascist Party, Mussolini suggested that in the ideal system the best citizens would emerge. They would be the people most in tune with the will of the state. Relying on racism, Hitler suggested the same dynamic, except that the German elite would be those who enjoyed the greatest amount of the volkish essence.

And, they declared, just as there are some people in society who are better than others, so too there is a single person who is qualified above all, and that person should be given total deference as the infallible leader. Truly good people in society would easily recognize their betters and defer to them without qualm.

Il Duce and the *Führer* were endowed with innate power: It could not be acquired. Their claim to power rested in their intuitive, unreasoned oneness with the will of the state or the will of the *volk*. It was not something that could be understood rationally or controlled; it simply existed. Mussolini said that the leader is "the living sum of untold souls striving for the same goal"; he is the embodiment of the state itself. And the Nazi philosopher Ernst Hubber said

> the *Führer* is no "representative" of a particular group whose wishes he must carry out. He is no "organ" of the state in the sense of a mere executive agent. He is rather himself the bearer of the collective will of the *volk*. In his will the will of the volk is realized. He transforms the mere feelings of the *volk* into a conscious will.

Thus, the leader was the indispensable and infallible conduit of the nation's will. He (it was assumed the leader would be male) crystallized and articulated the will of the state or *volk* and was therefore to be relied on for the most authoritative expression of truth. Accordingly, the leader was to receive complete obedience. The people were not to question the leader's commands since his will was actually that of the society itself. To cement the point early in life, Italian schoolchildren were required to begin each day with the assertion "Mussolini is always right!"

The Corporate State

Fascist totalitarianism and elitism manifest themselves economically in the **corporate state.** Based on **syndicalism,** a democratic idea advocated by Pierre Joseph Proudhon and Georges Sorel, it suggests that people should channel their political ideas through giant trade unions to which they belonged. But Mussolini stood this concept on its head, reversing the power flow. Instead of the people running the government through the syndicates, Mussolini intended that the *government would control the people through the trade unions.* The corporate state was based on a foundation of *syndicates* (trade unions) to which both workers and owners *were required to belong.* Strikes and boycotts were made illegal; the syndicates were supposed to settle disputes between management and labor. By the same token, prices, profit margins, production standards, and the like were set by the state, leaving very few important decisions to the owners. In fact, though the Italian economy was privately owned, it was actually completely controlled by the state.

The local syndicates were brought together in regional federations, which, in turn, became members of one of twenty-two governing *corporations.* Actually official government agencies rather than private entities, the Italian corporations directly controlled the economy. The heads of the corporations were members of the National Council of Corporations, by which the economy was centrally controlled and directed. The members of the National Council of Corporations automatically became members of the Chamber of Fasces and Corporations, Italy's highest governing body, which was, of course, headed by *Il Duce* himself. To be assured of absolute obedience at every level, the state appointed the heads of all the corporations, regional federations, and syndicates.

Besides serving as a tool for directing the economy, however, the corporate state was the primary means by which the state controlled its citizens. Through this mechanism, almost every aspect of daily existence was monitored. Jobs, wages, fringe benefits, social programs, housing, retail goods, recreation, entertainment, and education were all part of this elaborate organization.

By these means, the state controlled and regulated almost every conceivable social, economic, and political activity of its citizens. This made it relatively easy for the government to reward supporters and punish dissidents. Along with the party and the police, the corporate state was Mussolini's principal mechanism for maintaining control.[3]

Unlike the Italians, the Germans did not establish a corporate state, though there was considerable talk about doing so in the early days of the regime. All the same, while the German economic structure differed from Italy's, the result

---

[3]The Soviet Union adopted a very similar mechanism, except that the corporate enterprises were owned by the state. Additionally, a 2009 U.S. Supreme Court case (*Citizens United* v. *FEC*) held that corporations have all the same free speech protections as do people under the First Amendment. Thus, corporate America is virtually unrestrained in making political comment. Combining corporate economic power with unlimited political speech causes several to wonder if the Court has taken a large, dangerous step toward creating a corporate state in the United States.

was largely the same. The economy was tightly controlled by three superagencies. Industrial production was managed by the Estate of Industry and Trade, and the agricultural sector was controlled by the German Food Estate. As in Italy, strikes and boycotts were made illegal and German trade unions were dissolved. In their place Hitler created the Labor Front, a federation of worker and professional associations. Through these mechanisms, all economic functions were manipulated by the state.

Imperialism

As we have seen, Mussolini and Hitler viewed society in terms of human conflict: Good combated evil, strength fought weakness, purity struggled with decadence. Mussolini, in a chauvinistic fury, claimed that just as people within society were not equal, states and their wills were not equal, and justice demanded that the most powerful will of the state should achieve supremacy over all others. Applying his racist theories, Hitler concluded the same. Since the German *volk* enjoyed the purest blood, they had the right to impose their will on all lesser races. To shirk this responsibility would be to deny destiny, rejecting rightful heritage, thus betraying the natural order of things.

Imperialism (one nation dominating others) became the paramount mission for both societies. Exerting power over others within a society is a vital function of those who are best able to rule; imperialism is simply an extension of this principle to a higher, more important level of human relationship. Imperialism, Mussolini claimed, is the most advanced form of this natural regulator, which he called *the will to power* "The highest expression of human power," he said, "is Empire."

Arguing that the "higher life" is possible only when the greatest will dominates all lesser personalities, Mussolini gave imperialism a moral justification. In *The Doctrine of Fascism*, written in 1932, he said, "For Fascism the tendency to empire, that is to say, to the expansion of nations, is a manifestation of vitality; its opposite, staying at home, is a sign of decadence: people who rise or re-rise are imperialist, people who die are renunciatory."

As one might expect, Mussolini saw Italy as an imperialist state. Once great, Italy was regaining its status as a world power. Accordingly, Mussolini assigned it the task of re-creating the Roman Empire. This goal became the national myth, compelling the Italian nation to action. The absurdity of equating modern Italy with ancient Rome was ignored, since as we have already seen, fascists consider the veracity of a myth unimportant; its great value is inspiring people to act.

Hitler's justification of imperialism was basically the same as Mussolini's except that the Nazi dictator substituted the will of the *volk* for the will of the state. Believing that the strong must dominate the weak in an ongoing process of Social Darwinism, Hitler lusted for territorial acquisition. Sending out an ominous warning of this suicidal tendency in 1929, Hitler said

> If men wish to live, then they are forced to kill others. . . . As long as there
> are peoples on this earth, there will be nations against nations and they will
> be forced to protect their vital rights in the same way as the individual is

forced to protect his rights. . . . *There is in reality no distinction between peace and war.* . . . One is either the hammer or the anvil. We confess that it is our purpose to prepare the German people again for the role of the hammer. (Emphasis added.)

Thus, each expansionist dictator threw the war machine against his weak adversaries even as Britain, France, and the United States appeased them in an effort to placate the aggressive titans. Italian armies were sent to conquer Abyssinia (Ethiopia), Albania, and Greece, whereas Hitler's *blitzkrieg* (lightning war) was hurled against Poland, and *fifth column* (collaborationist) reactionary movements seemed to arise everywhere. Finally, France and England resolved to allow no more aggression, and World War II began in 1939.

Militarism

The tool of fascist and Nazi imperialism is, of course, militarism. Yet, according to these ideologies, war is actually much more than simply a means of asserting the national will: War is the prime goal. Indeed, when referring to Nazi Party members, Hitler did not call them people or leaders; he called them *fighters.* Rather than something to be used only as a last resort, war is a spiritually creative and positive feature of life. It should occur often and should never be avoided merely to achieve peace. Peace is not a positive condition but rather an interlude between national struggles for imperial dominance. Indeed, permanent peace is equated with cowardice and is not to be tolerated because it robs society of its vitality. "Fascism," Mussolini wrote,

> believes neither in the possibility nor the utility of perpetual peace. It thus repudiates the doctrine of Pacifism—born of a renunciation of the struggle and an act of cowardice in the face of sacrifice. *War alone brings up to its highest tension all human energy and puts the stamp of nobility upon the people who have the courage to meet it.* (Emphasis added.)

Hitler chose to express the same sentiment with the racist attitudes of von Treitschke. War, von Treitschke believed, was good in itself because states, like people, were driven to dominate each other and warfare was the process by which national domination was achieved. Consequently, war was a normal condition of human life. "That war should ever be banished from the world," von Treitschke wrote, "is not only absurd, but profoundly immoral." Permanent peace, he argued, would be a crime, and societies that wanted peace were obviously decaying. The entire society was therefore channeled into preparation for war. Every possible pursuit, be it school, work, or pleasure, served a martial purpose.

Struggle, conflict, fight, discipline, courage, obedience, and *the holiness of heroism* are among the terms that occur often in fascist literature. Dueling, swordsmanship, pistolry, riding, uniforms, weapons, discipline, and other martial trappings were valued. Masculinity and virility were prized, women being confined to the kitchen and domestic duties. "War," Mussolini said, "is the most important thing in a man's life as maternity is in a woman's."

Fascism's and National Socialism's attempt to create *warrior states* is an important reason they are classified as reactionary ideologies. Denying the value of peaceful, amicable human relationships amounts to favoring a return to an ancient era during which those who were physically strong dominated everyone else and people were judged and ranked by their ability to fight. Accordingly, martial activities, emotional causes, and domination become the goals of such a society, whereas values like human refinement, rationality, culture, peace, equality, and brotherhood are rejected.

Despite all the rhetoric and emotionalism of these assertions, perhaps the essence of fascism and National Socialism was captured in the fascist slogan "Believe, Obey, Fight!" Nothing better expresses the irrationalism, elitism, militarism, or contempt for the masses so prominent in these ideologies. This simple phrase says it all. It demands blind faith rather than intelligent commitment, it insists that people follow the orders of their superiors without hesitation, and it pits people against each other for no other reason than love of struggle itself.

Romantic, emotional, and violent creeds based on a militant rejection of the modern rational and scientific world, these reactionary movements offer little save the perverted sense of glory derived from annihilation and carnage. In a sentence that surely would have enjoyed Hitler's agreement, Mussolini said, "Fascism brings back color, force, the picturesque, the unexpected, the mystical; in short, all that counts in the soul of the crowds."

CONTEMPORARY FASCIST AND NEO-NAZI MOVEMENTS

Perhaps the four best examples of post–World War II fascist states are Spain, led by Generalissimo Francisco Franco; Argentina, under Juan Perón and the military juntas which succeeded him; Chile under Augusto Pinochet; and South Africa during the time of *apartheid*. Human rights suffered egregiously in each regime. Murderous Nazi fugitives, some of whom were spirited out of Europe with the help of U.S. and British intelligence organizations, were given shelter in each of these countries.[4] By the 1990s, however, each of these notorious

---

[4]Still other fugitive Nazis hid out in their home countries or fled the Axis states after the war, and some came to the United States. Most came illegally, but, regrettably, some enjoyed official help. In 1979, *but not until then*, the U.S. government created an Office of Special Investigations (OSI) in the Justice Department to locate these fugitives. Since then over one hundred former Nazi leaders, former guards at the Nazi death camps, and other war criminals—many of whom had by then become U.S. citizens—have been ferreted out, prosecuted, or deported from the United States. How many more of these criminals might have been brought to justice had a serious effort to catch them been started earlier is impossible to say. Even so, eventually the United States became the most proactive country, outside of Israel, in efforts to punish Nazi war criminals. At this writing, a few octogenarians are standing trial for their alleged crimes, while a few others serve time in prison. But this effort is necessarily slowing to a halt because the fugitives, as well as the witnesses to their horrendous crimes, are dying.

societies had moderated significantly, whereas fascism became popular elsewhere. The past two decades have seen startling increases in neo-Nazi organizations' memberships and activities, and right-wing parties have won larger shares of the electorate than previously in Austria, Belgium, the Czech Republic, Ukraine, Russia, Norway, Sweden, Latvia, France, Switzerland, Germany, and Japan. In Hungary, the Jobbik Party has rapidly become the fastest growing party in the country. Overtly racist, it demonstrates against Jews and the Romanies (Gypsies). Its Hungarian Guard, behaving very much like the Nazi Brown Shirts, sports a red-and-white striped flag looking suspiciously like that of the Hungarian government that allied with Hitler. This neo-fascist group terrorizes those it hates in order to "protect" the "true Hungarians." The understaffed national police force is unable to exert civil control over large parts of rural Hungary and the Hungarian Guard has stepped in to assume that role. While the Hungarian Guard has been legally banned, it and the Jobbik Party ignore court orders to stand down.

In Italy, another far-right movement is popular. Silvio Berlusconi, a media mogul and among Italy's wealthiest people, was elected to his third stint as prime minister in 2008. He is the only prime minister in post–World War II Italian history to serve a full term. At his third election, Italy, hobbled by a seriously split multiparty system, had had sixty-two prime ministers in sixty-three years. Profoundly conservative, Berlusconi's government is a coalition including the National League, a neo-fascist party. Berlusconi has embarrassed himself and enraged his European Union counterparts by making outrageous neo-fascist, sexist, and other inappropriate comments. Very popular with the Catholic conservatives in Italy, he has managed to survive challenges to his government based on his legislation, some of which allegedly benefit his business interests and other charges of corruption.

Beyond Italy, however, the rise in public interest in Nazism, fascism, and racism has become unsettling. Iranian president Mahmoud Ahmadinejad openly denies the Holocaust occurred and loudly proclaims that the state of Israel must be erased from the globe. Former Nazi collaborators march in celebration in Latvia, and marauding Russian skinheads and other racists have participated in attacks that have left dozens of migrant workers dead and hundreds injured. Meanwhile, the Swiss passed a referendum forbidding Muslims in the country to build minarets. The French, under conservative president Nicolas Sarkozy, have banned students from wearing conspicuous religious symbols to school (Muslim headscarves, Jewish skullcaps, large Christian crosses). While the law is technically neutral regarding various religions, it is popularly known as "the veil law" because it is aimed at discouraging the use of the Muslim scarf. France has also banned wearing burkas (a robe and headdress covering the entire woman's body) in public (the Dutch, Hungarians, Belgians, and others are considering the same prohibition), and it engaged in a government-sponsored public debate about banning minarets and discussions about what values and heritage one must have in order to be truly French. This, from a government led by a president of Hungarian and Turkish descent.

The debates were openly opposed by prominent academics as "racist" and "Vichy-style" efforts to "stigmatize" French Muslims. Together with these events, a French court, for the first time, formally recognized the Vichy (1940–1944) government's cooperation with Hitler in shipping 76,000 Jews—including 11,000 children—to Nazi concentration camps. However, even though fewer than 3,000 of these hapless people returned alive, the court refused to grant their families any sort of reparation. And, disturbingly, only days before the British royal family was to play a major role at the sixtieth anniversary of the liberation of the death camp Auschwitz, where 1.1 million victims of the Nazis perished, Prince Harry shocked many when he attended a London costume party dressed in a Nazi uniform, garnished with a swastika armband. Harry's racist proclivities came to light again in 2009 when a British newspaper reported that in 2006 he had used "offensive terms" when speaking about people of Arab lineage. Meanwhile, Britains right-wing English Defense League has engaged in anti-Muslim protests and riots.

Strikingly, the most frequent, brutal, and lethal episodes of right-wing extremist violence have occurred in Germany, especially in what used to be East Germany. Experiencing much lower wages and higher unemployment than their compatriots in the West, young people in the eastern part of the country manifest palpable angst. Not content only to vent their anti-Semitism, these youths attack "guest workers" from Turkey, the Balkans, and North Africa as well. Neo-Nazis in Germany vandalized a memorial to *Kristallnacht* on the date of its sixty-eighth anniversary. (*Kristallnacht,* the "Night of Broken Glass," occurred in 1938 when the Nazis vandalized Jewish homes and businesses, causing huge damage to property, brutalizing thousands of people, and even killing some.) In another episode, a copy of Holocaust victim Anne Frank's diary was publicly burned by right-wing extremists at an anti-Semitic demonstration in Saxony-Anhalt. While the state has tried to crack down on its ultra-right-wing elements, the center-right government of Angela Merkel urged that Germany's Muslim population observe the legal norms of the country if they want to continue living there.

In an unrelated episode, a Swede and several Polish vandals stole and dismantled the sign over the main gate at the Auschwitz death camp. The culprits were arrested and the sign saying *"Arbeit Macht Frei"* (Work Sets You Free) was restored. However, whether this was an act driven by racial hatred is not yet settled. It may have been a simple, but unforgivable, commercial theft.

Auschwitz, the most lethal Nazi death camp, was actually designed and built for the purpose of the mass extermination of Jews, Romanies, socialists, and communists. A copy of the blueprints for the camp was found in 2009 and was given to Israeli Prime Minister Benjamin Netanyahu to be kept in the Israeli capital. In accepting them, Netanyahu said, "There are those who deny that the Holocaust happened. Let them come to Jerusalem and look at these plans for the factory of death."

The German government recently opened a memorial to the Holocaust in Berlin. Ironically, the German chemical giant Degussa, which earlier admitted it had helped Hitler's government's extermination of Jews by producing Zyklon B (the gas used to kill millions of people in the death camps), became a subcontractor in the construction of the museum. In 2009, the museum was vandalized. Swastikas and anti-Semitic epithets were painted on part of the building and its contents.

The Catholic Church also bears some responsibility for the Holocaust. It, and several Protestant sects have apologized for not doing more to stop the slaughter of Europe's Jews and even for profiting from slave labor in Nazi territories. Further, Pope Benedict XVI agreed to open formerly closed files that shed some light on the suspected cooperation of Pope Pius XII, (called "Hitler's Pope") by some, with the Nazis and fascists during World War II. Yet, the Church continues to struggle with its long history of anti-Semitism. In early 2009, Pope Benedict XVI revoked the excommunication of four bishops belonging to the ultraconservative order, the Society of St. Pius X. Among the four reinstated bishops was Richard Williamson who publicly denied the Holocaust happened. The public uproar among Jews and others at Benedict's absolution of Williamson was so strong that Benedict quickly reversed his reinstatement and demanded that Williamson retract his statements. The twice defrocked bishop apologized but refused to retract his comments, so he remains excommunicated and the Church continues to suffer from the perception that it remains anti-Semitic.

Besides the Jews and Muslims, the Romanies continue to feel the sting of European racism. Numbering between 7 and 9 million people, most Romanies live in Eastern Europe, although they can easily be seen throughout Europe. A nomadic people who probably originated in India, they are often suspected of theft and confidence crimes. How much crime they are guilty of is impossible to say, but it is undeniable that they suffer from enormous prejudice. For example, the Czech Republic has been called to task by the European Parliament for banishing Romani children to schools for the mentally disabled. Indeed, about 80 percent of the children in these schools are Romani. In other cases, gangs of thugs have attacked, beaten, and even killed Romani people. In June of 2009, over 100 Romanies who were attacked in Belfast, Northern Ireland, fled to Eastern Europe. Italy's Berlusconi government has also been chastised by the European Parliament for its "crack down on crime" which saw the forced fingerprinting of Romanie, including children. Hungary's extreme right-wing party, Jobbik, frequently agitates against "Gypsy criminals" and the French government's secret policy of systematically tearing down Romani unauthorized shanties and deporting the Romanies to Romania and Bulgaria was recently exposed by the French media.

These expressions of racism and the rise of interest in fascism and Neo-Nazism in Europe are not new. They generally accompany economic downturns and high immigration of poor, dark-skinned people. While it is not unique, the resurgence of reactionaryism anywhere, but especially in Europe, cannot be ignored, given the history of the 1920s, 30s, and 40s. But, Europe is not the only place where right-wing extremism can be seen festering.

Right-Wing Extremism in the United States

Right-wing extremism is also gaining popularity again in the United States. The collapse of the Soviet Union eliminated a traditional negative focal point of the extreme right. With that external danger removed, those Americans who tend to look for sources of great evil in their midst came to see the federal government as a threatening and oppressive force that must be resisted—violently, if necessary. This political paranoia, fed by exaggerated notions of individual rights, xenophobic Christianity, and even a revival of paganism, has often been reinforced and strengthened by alliance with profound racial hatreds brought to a new pitch by the enormous recent immigration of Hispanics and Asians to the United States. Aggravating the situation, the 2000 census revealed that these populations have spread from their usual focal points (New York, Florida, Texas, Arizona, New Mexico, and California) throughout the country.

The 2001 attacks on the New York World Trade Center and the Pentagon by Muslim terrorists also contributed to the alarm of the far right. Since then, the Southern Poverty Law Center, echoed by the Department of Homeland Security, has warned that, spurred by a serious economic decline, the election of an African American president,[5] and fear that a Democratic Congress will severely restrict gun ownership, membership in right-wing extremist groups has greatly increased and become a font of conspiratorial theories, so favored by these reactionaries. As a consequence, traditional right-wing hate groups like the Aryan Nation, the Ku Klux Klan, Neo-Nazis, militant civilian militias, and belligerent survivalists have rapidly developed new vitality.

At the same time, these movements have changed with the times and evolved modernized ideological doctrines that resonate with new generations of Americans. Joining the more traditional hate groups, for example, are new organizations with similar extremist leanings. Racist *skinhead* (because of their close haircuts) groups attract young people with anti-Semitic, anti-Hispanic, anti-African American, anti-Muslim, homophobic rhetoric punctuated with vile music encouraging hate and violence. Besides the skinheads, Christian Identity, neo-Confederate, and black separatist groups are springing up with new vigor.

Christian Identity espouses virulent race hatred. Claiming that the Aryan people are the offspring of Adam and Eve, whereas the Jews are descended from Satan, these devout people look forward to a race war in which the whites will finally subjugate the "mud people" (Jews, African Americans, Hispanics, and Asians). There are several black separatist groups that advocate either returning

---

[5]So far, there have been four discovered plots to assassinate President Obama. None of them actually resulted in an attempt, all were amateurish, and all were race motivated. One involved two gunmen who planned to kill 102 African American schoolchildren, and then, dressed in white tuxedos and top hats, they planned to shoot the president. In an equally chilling case, a poll on Facebook was entered by an unknown correspondent asking "Should Obama be killed?" Similarly, for about a year following Obama's election buyers depleted merchant stores of guns and ammunition. Listed as reasons for the unprecedented shopping spree: guns will soon be outlawed, a crime wave is coming, and a race war threatens.

to Africa or reestablishing a segregated society in which black people will be isolated from white oppression. Among the groups that fall into this category are the New Black Panther Party, the House of David, and the Nation of Islam. Meanwhile, neo-Confederate groups that want to re-create the Confederate States of America are spreading across the southern states. This new country would reinstate old mores and laws, making even slavery possible again.[6]

Traditional American hate groups often extol patriotism and Christian values. But some new groups, like the neo-Confederates, abandon loyalty to the United States and call for a new political entity. At the same time, many of the young people recently drawn to hate groups eschew Christianity. The World Church of the Creator, now known as the Creativity Movement, headquartered in East Peoria, Illinois, has several chapters across the country and is one of the fastest growing hate groups in the United States. The church is led by the Reverend Matthew Hale, who is now serving a 40-year sentence in federal prison for soliciting the murder of a federal judge. The Creativity Movement believes that white people are superior to all others and that Jews, African Americans, Asians, Hispanics, and homosexuals are degenerates and will ultimately destroy themselves. Although Hale claims that he does not advocate violence, "RAHOWA" is an important mantra for his followers: It stands for Racial Holy War. After a follower went on a shooting spree in the Midwest, killing two and wounding seven, and then killing himself to avoid capture, the Reverend Hale ignored the victims' plight, saying "As far as we are concerned, the loss is one white man."[7]

Moving even further from Christianity is another group of young people currently attracted to hate. They are drawn to neopagan beliefs in multiple gods. Attracted principally to Nordic gods like Oden, Thor, and Freya, these youngsters, like the Nazis before them, exalt in the purity of Nordic blood and resent the decadence they believe the "lower" races have forced upon it.

Racism is obviously the dominant focus among these groups, but recently, another issue has also come to the fore. Homophobia, long a source of angst among American right-wing extremists, has suddenly assumed huge proportions. During the Clinton administration, the requirement that homosexuals and bisexuals remain anonymous in the military resulted in the "don't ask, don't tell" policy. Later, in 1996, the Defense of Marriage Act was passed, ignoring the Constitution's Full Faith and Credit clause by allowing states not to recognize as legal same-sex marriages performed in other states. Passions on the subject rose even further with the 2001 Vermont law allowing same-sex civil unions. Then the U.S. Supreme Court in 2003 struck down state laws making sodomy a crime, and same-sex marriages or civil unions have now been legalized in some states. Expressing moral qualms but also facing the 2004 election, President Bush brought the "cultural wars" issue even more

---

[6]Perhaps the best source on hate groups, their growth, and their varied ideologies is the Southern Poverty Law Center. Its quarterly publication, *Intelligence Report*, is relied on heavily for this material.

[7]*The Los Angeles Times*, "Leader of Hate Church Mourns 'One White Man,'" July 6, 1999.

into the spotlight by calling for a constitutional amendment to define marriage as a legally sanctioned union of one man and one woman. Perhaps more than any other recent issue, homophobia has given American reactionaries an ideological compatibility with other, less extreme elements of society, thus giving them entry into mainstream political debate.

Irresponsibly encouraged by right-wing radio talk show hosts and musical groups, there is also a profusion of **militant civilian militia** organizations that complicate and heighten the lethal potential of right-wing extremism in the United States. Generally, these groups are convinced that the federal government has been taken over by the "mongrel races" and that it is being used to deny liberty to the more deserving whites. Thus, they are preparing to defend themselves from government oppression, and they look forward to a race war in which the whites can forcefully reassert their dominance in the land. Militia groups have tripled in number since Obama's election.

At the other strategic extreme are many new young converts to violent hatred. These stalwarts eschew joining hate organizations because they believe, perhaps correctly, that the Ku Klux Klan, skinheads, militias, and so on are heavily infiltrated by the FBI and other police units. Instead, they advocate individual random acts of violence by racist terrorists. A leading member of this genre is Alexander James Curtis, who engaged in acts of harassment against a Jewish congressman, a Latino mayor, and two other local officials in San Diego County. Using the Internet, he called on white supremacists to strike out like "lone wolves" in individual terrorist attacks. Curtis, a protégé of longtime racist leader Tom Metzger, called for racists to form small, leaderless, anonymous cells of terrorists who would attack targets of opportunity at random.

This anarchistic approach to engaging in race war grew in adherents in the 1990s. Lone-wolf attacks took several lives throughout the country. However, since the turn of the century, a decline in lone-wolf attacks seemed to occur, but beginning in 2009, the number of these anarchistic killings has increased again. Some graphic, recent examples are the assassination in a Kansas church of Wichita abortion provider, Dr. George Tiller, by Christian fundamentalist Scott Roede, who is said to have been connected to the Freemen of Montana at one time; the shooting by neo-Nazi James von Brunn of an African American Holocaust Memorial guard in Washington, D.C., Stephen T. Johns; and the murder of a gay California high school classmate by 14-year-old, neo-Nazi Brandon McInerney. In Philadelphia a white supremacist shot three police officers to death because he feared his guns would be taken from him, and two Florida deputy sheriffs were killed by a National Guard soldier because he was angered by Obama's election in 2008.

Regardless of the circumstances of organized hate groups in America, there remains a virulent strain of hatred among elements of ordinary people in this country. The truth of this assertion is verified repeatedly and need consume little space here. The events in 2007 in Jena, Louisiana, will suffice as an example.

An oak tree on the grounds of the high school in this tiny rural town served as a meeting place of white students. The day following a request by a black student to enjoy the tree's shade as well, several hangman's nooses were suspended from the tree's branches. Fights among the students broke out, some started by white students and others started by black students. The upshot of these fracases was that the white students were suspended from school for a few days while the black students, the "Jena Six," were charged with felony assault which could end in sentences of up to fifteen years in the penitentiary.

This obvious racially inspired handling of students caused an international scandal. Ultimately, public pressure forced reductions in their sentences, and, in the end, only one of the Jena Six, Mychal Bell, actually served time. Tragically, this young man, who once aspired to a college athletic scholarship, committed suicide when he was later arrested on a shoplifting charge. But, the South is not alone in hosting racial hatred. In 2010, a KKK-like hood on a statue was found and a noose hanging from the library was discovered, both at the University of California at San Diego.

Right-Wing Extremist Ideology Analyzing the ideology of recently popular strains of American right-wing extremism is difficult because not all groups agree about their goals. Common themes among all of them, however, can be identified. They include an absolutist value system in which hatred plays a large part; a view of the world in which the players are either good or bad; the certainty that religious fundamentalist ideas are true and constitute the foundation of a good society; a belief in the "sovereign individual," meaning that people and their property are virtually sacrosanct, and government regulation and taxation are unwarranted intrusions on the sacred rights of the individual; a profound sense of foreboding about the future, punctuated by the conspiratorial belief that sinister forces are controlling society and sapping it of its goodness and vitality; the persuasion that the nation's strength rests with its fundamental values and that evil people are destroying the moral fiber of the society; the conviction that the good people must be ever vigilant against unceasing and insidious efforts of sinister forces to infiltrate and destroy the organizations that good people use to identify and resist the bad; the commitment to defending their liberties with violence if necessary; and finally, the belief that life is meaningful only when struggle against the ingrained enemy is occurring.

These ideas are not new in the American experience. Exaggerated notions about personal liberty, mistrust of government, and beliefs in racial and moral superiority have been present since the earliest days of colonial America. Even political paranoia is no stranger to our shores: Consider the lynchings following the liberation of the slaves (an estimated 5,000 occurred between 1880 and 1940 alone), the various nativist movements in the last two centuries, the Great Red Scare of 1919, the McCarthy hysteria of the 1950s, and perhaps this moment in our history if current ominous trends of our dwindling civil liberties, justified by our response to the war on terrorism continue. These restrictions include imprisoning people for indefinite terms without charge or trial in the vast majority of cases. While there are general commonalities among right-wing extremist groups, there is also diversity. White supremacism is a very strong factor among most extremist groups, but there are a few that specifically disavow this bias. Most extremist groups view environmentalism as a dangerous threat to individual and property rights, but there are a few that call for an end to both racial pollution and environmental pollution in America. A militant opposition to taxation is not only a very common stance among these groups, but taxation is also among the oldest specifically identified evils in this movement's ideology. Gun control legislation is also a very common evil, so far as these groups are concerned. Indeed, if there are two specific policies with which these groups find themselves most at odds, they are taxes and gun control legislation. In a more general sense, socialism and liberalism seem to be used as catchalls for whatever is suspicious or bad.

Left with no villain when the Soviet bloc collapsed in 1991, right-wing extremists began searching almost desperately for a new bad guy, because conspiratorialists are fixated on the belief that someone evil is about to take over society and enslave the innocent. Robbed of the "evil empire" for a villain, American reactionaries focused on the federal government as the new ogre. The precise danger seen depends on the particular extremist group, but usually a massive conspiracy threatening civilization is suspected. The people perpetrating this potential holocaust are described variously as yet-to-be-vanquished communists, Jews, international bankers, the UN, and foreigners of one kind or another. And, to be sure, it is often suggested that the identity of the evil ones is not yet known but that it is well known that they do exist and portend imminent danger. Not uncommonly, these groups are seen as being in league with the United States government.

As mentioned above, suspicion of the government has long been a tenet in American politics, but the suspicion is usually born of a contempt for bureaucracy and as a defense against individual politicians who may trounce on the people's rights in pursuit of their own selfish ambitions, or out of the belief that some evil people—the communists, for example—have infiltrated the government and want to use power for nefarious reasons. The current reactionary phobia about the government, by contrast, is founded on a much more sweeping fear. Right-wing extremists believe that the government's authority is totally evil and cannot be reconciled with individual freedom, Americanism, or "God's true will"—that they are so incompatible as to be mutually exclusive. To these people the government of the United States is un-American and oppressive. "I love my country but I fear my government" the bumper sticker reads.

Strangely romantic and pseudo-chivalrous, these reactionaries see themselves as soldiers in a righteous cause. They are called by a higher power to resist satanic control, and they seem almost to welcome an apocalyptic fate in resisting evil. For example, about a year before she was shot to death in a 1992 standoff with federal agents at Ruby Ridge, Idaho, Vicky Weaver addressed two letters to "The Queen of Babylon" and mailed them to the United States Attorney's office in Boise. "A long forgotten wind is starting to blow," she wrote,

> Do you hear the approaching thunder? . . . The stink of your lawless government has reached Heaven, the abode of Yahweh or Yahshua. Whether we live or whether we die, we will not bow to your evil commandments.

© Leon P. Baradat

Prominently displayed on Interstate 5 in California, close to Tejon Pass in the mountains between Los Angels and Bakersfield, this sign expressed the militant and violent frustration with authority harbored by right-wing extremists. Presumably, the misspelling of the word "bullet" was intended to give deniability to the owners should they be accused of inciting violence against the authorities. Other signs seen along California's Great Central Valley, to which the I-5 leads, are "IRS Means In Range Shoot," "Keep Your Car Use A BAR" (a BAR is an automatic rifle), and "Follow Jesus or Go to Hell."

There is little or no recognition in this ideology that government does at least some good things, and the extremist firebrands offer no coherent suggestion for what institutions society might use to resolve its problems in the absence of government. These blind spots are particularly ironic since several leaders of this movement, including Randy Weaver, who battled with federal agents on Ruby Ridge, and Jack Maxwell Oliphant of Arizona, who was among the founders of one of the first militant civilian militias, the Arizona Patriots, long depended on Social Security checks and other government assistance for their economic well-being. Presumably, Weaver is now financially independent, having been given a $3 million settlement by the government for the shootings of his son and wife during the Ruby Ridge standoff. (Oliphant has passed away.)

Convinced as they are that the government is conspiring to enslave them, these reactionaries often oppose government policies as plots to unjustly deny the individual's liberties. The measures that have been pointed to as repressive range from local zoning laws to the North American Free Trade Agreement (NAFTA), from city decisions to fluoridated drinking water to the monetary policies of the Federal Reserve Board.

More recently (in 2010), a group of extremists calling themselves. The Guardians of the Free Republic sent letters to several state governors demanding that they resign office immediately, thus—they hoped—beginning the first step to dismembering the U.S. government. Even more extreme, nine members of a group they call Hutaree, describing themselves as "Christian warriors" and sporting shoulder patches showing "CCR," for Colonial Christian Republic, were arrested by federal agents and accused of plotting the overthrow of the U.S. government. Anticipating "the end times,"[8] this group allegedly plotted killing several people and sought to obtain bomb-making materials.

A common complaint by the right-wing extremists is that the federal government is the willing agent of the UN, or some other equally threatening international group, in plots to demolish U.S. power and to surrender the society to them. Another conspiracy theory currently circulating on the far right is that President Obama is conspiring with the Mexican government to take over the southwestern United States.

The origins of the reactionary movement that currently has become so prominent in the United States can be traced at least to the 1970s. William L. Pierce, a former professor of physics at Oregon State University, wrote a novel entitled *The Turner Diaries*.[9] Self-published under the pen name of Andrew Macdonald, the book calls for violence against African Americans, Jews, journalists, liberals, immigrants, gun control advocates, the federal government, its agents, and anyone else who supports it. The FBI suspects that the book, which the agency refers to as "a blueprint for revolution," was used as a model for at least one terrorist escapade in which a man stole $500,000 at gunpoint and later died in a standoff with police. The money, it is believed, was to be used to fund the overthrow of the government. The book, which calls for cutting the throats of newspaper editors and which imagines Jews being herded off to a remote canyon—reminiscent of the Babi Yar massacre in which the Nazis murdered over 100,000 Ukrainian Jews at a ravine in which they were then covered in a mass grave outside of Kiev during World War II—also describes destroying an FBI building with a car bomb made of ammonia nitrate fertilizer. Such a bomb was used in 1995 by a disgruntled right-wing extremist, Timothy McVeigh, to demolish a federal building in Oklahoma City. The blast took the lives of 168 innocent people.

Until his death at age eighty in 2002, William Pierce headed the National Alliance, one of the most successful hate groups in the country. Its membership may have been as high as 1,400 throughout the country, and it financed

---

[8]"The end times" is thought by some to mark the end of the earth. This view is popular among many Christian fundamentalists on their reading of the Bible, but other people see the apocalyptic times coming for other reasons; race war, earthquakes, floods, even when the Mayan calendar ends on December 21, 2012. In fact, there is a growing business for some New Aged entrepreneurs selling berths in deeply buried bunkers in remote parts of the country, the Mojave Desert in California, and in Kansas. These are being sold to people who wish to try to survive the "inevitable."

[9]Copies of this book are usually on sale at gun shows across the country.

itself by sales of the products of its companies: Resistance Records and Vanguard Books. Each of these enterprises tried to popularize right-wing beliefs of the most vile type. Since Pierce's death, the National Alliance's membership has declined dramatically.

The White Aryan Resistance (WAR) and the Aryan Nations were two other very important hate groups. WAR, founded by Tom Metzger, became an influential propaganda and organizational advisor to right-wing extremists. Using considerable political savvy and electronic and print media skills, Metzger has become something of a guru to violent reactionaries. His literature and broadcasts extol white supremacism and advocate violent attacks on Jews and African Americans. Answering his call, some skinheads attacked and even killed innocent people. The Aryan Nations, the political wing of the Christian Identity Church of Jesus Christ Christian, was headquartered in Idaho. The movement's founder, Rev. Richard Grint Butler, had an office adorned with pictures of Adolf Hitler situated inside a compound that warned "Whites Only." This sect, which also believes that bar codes on food products are a Jewish plot to poison whites, had an influence on Randy Weaver and his wife.

The Aryan Nations was finally brought low after a group of its armed security guards raced out of their Hayden Lake, Idaho, compound and attacked Victoria Keenan and her son. Claiming that they thought the backfire of her car was actually a shot fired at the compound, they viciously beat the two. In the resulting lawsuit, paid for by the Southern Poverty Law Center, Butler was forced to pay the plaintiffs $6.3 million. This settlement drained the financial resources of the Aryan Nations. Butler has died, but his followers are still active. The Southern Poverty Law Center also dealt a debilitating blow to WAR. Following a brutal beating death of an Ethiopian emigrant by skinheads in Portland, Oregon, the Law Center sued Metzger and his son John for their part in inciting the killing. The ultimate judgment of $12.5 million has quieted the Metzgers, at least for now.

The Council of Conservative Citizens (CCC) is distinguished among reactionary groups because of its mainstream prominence. It was once dominated by legitimate conservatives; 34 percent of its members served in the Mississippi legislature. However, under the leadership of Gordon Lee Baum, it has moved to the right at warp speed, becoming a vociferous and openly racist organization. Perhaps even more disturbing, this group is courted by powerful Mississippi Republican politicians, including the former U.S. Senate majority leader Trent Lott, and former Republican National Committee Chairman Haley Barbour. In 2003, Barbour was elected governor of Mississippi, even though he refused to dissociate himself from the CCC, which had endorsed his candidacy. Barbour is currently contemplating a run for the Republican presidential nomination in 2012.

Another movement that achieved prominence in the 1990s is the militant civilian militias. The militias declined in popularity briefly in the first decade of this century, but now their membership is once again increasing. The greatest amount of militia activity is found in Arizona, California, Florida, Michigan,

Montana, and Texas, but these paramilitary groups have been formed in virtually every state. Their avowed purpose differs from group to group and ranges from an extremist neighborhood watch to militant neo-Nazi, Christian fundamentalist fanaticism.

Paralleling the militia groups are the "Common Law Courts." These groups consist of private citizens who claim the right to take the law into their own hands. The Freemen, who in 1996 barricaded themselves in a Montana farmhouse to fend off state agents and the FBI trying to arrest them on charges of fraud and tax evasion, were partisans of this view. Using tortured interpretations of the common law, the U.S. Constitution, and the Bible—for instance, they claim the "original" Thirteenth Amendment outlawed lawyers—these kangaroo courts insist they have the authority to overrule state and federal law. They encourage people to renounce any further financial responsibility for debts. They also have tried and convicted in abstentia certain real jurists whose rulings they opposed. They have attempted to intimidate jurists by summoning them to appear before them, by sending judges threatening letters, and, in one case, by attempting to assassinate a Missouri highway patrol officer.

Although they are spread throughout the country and are becoming increasingly militant and open about their beliefs, the number of people engaging in the militias and similar movements is still fairly small. However, it's clear that these reactionaries enjoy a rather large base of unofficial support among the general public. Elements of their ideology are often espoused by people in some gun clubs, certain groups in the military, survivalist organizations, and other groups.

There has even been a relatively successful effort to recruit hate group members in state and federal penitentiaries. Four Aryan Brotherhood members were convicted of murder, conspiracy, and racketeering in California in 2006. All these people were serving terms in penitentiaries while they organized the criminal ring and committed the crimes.

Meanwhile, longtime Klansman Edgar Ray Killen was finally convicted of the 1964 murder of three civil rights workers. Klan rallies are increasing. There have been notable Klan demonstrations in Ohio, Pennsylvania, Wisconsin, Kentucky, Mississippi, Georgia, Florida, and Virginia recently. Also, in 2006, six Klansmen pleaded guilty to plotting to blow up a North Carolina courthouse. Neo-Nazi groups have also seemingly stepped up their public protests and more violent activity.

While the Klan, the neo-Nazis, and the militant civilian militias have generally focused their venom on Jews and African Americans, Hispanics are beginning to attract more negative attention from these and other racists. This new interest is apparently driven by the rapidly increasing number of Hispanics in the United States, and that they are spread across the nation as a whole. Most alarming is the question of illegal immigration across the border of Mexico. Frustrated by what are seen as ineffective policies by the federal and state governments, some extremists have formed vigilante groups to patrol the borders in Texas, Arizona, and California. Indeed admitted neo-Nazi, Jason J. T. Ready, although he does not like the term, taking advantage of Arizona's lax gun-use regulations, currently leads his militia joining the vigilante elements who patrol the border with Mexico. (Ready believes only white heterosexuals should be citizen and live in the United States.) Encouraged by some conservative politicians, these self-appointed "guardians of freedom" are armed and quite dangerous. Not only do their activities, in and of themselves, constitute a public danger but one must also seriously question the wisdom of encouraging or even allowing people to arm themselves and take the law into their own hands. However, once regarded as a fringe element, reactionary groups are gradually being accepted by the mainstream, as are some of their previously thought unconventional ideas. The absurdly conspiratorial theories of some Tea Party members are becoming commonplace with some of its adherents being elected as Republicans to some of the country's highest offices, while even neo-Nazis and Aryan Nations followers are now seeking local offices, including school boards.

QUESTIONS FOR DISCUSSION

1. How can fascism and Nazism be compared and contrasted?
2. What are the fundamental features of fascism and National Socialism?
3. What seem to be the social conditions under which right-wing extremism develops?
4. What fundamental beliefs are common among American right-wing extremists?
5. What features and beliefs in the American political experience tend to encourage right-wing extremism?

SUGGESTIONS FOR FURTHER READING

Bosworth, R. J. B. *Mussolini*: Oxford: Oxford University Press, 2002.

Gregor, Neil, ed., *Nazism*. New York: Oxford University Press, 2000.

Hitler, Adolf, *Mein Kampf,* trans. Ralph Manheim. Boston: Houghton Mifflin, 1943.

Merkl, Peter, and Leonard Weinberg, *Right-Wing Extremists in the Twenty-First Century*. London: Frank Cass, 2003.

Mussolini, Benito, *Fascism: Doctrine and Institutions*. New York: Howard Fertig, 1968.

Paxton, Robert O., *The Anatomy of Fascism*. New York: Alfred A. Knopf, 2004.

Ryon, Mick, *Homeland: Into a World of Hate*. Edenburgh: Mainstream, 2003.

Shirer, William L., *The Rise and Fall of the Third Reich*. New York: Simon & Schuster, 1960.

Sonder, Ben, *The Militia Movement: Fighters of the Far Right*. Culver City, CA: Watts Publishing, 2000.

Southern Poverty Law Center, *False Patriots: The Threat of Anti-Government Extremists*. Montgomery, AL: Southern Poverty Law Center, 1996.

Ideologies in the Developing World

PREVIEW

Although the various Developing World countries have unique qualities, they also tend to exhibit certain ideological traits in common. Being divided along tribal, cultural, religious, and ethnic lines, many former colonies have adopted an exaggerated nationalistic posture in attempts to unify the diverse elements within their societies and to secure the state's interests against foreign aggression, real or imagined. In the past decade, many underdeveloped states have experimented with democracy and capitalism, but the lack of political and economic stability has already defeated several of these efforts and threatens even more. Struggling against extreme overpopulation, crushing poverty, and neocolonial exploitation, most Developing World states find socialism to be more compatible with their worldviews, since the individualism and aggressiveness of capitalism repel many.

Holding different perspectives than the world's economically advanced states, Developing World countries tend to evolve unique political and economic systems. Liberal democracy, although tried by many countries, has been found impractical by several and has been abandoned. Yet, totalitarian dictatorship is also rejected. Hence, many countries are governed by paternalistic authoritarian rulers. Lacking the individual freedom of the liberal democracies, these systems, which sometimes refer to themselves as *"guided democracies,"* vest powerful political controls in the hands of their leaders while denying them complete authority over other elements in the society. Under the most pleasant circumstances, some Developing World states may gradually improve their economic and political systems enough to maximize the benefits for all their citizens. Yet, in other cases, the combination of authoritarianism and nationalism may doom their people to fascist equivalents. At the same time, the growing popularity of religious fundamentalism in the Muslim world engenders reactionary revolutionary movements that would see modern political systems replaced by theocracies, even as terrorism threatens not only democratic systems in the underdeveloped world, but in economically advanced countries as well.

DEVELOPING WORLD DEFINED

To this point we have, with few exceptions, studied the ideologies that relate to the industrialized nations of the world. Such an approach is appropriate given the relationship between modern ideologies and the Industrial Revolution. There are, however, a large number of countries either still in the infant stages of their industrial development or have yet to undergo the Industrial Revolution at all. But, given the reality of the global economy, not yet having developed a mature industrial base does not prevent these societies from feeling the consequences of industrialization. Indeed, these peoples have been dramatically affected by its economic and political implications.

As with all generalizations, the term Developing World suggests a uniformity that in reality does not exist. Including the majority of the world's nations and a huge number of people and cultures, the Developing World is characterized by a bewildering diversity that virtually defies adequate generalization. There are similarities, however, and perhaps the most

© Mike Theiler/Reuters/Corbis

A worried Somalian mother comforts her starving child.

comprehensive similarity among these countries is poverty. The Malthusian calamity of population growth far exceeding the food supply is pressing hard on this sector of the world. Accordingly, feeding the multitudes is the most important preoccupation of many developing countries. At the same time, however, some of the Developing World countries have recently acquired vast wealth, largely through the production and sale of oil. So, even in its most obvious commonality—poverty—the Developing World is fraught with contradictions and exceptions.

As difficult as it is to generalize about the Developing World without hopelessly distorting the subject, this must be done if such an important element in the world community is not to be ignored. The following, therefore, is intended to be a broad approach to the politics and ideologies prominent among the world's underdeveloped countries.

POLITICS OF THE DEVELOPING WORLD

Essentially, the modern world has seen two periods of colonial expansion, each fundamentally representing the economically advanced powers forcing their domination over other parts of the world. The first colonial era spanned the period from 1492 to about 1785. During this time the trading countries of Portugal, Spain, France, England, and the Netherlands established some outposts in Africa, dominated the Indian subcontinent, and also established themselves in the East Indies and in some port cities in China and Japan. But the most extensive colonization was in the newly discovered Western Hemisphere. The colonies produced some precious metals, gems, and items of trade, but essentially they were given the task of providing agricultural goods to their European masters. Although private fortunes were made in the colonies, the military and administrative costs of maintaining them proved to be burdensome for the European governments. Gradually, as Spain, Portugal, and the Netherlands declined in power; as France was vanquished by England in North America and India; and as England lost its most prized colony to the American Revolution, colonialism came to be viewed askance, causing almost a century to pass in which relatively little more colonial expansion took place.

The second era of colonial growth ran from 1875 to the 1950s. Driven by the wish to feed their newly industrialized economies with cheap raw materials and labor, England, France, Belgium, Italy, and Germany began colonial expansion anew, rushing to take as much of Africa as they could; and, joined by Russia, the United States, and Japan, they also invaded large parts of Asia. By 1914, with the exception of Canada, Australia, and New Zealand (which had become independent from England), virtually all the world had succumbed to the industrial powers. This includes Latin America, which, while it became independent of its European masters during the early nineteenth century, was dominated by the United States through its application of the self-proclaimed Monroe Doctrine.[1]

In their rush to gobble up colonies, the industrial powers warred not only with their hapless captives but also with each other. For example, Japan fought with China (1894–1895); the United States warred with Spain (1898); Russia and Japan fought over Manchuria and Korea (1904–1905); and finally, all of the industrial powers entered in the titanic bloodletting of World War I, which, as Lenin observed, was motivated in part by colonial competition. The interwar years saw the rise of totalitarianism and a new spate of colonialism by Italy, Germany, and Japan, even as the Soviet Union expanded westward, taking the Baltic states and parts of Finland and Rumania.

To the industrialized nations, even though the Soviet Union added most of Eastern Europe to its empire and England and France tried desperately to hold on to their colonies in Africa and Asia, World War II is viewed as a struggle to conquer the chauvinistic, xenophobic ideologies of fascism, National Socialism, and Japanese militarism. With the war's end, the industrialized world put its faith in international cooperation; the UN, after all, promised security as a reward for such cooperation. Soon, however, the industrialized world found itself split again, divided ideologically in the East–West standoff called the Cold War. To the people in the world's colonies, however, World War II was seen as something more than a struggle against fascism. Abandoned during the war to the advancing Axis armies (Germany, Italy, and Japan) or left to fend for themselves by their preoccupied imperial masters, the colonies experienced an awakening of *nationalism* among their peoples.

As the economically advanced states became polarized ideologically, aligning themselves with one of the two great superpowers, the United States and the Soviet Union, the colonial countries went a third way: toward independence. Nationalist movements in the colonies organized to resist continued colonial rule by the industrial powers. Except for India, where Mohandas Gandhi used passive resistance to compel independence, long and bloody wars of national liberation were fought to loosen the colonialists' grip on Asia and Africa. Regrettably, despite the Good Neighbor Policy of President Franklin D. Roosevelt, the United States continued to insinuate itself in the affairs of its southern neighbors. Perhaps most notably, the CIA under President Eisenhower brought down the government of Iran in 1953 and the Guatemalan and Paraguayan governments

---

[1]The Monroe Doctrine, proclaimed by President James Monroe in 1823, is often presented to students in the lower grades as a beneficent policy by the United States to lift the heavy hand of European domination from the shoulders of the Latin Americans. In fact, since it proscribes only further European colonization in the Western Hemisphere, it does not place the same restriction upon the United States itself. The United States drew a line of demarcation indicating it intended to stay out of European affairs, but that the Western Hemisphere was uniquely within its sphere of influence. Accordingly, often citing the Monroe Doctrine as justification, the United States made a practice of intervening both economically and politically in the affairs of the "sovereign" Latin American states whenever it chose to do so, occasioning the poignant Mexican lamentation "Poor Mexico, so far from God, yet so close to the United States."

in 1954; President Kennedy supported the unsuccessful Bay of Pigs invasion of Cuba in 1961, and the general's coup against the Diem government in Vietnam in 1963, during which President Ngo Dinh Diem was assassinated. President Lyndon B. Johnson sent troops to put out the Juan Bosch government of the Dominican Republic in 1964; and in 1973, the CIA under President Richard M. Nixon "facilitated" the ouster of President Salvador Allende from Chile. In 1984, President Reagan ordered the invasion of Granada to displace its Castro-friendly government and he supported the Contras' efforts to overthrow Nicaragua's leftist government. Reagan even sold arms to Iran, which he had previously called a "terrorist state," to raise money to fund the Contras; President George H. W. Bush sent troops to Panama to remove Manuel Noriega in 1989; both President Clinton in 1994 and President George W. Bush in 2004 supported coups in Haiti; and President Bush supported an unsuccessful coup against Hugo Chavez in Venezuela in 2002. Beyond these coups, the United States has attempted several assassinations of various political leaders. There have been a number of U.S. attempts to assassinate Fidel Castro, including one by a loaded cigar, and another in cooperation with American Mafia figures.

Imperialism was also a crippling influence in the Developing World in other ways. It was not only politically and economically oppressive, but it tried to destroy the cultures, the social structures, and the political systems of the colonies. The imperialistic interlopers ignored the values of the people of their colonies. They minimized their histories, denigrated their traditions, disparaged their religions, and blatantly asserted Western superiority. Equally debilitating, the Western colonialists often created states with scant concern for the ethnic and cultural differences among people. When these countries became independent, they found little consensus among their peoples, thus making building a nation of people difficult.

These outrages ultimately became too much for the colonial countries to bear. Finally having recovered their equilibrium after the trauma of colonial rule, and emboldened by the weakness of the European imperialists following World War II, the militant elements in the colonies demanded, fought for, and eventually achieved independence.

The rallying cries of the colonial revolutionaries, however, did more than simply demand independence from the imperialists: Secularism was denounced, materialism was condemned, liberal democracy was often vilified as hypocritical, and, above all, individualism was excoriated.

In their place the old ways were exhumed, and liberation and prosperity were pledged. The aspirations of these new states were articulated in complicated hybrids of Western ideas and traditional values and institutions. Beyond question, however, the most striking political reality among Developing World countries was their enthusiastic *nationalism*. Used as the mantra to drive the hated colonial powers out, nationalism assumed enormous authority in the Developing World. Its importance in the newly emerged states is especially great because they have suffered a severe identity crisis resulting from the cultural imperialism endured.

Thus, when the former colonies emerged as independent states, they found themselves comprising varieties of tribes, social structures, and cultures, and were confused and disoriented about themselves. Grasping for unifying themes, their leaders have pursued contradictory policies of lionizing the traditional languages, art, religions, and cultures while championing national unity. Moreover, the weight of nationalism in the Developing World is compounded by the insecurity of its leaders. New to independence and power, they are anxious to prove the legitimacy of their rule. This concern often leads them beyond the occasional assertion of their national interests to bravado and bombast in world arenas such as the UN.

The exaggerated nationalism in the Developing World is also a by-product of anticolonialist emotions. Having experienced the humiliating exploitation of colonialism, the people of the emerging states will not be denied their independence. Yet, the power that foreign investors have in many developing countries, called **neocolonialism** (dollar, yuan, euro, yen, pound, and diplomacy), frightens the Africans, Asians, and Latin Americans. At the same time, the developing countries lack the funds for domestic capital investment and, therefore, are forced to encourage foreign investment, even though experience has painfully taught them that foreign influence can become oppressive. Understandably, this dilemma makes the people of developing countries defensive about their status in world affairs.[2]

Although nationalism is used to unify the people in the developing countries, several factors in these societies also tend to divide them. More often than not, as the residue of receding colonial empires, these states are composed of a number of different tribal, ethnic, cultural, and religious groups. Forging these diverse people into a single nation requires more than geographic proximity or political and economic necessity. Ordinary citizens of these states may be oriented entirely toward their own villages and feel little identification with their newly named country or its government. In such circumstances, leaders use exaggerated patriotic appeals to awaken national awareness in the minds of their provincial citizens. They often warn that a neighboring regime may take advantage of the new state, or that a former colonial oppressor wants to reestablish its control, still others demand cohesion so as to ward off the dangers of socialism or the threat of another right-wing military dictatorship; such warnings are intended to galvanize nationalist spirit. Frequent use of this technique has contributed to strong nationalistic ideologies among many emerging states.

At the same time, however, a true and deeply felt nationalistic attachment cannot be created by such techniques. Nationalism, as explained in Chapter 3, is based on a very personal identification with one's nation-state. For nationalism to develop, a nation must already exist. Shared traditions, history, and

---

[2]You will remember the consensus expressed in Cuba to oppose any effort by the United States to come into control of the island again. Cuban leaders repeatedly use threats of such renewed Yankee colonialism to remain in power, and American presidents, seemingly unable to learn the lesson, continue to pursue policies that look strikingly like such neocolonialist policies.

territory, although not essential, are very helpful in building a nation. Although Cuba had already developed an innate sense of nationhood long before Castro took power, and even somewhat before the United States intervened in the early twentieth century Cuban revolution to drive the Spanish out, most former colonial countries had not by the time they became independent.

Often the colonial experience failed to make a unified group out of the various peoples thrown together by foreign rule and later by independence. Too often a Developing World country becomes an independent state without a nation to serve as its foundation. Nigeria, for example, Africa's most populous country, is composed of at least ten major ethnic groups, including the Hausa-Fulani, the Yoruba, the Igbo, and the Nupe. The cultural and religious differences among Nigeria's people are so strong that civil war and military dictatorship are common. Unifying these diverse societies is a monumental political task. The collapse of the Soviet Union has, in fact, complicated the effort in that the titanic struggle between East and West is no longer a factor. Thus, it no longer distracts people's attention. Consequently, people of the Developing World have become even more focused on their own economic, social, and political difficulties. Moreover, the world seems to be evolving from one dominated by military confrontation to one absorbed in economic competition, a struggle for which most of the Developing World is poorly suited.

This situation creates a political paradox. Not only must the emerging states maintain their independence, sometimes against incredible economic and political odds, but at the same time they must also build a nation. So, paradoxically, though the emerging states are often the strongest supporters of nationalism in international affairs, they also often suffer the greatest disunity and separatism within their own borders. The ethnic and cultural differences within these states sometimes overwhelm efforts to unite people and create a nation; violence of the worst sort sometimes erupts, as in the 1990s in Rwanda and Congo, the current genocide in Darfur, Sudan, and the American invasion-induced chaos in Iraq, threatening to spread instability throughout the region.

Disunity within Developing World countries is matched by parochialism in international affairs. Although several attempts have been made to create regional international unions, none has succeeded very well. Divided by nationalistic jealousies and historical differences, the Arab states have consistently faltered in efforts to coalesce into larger political units. The Organization of African Unity has seldom been more than a forum in which the various members vent their frustrations, rarely being able to agree on united action. In 2001, several Caribbean states forged an economic Union, the Caribbean Community (CARICOM). Although CARICOM got off to a good start, largely because of its growing trade with Asia, in 2008 the global recession hit these countries hard. Hopefully, they will soon recover and get back on track building their economies. And the Organization of American States, perhaps the most successful Developing World organization because it makes no pretense at establishing permanent political unity, is often criticized as being a puppet of the United States.

The ideological themes in the Developing World are recognized, even if the political movements they inspire are unable to join together. Without question, *emancipation* is the dominant theme in these ideological appeals. Freeing themselves from the still-present shackles of colonialism and imperialism is the preeminent goal. Restoring broken cultures, political independence, economic self-sufficiency, and self-esteem are paramount.

Just as emancipation is the objective, militancy is increasingly the tone used to claim the goal. The faithful are called to battle for common goals. This tone reflects the tumultuous state in which much of the Developing World finds itself. Sub-Saharan Africa is ablaze with strife that runs from the East African horn (Sudan, Ethiopia, Eritrea, and Somalia) diagonally southwest across the continent to West Africa. The reasons for these many conflicts are varied and complex, but essentially they revolve around cultural, ethnic, economic, and political problems.

There are two conditions in the Developing World that must be examined in this regard. The first is the current decline of support for democracy in the Developing World and, second, the accompanying rise in the prestige of China. With the collapse of the Soviet Union, the last decade of the twentieth century saw an important increase of interest and commitment to democracy and capitalism. It appeared as though democracy was going to liberate people from political oppression, and capitalism would create economic improvement. Yet this unrealistic optimism turned to disappointment among many by the end of the decade. In reality, corruption and oppression can be visited upon a people by elected officials as well as by leaders put in power through military coups. In fact, it is true that like socialism and capitalism, democracy is also a rich man's sport. The individual liberty afforded by liberal democracy is expensive. That is, a society must be wealthy enough to allow its citizens to do almost whatever they like, even if what they want to do is not very economically productive. Poor countries often demand, if everyone is to be fed, a degree of organization and control that can stifle democracy. Africa is a good case in point. Faced with political reversals, Zimbabwe, Kenya, South Africa, Nigeria, Uganda, and Ethiopia are among the fledgling democracies in Africa where leaders recently resorted to authoritarian measures to retain power. As a rule, votes are seldom a match for machine guns among societies in turmoil and where democratic traditions and institutions are not securely established.

Meanwhile, in 2008 and 2009, the world economy came perilously close to complete collapse because the United States' financial houses engaged in unethical and irresponsible banking schemes and they were followed by the banks of most of the advanced economies on the globe. Suddenly, the capitalist juggernaut was brought to its knees, proving itself all too fallible. China, however, provided a different example. While it also had serious economic problems during the Great Recession, it was the first country to regain its economic equilibrium and quickly grew so fast, while the Western economies were still staggering, that its leaders had to take measures to avoid inflation.

China's economic success, while at the same time continuing to eschew calls for political liberalization, has given people in the Developing World a glimpse of another model: *authoritarian free marketism*. This model is very attractive to the power elites of many developing countries. Enhancing China's attractiveness further is the fact that it has used some of its immense foreign exchange earnings to invest in the underdeveloped countries in Asia, Africa, and Latin America. It has funded roads, bridges, hospitals, schools, joint ventures, and so forth, and it has bought large quantities of raw materials necessary for its own construction projects and for its growing industrial base. In short, because of its successful economic flexibility and its political stability, China is seen by many developing countries as a model worthy of emulation.

Another area of the world also should be given close examination: the Muslim world. With 1.2 billion believers, Islam is second in size only to Christianity. Although it is most prevalent at the world's midsection, it stretches through over forty states from West Africa to Indonesia. Interestingly, when we think of Muslims, we usually think of people in the Middle East, but actually, almost eighty percent of the world's Muslims live in Asia, and Indonesia is most populus Muslim state. Islam is among the fastest growing religions in the world. Indeed, it is among the fastest growing religions in the United States, having increased by one-third to over 6 million people in only thirty years. Today, there are more Muslims in the United States than Presbyterians. Originating in the same region from which Judaism and Christianity issued, Islam (meaning surrender to the will of Allah or God) worships the same God as do the Jews and their notion of God is consistent with the Christian God the Father. They accept the ancient Hebrew holy men as early prophets and also recognize Jesus as a prophet, but not as God. Muslims believe that Mohammed (570?–632) is the most important prophet, to whom Allah revealed the greatest truth. Like the Bible to Jews and Christians, the Koran is accepted by Muslims as the revealed word. Their religion is expected to be central to their lives, guiding them in all things. They accept the Ten Commandments but add to them the "five pillars" of faith: profession of faith, five daily prayers, giving alms, observing Ramadan (fasting), and making a pilgrimage to Mecca at least once in life. Beyond these revealed truths, Muslims are guided through the course of their lives by the *Sharia* (the path), a set of legal and moral precepts developed by religious leaders over the centuries. It is the Sharia, and not the Koran, that has been the most powerful force in relegating women to a subordinate role in Muslim society. For example, the Koran does not call for veiling women. That tradition evolved in the Sharia.[3]

In an earlier period, Islam was theocratic. That is, the religious leaders were also the political leaders. A dispute over who should become the next caliph (religious and political successor to the mantle of Mohammed) in the

---

[3]An example of growing paranoia about Muslims in Oklahoma is that its citizens in 2010 voted overwhelmingly to pass a state constitutional amendment prohibiting Sharia Law from being used in Oklahoma's courts, even though there is no indication that it would be.

late seventh century opened the most significant schism in Islam. Those claiming that the succession was wrongful are known as *Shiites,* and through the years they have also developed some doctrinal disputes with the much larger orthodox sect, known as the *Sunnis.* The Shiites are concentrated mainly in Iran, Iraq, and Azerbaijan, and the Sunnis hold sway in most other Islamic societies.

Complicating this ancient schism is a modern three-way split rending apart the Muslim world. On the one hand are oil-rich Saudi Arabia, Kuwait, and the United Arab Emirates struggling to hold together their lucrative but autocratic monarchies in the face of increasingly insistent demands for social and political reform. A second force includes the modernists like Muammar Qaddafi of Libya and the Ba'th parties of Syria and Iraq. These leaders propose to merge the traditions of Islam with their notions of socialism and Arab unity. Their regimes, however, are truculently nationalistic in foreign affairs, and they impose a heavy-handed despotism at home. Closely related to these regimes ideologically are Pakistan, Bangladesh, and Indonesia.

Islamism

The third element in the division of the Muslim world is the animus between secular government and **Islamism.** Islamism, more an ideology than a religious doctrine, is defined variously by different people. These interpretations range from the moderate view that it is a call to the faithful to rededicate to Islam as a lifestyle as well as a religious practice, to its most extreme form insisting Muslims welcome a society, government, and laws based on the traditional principles of Islam. It is this interpretation that is most pertinent to our study, because it has become a powerful ideological movement.

The term Islamism was first used almost three centuries ago but its use became most prominent since the last quarter of the twentieth century. While it enjoys less appeal in sub-Saharan Africa, Bangladesh, and Indonesia, it has become the most salient political idea in the Middle East and Pakistan, as previously popular secularism has declined in importance. Its appeal is even being felt in usually militantly-secular Turkey with the 2007 election of Islamist Abdullah Gül as president of the republic.

Interestingly enough, the most powerful recruits in this militant movement are not from the backward rural areas. Instead they come increasingly from middle-class people who have become disillusioned with Westernization—with "McAmerica," as one critic put it—and the drift away from the "true faith."

The extreme form of Islamism is a reactionary ideology, demanding the rejection of modernization (Westernization), and a return to the theocracies of old, where people and the state are governed by the principles of the Koran and the mandates of the Sharia; not by secular legislation and mores. It rejects Western values and institutions as contradictions of the true path. Smarting from former Western colonialism, its adherents suspect that Europe and the United States intend to reduce Islam to political insignificance by plundering the oil resources in the Middle East, which many Arab Muslims believe is Allah's gift to the faithful.

That Islamism finds itself directly confronting the West contributes significantly to its appeal in the Middle East, since Islam has been in conflict with Europe and Christianity for almost its entire existence. Bordering on Byzantine Europe, Islam spread east to Afghanistan, Pakistan, Bangladesh, Malaysia, and Indonesia. In the west it conquered North Africa and Catholic Spain, governing it for seven centuries. Its conquest of Spain was followed by the Western invasion of Islam by the Crusades. With the eventual defeat of the Crusades, Europe turned to the re-conquest of Spain, even as Turkey converts to Islam advanced from the east to vanquish Byzantium. As the caliphs aged, however, their previous superiority in education, culture, and trade was surpassed by a new era of Western technological development, and bureaucratic and military advances, as it turned to exploiting the Western Hemisphere and Asia. By the late nineteenth century Britain, France, and eventually the United States arrived to exploit the oil-rich but politically weak Middle East. Arabia, Libya, Syria, Palestine, Persia, and other states became pawns, manipulated by the West during its own titanic fraternal struggles of World Wars I and II. The nationalism, spiced with anticolonialism, that spread across Asia and Africa deeply affected the Muslim world as well as its anti-Western emotions that were further stoked by the creation of Israel in the midst of the Muslim homeland, brushing aside the Muslim residents in the area during the process.

As these political events played out, modern economic reality set in. The industrialized world became dependent on oil as an energy source and quickly used up most of its domestic reserves. Biding its time, the oil producing Muslim world quietly became increasingly stronger and more strategic. Finally, in the 1970s the mouse roared. The Organization of Oil Producing Countries (OPEC) was formed in 1960, and the Arab states used it to quadruple oil prices (1973–1974) in retaliation for U.S. support of Israel during the Yom Kippur War (1973), and another large boost to prices was executed in 1979 during the U.S.-Iran crisis which saw the staff in the American embassy in Tehran held hostage until 1981. Since then, although not able to completely control oil prices, the Middle East oil states have been able not only to influence the price of oil but also influence the foreign policies of the West. And, Islamism has greatly benefited from the anticolonial emotions and the economic power of the Middle East.

When, during the Gulf War of 1991, Saudi Arabia allowed United States and allied forces on its territory—sacred land to Muslims—the Islamists, whom the Saudi's had previously encouraged, lost confidence in the Kingdom. The most extremist elements among them, led by Osama bin Laden, determined that the infidel Americans must be driven from the sacred soil of Arabia. After having received substantial aid from the United States during the Afghan-Soviet War in the 1980s, bin Laden fostered a terrorist organization, **Al Qaeda,** and after several terrorist strikes at the United States abroad, he ordered the attacks on the Twin Towers[4] and the Pentagon on September 11, 2001. Although it was never established that any links existed between Iraq President Saddam Hussein and Al Qaeda before the United States invasion of Iraq, the invasion confirmed in the minds of the adherents of Islamism that the United States intends to dominate the Muslim world. Upon learning that no weapons of mass destruction (WMDs) existed in Iraq and that no connection between Hussein and Al Qaeda existed, the Bush administration, for reasons never adequately explained,[5] was intent on conquering Iraq anyway, an ambition proving to Islamists that the United States was fixed on gaining a physical foothold in the Middle East, regardless of the facts. Ironically, subsequent elections have produced a Shiite government in Iraq, much more partial to their co-religionists in Iran and Islamism than to the United States; an extremist-led government in Iran; the Hamas government in Palestine; and the Muslim Brotherhood and Hezbollah have gained in power in Egypt and Lebanon, respectively. Other manifestations of the political potence of Islamism include an important Muslim cleric in Indonesia demanding an end to secular government there and an influential Pakistani cleric establishing an Islamic court to enforce strict adherence to the Sharia and threatening the Pakistani government with suicide bombings if it tried to obstruct his self-anointed authority. Islamic fundamentalism has fostered civil disorder in Turkey; political assassinations in Egypt, Algeria, and Israel; a civil war in Algeria; and suicide bombings throughout the world. Islamism has spread beyond the Muslim world as well. Citizens of Denmark, Germany, England, Canada, and the United States have been arrested on suspicion of plotting terrorist attacks in their respective countries.

Quite beyond these instances, the most important successes in Islamism have been the Shiite takeover in Iran by the Ayatollah Khomeini and his successors and the emergence of the Taliban in Afghanistan. Also, a little-recognized

---

[4]This was the second attempt by Muslim terrorists to bring down the Twin Towers. The first occurred in 1993. Exactly who is responsible for that attack is still a matter of dispute.

[5]Once no WMDs were found in Iraq, a fact long asserted by the UN arms inspectors in Iraq, commentators and scholars tried mightily to discover the real motivation for the U.S. invasion. To date, no consensus has developed. Besides the nonexistent WMDs and Hussein's alleged connection to Al Qaeda, which very few authorities on Middle East politics ever believed owing to the fact Hussein was a secular leader and bin Laden is an extreme Islamist, several other motives have been proposed. With no WMDs in evidence, Bush claimed the goal was to remove a dictator and establish democracy in the Middle East. Others have suggested control of Iraqi oil or Bush wishing to avenge his father, who Hussein allegedly tried to have assassinated, were the objectives. Adding to the guessing game, it was reported by GQ Magazine in May of 2009 that during the run-up to the war, several U.S. intelligence reports were passed to President Bush by Secretary of Defense Donald Rumsfeld headed by biblical quotes like "put on the full armor of God," and "open the gates that the righteous nation may enter." This revelation (no pun here), together with the fact that in 2001 Bush referred to the war on terrorism as a "crusade," and the Deputy Undersecretary of Defense for Intelligence in 2003, General William G. Boykin, compared the war to a struggle against Satan, has caused many analysts to wonder anew if the war was religiously motivated. Unfortunately, it is possible that we shall never learn the true reason we were led into such a tragic waste of blood, treasure, and prestige.

bridge Islamism has made between Sunni and Shiite should be considered. The usual animosity between the two sects has been tempered somewhat by events. Iran, a Shiite country, led by President Mahmoud Ahmadinejad, has favorably impressed its Sunni neighbors. It materially contributed to the abject embarrassment of Israel by its support of Hezbollah during the 2006 Israel-Lebanon conflict. It has also twisted the tails of two Western lions: the United States and Great Britain. Clearly, if anyone has won in the Iraq War, it is not Iraq or the United States, but Iran. Iran has gained great stature in Iraq through its steadfast support of an independent Shiite government there. It has also refused to tailor its nuclear power development policy to United States or international standards. Each of these policies has virtually electrified Sunnis as well as fellow Shiites who ascribe to the traditional ideas of Islamism. Thus, in the eyes of Islamists of all ilks, Iran has surfaced as a leader.

Besides this bridge between Shiites and Sunnis, however, the awakening of Islam has also become the catalyst for bloody divisions within the Developing World, as the civil strife in Lebanon, the war between Iraq and Iran, the Persian Gulf War, and the U.S. invasions of both Afghanistan and Iraq have shown. Moreover, the collapse of the Soviet Union resulted in its Muslim republics (Kazakhstan, Uzbekistan, Turkmenistan, Kyrgyzstan, and Tadzhikistan) becoming independent. These countries, containing some 50 million people, are torn by civil strife as they try to find their way toward sovereignty in a confusing and dangerous political environment.

Sadly, caught in a murderous crossfire among those who wish to prevent change, those who insist on modernization, and those who demand that the clock be turned back, the Middle East squanders its youth and resources in desperate struggles with the shattering realities of the twenty-first century. It must also be quickly added that the recent policies of the United States and Great Britain have done little but exacerbate this political chaos.

Other Religions in Politics

Religion is also playing a major role in the politics of other parts of the Developing World. Cyprus continues to be divided among its Greek Christians and Turkish Muslims. In Sri Lanka, Christians war with Buddhists. On the Asian subcontinent, strained relations persist between Muslim Pakistan and Hindu India; and within India itself, Sikhs and Hindus have come to bloody clashes over religious, economic, and political issues. Finally, several African states are rent by conflict between their Muslim, Christian, and even pagan believers, and China's Falun Gong continues to be a political factor.

In Latin America, a quite different phenomenon is occurring. Inspired by European liberalism and even Marxism, some Roman Catholic clerics and laypeople have become political activists in struggles to combat poverty, ignorance, and powerlessness among the masses. They believe that scripture demands the Church be a force to liberate people from political and economic oppression as well as being a guide for people to reach heavenly reward.

Hearkening to the trumpet call of **Liberation Theology,** these leftists decry the exploitation of capitalism and neocolonialism and insist that the Church lead the poor in political efforts to restructure their societies and redistribute wealth and power more equitably. Socialist in concept and sometimes Marxist in rhetoric, this movement has achieved significant followings in Guatemala, El Salvador, Nicaragua, Peru, Brazil, Chile, and Colombia.

In the late 1800s, the Church abandoned its previous posture of focusing only on the spiritual needs of its flock while remaining uninvolved in social and political questions. Instead, today it recognizes the validity of the Church's engaging in a broader mission. Pope Leo XIII (1878–1903), among the greatest of modern pontiffs, wrote a number of encyclicals (public letters) at the turn of the twentieth century. These appeals called for social justice (at the time, the primary focus of these thoughts was Europe) and nurtured the Christian socialist movement in Europe. This movement saw a connection between the egalitarian goals of humanitarian socialism and the teachings of Christ. Following a conservative resurgence in the Church's focus during the first half of the twentieth century, in the 1960s it again gave impetus to its social and political role with a new set of encyclicals emanating from the work done at the Second Vatican Council (1962–1965) and with subsequent papal comments condemning economic and social exploitation of the poor. Although other religions in other areas have also begun to take a greater part in improving the social conditions of the world's poor, the Catholics in Latin America, albeit not unanimously, have taken the lead. But the Vatican has greeted these activists with ambiguous feelings. Pope John Paul II was genuinely committed to social and economic egalitarianism and to an activist Church, but he recoiled from the Marxist tendencies of some zealots. Accordingly, he supported efforts of Latin America priests and nuns to combat poverty and political oppression, but he condemned their involvement in revolutionary and other directly political activities. This admonition affected the movement of liberation theology somewhat negatively, although it certainly has not ended it. Pope Benedict XVI is also an opponent of the more radical trends in the movement, which may further take the edge off pressure to make the Church an agent of social change.

ECONOMICS OF THE DEVELOPING WORLD

As pointed out at the beginning of this chapter, poverty is probably the most common single feature in the Developing World. In fact, the situation is becoming very complicated and potentially catastrophic. The ongoing population explosion combined with a lack of capital, changing economic conditions, a disturbing decline in the food supply, and the almost certain fact that the people of the Developing World will suffer most from the consequences of global warming—a problem which they had little to do with creating—are fostering increasingly hopeless circumstances and potentially explosive political

TABLE 11.1

Ranking of the World's Most Populous Countries (in millions)

1950		2000		2050	
1. China	554.8	1. China	1,275.1	1. India	1,572.1
2. India	357.6	2. India	1,008.9	2. China	1,462.2
3. United States	157.8	3. United States	283.2	3. United States	397.2
4. Russia	102.7	4. Indonesia	212.1	4. Pakistan	344.2
5. Japan	83.7	5. Brazil	170.4	5. Indonesia	311.3
		7. Japan	127.1	16. Japan	109.2

Source: United Nations Population Division

conditions among these unfortunate societies. A UN study estimates that the total world population reached 1 billion people in 1804; but by 1960, only 156 years later, the world's population stood at 3 billion, and in 1999, barely 29 years after that, the 1960 figure doubled, reaching 6 billion. At the current growth rate, 213,696 people are added to the world's population each day. That means the world's population increases by 78 million people annually, a number slightly larger than the population of the Philippines. At this rate, assuming that such growth can be sustained, the world's population in 2040 will have reached 9 billion.

Even though China, the world's most populous country, has managed to significantly slow the pace of its population growth (largely by the desperate measure of its one-child-per-family policy), in 2000 its population stood at 1.28 billion, or double its 1953 figure. Rapidly gaining on China, India reached a population of 1.009 billion in the same year.

Table 11.1 illustrates four factors. First, it shows the phenomenal population growth of India. Second, it illustrates the inability of the developed states, except for the United States—which at 1.96 children per woman has the highest fertility rate in the industrialized world—to maintain their relative status among the world's populations. Third, the table shows Japan's population actually declining in absolute numbers in the next half century. Indeed, Russia's population is expected to drop even more precipitously. Fourth, the great explosion in the world's population is shown to be occurring in the Developing World. In the coming generation, the growth rate is expected to be 1 percent in Europe, 24 percent in North America, 47 percent in Asia, 52 percent in Central and South America, and a whopping 116 percent in Africa.

The population of sub-Saharan Africa is doubling each twenty-four years, despite the political turmoil in which it finds itself. In 1996 it had 600 million people. At the current rate of growth it will have about 1.2 billion people (the

> ### TABLE 11.2
>
> **2008 Estimates of World Populations**
>
> | Year | Asia | Africa | Europe | Latin America | North America |
> |------|------|--------|--------|---------------|---------------|
> | 2010 | 60.3% | 15.0% | 10.6% | 8.5% | 5.1% |
> | 2030 | 59.2% | 18.3% | 8.7% | 8.3% | 4.9% |
> | 2050 | 57.2% | 21.8% | 7.6% | 8.0% | 4.9% |
>
> *Source:* United Nations

current population of China) by the year 2020. The average fertility rate for women worldwide is 3.5 children, but in sub-Saharan Africa it is 6.2.[6]

Almost 98 percent of the annual increase in the world's population takes place in the Developing World. In a report released by the UN in 2008, Asia was expected to have 60.3 percent of the world's people by 2010. But Asia, Europe, Latin America, and North America are expected to decline while only the population of Africa is expected to increase as a percentage of the world's people by 2050, when the world's population will be 9.4 billion. (See Table 11.2.) At the same time, the populations of Europe and North America will grow older, while in Asia, Africa, and Latin America they will become younger.

In Asia, 32 percent of the population is below the age of fifteen. The figure is 35 percent in Latin America and 46 percent in Africa. In 1998, the population of the industrial countries stood at about 20 percent of the world's people, but by 2020 it will be only 16 percent.

The growth rate of the world's population reached a historical peak during the twentieth century, with the highest point of 2.2 percent in 1963. Since then, although it is still increasing, the rate of growth has been cut in half. Even so, it is clear that the earth will be sorely taxed to provide enough to accommodate the anticipated growth of 2.1 billion people in the thirty years from 2010 to 2040. Food alone, saying nothing of fresh water, energy, clothing, and everything else necessary to support life, will become an even greater problem than it is now. At present 1.2 billion people haven't enough to eat on a regular basis. In 2007 and 2008 alone the world's hungry increased by 110 million people in response to the leap in food prices: The price for cereal in 2009 was 71 percent higher than in 2005. Disturbingly, while an extraordinarily generous, but temporary, aid program salvaged the situation, nothing has been done to ameliorate

---

[6]It should be noted that the population explosion is not the result of an increased fertility rate around the globe. The number of births per woman has been brought down in the last forty years. However, modern medicine has expanded the life expectancy so greatly that it easily overwhelms the gains made by the declining fertility rate. This is true even though 12.2 million children under the age of five die each year of diseases that are easily treated, such as cholera, measles, pneumonia, and shigellosis. An additional 6.6 million children die each year of hunger and malnutrition. In other words, 1,808 children die of starvation/malnutrition each day.

the cause of the problem. A little over 900 million of the 1.2 billion hungry live in the Developing World, and it could become a powder keg in consequence.

Hunger falls most heavily on women and children. Sixty percent of the world's hungry are female and the death rate from hunger among children is frightening, with one child dying of hunger every six seconds. Besides hunger, the major killers of children in the Developing World are vitamin deficiency, iron deficiency, tainted water, and poor medical care.

You will recall the Malthusian dilemma, the calculation that saw population growth out-stripping the food supply. Almost immediately after Malthus's death, however, mechanized production and other advances increased the food supply and it appeared that the old English economist was wrong in his gloomy prediction. Eventually, however, growth of population surpassed previous increase in the food supply, leading many authorities to rethink their former disregard for the Malthusian dilemma. The current population explosion, of course, exacerbates already serious problems attendant on great poverty. The Developing World has 80 percent of the world's population but spends only 5 percent of the total money annually devoted to health care.[7] Half a million women die in childbirth each year, 99 percent of them in the Developing World. Three million children die annually in the Developing World due to lack of immunization. These circumstances are serious enough by themselves, but matters are even worse because the Developing World also hosts the greatest rate of human immunodeficiency virus (HIV) infection and acquired immune deficiency syndrome (AIDS) in the world. The most serious problem is in sub-Saharan African countries. Ignorance about the disease, poor medical treatment, lack of funds to buy medication, and superstition contribute to the pandemic. Not since the bubonic plague in Europe in the 1300s or the smallpox epidemic among Aztecs in the 1500s have we faced a medical threat of these proportions. The disease is also spreading rapidly in Russia, China, and Southeast Asia, and it is soon expected to become worst of all in India.

Of course, health problems in the Developing World are made worse because more than 1 billion people must use unsafe water, and 300 million people live in areas that have dangerous shortages of water. Because of exploding populations, it is estimated that this figure could rise to 3 billion by 2025—almost half of the current world population. This figure, startling as it is, will be seriously exacerbated by the warming of the earth's surface, which will be discussed in the next chapter. For now, suffice it to say that 10 million people have already been forced off land so dried by global warming that it can no longer support them. The number of "climate refugees" is expected to grow to more than 25 million by 2050. It is likely that the 1.2 billion currently hungry people will soon increase in numbers significantly, despite expanded

---

[7]Of course, great wealth does not ensure good health care. A study by the World Health Organization in 2000 ranked the United States—among the world's wealthiest countries, spending more on health care than any other, 14 percent of its GDP (in 2010 it had risen to 16 percent)—thirty-seventh in the world in health care quality. Only Russia scored lower among industrial states.

aid programs by the UN and some wealthy countries. Making things worse, global warming is expected to drastically reduce the food supply in the equatorial countries. Ironically, the United States alone produces about 20 percent of the greenhouse gases that cause global warming, but it is expected to incur from it only marginal negative consequences in the next 100 years. It is the relatively innocent people of the Developing World who will pay for our negligence and irresponsibility.

Beginning in the 1940s, the world's supply of grain, meat, and fish increased, but in the 1990s the UN reported dramatic declines in the production rates of each of these staples. By 1998, the increased production of rice and wheat had fallen to less than half of the 1950 rate. The principal causes of this serious decline in grain production are soil depletion, overuse of fertilizers, and a growing scarcity of fresh water. Since the annual world population increases by about 1.1 percent, a severe food shortage is clearly developing. Beyond grains, protein sources are also in trouble. Overfishing has brought 70 percent of the marine fish stock to the verge of depletion or beyond.

Although since 1950 the Developing World has quadrupled its food production, this advance is insufficient to match the needs of its population growth. In Africa alone, 80 percent of the continent's countries cannot feed themselves. Asia, with half of the world's population (China and India combined account for 40 percent of the human beings living today) and 60 percent of the population growth, has made some important isolated gains in food production, but overall, it has fallen behind so significantly that there is serious question as to whether grain-exporting countries will be able to satisfy future Asian grain import needs. In 1950, Asia's net grain imports were 6 million tons, in 1990 it imported a net of 90 million tons, and estimates are that by 2030 it will need to import a net of 300 million tons.

Clearly, the world population growth rate must be dramatically slowed, even as food production is increased, if a crisis of calamitous proportions in the Developing World is to be averted.[8] Demography experts, and the UN, have concluded that the best chance of solving these two problems rests with the women of the Developing World. The paternalism endemic in most developing countries must be challenged and women must be better educated. Although women are heavily engaged in agriculture, they are largely denied knowledge of modern methods of crop management, land use, and animal husbandry. Because their years in school lengthen the time before they marry, educated women are also less likely to have children out of wedlock and are apt to have fewer children when they are married. Consequently, it appears that a large part of the solution to the problems of the Developing World rests with liberating and educating its women. Hopefully, the men of the Developing World will recognize these critical necessities before it is too late.

---

[8]In 2007–2008, a price spike on food by as much as 30 to 50 percent in some countries imposed food riots on 30 countries in the Developing World.

Unequal wealth among the world's people is also a compelling problem. In 1998, the world's 358 billionaires collectively owned as much wealth as was owned by the poorest 45 percent (roughly 2.75 billion) of the people on earth. A more recent UN study revealed that in 2000, 1.3 billion people lived on less than $1 a day, whereas the 18 richest countries in the world, which together account for only 15 percent of the global population, control about 70 percent of the world's wealth. By contrast, the 73 poorest countries on earth, comprising almost three-quarters of the total population, produce less than $1,000 in annual per capita income. For perspective, the United States, with about 4.5 percent of the world's population in 2007, produced a per capita gross national income (GNI) purchasing power parity of $46,970. Luxemburg, the highest, produced a per capita purchasing power GNI of $64,320. At the other extreme, the Democratic Republic of the Congo has the lowest per capita GNI of $290.[9]

Years ago, some observers predicted that the East-West standoff of the Cold War was not in the long run the most intractable problem we faced. Instead, they suggested, correctly as it turned out, that a far more complicated confrontation was looming on the North-South axis.

Even poverty is not universal in the Developing World, however. I mentioned the oil-rich states earlier, but there are other successes as well. The 1980s saw a worldwide recession, and while a few developing countries (China, India, Brazil, Indonesia, Mexico, Thailand, and Turkey) prospered in the 1990s, the rest of the Developing World continued to languish in relentless poverty. So, many never quite recovered from the recession of the late 1980s before being struck by the "Great Recession" beginning in 2007.

A couple of positive notes can be struck in this otherwise bleak story. The foreign debt owed by many Developing Countries to the industrialized economies was so heavy that several countries spent a greater share of their budgets on interest payments than they could spend on education or health. Coaxed by the United Nations, many advanced countries restructured or simply forgave much of the debt owed by these destitute countries. Also, the Bush administration joined several advanced societies in significantly increasing their foreign aid to the Developing World.

However, whatever aid to the Developing World equals in the future, from the end of the Cold War until now, it has actually declined, since much of Western aid was diverted to the former communist bloc. Other impediments to aiding the needy societies are "donor fatigue" born of disappointing results from previous aid, government corruption and mismanagement among the developing countries, and a "what's the use" attitude prompted by the sheer magnitude of the problems in the poorest developing countries. Furthermore,

---

[9]The purchasing power parity is a calculation of relative purchasing power. People in the Democratic Republic of the Congo do not actually earn $290 annually; they earn far less, but because of lower prices for labor and most other basic goods, their relative per capita purchasing power reaches this figure.

the recession beginning in 2007 has limited the amount of aid the wealthy states feel free to give to the less fortunate societies.

In 2007, the UN estimated that starvation and malnutrition could be ended with an annual gift of only $80 billion, and that the total cost to feed people adequately, inoculate them properly, educate them sufficiently, clean up their water, and address their health problems was about $175 billion annually. As a stand-alone number, $175 billion is large, but, in fact, it amounted to only seven-tenths of 1 percent of the combined income of the industrialized countries. (The U.S. government alone spent almost three times that amount on its annual defense budget.) Currently, the industrialized world contributes less than two-tenths of 1 percent of its income to Developing World relief. Interestingly, U.S. public opinion polls repeatedly indicate the American people believe that the United States is by far the largest foreign aid donor in the world. While the United States gives the greatest number of dollars in foreign aid among advanced countries, only Russia gives less than the United States as a percentage of GDP and, as you can see from Table 11.3, several states not even listed among the leading industrial countries give more of what they have than does the United States. In fact, while France has a GDP only 20 percent as large as the United States, it gives well over twice as much of its GDP in aid as does the United States.

Not only is the U.S. contribution relatively low, but a huge amount of its aid is in the form of military, as opposed to social and economic aid. You can also see that, ironically, the two industrialized countries with the largest GDPs, the United

TABLE 11.3

Foreign Aid Contribution of Industrialized Countries

Country	% of GDP in Aid to Developing World	Country	% of GDP in Aid to Developing World
Sweden	.98	Switzerland	.41
Luxemburg	.92	France	.38
Norway	.89	Germany	.37
Denmark	.82	Austria	.35
Netherlands	.79	Canada	.33
Ireland	.58	New Zealand	.31
Belgium	.47	Portugal	.28
Finland	.44	Greece	.20
Spain	.44	Italy	.20
United Kingdom	.44	Japan	.18
Australia	.43	United States	.17

Source: Organization for Economic Cooperation and Development, 2008

States and Japan, give the smallest percentage of their respective GDPs to foreign aid, and only the Scandinavian countries, Luxemburg, and the Netherlands are so generous as to give more than the 0.7 percent the UN considers is needed from each industrial state to properly fund the Developing World's needs.

Clearly, political tranquility is closely related to economic well-being. People of the Developing World, in their multitudes, see their lives becoming hopelessly mired in the squalor surrounding them, even as modern communications graphically illustrate the chasm dividing the haves from the have-nots. Frustration mounts as these people seek solutions that seem never to materialize.

Historically, the Developing World's approach to economics was heavily influenced by cultural proclivities and traditional practices. Capitalism seemed unattractive because its individualist bent and its materialism were foreign to many cultures, to say nothing of the fact that it was used to suppress the colonial peoples. Socialism seemed much more compatible with these societies, but the fall of the Soviet Union and socialism's temporary demise caused several developing countries to attempt to adopt market economies. As you have already learned, a few countries seem to have made at least the beginnings of a successful transition, but most of the Developing World was left behind during the economically prosperous 1990s and mid-2000s, and they found themselves in even more desperate straits since the global recession beginning in 2007. As a consequence, many developing countries suffer from a growing indecision about how to proceed. As mentioned earlier, China's economic success and its refusal to liberalize politically tempts some elites. Still, traditional communal values beckon, but the still heavy burden of debt and the reality that most of these societies depend on only one or perhaps two cash crops (peanuts, bananas, sugar, and cotton) make them almost hopelessly dependent on economic forces over which they have almost no control.

Public impatience with poverty is rising, and people are increasingly demanding solutions. The pressure on national leaders to produce instant prosperity is often disastrous because such demands are impossible to satisfy. The inevitable failure of leaders to meet the needs of impatient citizens leads to conflict, resulting in either a rapid succession of unstable governments or **dictatorship** imposed by force.

Certainly among the greatest threats to the independence of the Developing World countries is the role of international corporations in political affairs. With annual revenues larger than the national budget or even the gross national product (GNP) of many of the countries in which they do business, the power relationship between the international corporations and the host countries is frequently so uneven that the developing nations find themselves needing the companies more than the companies need them, and they are forced to sell their labor and resources at what they consider unfair rates. Once a corporation has made heavy investments in a developing country, it understandably becomes interested in its politics. This interest sometimes leads to improper involvement in the domestic and international political affairs of the host country, evoking charges of oppression, exploitation, and neocolonialism.

On a more positive note, a serious concern for several developing countries has, at least for the moment, lost prominence. *Neoconservative imperialism* from the United States gave the Developing World serious pause. As you know, the "neocons" are a small group of people who, despite their size, are well organized, well funded, and they enjoy a significant intellectual base of support. These people believe that the United States is morally and culturally superior to all others and that now, with the United States as the sole superpower, we have a golden opportunity to bring peace to the world. They believe that using our incomparable military resources, we can enforce our hegemony on the world. Highly placed in the George W. Bush administration—former Vice President Dick Cheney and former Secretary of Defense Donald Rumsfeld are among its leaders—this aggressive theory held sway in U.S. foreign policymaking for most of the Bush years, and it is responsible for the ill-fated U.S. invasion of Iran.

With the election of Barack Obama the neocon mentality no longer dominates White House policy. Gone is reference to the "axis of evil" (Iraq, Iran, and North Korea) and presidential expressions of the need for "regime change" in the Developing World are no longer heard. Yet, while Obama has publicly disavowed torture as a means by which to extract information from suspected terrorists, he has allowed to continue *extraordinary renditions,* by which suspected terrorists are forcibly kidnapped and delivered to countries known to use torture; while he has apparently expedited the trial or release from Guantanamo most of those people no longer considered a threat, he has admitted that some of those held by the United States cannot be convicted because much of the evidence against them was obtained through torture during the Bush years, but still they are too dangerous to release. Thus, they will remain in prison indefinitely. Further, Obama has allowed the CIA to continue to engage in *targeted killings,* by firing predator missiles at suspected terrorists in the Middle East, and presumably by other means as well. Critics claim, and the government does not deny, that innocent people are sometimes killed along with the suspected terrorists.

DEVELOPING WORLD DEMOCRACIES AND DICTATORSHIPS

As the Soviet Union began to collapse and its empire unraveled, democracy suddenly became very popular where it had been ignored before. During the 1980s, virtually every Latin American country shook off the shackles of petty military dictators and inaugurated a more open political system. By the early 1990s, a large part of the Developing World was experimenting with democracy of some sort. This trend is continuing in many areas but seems to be unraveling in others. The Baltic states, Poland, Hungary, Ukraine, and the Czech Republic appear to be developing more responsive political institutions. Because the Soviet threat has ended, the United States has become less prone to supporting right-wing dictators abroad, but its foreign policy shifts have caused it to lose much of its moral authority, thus erasing a once powerful exemplar of democracy. To the Developing World, the Bush foreign policies resemble a new colonialism more than democracy, a suspicion we have, regrettably, largely brought on ourselves.

But the slide back toward dictatorship in the Developing World had, in fact, begun before George W. Bush took office. Since the mid-1990s, there has been a trend of regression toward authoritarian systems in several important places. Democracy seems to have been snuffed out in Russia and other parts of the former Soviet Union. In Southeast Asia, authoritarianism is again on the rise; at least two-thirds of sub-Saharan Africa is reverting; and although Jordan, and Morocco have recently shown liberal tendencies, the Middle East remains the least hospitable part of the globe to democracy. Pakistan's dissent into political chaos threatens peace on the Asian subcontinent. Equally disappointing is Latin America, where more than a decade of economic decline, social turmoil, and political upheaval is being blamed on the advent of democracy in almost half of its states.

Guided Democracies

Although many factors such as national tradition and cultural habits are important, the recent reversion toward authoritarianism in so many developing countries underscores the basic point that the most fundamental source of the problems plaguing the fledgling democratic states is economics. Perhaps more than any other political system, democracy depends for success on wealth. For example, in 2001 all but three (Saudi Arabia, Kuwait, and the United Arab Emirates) of the twenty-four richest countries were democratic. By contrast, of the forty-two poorest countries only two (India and Sri Lanka) enjoyed democratic systems. And, even today, it is either the states with the closest ties to the West or the wealthier areas that seem best able to adopt democratic systems, whereas poorer countries falter. Indeed, democracy seems to work best in societies that have a large middle class, with few outstanding issues regarding the distribution of power and wealth within the social class structure and a well-organized bureaucratic structure.

Democracy is, of course, defined in many different ways. The term **guided democracies** is sometimes applied to the centralized systems that tend to develop among Developing World states. A euphemism for **authoritarian dictatorship,** or *soft authoritarianism,* this concept is worth some examination. Unlike a **totalitarian state,** in which a ruler controls every aspect of the society—be it cultural, economic, historical, social, or political—an authoritarian dictatorship is less complete. Although the authoritarian dictator is in firm command of the political system, he or she has less control over other aspects of the society and is checked by other institutions, such as the church, the military, or a property-holding class.

Interestingly, most underdeveloped states are no more attracted to totalitarianism than they are to liberal democracy. Although Saddam Hussein's

Iraq was totalitarian, and there are some others, such centralization of power is not the norm in the Developing World. The enormous variety of tribal loyalties, religious beliefs, and traditional attitudes found in many of the Developing World states makes totalitarianism impractical. Recalling the Indonesian experience with the leftist policies of the 1960s under Sukarno, President Suharto—himself deposed in 1998—said in the early 1990s.

> We have taken a path that corrects the mistakes we made in adopting open democracy and communism based on class conflict. They may work in other countries but liberalism and communism don't work here.

Guided democracy gets its name from the authoritarian administration of "democratic" policies. In the developing countries, political power tends to become centralized for three basic reasons. First, the communal spirit of tribalism encourages a collective rather than a competitive approach. Second, the politically aware people in a developing state were often united in a single movement organized to liberate the society from colonial control. When a single movement did evolve, it became easier to centralize power. Since these movements usually benefited from experienced, politically aware, and popular leadership, they often remained in existence after the state won its independence and tended to dominate the political system.

Third, faced with serious political and economic conditions, together with urgent demands for material progress, many Developing World leaders have been forced into a corner. When the government fails to overcome the problems of the new nation, the response of the impatient masses is often violent and negative. The ruling group must then choose between riding out the period of disorder, taking the chance that the resultant chaos will bring about their fall from power or even lead to foreign intervention, and dealing with the dissidents sternly, thereby stifling free political expression. A brief glance at many governments in Africa and Asia will reveal a clear preference for the latter policy. Hence, most developing societies are "guided" by an authoritarian government supported by and often controlled by the military. How can such a system be considered democratic?

The argument is that the people in a developing country are basically united. Although some rule while others are ruled, and although they are divided by tribal, cultural, ethnic, and religious differences, still they remain in the same social group. Regardless of the present status of any individual, all have shared in or have been taught about the humiliating experience of exploitation by the country's former colonial masters.

True or not, this concept of the basic equality of all the citizens of a Developing World country has great political resonance. It tends to legitimize the ruler's power and gives an aura of democratic respectability to the government even as dissent is forcefully muffled. Having the same origins as the people, the rulers suggest that they are united by common interests and goals. This makes the system democratic in the eyes of some of its citizens. Though most of the people have had little say in developing the nation's policies, they still consider the system democratic. To do otherwise, it is argued, would be to put democratic procedures above the ultimate democratic goal: the common good. Though this vision of democracy is unlike the ideals of the liberal industrial states of the West, we must remember that no society has a monopoly on the political dictionary; consequently, other countries' definitions of democracy may legitimately differ from our own. Whatever the case, the guided democracy may soon be replaced by something much more severe. Democracy, with its need for tolerance and its requirement for public consensus, often does not fare well during periods of severe economic privation. If the long-term economic difficulties in the Developing World are not overcome, soon a new era of social insecurity could cause much harsher dictatorial ideologies to arise.

Terrorism

Terrorism has been practiced, by the right and the left of the political spectrum, probably since the beginning of human history. Descriptions of it reach back at least as far as the ancient Greeks. The objective of political terrorism is to take action that will visit psychological discomfort upon the target group and, at least eventually, illicit desired political actions or acquiescence from that group.

Historical and contemporary examples of terrorism are abundant, only a few will be highlighted here. Perhaps the most notorious terrorist from premodern times is Hasan ibn al-Sabbah, the "Old Man of the Mountain," who created an order of assassins (c. 1090) who descended from Hasan's northern Persia mountaintop stronghold to assassinate political enemies. These killers, it is said, would be emboldened in their murderous quest by using hashish, from which Europeans developed the word "assassin."

Some historians consider the tar and feathering, rail riding, and other violent protest activity as terrorist acts against British rule by American Revolutionaries. The violent anarchists, Bakunin and the Narodniks introduced in Chapter 7, and the Ku Klux Klan in the United States from the 1860s to the present are well-known terrorists. The Irish Republican Army (1916–1921), and the Secret Army Organization (OAS) in the 1960s that tried to foil President Charles de Gaulle's plans to give Algeria its independence are each examples of terrorists. Some terrorist organizations extant today are *Euskadi Ta Askatasuna* (ETA), Basques fighting for independence from Spain; the Tamil Tigers who struggle to preserve the identity and independence of the Tamil people, a minority in Sri Lanka; the Egyptian Islamic Jihad, which is fighting for creation of an Islamic state in Egypt; and Hezbollah and Hamas struggling for the same in Lebanon and Palestine. Also, of course, Al Qaeda, founded by Osama bin Laden in the late 1980s and struggling to vanquish Western influence in the Islamic world and to create Islamic theocracies there.

The simplest form of terrorism is seen in acts of destruction perpetrated by individuals or groups with no apparent official backing. The bombing of the federal building in Oklahoma City by Timothy McVeigh and the lethal attacks on the subways of Tokyo, Moscow, and London and the commuter trains in Spain and

© AFP/Getty Images

Osama bin Laden sprang from the second most wealthy family in Saudi Arabia to become history's most notorious terrorist and the world's most wanted man.

Russia are examples. Also, there are the acts of Shining Path in Peru, Colombia's Self Defense Force, the Kurdistan Workers Party, Yemen's Al Qaeda in the Arabian Peninsula (currently Western terrorism experts believe Yemen is becoming the next training ground for Al Qaeda terrorists), and the suicide bombings in U.S.-occupied Iraq and Afghanistan, as well as suicide bombings throughout the Middle East. In the United States itself, there have been almost 50 attempted or plotted terrorist attacks between September 11, 2001, and mid-May of 2010, according to a Rand Corporation study.

When a government supports wanton acts of destruction by unofficial or even official organizations, on the other hand, it is called *state terrorism.* Examples of this phenomenon are the pogroms, officially sanctioned persecution of Jews, used by the Russian Empire at the turn of the twentieth century; Stalin's and Hitler's use of terror to govern their societies; the Nazi bombing of the Basque town, Guernica, in 1937; the Japanese rape of Nanking in 1938; and the brutal firebombing of Dresden in 1945. All are recent examples of the use of state violence to terrorize a particular public. More contemporary examples are Syria supporting the Hezbollah or Afghanistan harboring Al Qaeda.

Clearly, the United States itself has been involved in systematic efforts to execute its own forms of terrorism. Its firebombing of Tokyo and the use of atomic warheads on Hiroshima and Nagasaki were openly used to terrorize the Japanese and bring an end to World War II. More recently, the infamous School of the Americas run by the Defense Department was located at Fort Benning, Georgia, until it was closed in 2001. There, military personnel of Latin American countries—many of them governed by right-wing dictatorships—were trained, including Luis Posada Carriles himself in 1961. Many of these officers returned home with their new skills and brutalized their people with torture, death squads, and other forms of terror. The closing of the School of the Americas has not assuaged critics, however. It was quickly succeeded by the Western Hemisphere Institute, also at Fort Benning and also run by the Defense Department. Although officials claim the Institute's mission is to teach democratic values, skeptics assert otherwise. Also held to be state terrorism by a multitude of people across the globe is the 2003 U.S. preemptive attack and occupation of Iraq for no discernible reason. The current officially sanctioned CIA extraordinary renditions and targeted killings are regarded as terrorism as well by millions throughout the world. "Fighting fire with fire" some say, but terrorism nonetheless.

The end of the Cold War has negated the previous polarization between the Soviet Union and the United States and has tended to mute the resolve of ideological terrorist groups like the Red Brigade, the Red Army Faction, and the Japanese Red Army. But Neal A. Pollard of the Terrorism Research Center warns that the void is being filled by ethno-religious and single-issue terrorist groups. Many of these groups distrust highly centralized efforts to create destabilization. Instead they practice a potentially more frightening and dangerous form of terrorism. This new methodology might be called *noncoalescent* terrorism. Similar to the lone-wolf terrorist activities of some extremist racists (see Chapter 10), this approach relies on *terrorist cells*—small, loosely connected groups that engage in individualistic and almost random acts of terror. Although at this point one cannot be sure, it is possible that some recent terrorist attacks besides McVeigh's may be perpetrated by loan-wolfs. Umar Farouk Abdulmutallab, a Nigerian, tried to detonate a bomb in his underwear in the skies over Detroit in December of 2009. Faisal Shahzad, a Pakistani-American tried to explode a homemade bomb in his SUV parked in New York's Time Square, in May of 2010. And, United States Army Major, Nidal Malik Hasan, killed thirteen people in a shooting spree in late 2009 at Fort Hood, Texas.

It is worth noting that two of these terrorists are Americans. In fact, "homegrown terrorists," many of them recruited on the Internet, are becoming a serious concern to authorities. For example, Pakistani-American Daood Sayed Gilani, who changed his name to David Coleman Headly, presumably to avoid drawing attention to himself and his activities, was a major participant in the preparations for the 2008 terrorist attack on Mumbai, India. Also five Pakistani-American youth were convicted in Pakistan of plotting terrorist acts in 2010. And, Anwar Awlaki, and American Muslim cleric (who reportedly is on the CIAs unacknowledged list for targeted killings) has become an important Al Qaeda operative in Yemen and is also thought to have influenced Hasan's shootings in Texas. Late in 2010, Awlaki publically called on Muslims to kill Americans.

Of course, the most notorious figure in the terrorist movement is Osama bin Laden. A shadowy character who was sheltered in Afghanistan and receives heavy support from sources spread throughout the Middle East, bin Laden has devoted a large portion of his vast resources to supporting terrorism of this sort. It is believed that at his disposal are terrorist *sleeper cells* or sleeper agents across the globe. Like the Russian Nihilists, these cells are quite independent of, and perhaps even ignorant of the existence of, the other cells. Cell members lead normal lives until they are activated by orders from bin Laden. Ahmed Ressam, who was caught crossing from Canada into the United States just before the dawn of the new millennium with 130 pounds of explosives that he planned to use in a terrorist attack, is allegedly one of bin Laden's terrorists. A more successful attack of which bin Laden is suspected is the 1998 bombing of the U.S. embassies in Kenya and Tanzania, which saw hundreds killed or wounded. The most lethal assault to date, however, was the 2001 suicide attack on the World Trade Center in New York City and on the Pentagon near Washington, D.C. This attack, perpetrated by sleeper cell members in the United States, killed almost 3,000 people. Other known or suspected followers of bin Laden are the terrorists who bombed a commuter train in Madrid, killing over 200 people; Ali al-Marri, convicted of plotting with Al Qaeda but who was given a relatively light sentence because of what the federal judge called the "very severe" conditions al-Marri endured for six years in a U.S. Navy brig before being given a trial; eight Somali Americans in Minneapolis charged with recruiting people to go to Somalia to fight for the Islamic cause there; and a Jordanian physician who, in 2009, killed seven CIA officers in Afghanistan in a suicide bomb attack. It is thought that contact with Al Qaeda is facilitated by the Internet.

The picture is not totally bleak, however, as there are faint, but important signs that many people in the Middle East are becoming resentful of suicide bombings and other terrorist attacks that kill and maim innocent friends and relatives. Such a feeling in Anbar Province, Iraq, took a great deal of steam out of the deadly resistance to the American occupation. In 2008, Muslim leaders from fifty-seven states condemned terrorism as antithetical to Islam, and the Libyan Islamic Fighting Group, once allied with Al Qaeda, broke off that relationship and renounced terrorism.

However, the struggle is far from over, as the extent and deadliness of terrorism seem to be growing, threatening the stability of world politics in general and of many national governments in particular. Thus, a vigorous multinational struggle against terrorism is in progress—but the cost of rooting out an enemy so amorphous, so stealthy, and so widespread will be extensive. It will, of course, demand the sacrifice of many lives—both innocent and guilty—and much treasure. But perhaps the greatest cost, if matters get out of hand, is the loss of individual liberties. It will be the height of ironic tragedy if in an effort to eradicate terrorism, our country, and countries elsewhere, adopt the same methods that we claim we are trying to stamp out. Clearly, this first war of the twenty-first century, as it is now being called, not only threatens the existence of the fledgling democracies of the Developing World but also jeopardizes the established democracies.

QUESTIONS FOR DISCUSSION

1. In what ways do colonialism and nationalism influence the Developing World?
2. How has the collapse of the Soviet Union affected the Developing World?
3. What social and economic problems confront the Developing World?
4. How can the Developing World's view of democracy be compared and contrasted with the Western notion of democracy?
5. What are the two major kinds of terrorism, and what are examples of each?

SUGGESTIONS FOR FURTHER READING

Beck, Ulrich, *What Is Globalization?* Cambridge, MA: Polity Press, 2000.

Benjamin, Daniel, and Steven Simon, *The Age of Sacred Terror.* New York: Random House, 2002.

Burnell, Peter, and Vicky Randall, eds., *Politics in the Developing World.* New York: Oxford University Press, 2005.

Cammack, Paul, David Pool, and William Tordoff, *Third World Politics: An Introduction,* 3rd ed. Baltimore: Johns Hopkins University Press, 2001.

Diamond, Larry, and Marc F. Plattner, *The Global Divergence of Democracy.* Baltimore: Johns Hopkins University Press, 2001.

Esposito, John L., *What Everyone Needs to Know about Islam.* Oxford: Oxford University Press, 2002.

Haynes, Jeffry, *Democracy in the Developing World.* Malden, MA: Blackwell, 2001.

Kepel, Gilles, *War for Muslim Minds: Islam and the West,* trans. Pascale Ghazalch. Cambridge, MA: Belknap Press, 2004.

Lewis, Bernard, *The Crisis of Islam: Holy War and Holy Terror.* New York: Modern Library, 2003.

———, *What Went Wrong? Western Impact and Middle Eastern Response.* Oxford: Oxford University Press, 2002.

Simon, Julian, *Population and Development in Poor Countries.* Ewing, NJ: Princeton University Press, 1992.

Taylor, Robert H., ed., *The Idea of Freedom in Asia and Africa.* Stanford, CA: Stanford University Press, 2002.

Tibi, Bassam, *The Challenge of Fundamentalism: Political Islam and the New World Disorder.* Berkeley, CA: University of California Press, 2002.

Weatherby, Joseph N., et al., eds., *The Other World: Issues and Politics of the Developing World,* 5th ed. New York: Longman, 2003.

Feminism and Environmentalism

PREVIEW

Consistent with the growing political viability of democratic ideals such as equality and social justice, the social, economic, and political plight of women became a matter of growing concern beginning in the late eighteenth century. Gradually, feminism emerged as a protest against male domination of women, but as with all other ideologies, there are several different approaches to feminism. Reform feminism recognizes that although men and women are different, they are fundamentally equal. Thus, in this view, society's norms and institutions must be changed to include consideration of previously ignored feminine uniqueness and needs.

Revolutionary feminists disparage any possibility of cooperating with men to change the world to include feminine interests. Instead, they call upon women themselves to restructure society to reflect feminine interests, with no concern for male cooperation. The most radical feminists, the separatists, advocate ignoring men entirely and creating a parallel culture, one that fosters the best interests of women.

The environmental movement began at roughly the same time as feminism, but it did not become politically important until the turn of the twentieth century. Environmentalists decry the anthropocentrism evident in the modern world. They warn that science, technology, urbanism, the population explosion, and global warming combine with anthropocentrism to create a desperate circumstance in which the very existence of the Earth is threatened. Deep ecologists, the most extreme segment of the movement, demand that people see themselves as little more than creatures who, along with all others, are passengers on Spaceship Earth, and that they subordinate their interests to those of nature as a whole. Humanistic ecologists argue instead that while people may exploit the earth's resources, nature must be respected so that humanity can survive.

So compelling is the logic of environmentalism that it has been integrated into several other ideologies. Conservatives, liberals, anarchists, socialists, feminists, and religious people have all developed ecologist viewpoints that are subscribed to by some of their adherents.

FEMINISM

Imagine a world in which, only because you were a woman, you could not own property, bring suit, or sign contracts. You were denied significant positions of leadership in business, government, religion, and other important gender-integrated institutions. You could not attend a university or enter the professions. You were expected to stay at home and content yourself with domestic chores—but when you did go out in public, fashion dictated uncomfortable clothing (toe-to-neck dresses, punctuated by laced corsets and bustles) that suggested a prim and proper person, while, not too subtly emphasizing your sexuality. The purpose of this costume conundrum was in large measure to display the bearer as an object of pleasure that was unavailable to anyone except the man to whom she *belonged*. Consider the moral content of a world that bathed itself in stated aspirations of human equality, yet where married women not only took the last name of their spouses but assumed their entire name (e.g., Mrs. Henry Clay Frick), as if to say that the woman's identity apart from her husband's was irrelevant. Such a world is not very distant in time from the present.

Now imagine a world where young mothers are often abandoned by their children's fathers and little official help is rendered, a place where women hesitate to report rape or battery for fear of retaliation or out of concern that officials will hold the victim responsible. Think about a world where the gender double standard is so endemic that at their weddings women are supposed to broadcast their virginity by wearing white, whereas men sport mute tuxedos. Ponder the ethical efficacy of a society where sexual harassment and unequal pay for equal or comparable jobs are commonplace. Consider the moral legitimacy of a world in which dowry murders, bride kidnapping, and genital mutilation of women are not unusual and where honor killings of girls, selective abortions of female fetuses, and even infanticide of girls are the cultural norms. This world is not of the past but exists in the present.

Feminism may not be as prominent as it once was in the United States. Writer Barbara Ehrenreich recently lamented that one could hear barely a whisper of discontent from American women when, in 2009, Congress passed a provision that women could not receive insurance payments for abortion if the insurance was paid for by federal money. Be that as it may, feminism spawned a dynamic, complex ideology. Its purpose is to end gender inequality, and it also often combats racial, ethnic, and other forms of inequality. At minimum, feminism seeks to liberate women from the artificial restraints historically placed on them and enable them to take charge of their own personal, professional, and political destinies.

Although some feminist literature about men is negative, most feminists do not endorse this view, but they do insist on equality with men. Indeed, almost from the beginning of the movement, feminism has asserted that everyone, man, woman, and child, will benefit from the liberation of women. For example, feminists contend that conditions in the family will become less strained, society will benefit from maximum use of the human potential available to it, and men will not have to shoulder alone the burdens of supporting the family and serving in the military. To those who suggest that women's lives, at least in this country, are not all that bad because their life expectancy is longer, they inherit most of the personal wealth, they are given privilege in much of family law, and they usually receive lighter judicial penalties for crimes than men, feminists argue that, if true, this is scant reward for the burden of inequality they endure, and say they would gladly sacrifice such advantages in exchange for a more just society. At the same time, many feminists believe that most men are also victims of the oppression perpetrated by the dominant elements in society.

Endemic Sexism

Sexism—prejudice based on gender—is so deeply rooted in virtually every culture that it almost appears natural and often goes unnoticed and unchallenged. Moreover, although the degree and kind of sexism differ from culture to culture, one constant exists: Official, as opposed to individual, sexism is usually directed against women—the "weaker sex."

Consider our own society. Traditionally women have been seen as more emotional than men, less rational, weaker, and dependent. At the same time, women are often portrayed as seducers of innocent males. The Bible suggests that the first intergender relationship was laced with such insidious behavior when Eve brought Adam down by tempting him with material things to disobey the word of God. Women must pray behind the men in Islam, women are largely observers rather than full participants in Orthodox Jewish ceremonies, and women have only recently been allowed to become pastors, and even bishops, in some Protestant religions, whereas Mormons still illegally practice polygamy,[1] in which men have multiple wives but women share only one husband. In 1998, the South Baptist Church called upon its women to "graciously accept" the superiority of their men, and other fundamentalist sects insist that God intends women to keep to home and family. In 2004, the Catholic Church issued a letter to its bishops written by Cardinal Joseph Ratzinger, who has since become Pope Benedict XVI, attacking the "lethal effects" of feminism because it undermines the "natural two-parent home structure" and it encourages homosexuality. The letter claims that the Church supports equality of the genders and it rejects subjugation of women, although it continues to reserve the priesthood exclusively for celibate men, it claims, because all of the apostles were male. Further, Pope Benedict XVI welcomed as converts several Anglican bishops who converted to Catholicism in protest of the new Anglican policy of ordaining female bishops.

---

[1]While there is an estimated 37,000 polygamists in the state of Utah, the attorney general recently publicly said that the state is not likely to prosecute anyone just for polygamy since the state's 4,000 jail beds could not possibly hold everyone who could be convicted of the crime.

Besides religion, our art, literature, politics, economies, and other deeply rooted institutions are heavily laced with gender bias. Perhaps nothing is more influential on the values and beliefs of a society than its language. An objective examination of the English language finds that women are almost constantly relegated to secondary status relative to men. For example, one can easily refer to males without reference to *females* or wo*men,* but the reverse is impossible. Vulgar descriptions of sexual intercourse usually refer to what men do to women, thus demonstrating male power and feminine passivity. Even terms of endearment for women are often diminutive, and a common way to denigrate a man is to suggest that his mother is a female dog. It is left to the imagination to conjure what the character of the father might be.

It is true, however, that sexism works both ways. In recent years the feminist movement has sensitized us to a problem that previously received little attention. Its success is attested to by the number of efforts corporations make—ironically, many of which pay women less than men for comparable jobs—to sell products to female consumers by reversing the bias, portraying women as brighter, better informed, more mature, more serious minded, and stronger in character than men. Although this newfound sensitivity demonstrates some movement on the matter of gender bias, it's unfortunate that the vehicle for expressing it is reverse sexism. In fact, denigrating men is seen by some as empowering women. Further, the fact that the technique has been used so long and so frequently indicates that, in at least this case, selling products by massaging bigotry is acceptable *and effective.* Commercials portraying a particular race as smarter or more sensible than the rest would certainly be cast out by people as unacceptable bigotry, as would suggestions that men are smarter, more mature, and better informed than women—although forty years ago this approach was common.

All the same, we have made important advances from the traditional bias, when as recently as the twentieth century women were assigned a status no more empowered than that of children. Much remains to be done, however. The economic and social exploitation of women is still a serious problem in our society. As late as 1961, in *Hoyt v. Florida,* the United States Supreme Court—at the time perhaps our most liberal governmental institution—rendered an opinion in which it suggested that a woman's place was in the home. At present, housework is still considered women's work, and occupations dominated by women (nursing, elementary school teaching, child care, domestic services, etc.) are invariably poorly paid. In the 1970s at my own college, the male towel dispenser in the men's gym was paid at par with the faculty secretaries. Women are still badly underrepresented in leadership positions in business, academics, government, and the military, suggesting that indeed the glass ceiling persists. Women's clothing is generally more poorly made, yet more expensive, than men's; women are often charged more for dry-cleaning services than are men; and women's fashions are usually more uncomfortable, more suggestive, and less practical than men's. Furthermore, women scantily clad and/or suggestively postured are frequently used as attention getters in ads. (This message is more complex than it first appears. Clearly, it is designed to suggest to men that their sex life will improve markedly if only they will drive a certain car, use a particular aftershave, or sleep on a given mattress, but it also tells women that the best way to please a man is by flaunting their sexuality.) All these features are manifestations of the secondary and dependent status to which our society relegates women.

More dangerous manifestations of the unfortunate circumstances in which women find themselves in our culture can be seen in pornography, which exploits and abuses women by portraying them as witless, powerless, willless objects of male sexual gratification. Women are also subject to degrading aggressions such as sexual harassment, and women are usually the victims of the most common form of violent crime, domestic violence. Women endure mental abuse and battery and are the second most frequent victims of murder after black men.

Despite concerted efforts to change, our own society remains stubbornly sexist, although progress has been made here. But in many parts of the Developing World women suffer much more egregiously. They are denied opportunity, careers, civil liberties, and even driver's licenses. Frequently women are allowed little control over their reproductive lives. Contraceptives are often discouraged and abortions are illegal, except—in most cases—for health reasons. (Nicaragua, for example, in 2009 joined only 3 percent of the world's states to make abortion illegal, for any reason whatever.) Women can be denied the right to vote or hold public office, although the former is now rare outside of the Middle East. They can be forbidden to go out in public unless they are accompanied by a trusted male. Women out in public are sometimes required to be covered from head to foot by a loose fitting garment, the burka, called a moving prison by critics. Even the United States supported president of Afghanistan, Hamid Karzai, supported such a law in 2009, and it was similar to the discipline imposed on Afghan women by the Taliban. This law also provided that Afghan Shiite women must submit to their husbands' sexual demands at least every four days. In Saudi Arabia, a 75-year-old woman was recently sentenced to forty lashes and four months in jail for being seen in public with two unrelated men, while ten Sudanese women were flogged in Khartoum for wearing long pants in public. Meanwhile, female attorneys have been ordered in the Gaza Strip to wear a scarf over their heads while in court, so as not to "corrupt society's morals." It must be pointed out, however, that many Islamic women wish to wear headscarves or burkas as symbols of modesty, piety, or feelings of safety from being ogled as sex objects.

Women are often held to a much higher standard—a double standard—than men, especially in sexual matters. Rape in the Muslim world is usually considered the woman's fault and she can be punished by the courts (five years in prison and 200 lashes in Saudi Arabia), while the rapist is held harmless. Worse, a raped woman is often considered to have dishonored the family, and while the law usually forbids it, authorities often close their eyes to the woman's murder by family members in what is called "honor killings." Such things are possible even in the United States. In 2009, Muzzammil Hassan was charged with murdering and decapitating his wife, Aasiya, in a suspected honor killing.

Female adultery can also end in an honor killing, stoning, or divorce. Divorce in the Middle East is often solely a male prerogative. Of course, severe beating is another recourse open to a husband, for a wife that displeases him.

The recent civil wars in West Africa have been dubbed by some "wars against women." While no one has escaped the brutality, the worst ravages by marauding armies were perpetrated on women. Captured women have been sold into slavery or imprisoned as camp followers. Forced to watch their husbands and parents executed, some women were then gang-raped by dozens of men in front of their children.

Several societies practice arranged child marriages. Parents, wanting to secure a future for their daughters, or less nobly, wishing to collect a sum from the groom, the *bride price*,[2] marry off their female children, as early as age eight. This practice is employed throughout the Middle East and it is prevalent in India and Africa as well. In the Middle East, a few girls have been granted divorces. Recently, a girl of nine, who had been married at the age of eight, was granted a divorce from her 50-year-old husband. Often, these child brides' parents insist as part of the marriage agreement that the groom not consummate the marriage before the bride reaches puberty, but this pledge is often ignored, endangering the child's health. In some cultures women can be circumcised, and in others, unwanted female children are sometimes abandoned, sold, or even murdered. In fact, the use of sonograms in China to determine the gender of a fetus is a serious problem because female children are often aborted.

Women often suffer economic exploitation as well. Although it exists worldwide, the *"feminization of poverty"* is most desperate among the poor countries. With divorce becoming more common, female-headed households are no longer unusual, and these family units are almost always confronted with crushing poverty.

Among the factors leading to this circumstance are the social biases in their societies. Although women are becoming more and more responsible for growing food as the men go off to the cities to find work, they suffer prejudicial land tenorship laws, they receive less education and worker training, and they enjoy less health care. Generally, they have less access to technology and machinery, and they are less able to keep up with modern farming policy. All of this makes them less productive than they would be in more equitable circumstances.

Still, significant progress by women is being made in important areas. Perhaps the most encouraging advances are in the field of politics. Women are becoming increasingly active in politics. Greater numbers of women are

---

[2]In 2010, a 49-year-old Nigerian politician paid $100,000 as dowry to the parents of the 13-year-old girl he married.

being elected to public office on both local and national levels, and they are even reaching the highest levels—witness Angela Merkel of Germany, Mary McAleese of Ireland, Vaira Vike-Freiberga of Latvia, Janet Jagan of Guyana, Helen Clark of New Zealand, Corazon Aquino of Philippines, Yulia Tymoshenko of Ukraine, and Sirimavo Bandaranaike of Sri Lanka. Bandaranaike is exceptional in that she was the first female prime minister in history and she is also the only woman to serve three terms as PM (1960–1965, 1970–1977, and 1994–2000).[3]

UN statistics reveal that for every 100 men in the world there are 98.6 women; and although women comprise 47 percent of the global workforce and are often the major producers of agricultural goods in the Developing World, only about 13 percent of the legislators in the world are women. In an effort to increase women's political influence, over thirty countries have established numerous political positions that must be held by women.

Even where quotas are not imposed, several countries have significant numbers of women serving in national executive and legislative roles. For example, in 2009, Rwanda had the highest percentage of women in its parliamentary body (56.3 percent). Sweden, in second place, was the first country (in 1995) to have equal numbers of women and men on its cabinet. In 2009, there were twenty-five countries (up from ten in 2000) in which 30 percent of the national legislature were women. By contrast, in the same year, the United States Congress had only 17 percent—just over the world average—of its seats occupied by women. Also, in 2009, there were ten countries with no female legislators at the national level, one more than in 2000. (See Table 12.1.) Although India did not make the list, its constitution requires that no fewer than one-third of the seats on its village governments be occupied by women.

Further, the 2004 constitution of Iraq, negotiated by the Bush administration and the various Iraqi stakeholders, guarantees that 25 percent of the seats in the national legislature will be filled by women. Perhaps the greatest advance for women in politics is that Kuwait and Saudi Arabia have finally consented to at least limited female voting rights. Until recently, women had no political rights in either society, and they are still deprived of the right to vote and hold office in several other Persian Gulf States. This positive development is due, in part, to the emerging, but struggling, Islamic feminist movement.

Although there is no evidence to sustain the often heard suggestion that women in government would reduce belligerence and warfare among states, experience does demonstrate that female legislators and executives tend to focus attention on such issues as child labor protection, prenatal care, education, family law, and women's rights. These issues are often of only secondary importance to male politicians.

---

[3]In an interesting reversal, the tiny kingdom of Kumbwada, located in Nigeria, allows only women to rule.

TABLE 12.1

Percent of Female Legislators in 2009

Country	Rank	% of Women Legislators
Rwanda	1	56.3
Sweden	2	46.4
South Africa	3	44.5
Cuba	4	43.2
Iceland	5	42.9
Greece	86	17.3
Mauritius	87	17.1
United States	88	17*
Turkmenistan	89	16.8
San Marino	90	16.7
Belize	138	0
Oman	138	0
Qatar	138	0
Saudi Arabia	138	0
Tuvalu	138	0

*This number was taken from congressional data in 2010.
Source: Inter-Parliamentary Union

The United States' record, while still below the world average, is slowly improving. For example, Nancy Pelosi was the Speaker of the House of Representatives from 2006–2010 and history's highest ranking woman in U.S. government. Also, Sarah Palin, former governor of Alaska, was the second woman in U.S. history to run for vice president on a major party ticket.

Yet, to date, the electoral success of women in the Middle East is disappointing. Although Tunisia, Afghanistan, and Iraq have percentages of women in their legislature higher than the world average and higher, indeed, than the United States, the rest of the region's states lag far behind. Afghanistan's constitution, written after the Taliban was driven from government in 2001, reserves about one-quarter of its national legislative seats for women. Yet, in the parliamentary elections of 2010, after the Taliban had reestablished control in several parts of the country, women candidates were so intimidated by threats of violence, that several had to resort to "proxy campaigning," sending male stand-ins to ask people for their votes.

Saudi Arabia's laws are among the most restrictive on women's political involvement. Prohibited by law even to drive, women may vote and be candidates only for local offices. Males monopolize higher offices. Even female voting is sometimes filtered. In some Saudi cities, women may be allowed to vote, but their vote can be cast only by a male "guardian."

In recent years, however, women have made significant advances in executive positions. So far, sixty-seven women have served as governor general (an appointive office, equivalent to head of state), president, or prime minister of forty-four countries. Chile, in 2006, elected Michelle Bachelet, making her South America's first woman president who did not follow her husband to office. A socialist, she had been tortured during the Pinochet regime in the 1970s. Limited by the constitution to only one term, Bachelet, immensely popular, stepped down in 2010.

Similarly, Ellen Johnson-Sirleaf, known affectionately as "iron lady," also endured torture and exile before being elected president of Liberia in 2005. She is the world's first black woman to be elected head of state.

Liberia is a political and economic basket case, hobbled by decades of dictatorship, crushing foreign debt, and widespread corruption. With characteristic resolve, Johnson-Sirleaf has attacked these problems by slashing the size of the nation bureaucracy, punishing corruption, improving the production and distribution of public utilities, and negotiating economic concessions with Liberia's creditors. Two other black women have served as heads of government: Eugenia Charles of Dominica, 1990 to 1995 and Sylvie Kinigi of Burundi, 1993 to 1994.

Meanwhile, Cristina Fernández de Kirchner is the first female president elected in Argentina and in Jamaica, Portia "Mama" Simpson-Miller successfully campaigned for the leadership of the Peoples' National Party. Being the majority party, its election of a leader in 2006 was tantamount to choosing the prime minister. Her compatriots hope that she is able to do for Jamaica what Johnson-Sirleaf is trying to do for Liberia.

In India, Pratibha Patil has been elected president while Sonia Gandhi (Italian-born wife of assassinated prime minister Rajiv Gandhi and daughter-in-law of assassinated prime minister Indira Gandhi) has been the leader of the Congress Party, the nation's largest, since 1998. And finally, as already noted Angela Merkel became Chancellor of Germany in 2005 and is serving her second term as leader of one of the world's most important states.

These and other women have been successful in rising to the top of the political ladder. Yet, others have so far failed to succeed. Beyond question, one of the most distinguished female political leaders today has never held office. Aung San Suu Kyi of Myanmar (formerly Burma) has led a nonviolent, democratic movement in her country since 1988. In 1990 her party enjoyed a smashing victory at the polls, capturing 80 percent of the seats in parliament. Rather than allow Suu Kyi to become prime minister, the military refused to honor the election. Suu Kyi was placed under house arrest and has spent fifteen of the last twenty one years in detention. Recognized throughout the world for her commitment to democracy and nonviolence, she was awarded the Nobel Peace Prize in 1991. Suu Kyi did not vote, nor did her party participate, in Myanmar's 2010 elections—the first since 1990—because the rules for the election, written by the military dictators, assure victory for their supporters. Following the sham election, the government freed Suu Kyi from her long incarceration, but her liberty remains very tenuous.

The History of Feminism

Women's social equality with men has been a goal throughout history. Indeed, even Plato, although not endorsing equality for women per se, did assert that women should be allowed a much greater role in government than was traditionally the case in ancient Greece. Women's liberation, however, remained an issue without a movement until the late nineteenth century.

Perhaps history's first feminist was **Mary Wollstonecraft** (1759–1797). Challenging the conventions of the day, Wollstonecraft was welcomed into radical political circles even though she openly practiced free love, and in 1796 she married the anarchist **William Godwin** (1756–1836). Wollstonecraft wrote *Thoughts on the Education of Daughters* (1789) and *A Vindication of the Rights of Woman* (1792). By these books, especially the latter, she established herself as an important intellectual. She demanded equal rights for women in politics, employment, and education and rejected the common belief that women's sole purposes were to bear and raise children and to please men. She decried the social and economic subordination of women and anticipated contemporary feminists by claiming that the imposed inferiority of women in society did much to encourage social deviance of both men and women and actually prevented women from being the best possible wives and mothers.

Yet, a popular feminist movement was not yet to be. Indeed, throughout the early to mid-nineteenth century, the only political philosophers to call for equal rights for women were Godwin, **John Stuart Mill**, and **Karl Marx**.

The earliest feminist movement spun off two other liberationist endeavors: the drive to abolish slavery and the temperance (anti-alcohol) movement. Women participating in these two movements learned valuable lessons about bringing pressure for change on official agencies and about how to organize activist causes. More importantly, these two issues did much to validate female political activism.

New York was the home of early women's leaders **Elizabeth Cady Stanton** (1815–1902) and **Susan B. Anthony** (1820–1906), as well as the birthplace of the temperance movement in 1808 and the suffragettes. Stanton was the daughter of a progressive congressman and she married an abolitionist, and Anthony's father was also an abolitionist. Stanton originally advocated women's rights on a broad front, but she gradually came to focus on obtaining the right to vote for women.

Stanton helped organize the first women's rights convention at Seneca Falls, New York, in 1848, the same year Marx wrote the *Communist Manifesto*. She drafted and pushed through to a successful vote the *Declaration of Sentiments*. Patterned after the Declaration of Independence, it encouraged women to disobey laws that impeded their social development. A strong statement claiming women should have the right to vote was also included. Later, Stanton and Anthony joined in the publication of *Revolution* (1868–1870), a newspaper that addressed women's rights and advocated equal pay for equal work. Unfortunately, neither of these reformers lived to see women receive the right to vote with the passage of the Nineteenth Amendment in 1920. By that time, women had also won at least the most basic legal rights: to own property, to sue, and to sign contracts.

In the early period, the women's rights movement was not solely devoted to suffrage and economic issues, however, sexual freedom and control over one's body were also goals. Contraception was often illegal, and certain feminists demanded that women should be able to control and use contraceptives, thus liberating them from the tyranny of unwanted motherhood. Indeed, women controlling their own pregnancies became one of the major issues advocated by anarchist **Emma Goldman** (1869–1940). There were other goals that had to do with sexuality. **Victoria Woodhull** (1838–1927) was the most notorious advocate for women's sexuality. Besides demanding suffrage for women, she scandalized society by campaigning for free love as well as socialism. In 1872, as a candidate of the Equal Rights Party, she became the first woman to run for president of the United States. At first, Woodhull shunned traditional marriage and family. Children from free love liaisons were to be cared for by communal support groups. Woodhull also insisted that an end be put to society's double standard. Each gender, she insisted, should be subject to the same social expectations. Ironically, Woodhull finally settled in England as the wife of a respectable banker. Gradually, she was accepted into society and became admired as a humanitarian and philanthropist.

Eventually the goal of sexual liberation was suppressed as feminists focused all their attention on winning suffrage. Even so, with the exception of Australia, no country allowed its women to vote until after World War I.[4] (See Table 12.2.) The war called women to the fields and factories as the men marched to the front. Women proved that they were quite capable of taking care of themselves and of performing critical economic tasks.

Sadly, great advances in the legal or social conditions of women failed to follow procurement of the right to vote. In fact, the feminist movement seemed to lose momentum following its suffrage victory. Only in the Soviet Union did women gain appreciably. Yet, even there, the state's motive gradually became more a matter of getting women into the labor force than truly liberating them. It was not until after World War II that the feminist movement got its second wind.

In 1949, French writer Simone de Beauvoir published *The Second Sex*. Rapidly achieving popularity across the world, the book argued that male dominance over women was a social, not a biological, phenomenon. De Beauvoir argued that the man's world was detrimental to both women and men, and

---

[4]Almost every extant state of the union, beginning in New Jersey with a 1790 law that was later amended to exclude women voters, allowed women to vote in some kinds of elections at one time or another. Generally, the western states, hoping to attract women settlers, were the most generous with their franchise. However, the right of women to vote in the United States as a whole was first proposed in Congress just after the Civil War, but the Constitution was not amended to allow it until 1920, following repeated annual attempts to force the issue through Congress.

> **TABLE 12.2**
>
> **Women Given the Right to Vote[5]**
>
> | Country | Year | Country | Year | Country | Year |
> |---|---|---|---|---|---|
> | Australia | 1902 | Thailand | 1932 | Syria | 1949 |
> | Soviet Union | 1917 | Cuba | 1934 | Greece | 1952 |
> | Canada | 1918 | Turkey | 1934 | Mexico | 1953 |
> | Poland | 1918 | Philippines | 1937 | Nigeria | 1954 |
> | Germany | 1919 | France | 1944 | Nicaragua | 1955 |
> | Sweden | 1919 | Italy | 1945 | Egypt | 1956 |
> | United States | 1920 | Japan | 1945 | Algeria | 1958 |
> | Ireland | 1922 | Argentina | 1947 | Iran | 1963 |
> | England | 1928 | China | 1947 | Kenya | 1963 |
> | South Africa | 1930 | Israel | 1948 | Kuwait | 2005 |
> | Brazil | 1932 | India | 1949 | | |

that both genders could benefit from women's liberation. The book raised compelling points, yet the time was still not yet ripe for the rebirth of the feminist movement.

Once again energized by companion movements, feminism began to attract a large following in the 1960s. The civil rights movement and the antiwar demonstrations mobilized millions, and the high moral and egalitarian tone of the day lent impetus to the righteousness of feminism. Another factor that helped rejuvenate feminism was the socioeconomic fact that fewer and fewer men were able to support their families by themselves. They needed the help of their working wives. The flood of women entering the workforce encouraged them to become more independent and to demand that their husbands share in household and child-rearing duties.

Amid this change, **Betty Friedan** (1921–2006) in 1963 published *The Feminine Mystique,* in which she pointed to women's frustration with social norms that were prejudiced against them and that conditioned them to passively accept male domination. Electrifying the country with her critique, Friedan became an icon of the feminist movement. (Toward the end of her life she alienated some of her feminist compatriots by suggesting that elements of the movement may be going to unwise extremes.) In 1966 she helped found, and became the first president of, the National Organization of Women (NOW). Since then, feminism has blossomed into an international movement of considerable consequence. It has made great strides in the United States and

---

[5]Saudi Arabia allowed men to vote in national elections beginning in 2005, but not women. The United Arab Emirates and Brunei have no elections at all. The only election held in the Vatican City is the election of the pope, by the all-male College of Cardinals.

Betty Friedan

the West, and important progress has occurred in the Developing World. There have been failures as well, however. For example, in the 1970s the United States refused to pass the Equal Rights Amendment (ERA) to the Constitution. This proposal said simply, "Equality of rights under the law shall not be denied or abridged by the United States or any state on account of sex."

Clearly, if such a straightforward expression of equal rights could not be made as recently as the 1970s, much is left to be done. However, as already pointed out, the current generation seems much less interested in feminist goals than was the previous generation.

Feminist Thought

As with any other dynamic movement, the goals of feminism and the methodology by which the goals are to be reached are unsettled. Feminists wonder whether the goal should be that women be treated *equally* or *equitably*. Those arguing for equal treatment for women believe that the differences between men and women are relatively inconsequential, their similarities being fundamental. Those who want equitable, or fair, treatment for women suggest that the differences between men and women are important and should be recognized. However, women should receive fair treatment from society because, although there are important differences between the genders, women have a right to be treated without prejudice.

Another debate among feminists focuses on the question of how the problem of gender bigotry can be best combated. Should feminists concentrate on getting government regulations that ensure appropriate treatment, or should the focus be on bringing about changes in behavior and of understanding within the family?

As the feminist movement develops, it becomes more diverse and complex. Argument about its goals and how they are to be met has increased until at least a dozen different well-defined variants have emerged. These variants include socialist feminism, lesbian feminism, multiracial feminism, and even men's feminism. In general terms, however, each of these varied feminist strains can be associated with one of three broad categories of feminism: reform, revolutionary, and separatist.

Reform Feminism   The most moderate of the three, **reform feminism,** demands important changes within society but does not demand that the institutions of society themselves be changed. Reform feminists argue that men and women are different in important ways, but that being different does not mean that one gender is subordinate to the other. Equal does not mean identical.

Reform feminists are philosophically wedded to the liberal political tradition. Although they are quick to recognize the differences between the genders, they argue that the fundamental fact is that women and men are equally human and that this fundamental sameness demands that each individual has an equal claim to human rights.

Yet, men have used social norms, religion, the political system, the economy, and the law to suppress women. Ironically, nature has given women its most fundamental and important task, that of preserving the species, yet the male-dominated society devalues and undermines this role. At the same time, the man's world affords few opportunities for women outside of materialism and nurturing.

The remedy the reformers propose is to create a partnership with men in revamping society's values and laws so that they treat women and men the same with regard to occupational and social matters and reflect the importance of women's unique role by providing ample medical and prenatal treatment, maternity leave, child care facilities, and so forth. Additionally, men must be expected to shoulder more of the housework and the child care duties.

Revolutionary Feminists   Whereas the reformers seek a cooperative relationship with men in pursuing the goal of changing society's anti-feminine biases, the **revolutionary feminists** argue that such a liaison is doomed. They believe that the anti-feminine bias is so deeply rooted in men that they are useless as agents of change. Rather than promote a joint effort to change society, the revolutionists want to force change on society regardless of how much or how little male support they receive.

Furthermore, the revolutionary feminists assert that *patriarchy* (government or control by men) is so strong in the male psyche that a gender-neutral society, as the reformers advocate, is impossible. To believe that women should only be given equal opportunity to succeed at jobs and tasks as they are currently constituted is to perpetuate the male-dominated world, because the values upon which these things are based and the very definition of success are all determined by the male view.

Instead, the revolutionaries demand that women create a world based on feminine-oriented values. Society should be recast to reflect women's perspectives. Political, social, and cultural institutions, art, religion, education, government, law, science, and academics should be made to turn away from male-oriented power relationships and adopt feminine values of mutual consideration and nurturing.

As in previous eras of the feminist movement, this variant of feminism has gravitated toward union with other liberationist movements. Resisting the subordination of women to men, revolutionary feminism has recognized kinship with racial and ethnic egalitarianism, religious dissenters, opponents of social class divisions, and the gay rights movement.

Another distinguishing feature of the revolutionaries is that their most immediate focus is on sexual oppression and violence. They oppose pornography, sexual harassment, battery, and rape, believing these most painful manifestations of male power over women must be stamped out, if women are ever to be successful in changing the world they now endure.

Separatist Feminists   Finally, there are the **separatist feminists** who posit that rather than reforming with men or rebelling against them, the feminist movement can succeed only by ignoring the male culture and creating a female culture parallel to it. Basically, the separatists agree with the revolutionaries that the male culture is so strong and so corrupt that it cannot be accommodated in the changes that must be made. Where they differ is in the method they believe will most effectively change things.

The separatists disagree among themselves about the reasons for the strategy. Some argue that gender differences, outside of certain physiological factors, are more a matter of social expectation and selected behavior than of anything natural to the species. Others contend that the differences between men and women, although in part contrived, are mostly real and important. Thus, uniting women is essential for their own well-being, given the totality of the male-dominated world.

Among the most oppressive phenomena in the male world is heterosexual lovemaking. It is seen as a quintessential power trip, with the man usually on top, subjecting the woman to receive his penetration. Modern science and technology have made this heterosexual relationship unnecessary, the separatists say; the species can easily be perpetuated without it, and they demand that it be abandoned as archaic. Women can develop more egalitarian and loving sexual relationships among themselves, they assert.

With this heretofore essential reason for community among women and men now made irrelevant, in the separatist view, women can live out their lives ignoring their former oppressors, thus liberating themselves from centuries of dependence on hopeless exploiters. Women should begin immediately, creating their own world based on their own values and norms and encouraging themselves to flourish.

ENVIRONMENTALISM

The Industrial Revolution, the font of modern political ideologies, has, for the first time in history, made it possible for humans to improve their material lives on a vast scale, but at the same time to so influence the natural environment as to actually threaten human existence itself. Focus on this paradox has fueled the emergence of a new ideology. **Environmentalism** is an idea system demanding fundamental philosophical reorientation and mandating diametric political, economic, and social change.

Beyond question, the most profound philosophical reorientation demanded by environmentalism is that humans reject their **anthropocentric** belief that human beings are the source of all value, so that the worth of all things should be measured by how they affect the human condition. This view is buttressed by Western religious tradition. Genesis 1:28 entreats people to subject nature to their will.[6]

Instead, environmentalists insist that humans see themselves as only a part of nature, constituents of a universe that is composed of numerous interactive and interdependent beings, both living and nonliving. This new perspective, they aver, is not only ethically right but essential for human survival.

Concern for air pollution and poor sanitation brought on by industrialization and urbanization was registered from the beginning of industrialization in England. By the end of the nineteenth century, serious concern about environmental degradation resulted in efforts to preserve the wilderness. Eventually national parks were created throughout Europe, the Americas, Asia, and Africa to protect the wilderness. But it was not until the 1960s that people awakened to the danger posed to human survival itself by industrialization. In 1962 biologist Rachel Carson published *Silent Spring*. Principally about the deadly and broad effects of the pesticide DDT, the book awakened the world to the mounting problems of environmental degradation. *Silent Spring* was quickly followed by other books decrying the population explosion, air pollution, and the spiritual morbidity of gross materialism, and the environmental movement was born. Soon, Paul Ehrlich, Barry Commoner, Ernest Schumacher, Peter Singer, and others gained a public hearing as they extrapolated the consequences of uncontrolled population expansion, explained the concept of ecology (a biological universe in which species are interdependent on each other and the environment), and advocated abandoning abject materialism.

Environmentalism is a reaction against the predicament we have created through the combination of anthropocentrism and modernization. Environmentalists believe that we have wrongfully violated nature by attempting to become its master. Humans see nature as an economic resource to be harnessed rather than a domicile to be nurtured. As a result, humans have created an artificial world, one that fouls the air and water. The great rain forests that do so much to regulate the earth's climate and oxygenate the air are disappearing beneath the treads of giant mechanical forest harvesters and earth movers. Meanwhile, the still depleted ozone layer threatens us with lethal solar radiation, and global warming is causing a dangerous melt of the earth's glaciers and ice caps. The melt-off in the Arctic has reached a rate previously predicted for fifty years hence, baring an area three times the size of California, while the Antarctic also is melting much faster than previously believed. The polar and Greenland ice fields, like giant mirrors, reflect the sun's heat. With these

---

[6]Recently, several religious leaders have taken a less aggressive stance, including the Southern Baptists and the Catholic Church. Pope Benedict XVI, in fact, is sometimes called "the green pope."

One can almost see the retreat of this glacier on the Tibetan plateau. The glaciers of the Himalayas provide water to almost one billion people. The effects of global warming are causing serious flooding at present, but when the glaciers have disappeared, as they soon will, drought is expected to set in in parts of India, China, and other societies dependent on Himalayan waters. The political destabilization this scarcity of a vital resource will cause is a very troubling prospect.

new melts, more heat is absorbed, thus increasing the rate of global warming. Faced with a looming debacle, most of the world's governments are taking the threat of global warming seriously. But the questions impeding needed action are who sacrifices what and who pays the bill. Yet, inexplicably, the people of the United States have shifted away from believing there is a problem. A 2009 poll by the Pew Research Center found that public belief that global warming is occurring dropped to 57 percent from 77 percent only three years earlier and only 36 percent believe that human activity is contributing to the problem.

Despite this irresponsible denial, the evidence is overwhelming that human activity is contributing seriously to these problems and these effects are exacting a huge toll among other animal species. We have accelerated the annual rate of species extinction 200-fold over the pre-industrial rate, until now it is estimated that a species of animal is irrevocably lost every twenty minutes. The rate of loss is so great that scientists consider this the sixth largest of the earth's great extinctions. Estimates vary, but some authorities fear that 40 percent of the animal species alive today will become extinct by 2050. These species may include such favorites as polar bears, manatee, sea turtles, coral reefs, mountain gorillas, the Sumatran elephant, and certain kinds of

TABLE 12.3

World Population Projections

Year	World Population in Billions	Percent in Africa	Percent in Asia	Percent in Europe	Percent in Latin America (Mexico, South America)	Percent in North America (Canada & the United States)	Percent in Oceania
2010	6.8	14.4	60.7	10.5	8.7	5.1	0.5
2020	7.6	15.7	60.6	9.4	8.7	5.0	0.5
2030	8.3	17.2	60.1	8.4	8.7	5.0	0.5
2040	8.9	18.7	59.4	8.0	8.7	5.0	0.5
2050	9.4	20.2	58.5	7.3	8.6	5.0	0.5

Source: United States Census Bureau

pelicans, penguins, and whales. Among the principal causes of this immense die-off are human encroachment on habitat, global warming, toxic chemical pollution, overfishing, and illegal poaching and trade in exotic animals.

Ironically, the earth's human population (now approaching 7 billion) is growing to unsustainable levels, even as other animals are dying out. The current rate of human growth is just under 2 million per week and the total is expected to reach 9.4 billion in just forty years, unless the current growth rate is curbed. (See Table 12.3.) If it is not, the awful prediction of **Thomas Malthus** would seem to be looming as we approach the limits of the earth's ability to provide. This day, 1 billion people will go to bed hungry and 10,000 will die of hunger.

As you know, fresh water scarcity is among the most serious problems confronting us. The world population quadrupled in the twentieth century, yet the per capita fresh water use went up ninefold. Major rivers are now imperiled. The most threatened are the Colorado in the United States, the Nile in Africa, the Volga in Russia, the Ganges in India, and the Yellow in China. The Yellow River spawned the oldest extant civilization in the world. For thousands of years, millions of people have relied on its abundance of water, fish, and fowl; now, however, with China's huge population and its voracious industrial demands for water, the Yellow is so depleted that it fails to reach the sea for several months of the year. In fact, 60 percent of China's 669 cities suffer water shortages. Moreover, almost 1 billion people rely on the glaciers of the Himalayas for water. But, due to global warming, they are melting at an alarming rate, threatening floods now but only a trickle later. The political and social instability to be caused by water shortage is likely to become severe. So urgent is China's fresh water problem, that the government is "re-plumbing" the country by way of a huge project to redirect river flows from the flood plagued south to the parched north. A massive undertaking, it is to be done in three stages. The eastern and central legs are currently under construction and total 1,650 miles. The western section is not yet begun. The series of canals and tunnels will transport millions of gallons of water daily, piped under existing rivers and through mountains using only gravity as a propellant.

The world's ocean waters are experiencing a different set of problems. For example, the waters of the Aleutian Islands, jutting northwestward off the Alaskan coast, were teeming with wildlife only twenty-five years ago. Rich in plankton, shrimp, smelt, and crab, the area attracted vast herds of sea lions, otter, and seal. Today, however, the sea mammals are gone, as are the rich kelp beds, forage fish, and shrimp. In their place are urchins, salmon, pollock, and shark. Scientists point to global warming as the cause. Since 1981, the water temperature in the Gulf of Alaska has risen by 2°C, compromising the plankton. It is extremely sensitive to temperature, so as the Aleutian waters warmed, it began to vanish, along with the shrimp and fatty forage fish that fed on plankton, and the sea mammals and birds who were also deprived of their food source. At the same time, the warmer water attracted salmon and bottom fish, so sharks that feed on them followed. Thus, the Aleutian waters have been transformed from an environment abundant in a rich variety of sea mammals and birds into a predators' haven. If such a dramatic change can accompany a 2° warming of the Arctic waters, one wonders what is in store for the world as the process of global warming accelerates over the next half century, as now appears all but inevitable. One consequence is almost certain, however: As the earth warms, the ability of people in the tropical regions—where the human population is increasing most rapidly—to grow food will be significantly reduced. Thus, famine among large populations on earth is virtually unavoidable. Other early manifestations of global warming's threat can be seen in Bangladesh. Situated between India and Myanmar, it has the largest expanse of land in the world resting just above the current sea level, and its population of nearly 150 million is desperately poor. Most of the country is a delta, creased with waterways. A minute change in sea level caused by melting glaciers and ice caps as well as by sea water expanding as the weather grows warmer has caused the salinization of drinking water aquifers. This is happening today. If the earth warms enough to cause the sea level to rise by 1 foot—a possibility by 2040—an estimated 12 percent of the Bangladesh population will be driven from their homes, becoming climate refugees for the opposite reason mentioned in Chapter 11. By the end of the century the sea level could rise by 3 feet, displacing a quarter of the land's population. Either of these population shifts will likely be far beyond the capacity of Bangladesh to accommodate economically or politically. But the United States will not escape unscathed. New Orleans and almost the entire state of Florida could become uninhabitable in a century. A study published online in 2007 by the journal *Science* projects that the American Southwest may have already entered a period of prolonged drought and may suffer "dust bowl" conditions similar to those experienced in the southern Midwest in the 1930s; only this condition could be permanent. The American Southwest's population, part of the "Sunbelt," is growing by leaps and bounds. How will scarce water supplies be divided among the parched states of Colorado, Wyoming, Utah, California, Nevada, Arizona, New Mexico, and Texas? Within these states, some of them the homes of our rich agricultural producers, the competition for water between the cities and the farmers—who now use most of the water—will become intense. Beyond these areas, just a slight increase in sea level could completely submerge whole island nations in the South Pacific and the Indian Ocean. Furthermore, demographers and others warn that the drying of the earth's farmland will launch large, perhaps vast, migrations of refugees for the hard-hit Developing World. Perhaps as many as six million Mexicans alone, fleeing their scorched farmland, could come to the United States in the next half century.

Global warming is virtually certain and is largely caused by human activity, in the view of the vast majority in the climatology community and a large number of the world's political leaders. Leading the charge against them is the likes of gasbags, Glenn Beck and Rush Limbaugh. Perhaps it's time for a little critical thinking!

In 2008, the National Oceanic and Atmospheric Administration (NOAA) reported that carbon dioxide was accumulating in the atmosphere now at a rate of 2.4 parts per million (ppm) annually, much faster than originally thought. In the same year, famous NASA climatologist, James Hansen, published a paper saying that the carbon dioxide (CO_2) content in the atmosphere was at about 385 ppm and that it must be reduced to no more than 350 ppm "if humanity wishes to preserve a planet similar to that on which civilization developed. . . ." The NOAA report estimated that the CO_2 level at preindustrial times was about 280 ppm. Tellingly, nineteen of the twenty hottest years on record have occurred since 1980 and the first decade of the current century was the hottest on record, easily surpassing the previous record holder, the 1990s. The hottest year on record so far was 2005 at 1.11 degrees above normal, according to the U.S. National Climate Data Center in a 2010 report. Scientists warn that these temperature increases, if sustained, portend intense heat waves, extensive drought, wildfires, more volatile typhoons and hurricanes, deforestation, and declines in food production. Indeed, there is strong evidence that these consequences have already begun.

Beyond these potential large-scale crises, it is worth briefly considering specific vestiges of global warming occurring now. The permafrost in eastern Siberia is melting, exposing vast amounts of formerly frozen carcasses and dead plant life which, as it spoils, will release billions of tons of carbon dioxide and methane into the atmosphere already congested by CO_2. Because of its having been frozen for so long, scientists estimate Siberia contains ten to thirty times the carbon as deep soils elsewhere.

As ice flows melt, polar bears are drowning or starving since their hunting grounds are disappearing. Walruses are experiencing similar problems with their habitat. As the Arctic and Antarctic become warmer, certain species of fish, sea birds, and whales are driven further north, perhaps transforming the entire ecosystem. Warmer temperatures now allow disease-bearing insects to spread farther afield. For example, encephalitis, spread by ticks, is now occurring farther north in Europe than it did before the 1990s. Similarly, mosquitoes are spreading malaria to higher elevations in Africa than was the case in cooler eras. These changes are fundamental and may not be reversible, even if global temperature is stabilized.

To combat global warming, scientific authorities are in almost unanimous agreement that the amount of greenhouse gases must be reduced dramatically. In a world dependent on petroleum and coal for the bulk of its energy, any effective combat of global warming will require profound changes in lifestyle: changes in how we live, how we travel, what we eat, and so on. To date, however, precious little has been done to reverse or even stabilize the problem. In fact, greenhouse gas production is up across the board in the industrialized world. The 1998 Kyoto Accord called on signatories to reduce greenhouse gas emissions by 5 percent from 1990 levels by 2012, the date its authority ends. Although Europe and Japan made important strides toward the goal, they missed the mark, and President George W. Bush refused to sign or cooperate with the treaty. His administration even deliberately suppressed a 2007 EPA report warning that immediate attention be given to substantially reducing greenhouse gas emissions and asserting that the damage done already could take the earth 1,000 years to completely restore the climate to normal, even if greenhouse gas emissions were somehow immediately returned to preindustrial levels. This shortsighted, irresponsible policy has helped set the United States far behind other industrial states in combating global warming. (See Table 12.4.)

TABLE 12.4

Top Ten Carbon Dioxide Emitters in 2007

Country	Percent of World Emissions	Per Capita Emissions by Metric Tons
China	22.30	4.9
United States	19.91	18.9
India	5.50	1.4
Russia	5.24	10.8
Japan	4.28	9.8
Germany	2.69	9.6
Canada	1.90	16.9
United Kingdom	1.84	8.9
South Korea	1.72	10.5
Iran	1.69	6.8

Source: United States Department of Energy Carbon Dioxide Information Center

While President Barack Obama declared a strong commitment to join the world community in reducing emissions of greenhouse gases, he has not yet gotten Congress to pass a climate bill. The UN Copenhagen Conference on the subject late in 2009 ended with ambiguous results. The rub came over the question of who should pay how much for the solution. Basically, the Developing World contends that the developed economies created the problem and have long profited from the offending technology; thus, they should pay the lion's share in resolving it. The advanced countries demurred. While such dithering is understandable, from a political point of view, it is terribly counterproductive as the world approaches a crisis of epic proportions.

While global warming is, without question, the most serious environmental problem we face, it certainly is not the only one. The BP oil blowout in the Gulf of Mexico has become the largest man-made environmental disaster in our history and portends consequences we may not even be able to yet imagine. Concentrations of mercury in marine fish from industrial discharges are growing to dangerous levels. This very toxic metal causes serious and permanent declines in the physical and mental development of children. Polychlorinated biphenyls (PCBs), polybrominated diphenyls (PBDEs), used in the manufacture of fire-retardant materials, and DDT from industrial waste, drawn by the winds, rains, and ocean currents, are concentrating in the Arctic region, threatening its wildlife. Pesticides used on commercial crops have been shown to weaken and reduce sperm counts in human males. Recent research strongly suggests that widespread use of pesticides explains the global disappearance of frogs and other amphibians. At least one-third of the 1,856 species of amphibians worldwide are in danger of extinction.

An island of plastic, three times the size of Texas, washed from the land and broken into tiny bits is floating just beneath the surface in the Pacific Ocean. Not a lot is known about it, but it is suspected to be dangerous for sea animals that may mistake it for food. There are over 400 huge "dead zones" in the world's seas in which oxygen is so scarce fish and other animals cannot live there. There are two causes for these vacant expanses. First, chemical fertilizers wash down rivers and these nitrogen-rich pollutants feed massive algae growths, which then use up the oxygen in the water. These kinds of dead zones are found at the mouth of the Mississippi River, in the Chesapeake Bay, in Lake Erie, and in waters off India, Japan, Australia, Brazil, Mexico, and in the Baltic Sea. There are also huge dead zones running along the Pacific Coast from the state of Washington to Peru and off of South Africa. Scientists are not sure why these occur but they posit it has something to do with the warming air over the Pacific and South African waters. Second, plankton increase but overfishing has depleted stocks of fish to eat it. The plankton die, drift to the bottom, and the decaying process sucks oxygen from the water, making other life there impossible. Whatever the cause, the number of dead zones is thought to be doubling each decade.

On land, a fungus called Ug99, named after Uganda and 1999, the place and year it was discovered, threatens to eventually wipe out as much as 80 percent of the world wheat crop, the most common of all cultivated grains. The wind, or people inadvertently carrying the fungus, have spread it across the Red Sea and it is now rapidly moving toward Pakistan and India. Unless it can be stopped, it is expected to sweep across Russia and China and finally be carried to the Americas and Europe.

After three decades of breakneck industrial development, China finds itself among the most polluted countries in the world. (According to the World Bank, of the thirty most polluted cities in the world, twenty of them are in China.) Because China burns more coal than the European Union and the United States combined, asthma and other respiratory diseases are growing, especially among children. Heart disease and ailments have become the leading causes of premature death in China. About 10 percent of China's arable land is now contaminated by overfertilization, use of solid waste, and heavy metals coming from industry. With about 30 million acres now damaged, authorities are beginning to worry that China will become unable to produce all the food its bulging population needs. Green spaces are shrinking, endangering unique wildlife including the panda bear. Many of its rivers have become open sewers carrying deadly industrial chemicals to the sea and poisoning people and the land along their banks. The government has pledged to deal with the problem, but so far the most concerted effort to clean up the air and water was directly related to preparing for the 2008 Olympics.

But China's record is not completely negative. Although still relying heavily on coal for energy, China has spent a considerable sum on building power plants fired by nuclear energy. Further, resurrecting a technology used in the United States at the turn of the last century but later abandoned for natural gas, China has become the world's leader in production and use of stainless steel solar water heaters. Moreover, China has also become a leader in producing solar panels and wind-driven turbines. In fact, most of the windmills purchased for President Obama's push for developing renewable energy sources were bought from China in 2009.

For its part, the United States, although developing a substantial record of concern for the environment, also has long been among the world's largest polluters. By far, the worst environmental record of any president in modern times has been George W. Bush's (2001–2009). Closely connected to the energy industries in the United States, the administration systematically ignored several important scientific studies, while actively distorting others, and even suppressing others that warned the nation of looming environmental problems. Its efforts to obfuscate the science was so blatant that hundreds of private and government-employed scientists associated with the EPA, the U.S. Fish and Wildlife Service, the Intergovernmental Panel on Climate Change, the Union of Concerned Scientists, and Nobel laureates repeatedly wrote letters condemning the administration for its obstructionist and disingenuous policies. Heedless of this opposition, the administration ignored global warming, opened vast acreages of pristine public forests to road building and logging, inhibited protections for several wildlife species, facilitated a huge expansion of natural gas and oil development on public lands, and exempted military bases from hazardous waste cleaning requirements. In other areas the Bush administration simply refused to enforce laws already on the books to protect the environment.

Finally, in the last few months of his term, Bush tried to ramrod, by presidential order, a number of benefits for the energy industry. Examples of these "midnight regulations" include rules facilitating exploration and development for oil and gas and opening the shale deposits for oil in huge parts of public lands in the western states. He eliminated rules requiring that experts be consulted before actions are taken that could endanger the environment. Pollution restrictions were eased, as were regulations of commercial fishing and drinking water standards, and rules regulating power plant pollutions and emissions from oil refineries were relaxed. In all, fifty-three of these gifts to industry and blows to the public health and the environment were promulgated. President Obama has reversed many of these presidential orders. Some cannot be negated so easily.

Yet, the Bush administration was not totally without some saving grace. In 2009, only fourteen days before his term ended, President Bush created three huge marine preserves off U.S.-controlled islands in the Pacific Ocean. These total 195,000 square miles and are added to the 140,000-square-mile preserve Bush previously created off the waters of Hawaii. These preserves protect species of sea life and unique geological formations. Together, they represent the largest expanse of protected seascape in the world.

Early in the first year of his term, Obama pledged U.S. commitment to significant reductions in its carbon footprint. He has supported a stronger role for the EPA, he has made getting passage of a bill to mitigate global warming a top priority, and he strongly supports an energy bill containing provisions allowing energy-efficient corporations to sell to less efficient companies energy credits toward ever-decreasing allowances: the "cap and trade" provisions. Obama has also encouraged development of renewable energy sources; wind, solar, and others, and anticipating a resurgence of the importance of railroads in our transportation system, he has pushed for high-speed rail services. However, Obama's environmental record is not without controversy. He has been taken to task by the scientific community for not yet keeping his promise to insolate government scientists from political pressure. In a much-deserved embarrassment, Obama authorized increased offshore oil well drilling in large sections of the Atlantic and Gulf of Mexico just weeks before the BP oil blowout ("spill" is inadequate) in Louisiana waters. Furthermore, Obama has proposed underwriting construction of new nuclear power plants, raising cries of "foul" from some environmentalists. Yet, many authorities admit that as the threat of global warming mounts, any real hope of significantly reducing carbon emissions of the country must include nuclear generated electricity. The major reason France's carbon footprint is the lowest among the industrialized states is that it has an extensive system of nuclear power plants. (See Table 12.5.)

TABLE 12.5

Carbon Dioxide Emissions and GDP of G-8, China, and India

	Carbon Dioxide (2006)		GDP (2008)		Total Per Capita (1,000)	
	Metric Tons	Rank	Metric Tons	Rank	in Dollars	Rank
Canada	544,680	8	16.7	7	$1,400,091	11
France	474,148	14	6.2	46	2,853062	5
Germany	805,090	6	9.7	27	3,652,824	4
Italy	474,148	10	8.1	26	2,293,008	7
Japan	1,393,409	5	10.1	20	4,909,272	2
Russia	1,564,669	3	10.9	16	1,607,816	9
UK	568,520	7	9.4	23	2,645,593	6
US	5,752,351*	2	19.0	6**	14,204,322	1
China	6,103,493*	1	4.6	50	4,326,187	3
India	1,510,351	4	1.3	83	1,217,490	12
EU***	3,914,359	NA	NA	NA	15,311,220	NA
World	28,431,741		4.4	NA	NA	NA

*China and the United States alone account for 41.7% of the world's annual carbon dioxide emissions.
**Those leading the United States are tiny states: Qatar, 56.2; UAE, 32.5; Kuwait, 31.17; Trinidad and Tobago, 25.29; and Bahrain, 28.82.
***Note: The European Union (EU), composed of 27 nations, has a total population of 187 million greater than the United States and a cumulative GDP of $1.1 trillion greater than the United States; still it has only 68% as great a carbon footprint as the United States.
Source: Carbon Footprint, U.S. Department of Energy, Carbon Dioxide Analysis Center, GDP, World Bank.

The Environmentalists

The Greens   Many political parties throughout the world associate themselves with the environmental movement and refer to themselves as "Greens." Perhaps nowhere has the Green Party become so powerful as in Germany. Founded in the 1970s, the Greens burst on the political scene as idealistic, impractical, and radical. They demanded dramatic reductions in the use of fossil fuels, immediate closure of nuclear power plants, unilateral disarmament, and other extremist policies. Gradually, however, the Green leadership in Germany has become more sophisticated. It has learned that to accomplish its principal ends it must moderate and expand the scope of its political involvement. Today, it finds itself among the strongest parties in Germany, and its approach has become the model of Green movements around the globe. There are Green Parties in virtually all industrial and in many other countries now (Antanas Mockus, a Green, is currently making a good showing in the race for president of Colombia), but the German party continues to be the most successful politically and the most creative ideologically.

The ideology of the Green Party, the *Green Ideology,* couches its goals in moralistic tones. It is committed to improving environmental policy through activist strategies, largely at the local level. The *Four Pillars* of the movement are *ecological sustainability,* environmental policies which, whenever possible, do not deplete resources but rather are focused on the use of renewable resources; *social justice,* social policies which elevate the material and social circumstances of the underclasses and give all people the same access to a clean environment; *grassroots democracy,* mobilizing the people at the local level in an effort to accomplish the above; and *nonviolence,* while assertively pressing the party's objectives, it eschews using violence to accomplish its goals. The Green Party is predominantly a leftist party, although it resists the label. Besides its emphasis on environmental objectives, it has broadened its platform to supporting feminism; full meaningful employment for all; respect for diversity; and encouraging people to take personal and global responsibility for the state of the world's environment.

Environmentalist Ideology Philosophically, ecologists divide into two basic categories as a function of the intensity of their beliefs. Norwegian philosopher Arne Naess in 1973 was the first to make the distinction between the **deep ecologists** and the **shallow** or **humanist ecologists.** Often associated with Asian mysticism, the deep ecologists are the more extreme of the two groups. Rejecting the anthropocentric approach for the *biocentric* (concerned with how policy affects all living things) view, these ecologists believe that all things in the universe have value in and of themselves and that the value humans may place on other objects is irrelevant. Rather than humans being the focus in this philosophy, nature as a whole is central, and the value of all things is measured by their contributions to nature. Accordingly, if humans threaten nature, they reduce their own validity and worth. Deep ecologists call upon people to abandon their anthropocentric view of the world and embrace the totality instead. This broader view is called **holism.**

Another, even broader approach, *terracentric,* is suggested in an essay by Bruce E. Marshall and F. Herbert Bormann, professor of ecology at UC Santa Barbara and professor emeritus at Yale, respectively. It eloquently contends that the economic model we employ, capitalism, is anthropocentric and has led us to the point at which we are about to—or perhaps already have—force unnatural changes on the earth from which it may not be able to recover. This result comes from an approach of trying to satisfy virtually unquenchable human demands for more. The problem arises from the fact that the earth is governed by an objective set of rules while our economic model is terribly subjective and too often in contradiction of the forces governing the earth.

To apply a value system which begins and ends with human benefit is wrongheaded because "that is not the way the Earth works." We must, they argue, stop our "reckless inclination" to do things that contradict the rules governing the earth. We must learn to nurture nature instead, because it performs tasks which we cannot and without which we cannot survive. In short, they

© Time & Life Pictures/Getty Images

James Lovelock (born 1919) is a principal advocate of the Gaia hypothesis.

entreat that we need "to become part of the Earth," not contradictory of it, or else it will become impossible for Earth to sustain us.[7]

This approach gives rise to important ethical questions. Do humans have a moral right to exploit and kill animals in pursuit of our economic and social ends? Is life itself not the great equalizer, thus requiring that humans respect the rights of all living things? Perhaps most expansive is the question of the *Gaia Hypothesis.* Hearkening back to ancient Greek mythology, which named its earth goddess Gaia, British scientist James Lovelock suggested in the late 1970s that earth was not simply an inert host to countless living and nonliving things. Instead, it was itself a living organism, with humans little more than certain cells in the earth's body. Like the cells of our own body, humans can contribute to the overall strength of the host and thus enjoy its fruits. But if our behavior becomes erratic and harmful, weakening the earth, then we, just like human cancer cells, will ultimately destroy ourselves as we kill the host.

Although the deep ecologist theories are often seen as extremist, the *ecoterrorists* or *ecowarriors* are much more extreme, at least behaviorally. These extremists engage in *monkey wrenching,* acts of sabotage against environmental degradation, construction, logging, hazardous waste disposal, cruelty to animals. An example of such behavior is the Earth Liberation Front (ELF). This is a terrorist group that strikes out at what it regards as threats to the environment. Founded in Britain in 1992, ELF has also engaged in several attacks in the United States, including torching large home construction projects, defacing and destroying Hummers, wrecking laboratories engaged in genetic engineering, loosening bolts on several electrical transmission wires across the West Coast states, and burning university buildings. Several people have been convicted of such acts, albeit one was freed in 2010 on a legal technicality. A different sort of ecowarriors are whale enthusiasts who annually confront whaling ships in Antarctic waters, usually Japanese because they take about 1,000 whales a year, ostensibly for research purposes, but their meat ends up in the markets.

Certainly not as violent a monkey wrenching technique, yet very disruptive, was the lone-wolf act of 27-year-old environmentalist, Tim DeChristopher. He attended a 2008 auction of Utah oil leases to be sold by the Bush administration.

---

[7]Bruce E. Marshall and F. Herbert Bormann, "It's No Longer a Garden Spot," *Los Angeles Times,* March 3, 2010.

In the end, he was arrested for buying, but not being able to pay for, 22,000 acres abutting Arches and Canyonlands National Parks.

Closely associated with the ecoterrorists are animal rights activists who have also resorted to violence. For example, a group calling itself the Revolutionary Cells has bombed firms that experiment with animals. Other animal rights activists have demonstrated at the steps of universities doing medical experiments on animals, firebombed cars owned by researchers, intimidated their family members with threatening phone calls and stalking, and other forms of terrorism. Over the past few years, several of these terrorists have been tried and punished.

Joining the deep ecologists in condemning the violent acts of the ecowarriors, shallow or humanistic ecologists also find the deep ecologists' demands impractical, given the high level of self-awareness among humans.

Rather, they aver that the gradual reduction of materialism, pollution, and population growth is essential for the well-being of the human condition. As an example, they point out that the industrialized world is almost totally dependent on oil as an energy source, and yet the known reserves of oil, at current rates of consumption, will probably become unable to satisfy all demand sometime in the 2020s and will be completely depleted in twenty to twenty-five years later.[8] Asserting the principle of *sustainability,* the humanistic ecologists call for immediate steps to conserve extant resources and to convert to the use of renewable resources (solar, wind, and hydrogen energy) so that humanity can be sustained. Humans are asked to think about their existence, to consider the long-term consequences of their current irresponsible economic and social behavior and then to develop policies that will sustain life rather than threaten it with disaster. In the words of philosopher Louis P. Pojman, people are asked to "live off the interest instead of the principal" of the environment.

Concern for the moral aspects of environmental degradation has spawned an entire field of philosophical inquiry called *environmental ethics.* Of interest to this new field are anthropocentric questions such as the morality of roughly 20 percent of the world's population (those in the industrial societies) enjoying most of the wealth, consuming most of the resources, and producing most of the pollution while the other 80 percent of humanity languishes in squalor and suffering. The ethical responsibility this generation has to ensure that ample resources remain for future generations is also examined. Perhaps the most articulate spokesperson for human ethical and spiritual responsibility to the planet was Thomas Berry (1914–2009).

Interestingly, environmentalism has become associated with a number of other ideologies. Some people on the right of the political spectrum warm to the romantic notion of returning to a lifestyle in which people depend on themselves and their immediate neighbors for sustenance. Liberals have become even more committed to environmentalism. Classic liberalism's

---

[8]Some authorities believe oil production has already peaked, and Saudi Arabia announced in 2004 that its production had already begun to decline.

founder, John Locke, called upon humans to possess nature, but humanistic environmentalism resonates strongly among contemporary liberals. Anarchists relate to environmentalism because both are reactions against the ravages of industrialization, urbanization, and bureaucratization. Each theory calls for the abandonment of modern institutions and for a return to a simpler, less centralized, more modest existence. Socialists also identify with environmentalism because they blame the degradation of the environment on capitalism. Exploitation of nature is as much a part of capitalism, these *social ecologists* claim, as is exploitation of the lower classes, which Murray Bookchin condemned as the exploitive mentality. It must be noted, however, that although capitalism indisputably drives much of the world's economic exploitation, socialism itself must also accept a great deal of the responsibility for environmental degradation. Beyond question, the greatest human-made environmental crises to date are those created in the Soviet Union, as is amply documented in Murray Feshbach and Alfred Friendly Jr.'s *Ecocide in the USSR.*

Coining the term ecofeminist in 1974, Françoise d'Eaubonne observed that the male trait of wishing to dominate had been manifested no less in attempts to subdue nature than in oppressing women. The suggestion that women are more in tune with nature and less threatening to it than men has gained resonance among some feminists. They claim that their biological role of giving birth and nurturing is more compatible with the Earth Mother than is the male drive to conquer. This notion has led some feminists to conclude that the fate of nature and the fate of women are joined, and that the salvation of each is dependent upon the same thing: vanquishing patriarchy.

Among the most recent converts to environmentalism is organized religion. Previously put off by the fear that environmentalism was the worship of nature (as in the Gaia Hypothesis) or of science, and repelled by the environmentalist thesis that we must reject the Christian notion that nature exists only to serve humans, religious movements and their hierarchy have tended to eschew environmentalism. Yet, some Christian and Jewish congregations have recently taken up the cause. "Redwood Rabbis," ministers, priests, and even the pope have admonished that people are God's stewards of the earth and have a responsibility to preserve nature as well as to use it for the good of humanity. Accordingly, several religious groups have become activists and have enjoyed significant successes in protecting ancient forests and endangered species of plants and animals.

Regardless of their varying ideologies and beliefs, environmentalists of all kinds point out that in the 4.5 billion years of the earth's existence, only during the last 200 years have any of the earth's occupants developed the capacity to seriously jeopardize it. Science and materialism led humans to the Industrial Revolution. It has created many wonderful things, but it has also brought us to a critical state, one that, if we are not careful, will bring humans to ruin and the earth to devastation. How could we do this to ourselves, to our children, to our progeny yet unborn, and indeed, how could we do this to nature? By what right do we trifle with that with which we are entrusted?

QUESTIONS FOR DISCUSSION

1. In what ways does sexism manifest itself in society?
2. How can the three varieties of feminism be compared and contrasted?
3. In what ways has the Industrial Revolution evoked the environmental movement?
4. How does environmentalism relate to other ideologies?
5. What are the basic philosophical questions revolving around environmentalism and feminism?

SUGGESTIONS FOR FURTHER READING

Carson, Rachel, *Silent Spring*. Boston: Houghton Mifflin Co., 1962.

Dale, Ann, *At the Edge: Sustainable Development in the 21st Century*. Seattle: University of Washington Press, 2000.

De Beauvoir, Simone, *The Second Sex,* trans. H. M. Parksley. New York: Knopf, 1953.

Friedan, Betty, *The Feminine Mystique*. New York: W. W. Norton, 1963.

Humphrey, Matthew, ed., *Political Theory and the Environment: A Reassessment*. London: Frank Cass, 2001.

Lovelock, James, *Gaia: A New Look at Life on Earth*. New York: Oxford University Press, 1981.

Mahanly, Chandra Talpade, *Feminism Without Borders*. Durham, NC: Duke University Press, 2003.

Moghissi, Hiadeh, *Feminism and Islamic Fundamentalism*. New York: St. Martin's Press, 1999.

Sandler, Ronald, and Phaedra C. Pezzullo, eds., *Environmental Justice and Environmentalism*. Cambridge, MA: MIT Press, 2007.

Saul, Jennifer Mather, *Feminism: Issues and Arguments*. Oxford: Oxford University Press, 2003.

Sunderlin, William, D., *Ideology, Social Theory, and the Environment*. Lanham, MD: Rowman and Littlefield, 2003.

Tong, Rosemarie, *Feminist Thought*, 2nd ed. Boulder, CO: Westview Press, 2009.

Valenti, Jessica, *Full Frontal Feminism*. Emeryville, CA: Seal Press, 2007.

Weigand, Kate, *Red Feminism: American Communism and the Making of Women's Liberation*. Baltimore: Johns Hopkins University Press, 2000.

Wollstonecraft, Mary, *A Vindication of the Rights of Woman*. New York: W. W. Norton, 2009.

GLOSSARY

Al Qaeda   A Muslim terrorist organization. While Osama bin Laden is the titular leader of the group, his influence is somewhat muted by his ill health and the fact that its various cells may not be under his absolute control at any given time.

Anarchism   An ideology opposed to all or much of institutionalized government. Some anarchists want to free people to make the greatest possible personal advancement; they are the *individual anarchists*. Others hope to free people so that they can make their greatest possible contribution to society as a whole; they are the *social anarchists*.

Anthony, Susan B.   (1820–1906) A leading figure in the struggle to secure the vote for women in the United States.

Anthropocentrism   The view that humans are the central focus in the universe, and, therefore the value of all other things is to be measured relative to them.

Aryans   In Nazi ideology, a race of people who have the best of all human qualities and are the creators of all culture. Science has so far failed to find any proof this race ever existed.

Atomistic society   A view of society in which the individual is believed to be central, whereas society itself is considered unimportant and coincidental.

Authoritarian dictatorship   A dictatorship in which the government has an extraordinary amount of control over society's political institutions (the police, the courts, the military) but does not control every major institution in society, as does a totalitarian dictator.

Babeuf, François-Noël   (1760–1797) History's first socialist, Babeuf talked about creating the workers' revolution as early as the 1790s.

Bakunin, Mikhail   (1814–1876) The founder of violent anarchism. He also competed with Marx for control of the international socialist movement.

Bentham, Jeremy   (1748–1832) The creator of utilitarianism and positivist law, he founded contemporary liberalism. He was also an important force in Britain's early nineteenth-century reform movement.

Bernstein, Eduard   (1850–1932) A revisionist socialist. See also *Revisionism.*

Bolsheviks Party   Followers of Lenin who believed that violence was necessary to bring about socialism and that Russia could be taken in a coup led by them. They were renamed the Communist Party after they came to power in Russia.

Bourgeoisie   The wealthy merchant and professional class that became the dialectical challenge to the feudal society.

Burke, Edmund   (1729–1797) The father of modern conservative philosophy. His ideas contributed heavily to neoclassical democratic theory, especially in making the property right a dominant theme. He thought that the people ought to be ruled by a benevolent aristocracy elected by them.

Capitalism   An economic system first conceived of by Adam Smith. It is based on individual competition in an unregulated marketplace.

Castro, Fidel Ruiz (born in 1927) A Cuban revolutionary and the founder of the current Cuban government.

Castro, Raoul (born in 1931) A revolutionary and longtime Cuban minister of defense, he succeeded Fidel as president in 2006, upon his brother's resignation for health reasons. So far, he has carried out several modest reforms.

Chamberlain, Houston Stewart (1855–1927) A friend and later the son-in-law of Richard Wagner, who shared Wagner's anti-Semitic views and developed a theory based on those views which were later admired by Adolph Hitler.

Checks and balances Madison's plan of government, in which each branch of government has the power to influence the others but no single branch can become too powerful. In addition, through staggered terms of office, indirect elections, and a specific election date, Madison hoped to prevent a permanent majority from controlling the government.

Classical liberal See *Liberal.*

Coalition government When no single party wins a majority of seats in parliament, sometimes two or more parties will unite to form a government. Such unions are usually unstable and short-lived.

Collective responsibility In the parliamentary-cabinet system, the notion that the members of the cabinet share responsibility for the government's successes and failures.

Comintern An organization, also called the Third International, created by Lenin to stimulate communist revolutions throughout the world, but under Stalin it became merely an instrument of Russian foreign policy.

Communism A very old term that originally meant a local communal relationship among a small number of people. Today it refers to a system based on Marxist-Leninist ideology.

Compulsive toil A term Marx used to describe Locke's notion of a condition in which people had to toil every waking hour just to make ends meet.

Concurrent powers Used in the U.S. federal system, these powers are exercised by both the state and national governments at the same time. If the two conflict, the laws of the national government prevail.

Conservative A person who is satisfied with the system as it is and tends to resist change. At its base, conservative resistance to change stems from lack of faith that people can improve conditions through deliberate action.

Conservative theory of representation A system in which an elite group is chosen by the people to govern. Yet although public officials should try to represent their constituents' interest, the people cannot compel them to vote in a particular way.

Conspiratorial theory The theory that a small group of powerful people is secretly controlling political and economic events.

Contemporary liberal See *liberal.*

Cooperatives Enterprises that are owned and operated by their members, who all participate in the enterprise directly.

Corporate state The economic system used in fascist Italy in which the state controlled the people by controlling labor unions and businesses. Production and prices were regulated, while strikes and boycotts were outlawed.

Cottage industry A preindustrial entity, although some survive to this day, in which the master craftsman owned a small shop and worked with apprentices as journeymen in the production of goods.

Cybernetics The study of the processing and exchange of information. This field includes computerization and robotics and is often involved in replacing workers with machinery.

It is the most advanced stage of the Industrial Revolution.

Deep ecology   The most extreme belief about the environment's relationship to humans. Human beings, it suggests, are no more important than any other species, and therefore they have no right to mold nature to their will.

Deng Xiaoping   (1904–1997) A pragmatic reformer who enjoyed great power in China, Deng managed to survive Mao and was responsible for the current modernization of China.

de Tracy, Antoine Louis Claude Destutt   (1754–1836) A French scholar who coined the term *ideology,* calling it the "science of ideas."

Dewey, John   (1859–1952) The philosopher of the New Deal. He called upon people to engage in social engineering by using their reasoning ability and their control of government to create a better life.

Dialectic   Georg Hegel's concept that historical progress is achieved through conflict between the existing order and challenges to it.

Dialectic materialism   The Marxist theory of history suggesting that human progress results from struggle between the exploiter and the exploited classes. This dynamic, Marx argued, would inevitably lead to socialism.

Dictatorship   See *Authoritarian dictatorship* and *Totalitarian state.*

Dictatorship of the proletariat   A temporary tyranny of the workers proposed by Marx that follows the revolution and lasts until all non-proletarian classes had been removed, at which time the state would wither away and a democratic utopia would evolve.

Direct democracy   A system in which there is no elected legislature and people make the laws themselves.

Divine right of kings theory   The belief that the king had been chosen by God to rule.

Divine theory of the state   The belief that God has chosen one people above all others and that, therefore, the state governing the chosen ones may do things to other people that could not be morally justified otherwise.

Division of labor   Economic specialization that Marx claimed led to the creation of private property, social classes, and human exploitation.

Economic determinism   The belief that all social and political features are conditioned by the economic environment.

Elite theorism   A theory suggesting that the political system is controlled by a relatively small number of people who head important interest groups.

Elitism   The assumption that some people are more deserving and qualified than others and that they ought to govern.

Engels, Friedrich   (1820–1895) The son of a wealthy Prussian textile manufacturer who became a close friend of Marx in 1844 and remained his collaborator and benefactor until Marx died in 1883.

Environmentalism   An ideology advocating human restraint in the use of resources and assuming a cooperative posture toward nature.

Exclusive powers   Used in the U.S. federal system, these powers may be exercised by either the state or the national government, but not by both. For example, education is an exclusive power for the states, whereas only the national government can make war.

Fabianism   Founded in 1884, the Fabian Society, cast in the tradition of John Stuart Mill and Robert Owen, advocated that the British adopt socialism gradually and peacefully.

Federalism   A system of government developed in the United States that divides the powers of government between the state and national levels.

Federalist Papers A series of articles written by James Madison, Alexander Hamilton, and John Jay, during 1787 and 1788, urging New Yorkers to ratify the proposed federal Constitution.

Feminism The belief that women are oppressed by men and that the oppression should be eradicated. Also see *Reform feminism, Revolutionary feminism,* and *Separatist feminism.*

Fidelismo Fidel Castro's adaptation of Marxism, which combines dialectic and idealistic rhetoric with anti-Yankee policies to create the new Cuba.

Force theory of the state The belief that the state was created by the forceful conquest of some people by others.

Foundation of Society Marx argued that economics was the foundation of any society, and that the economic foundation preconditioned the rest of the society (*the superstructure*).

Fourier, Charles (1772–1837) An influential utopian socialist. See also *Utopian socialism.*

Friedan, Betty (1921–2006) A social critic whose book *The Feminine Mystique* gained international acclaim and helped launch the feminist movement.

General will The all-powerful authority of Rousseau's organic society. The general will is created by the majority when it is acting in the best interests of all people.

Gobineau, Arthur de (1816–1882) A French noble who tried to prove that the French aristocracy was superior to the peasantry and should therefore rule France. In doing so, he claimed that the Aryan race was superior to all others. His theories deeply influenced Adolph Hitler.

Godwin, William (1756–1836) Once a Protestant minister, Godwin eventually became an atheist and founded anarchism.

Goldman, Emma (1869–1940) The leading anarchist in American history. Sometimes known as "Red Emma."

Gorbachev, Mikhail S. (born in 1931) General Secretary of the Communist Party of the Soviet Union from 1985 until its collapse in 1991. His profound reforms failed to prevent the Soviet collapse, but even so, he will probably be remembered as one of the twentieth century's most important leaders.

Great Cultural Revolution (1966–1969) A movement in which the Chinese radicals were unleashed against the moderate bureaucrats and intellectuals. The radicals favored greater personal sacrifice and stronger commitment to the goals of the revolution, whereas the moderates wanted to produce more consumer goods.

Great Leap Forward (1958–1961) An attempt to bring China into the modern industrial age through maximum use of the vast Chinese labor force; it failed miserably.

Green, Thomas Hill (1836–1882) A liberal philosopher who wrote that the government should actively promote material well-being for its citizens. His ideas offered an early justification for the welfare state, and his work redirected liberalism toward collectivism from individualism.

Guided democracies Developing World dictatorships in which the leaders claim to be carrying out the popular will.

Head of government The title given to the official who leads the government of a country (e.g., prime minister). In the United States, the president is the head of government, but he/she is also head of state. See *head of state.*

Head of state The title given to the official who symbolizes the history, traditions, and aspirations of a nation-state. In England, for example, the queen is the head of state, whereas the prime minister is head of government. See *head of government.*

Hegel, Georg Wilhelm Friedrich (1770–1831) A German political philosopher whose ideas were not only important in their own right but also greatly influenced both Marx and Mussolini.

Hitler, Adolf (1889–1945) A reactionary revolutionary and the founder of the ideology of National Socialism and the Nazi state.

Hobbes, Thomas (1588–1679) A social contract theorist who claimed that people had created an ordered society by surrendering their rights to the king.

Holism The anti-anthropocentric concept in environmental ethics that the universe must be seen and understood as a whole. Humans, therefore, should see themselves as no more than a part of nature rather than apart from it.

Hu Jintao (born 1942) The president of the People's Republic of China and the general secretary of the Chinese Communist Party. His policies seem to indicate that he is a genuine populist, but not a political liberal.

Humanitarian socialism Beginning with the Utopian movement, this variant of socialism suggests that people should work and share in common because of moral imperatives. This kind of socialism is distinct from Marxism or *scientific socialism.*

Human rights The rights listed in the Declaration of Independence and guaranteed in the Constitution of the United States. The question of whether or not property should be considered a human right is a subject of debate between liberals and conservatives.

Ideology Any of a number of action-oriented, materialistic, popular, and simplistic political theories that were originally developed as an accommodation to the social and economic conditions created by the Industrial Revolution.

Il Duce The Italian title for supreme leader, as used by Mussolini.

Imperialism (as used by Lenin) The most advanced state of capitalism.

It followed the stages of industrial capitalism and finance capitalism and represented the exportation of exploitation.

Imperialist capitalism Lenin's term for what he believed is the final stage of capitalism, in which capitalists exploit foreign labor classes in order to continue to increase profits but to avoid an uprising by their domestic workers.

Imperialist capitalists Members of the Chinese bourgeoisie who had ties to foreigners. They were held to be the most dangerous element in the society and were quickly eliminated after the communists came to power.

Individual anarchism See *Anarchism.*

Industrial Revolution A period beginning in the eighteenth century that consisted of several phases: Handcrafted goods produced in small shops gave way to *mechanization* (goods produced by machines). Labor then became concentrated in factories and cities. This phase was followed by *automation* (production of goods with machines powered by steam, gasoline, coal, running water, or electricity rather than by humans or animals). Today the advanced economies have reached the *cybernetic* level, in which machines are run by other machines.

Iron law of oligarchy Robert Michels's theory that only a very few people are active in any organization and that they therefore control it.

Iron law of wages David Ricardo's argument that the capitalist would pay the worker no more than a subsistence wage.

Irrationalistism The belief that human reason has definite limits and that people must depend on phenomena that are beyond reason for the explanation and solution to some of their most difficult problems.

Islamism A reactionary ideology suggesting that society should be governed by the principles of the Koran rather than by the dictates of secular values. Iran is currently a state subscribing to this approach.

Jaurès, Jean (1859–1914) A revisionist socialist. See also *Revisionism.*

Jefferson, Thomas (1743–1826) An American statesman and philosopher in the classical democratic tradition of Locke and Rousseau. He argued for a government that was much more directly controlled by the people than the one proposed in the federal Constitution.

Kautsky, Karl (1854–1938) A German Marxist who became the leader of the Orthodox Marxists following Engels's death.

Khrushchev, Nikita (1894–1971) The successor to Stalin and a political reformer in the Soviet Union.

Kropotkin, Prince Peter (1842–1921) A scientist and a communistic anarchist.

Kuomintang A Chinese nationalist political party founded by Dr. Sun Yi Xian and taken over by Jiang Jieshi after Sun's death.

Labor theory of value A theory espoused by David Ricardo and amplified by Marx suggesting the true value of any item was determined by the amount of labor it takes to produce it.

Laissez-faire Fundamental to capitalism, this belief held by John Locke, Adam Smith, and David Ricardo demands that government should not foster economic policies.

Lenin, Vladimir Ilyich Ulyanov (1870–1924) A Russian revolutionary who first adapted Marxism to a practical political situation; the founder of the Union of Soviet Socialist Republics.

Liberal A person who favors legal, rapid, substantial, and progressive change in the existing order. The *classical liberals* believed in natural law and that government was naturally oppressive. *Contemporary liberals* reject natural law and argue that government should be used by them to solve human problems.

Liberal theory of representation The belief that people should be able to compel their elected representatives to vote in a particular way.

Liberation theology A movement centered primarily in the Roman Catholic Church in Latin America, where some priests, nuns, and laypersons are committed to a socially and politically active Church to bring economic improvement, social advancement, and political power to the poor.

Locke, John (1632–1704) A social contract theorist and the leading philosopher of classical liberal democracy. He argued that people had created government to serve their needs and that most of the time government should have very little power over the individual.

Long March (1934–1935) A massive retreat from south to north China by the communists. A power struggle took place during the march, with Mao emerging as the dominant Chinese political figure.

Lumpenproletariat Vagabonds, prostitutes, and other social outcasts whom Bakunin wanted to mold into a revolutionary force.

Madison, James (1751–1836) The founder of the American federal system. He believed that people were base by nature and that governmental institutions should turn the people's vices into virtues. Accordingly, he designed a system of separate and diffuse powers with institutions that would check and balance each other.

Malatesta, Enrico (1853–1932) An implacable violent anarchist who demanded that leftists should engage in more revolutionary activities and less talk.

Malthus, Thomas (1766–1834) An English economist who postulated that since population increases more rapidly than food, calamity awaits those nations that do not exercise "moral restraint."

Maoism Marxist ideology heavily influenced by populism and traditional Chinese values. Like the ideologies of other developing countries, Maoism is heavily focused on anticolonialism.

Mao Zedong (1893–1976) A Chinese revolutionary and political leader. He founded the People's Republic of China and adapted Marxism to an Asian peasant society.

March on Rome A 1922 demonstration in which several thousand supporters of Mussolini successfully marched on Rome to demand that he be given power.

Marx, Karl (1818–1883) A scholar and the leader of the international socialist movement. He developed a theory of historical development—Marxism—based on the assumption that economic factors were the primary human motivation and that history was propelled by struggle among competing social classes.

Mass line A Maoist doctrine calling upon the masses of China to carry out the goals of the revolution.

Mercantilism An economic theory prominent in the 1600s and 1700s. Nations practicing mercantilism used economic monopolies and colonial exploitation in efforts to increase their wealth and political power. Today's vestiges of mercantilism are called economic nationalism.

Militant civilian militias Right-wing conspiratorial groups who believe that the U.S. government and other powerful institutions threaten their individual liberty and well-being. Racism, Christian fundamentalism, and survivalism are also themes commonly found among militia members.

Mill, John Stuart (1806–1873) A British philosopher who contributed greatly to the development of democratic socialism by questioning the

assumptions that people are naturally selfish and that government should have no economic role.

Moderate A person who is basically content with the political system but sees some flaws in it. Accordingly, a moderate will accept a small amount of progressive change.

Moral absolutism The belief that there is a set of absolute truths that apply equally to all people. Natural law is an example of these presumed truths.

Moral relativism The belief that truth at any given time is subject to the needs of society.

Multimember district An electoral district in which several people are elected to office. Legislative seats are awarded among parties in rough proportions to the votes they received.

Multiparty system A system in which there are several political parties that enjoy significant strength. This system gives the clearest voice to minority opinions but in doing so destroys the majority. Coalition governments and governmental instability may result from the absence of a majority.

Mussolini, Benito (1883–1945) An Italian reactionary revolutionary, the originator of fascism and the leader of the Italian fascist state.

Narodniki Russian populist anarchists of the late nineteenth century.

Nation A sociological term used to refer to a group of people who share a common language, ethnic relationship, culture, or history. The term does not necessarily have political significance.

Nationalism The ideology of the nation-state; the most powerful political idea to emerge in the past 300 years.

Nationalization Government expropriation, operation, and control of an industry by government.

National Socialist German Workers Party The official name of the German Nazi Party.

Nation-state A country that is dominated by a particular nationality. Nationalism is the ideological justification for the nation-state.

Natural law Rules of nature governing human conduct that can be discovered through the use of human reason.

Natural rights Rights believed to issue from the fact that natural law applies to all people equally, thus each individual has the right to expect certain rights and considerations from all others. Among the natural rights, according to John Locke, are life, liberty, and estate.

Natural theory of the state The belief that people are political as well as social animals and can develop their humanity only within the context of the state.

Neocolonialism A condition in which wealthy nations gain control of developing states by making vast economic investments in those states.

New Deal The 1930s policies of President Franklin Delano Roosevelt, which tempered capitalism with government regulation of business, collective bargaining for labor, and welfare state institutions including Social Security, housing loan guarantees, and welfare programs for the needy.

New Economic Policy (NEP) When his efforts to immediately socialize the Soviet Union failed, Lenin initiated the NEP reforms, privatizing small factories, retail, and agriculture, while finance, heavy industry transportation, communications, and foreign trade remained under state control. Stalin ended it in 1929 with the planned economy.

Nietzsche, Friedrich (1844–1900) A German philosopher who thought that power and strength were desirable qualities that justified all things.

Nihilism An anarchist theory of the mid-1800s; its goal was the complete destruction of society.

Organic theory of the state The belief that the state is similar to a living organism and that people are the cells of that organism.

Orthodox Marxists A group of socialists led by Engels and Karl Kautsky who followed the teachings of Marx without significant deviation. The movement failed because of its rigid dogmatism.

Owen, Robert (1771–1858) A self-made industrialist who recoiled at the suffering capitalism caused ordinary people. Wanting to reform capitalism, he became a utopian socialist and actually coined the term *socialism*.

Parliamentary-cabinet system A system in which the people elect the legislature, which then chooses a leader who is appointed prime minister by the head of state. The head of state also appoints members of the legislature to the cabinet on the recommendation of the prime minister. The cabinet acts as a plural executive, and its members stand (or fall) together on the government's policies.

Patriotism An act or gesture of loyalty or commitment to the nation-state.

Peaceful coexistence Khrushchev's policy of accommodation with the West, based on the recognition that neither side could win a nuclear war.

Permanent revolution A theory, supported by Leon Trotsky and Mao Zedong, favoring revolution as the best way to achieve meaningful reform even after Marxists have taken power.

Pluralism A decision-making process in which the people's interests are represented by various interest groups; governmental policy is a compromise among the competing interests of those groups.

Plurality The largest number of votes cast. A plurality is distinct from a majority because it need not be more than half; it is simply the most votes.

Political correctness The belief that certain words or phrases (racial epithets, for example) should be banned. Interestingly, this illiberal position is advocated by some liberals.

Popular sovereignty   The belief that the people are the sole source of political power; a fundamental idea in liberal democracy.

Populism   The belief that the common people are the soul of society. Among the great political leaders ascribing to this romantic notion are Thomas Jefferson, the Narodniki of Russia, and China's Mao Zedong.

Positivist law   Bentham's theory that the law should serve the people's interests and should be changed when it fails to do so.

Presidential-congressional system A system used in the United States in which the executive and the legislature are elected separately, resulting in less interdependence between the two branches than in other systems. Officials are elected to uninterruptible terms, a fact that adds stability to the system but tends to reduce popular control over the government.

Principle democrats   Those who believe that the process of making decisions is only part of democracy. More important are the basic goals of democracy, such as the freedom and independence of the individual.

Process democrats   Those who argue that democracy is simply a process by which decisions are made on a popular basis.

Proletariat   Industrial workers who, according to Marx, are exploited by capitalists and are supposed to rebel and eventually create a communist democratic utopia.

Proportional representation   A method of awarding legislative seats to parties or candidates in relation to the proportion of the vote won.

Proudhon, Pierre Joseph   (1809–1865) A leading anarchist socialist, sometimes called the founder of modern anarchism.

Putin, Vladimir   (born in 1952) Boris Yeltsin's successor to the Russian presidency in 1999. He served two terms until required to stand down by term limits. Succeeded in 2008 by his protégé, Dmitry Medvedev, Putin continues to dominate Russia as prime minister. Putin's authoritarian policies have apparently snuffed out a fledgling democracy.

Radical   A person who wants immediate, profound, and progressive change in the existing order. Some radicals insist that violence is the only way to bring about meaningful change; pacifist radicals oppose violence altogether.

Radical theory of representation   A theory that rejects elected representatives and holds that people should represent themselves in the policy-making process.

Rationalism   The belief that human problems can be solved through the use of human reason.

Reactionary   A person who would like to see the existing order reversed and favors substituting earlier political institutions for the contemporary system.

Reactionary theory of representation A theory stating that the monarch and parliament should represent the people's interests as they see them without necessarily consulting the people.

Reform feminism   The belief that women should join with men to reform the institutions, policies, and attitudes that treat women as inferior to men.

Republic   Also called *indirect democracy or representative government,* it is a system in which the people elect representatives to make laws for them. Traditionally the term has meant non-monarchial government.

Revisionism   A movement led by Eduard Bernstein (1850–1932) and Jean Jaurès (1859–1914) that challenged almost every major principle of Marxism. Abandoning scientific socialism, the revisionists returned humanitarianism to a central place in socialist theory.

Revolutionary feminism The belief that men are incapable of significant change; therefore, women must gain control of the levers of power and eradicate sexism without the help or cooperation of men.

Ricardo, David (1772–1823) An English economist who applied the capitalistic theories of Adam Smith to the British economy. He is particularly noted for articulating the *iron law of wages* and for his contribution to the theory of profit—"the leavings of wages," as he called it. His major work, *The Principles of Political Economy and Taxation,* earned him the title "Newton of economics."

Rousseau, Jean Jacques (1712–1778) A social contract theorist and founder of modern radical thought. He argued that people are free only when they subordinate their own interests to those of the group.

Saint-Simon, Claude Henri (1760–1825) A utopian socialist. See also *Utopian socialism.*

Schopenhauer, Arthur (1788–1860) A German irrationalist philosopher who thought that life was a meaningless struggle beyond human understanding.

Scientific socialism The term used by its supporters to describe Marxism; they called it scientific because it was based on certain principles of human conduct that Marxists believed were inviolable laws.

Self-alienation, theory of Marx's belief that bourgeois exploitation so denigrated working conditions that laborers came to hate their work—that is, their major means of self-creative expression. Thus, workers in capitalist societies became alienated from themselves.

Separation of powers The distribution of the powers of the national government among three branches: legislative, executive, and judicial.

Separatist feminism The most extreme form of feminism, it advocates that women should exist totally apart from men, relying on artificial insemination to propagate the species.

Sexism Bigotry based on gender.

Shallow ecology The view that humans should nurture and protect nature so as to preserve enough of the earth's resources for humans and other species to survive. Also called *humanist ecology,* this position is regarded by deep ecologists as hopelessly anthropocentric.

Siegfried The idealization of the Aryan superman. Richard Wagner immortalized this character in his operas, and Hitler made him the symbol of the Nazi racial ideal.

Single-member district An electoral district in which only one person is elected to office. Since only one person can be elected, those who voted for the losers go unrepresented. Used in the United States, this electoral system also tends to favor a single- or two-party system while working against a multiparty system.

Single-party system A system in which only one party has a reasonable chance of gaining control of the government. Although it can easily be used to create a dictatorship, it may exist in a democracy as well.

Smith, Adam (1723–1790) A Scottish scholar, he is considered the founder of economics. With the 1776 publication of *The Wealth of Nations,* he first articulated the basic principles of capitalism.

Social anarchism See *Anarchism.*

Social contract theory The notion, outlined by Hobbes, Locke, Rousseau, and others, that people joined together in a contract to create a government that would protect them from the tyranny inherent in the state of nature.

Social Darwinism A theory developed by Herbert Spencer, claiming the wealthy were superior to others and therefore benefited society more than others. If the poor perished from exploitative policies, the human race would be strengthened.

Socialism   The application of collectivist economics to a national economy. Socialism developed only after the Industrial Revolution increased productivity enough to make it possible to provide plenty for everyone.

Socialist ethic   The hope that true socialists will enjoy work and will voluntarily share the product of their labor with the whole community.

Socialist intent   A moral goal that must exist for a system to be truly socialist. This goal is to free people from material need, allowing them to develop and refine themselves as human beings.

Sorel, Georges   (1847–1922) A French philosopher who developed the ideology underlying syndicalism and encouraged the use of myth as a tool of mass politics. Though Sorel was a leftist, his ideas were adapted and modified by Mussolini.

Sovereignty   The highest legal authority in a given society. The term is also sometimes used to refer to a monarch.

Spencer, Herbert   (1820–1903) The founder of Social Darwinism, Spencer claimed that the wealthy were the select of nature and had a right to accumulate wealth at the expense of inferior beings. Spencer, not Charles Darwin, coined the phrase "survival of the fittest."

Stalin, Joseph   (1876–1953) A Bolshevik conspirator who succeeded Lenin and became the unquestioned leader of the Soviet Union. Although he made the Soviet Union a first-rate military and industrial power while successfully defeating the Nazi invasion, he imposed a cruel totalitarian system on his country, executing or imprisoning millions of people.

Stanton, Elizabeth Cady   (1815–1902) An early leader of the suffragist movement advocating that women should be given the vote in the United States. In 1848 she helped lead the first convention on women's rights.

State   A political term which includes people, territory, sovereignty, and government. In the United States, the term has also been used to refer to what are actually provinces.

Statism   The concept that the state is the focal point of human existence and that all citizens should therefore give it absolute obedience.

Status quo   The existing state of affairs in a given political environment.

Stirner, Max   (1806–1856) A leading individualist anarchist. He encouraged each person to ignore society and to focus only on "ownness," the self.

Sun Yi Xian   (1866–1925) A Chinese physician and revolutionary leader. He inspired the movement that eventually led to the ouster of the Chinese emperor in 1911.

Superstructure   All elements, according to Marx, that are built on the economic foundation of the society, including art, values, government, education, ideology, and the like.

Supply-side economics   Pursued by Republican presidents in the 1920s, by Reagan in the 1980s, and again by George W. Bush in the first decade of the twenty-first century, this policy reduces taxes and government regulation for large corporations while increasing government subsidies and other support for big business.

Surplus value, theory of   Marx's argument that the capitalist forced the workers to surrender their product for less than its true worth. The difference between the workers' wages and the true value of the item was the *surplus value* or profit.

Syndicalism   A radical theory suggesting that trade unions should become the primary social and political units in the society.

Tiananmen Square Protest (1989) A mass protest by Chinese students and workers that was forcefully put down. The number killed is not known, but it was certainly in the hundreds.

Tolstoy, Count Leo (1828–1910) A famed author and pacifist anarchist.

Totalitarian state A state in which the government controls the economic, social, and cultural as well as political aspects of a society. Totalitarianism was not possible before the development of early twentieth-century technology, but the late twentieth-century advent of computers, the Internet, FAX machines, cell phones, has now made totalitarianism less likely.

Trotsky, Leon (1879–1940) A brilliant Bolshevik revolutionary who was Lenin's intellectual equal but was no match for Stalin's ruthlessness; he suffered exile and was finally assassinated on Stalin's order.

Two-party system A system in which only two parties have a reasonable chance of winning control of the government. Though this system has the advantage of a loyal opposition, it gives the multitudinous minority views little voice.

Two swords theory The belief that spiritual and secular powers are each essential and should not be held by a single person.

Unitary system A system of government that centralizes all governmental power in the national government.

Utilitarianism Bentham's philosophy that the government should do whatever would produce the greatest happiness for the greatest number of people.

Utopian socialism A humanitarian socialist movement that unsuccessfully tried to create ideal collectivist experiments that would be imitated by the rest of the society.

Vanguard of the proletariat (as used by Lenin) A small, dedicated elite of professional revolutionaries who would lead the proletariat to socialism through revolution. The Bolsheviks were the Russian vanguard and the Comintern the internal vanguard.

Vanguard of the proletariat (as used by Marx) Those who, because of their superior intellect, could recognize the coming of socialism. Marx expected them to awaken the proletariat's class consciousness and thus stimulate the revolution.

Versailles Treaty The treaty ending World War I. It imposed very harsh conditions on Germany and was blamed by Hitler for Germany's severe postwar problems.

Volk The German people. See also *Volkish essence.*

Volkish essence A mystical power within the German people that supposedly makes them superior to all others.

Wagner, Richard (1813–1883) An operatic composer who popularized German mythology and the foundation for anti-Semitism.

Weakest link theory Lenin's theory that Imperial Russia was the weakest link in the capitalist chain because it had exploited its workers mercilessly to make up for the advantages enjoyed by the imperialist capitalists. This increased exploitation pushed the Russian proletariat to revolution before the proletarian classes of the more advanced industrial states.

Weimar Republic The constitutional government of Germany before Hitler came to power and abolished it.

Welfare state A society that provides a large number of social programs for its citizens, including Social Security, publicly supported education, public assistance for the poor, and public health services.

Will of the state The fascist belief that the state is a living being with a will or personality of its own. The will of the state is more powerful than that of any person or group within the state and must be obeyed without question.

Will to power An uncontrollable force spoken of in Nazi ideology that inspires people to try to dominate one another.

Wollstonecraft, Mary (1759–1797) Perhaps history's earliest feminist, whose avant-garde ideas about women's equality scandalized Europe. William Godwin, the founder of anarchism, became her husband.

Woodhull, Victoria (1838–1927) An advocate of equal rights for women, open-mindedness, free love, and women's suffrage.

Work, theory of Marx's belief that work was a form of self-creation and self-expression and was therefore good.

Yeltsin, Boris (1931–2007) The Russian president who courageously led Russia in succeeding from the Soviet Union, causing its collapse in 1992. However, his alcoholism and the corruption of his government forced him to resign in disgrace in 1999.

INDEX

AARP, 120, 121
Abdulmutallab, Umar Farouk, 66, 301
Abkhazi people, 51
Abortion, 23, 28, 29, 32, 39–40, 212, 305, 308
Absolute equality, 35
Absolute monarchy, 57, 58, 68, 73, 82
Absolute power, Hobbes, 84
Absolute power, Rousseau, 84
Abyssinia, 260
Acquired Immune Deficiency Syndrome (AIDS).
   See AIDS
Adam and Eve, 57, 265, 306
Adams, Samuel, 106
Adelphia, 91
Adoptions in China by Americans, 213
Affirmative action, 23, 146, 155
Afghanistan, 19, 23, 29, 30, 50, 56, 62, 285, 286,
   287, 300, 301, 302, 308, 311
AFL-CIO, 120
Africa, 59, 60, 65, 226, 245, 266, 277, 278, 280, 281,
   283, 285, 287, 289, 292, 298, 309, 319, 321, 324
   Sub-Saharan, 282, 284, 289, 290, 291, 297
African Americans, 34, 172, 173, 253, 266, 271
Afro-Asian colonial peoples, 60
Age of Enlightenment. *See* Enlightenment
Age of Ideology, The, 9
Aggressive interrogations, 23
Ahmadinejad, Mahmoud, 30, 262, 287
AIDS, 5, 215, 219, 291
Air pollution, 319
Alaska, 311, 322
Albania, 260
Alcohol, Tobacco, and Firearms Agency (ATF), 158
Aleutian Islands, 322
Alexander II, 152
Algeria, 286, 298, 315
Allende, Salvador, 136–137, 279
Alliances, mutual defense, 40
Al-Marri, Ali, 302
Alps, 49
Al Qaeda, 66, 285–286, 298, 300, 301, 302, 334
Al Qaeda in the Arabian peninsula, 300
Al-Sabbah, Hasan ibn, 299
Amaterasu, 55
America, 37, 65, 153, 268, 269. *See also* United
   States American:
   anarchist movement, Goldman, 153
   capitalism, 90–96, 178
   constitutional law, 118
   government, 115, 124–126, 182, 233
   invasion of Iraq, 50, 281
   Mafia, 279
   nation, 50, 51
   reactionaries, 267, 269, 298
   right-wing extremism, 266, 268
   socialism, 232–234
   values, 30, 122
   workers, 38, 178

American International Group (AIG), 92, 233
American Revolution, 37, 104, 105, 185, 277
American Society of Civil Engineers, 121
Americas, the, 59, 229, 319, 326
Amin, Idi, 245
Amphibian extinction, 325
Anarchism, 141–159, 235, 334, 342, 343
   definition of, 142–147
   development of, 141–142
   government, 142, 147
   individualism, 147, 155, 338
   labor unions, 143. *See also* Trade unions
   law, 143
   pacifists, 146, 147
   popularity, 142
   violent, 146, 147, 334
Anarchistic tendencies in the American political
   character, 157–159
Anarchists, 143, 144, 145, 146, 148, 149, 155, 157,
   304, 340, 344
   atheistic, 141
   capitalist, 141
   individualist, 141, 146–147, 155–157, 334
   militant civilian militias, 141, 158
   social, 141, 146, 334
Anarcho-syndicalism, 148
Anarchy, 142
Anbar province, Iraq, 302
Ancient Greeks. See Greeks, ancient
Angelican Church, 73, 306–307
Anglo-American colonies, 11, 97
Angola, 229
Animal rights activists, 331
Animals, land, 320, 321, 323, 326
Animals, sea, 320–326
Anschluss, 200
Antarctic, 319, 323, 330
Anthony, Susan B., 313, 334
Anthropocentrism, 304, 319, 329, 331, 334
Anthropology, 250, 253
Anti-African-American, 265
Anti-Bolshevik rebellion, 154
Anti-colonialism, 228, 280, 285
Anti-communism, 51
Anti-feminist bias, 317
Anti-Hispanic, 265
Anti-ideology, 9
Anti-labor, 91
Anti-landmine Treaty, 60
Anti-Muslim, 265
Anti-Semitism, 65, 243, 249, 250, 263, 264, 265, 335
Anti-socialist socialism, 170
Antithesis, 184, 185
Apartheid, 245, 261
Appenzell Innerrhoden, 117
Aquifers, 322
Aquinas, Thomas, 54
Aquino, Corazon, 310

Robertson, Pat, 28, 121
Rochester, New York, 153
Rockefeller family, 95
Roede, Scott, 267
Roman Catholic Church. *See* Catholic Church
Roman Catholic Bishop, 232
Roman Catholic clerics, 287
Roman Catholics, 28
Roman Empire, 54, 60, 71, 117–118, 259
Romania, 264
Romanies (gypsies), 253, 262, 263, 264
Romans, 243
Rome, 118, 252, 259
  march on, 242
Roosevelt, Franklin Delano, 90, 96, 166, 233,
  278, 340
Rousseau, Jean Jacques, 19, 33, 35, 36, 54, 59,
  68–69, 72, 82–85, 96, 97–98, 104, 105, 111,
  116, 137, 138, 148, 152, 169, 170, 255, 343
  direct democracy, 85
  general will, 83–84
  moral relativism, 83
Ruby Ridge, Idaho, 19, 158, 269, 270
Rugged individualism, 90, 157
Ruling class, 8, 149, 180
Rumania, 153, 204, 278
Rumsfeld, Donald, 286, 296
Russia, 6, 48, 49, 51, 64, 127, 143, 144, 151, 152,
  153, 154, 185, 197, 199, 201, 202, 206, 217,
  231, 235, 250, 262, 277, 278, 289, 291, 294,
  297, 300, 321, 324, 334, 345
  carbon dioxide, 328
Russian:
  Civil War, 202
  federation, 49
  government, 155
  Marxists, 197
  nationalism, 48–49, 199, 203
  Orthodox Church, 149, 150
  peasants, 149, 152
  people, 62, 150
  revolution, 57, 218. *See also* Bolshevik Revolution
Russian Federation, 49
Rwanda, 281, 310, 311

Sabine, George H., 75
Sacco-Vanzetti hysteria, 145
Safe zones, Mao, 220
Saint Ambrose, 55
Saint Augustine, 55
Saint-Simon, Claude Henri, 173, 174, 343
Salazar, Antonio, 245
Sales tax, 93
Same-sex marriage, 28, 29, 32, 120, 121, 266
Samuel, 55
San Diego County, 267
San Marino, 311
Sargent, L. T., 9
Satan, 123, 269, 286
Saudi Arabia, 40, 284, 285, 297, 300, 308, 310,
  311, 315, 331
Saul, 55
Savings and loans collapse, 92
Saxony-Anhalt, 263
Scandinavia, 69, 152, 182
Scandinavian countries, 295
Scandinavian people, 252
Schilling, Friedrich von, 247
School of the Americas, 300

School vouchers, 28
Schopenhauer, Arthur, 245–249, 251, 343
Schumpeter, Joseph, 88
Science, 322
Science, 5, 8, 21, 71, 239, 246, 253, 322
Science of ideas, de Tracy, 8
Scientific experiments, Nazi, 253
"Scientific socialism," 160, 171, 172, 195. *See also*
  Marxism
Scientists, pseudo, 161
Seattle, Washington, 144
Second International, 172
Second Sex, The, 314
Second Treatise, 75
Secret Army Organization (OAS), 298
Secretary of Defense, U.S., 286, 296
Secretary General of the United Nations, 243
Secular worship, 63
Secularism, 279, 284
Self-alienation, theory of, Marx, 187, 343
Self Defense Force, 300
Self-determination, 59
Self-government, 142, 239
Selfishness, 160
Senate, United States, 130, 137, 272
Senators, U.S., 132, 137, 158
Seneca Falls, New York, 313
Sentimental value, 188
Separation of church and state, 28, 74
Separation of powers, 102–103, 115, 125, 126,
  130, 343
Separatism, nationalist, 65
Separatists feminists, 304, 343
September 11, 2001, 63
Serbia, 323
Serfs, 184–185
Seventeenth Amendment, 72, 73, 103
Sexism, 36, 307, 343
Sexist, 262
Sexual:
  freedom, 314
  gratification, 308
  harassment, 305, 308
  intercourse, 307
Sexuality, 305, 308, 314
Shah of Iran, 30
Shahzad, Faisal, 301
Shallow ecology, 320, 343
Sharia Law, 283, 284, 286
Shaw, George Bernard, 45, 197
Shelley, Mary, 147
Shensi province, 209
Shiites, 50, 284, 286, 287
Shining Path, 300
Sichuan province, 213
Siegfried, 248, 253, 343
Sierra Club, 120
Sikhs, 287
Silk Road, 215
Silent Spring, 319
Simpson-Miller, Portia "Mama," 312
Single-member district, 115, 132, 133, 343
Single party democracy, 135
Single-party system, 115, 134, 135, 343
Skinheads, 262, 265, 267, 272
Slavery, 184, 186, 266, 313
  new kind, 4
Slavic people, 253
Slums, 178